ALSO BY JOHN EDGAR WIDEMAN

Slaveroad

The Homewood Trilogy

Look for Me and I'll Be Gone: Stories

You Made Me Love You: Selected Stories, 1981–2018

American Histories: Stories

Writing to Save a Life: The Louis Till File

Fanon Briefs: Stories

God's Gym: Stories

The Island: Martinique

Hoop Roots: Basketball, Race, and Love

Two Cities: A Novel

The Cattle Killing: A Novel

Fatheralong: A Meditation on Fathers and Sons, Race and Society

All Stories Are True: The Stories of John Edgar Wideman

Philadelphia Fire: A Novel

Fever: Stories

Reuben: A Novel

Brothers and Keepers: A Memoir

Sent for You Yesterday: A Novel

Damballah: Stories

Hiding Place: A Novel

The Lynchers: A Novel

Hurry Home: A Novel

A Glance Away: A Novel

LANGUAGES OF HOME

Essays on Writing, Hoop, and American Lives 1971–2025

JOHN EDGAR WIDEMAN

SCRIBNER

New York Amsterdam/Antwerp London
Toronto Sydney/Melbourne New Delhi

Scribner
An Imprint of Simon & Schuster, LLC
1230 Avenue of the Americas
New York, NY 10020

For more than 100 years, Simon & Schuster has championed authors and the stories they create. By respecting the copyright of an author's intellectual property, you enable Simon & Schuster and the author to continue publishing exceptional books for years to come. We thank you for supporting the author's copyright by purchasing an authorized edition of this book.

First Scribner hardcover edition November 2025

SCRIBNER and design are trademarks of Simon & Schuster, LLC

Simon & Schuster strongly believes in freedom of expression and stands against censorship in all its forms. For more information, visit BooksBelong.com.

For information about special discounts for bulk purchases, please contact Simon & Schuster Special Sales at 1-866-506-1949 or business@simonandschuster.com.

The Simon & Schuster Speakers Bureau can bring authors to your live event. For more information or to book an event, contact the Simon & Schuster Speakers Bureau at 1-866-248-3049 or visit our website at www.simonspeakers.com.

Interior design by Julia Jacintho

Manufactured in the United States of America

10 9 8 7 6 5 4 3 2 1

Library of Congress Cataloguing-in-Publication Data is available.

ISBN 978-1-6680-3637-2
ISBN 978-1-6680-3639-6 (ebook)

CONTENTS

Introduction by Mitchell S. Jackson (2025)   ix

Fear in the Streets
The American Scholar (1971)   **1**

Review: *The Marrow of Tradition* by Charles W. Chesnutt
The American Scholar (1972)   **15**

Review: *The Unfinished Quest of Richard Wright* by Michel Fabre
The New York Times Book Review (1973)   **29**

Defining the Black Voice in Fiction
Black American Literature Forum (1977)   **35**

Review: *Stomping the Blues: Ritual in Black Music and Speech*
American Poetry Review (1978)   **47**

The Language of Home
The New York Times Book Review (1985)   **59**

Preface: *Charles W. Chesnutt and the WPA Narratives*
ed. Charles T. Davis and Henry Louis Gates, Jr. (1985)   **67**

What Is Afro, What Is American?
The New York Times Book Review (1986)   **91**

The Black Writer and the Magic of the Word
The New York Times Book Review (1988)   **97**

Michael Jordan Leaps the Great Divide
Esquire (1990)   **107**

Preface: *Breaking Ice*
ed. Terry MacMillan (1990)   **135**

Introduction: *The Souls of Black Folk*
by W. E. B. Du Bois (1990)   **143**

Dead Black Men and Other Fallout from the American Dream
Esquire (1992)   **149**

Monument to Malcolm
Vogue (1992)   **173**

Malcolm X: The Art of Autobiography
In Our Own Image, ed. Joe Wood   **183**

Preface: *The Homewood Books*
by John Edgar Wideman (1992)   **203**

Father Stories
The New Yorker (1995)   **209**

Introduction:
Live from Death Row by Mumia Abu-Jamal (1995)   **223**

Playing Dennis Rodman
The New Yorker (1996)   **233**

Justice: A Perspective
Outside the Law, ed. Susan Richards Shreve and Porter Shreve   **239**

The Silence of Thelonious Monk
Callaloo (1997)   **247**

In Praise of Silence
Callaloo (1998)   **259**

This Man Can Play
Esquire (1998)   **265**

What Is a Brother?
Esquire (1998)   **281**

The Night I Was Nobody
McCalls (1999)   **285**

Foreword: *Every Tongue Got to Confess*
by Zora Neale Hurston (2001)   **291**

Whose War: The Color of Terror
Harper's (2002)   **301**

Looking at Emmett Till
In Fact: The Best of Creative Nonfiction (2005)   **311**

At the Island's End
The New York Times Magazine (2006)   **333**

***from* The Louis Till Blues Project**
Callaloo (2011)   **337**

Witness: A Letter from France
The New Yorker (2015)   **365**

Doo-Wop
(2025)   **379**

INTRODUCTION

2025

Let me call the ways.

That's on my mama. On my grandmama. On my daddy. On my kids. On my blood and kin. That's on my set. On my block. On my hood. On the dead homies. That's on Jesus, Mary, and all the saints. On God. On everything God loves. On everything I love. That's on my life.

A litany that cites the ways we—and by *we*, I mean my people—affirm our truth telling. Or at least a need for the trust of our audience. The cultural practice of *puttin that on somethin* is a rhetorical tool somewhere between a casual request and baldface beseeching—a latter-day verily, verily, but even more insistent since it belongs to a people whose ethos (which I'm defining the same way Aristotle did) has been maligned from the time white folks usurped us to these shores; since it's the domain of a people whose credibility and legitimacy has been challenged, undermined, assailed during every damn epoch of this sundered republic.

To challenge that constant harm, we've birthed a whole lexicon that, at the crux, is this:

Believe me. Trust me. Trust and believe me, please.

Ethos. It's essential to the power of nonfiction and given that the character, reputation, and good judgment of Black people has been beset far and wide, it's tougher for us to reap. We shall overcome—but how? One way is to foster as much ethos as we can, to be excellent in ways impenetrable to the criticisms of even the Ivory Tower panjandrums.

What you have in your hands is the collected nonfiction of a writer who, more than anyone I can think of, owns unimpeachable ethos, someone whose work is furthermore never of want for wisdom.

Such as:

"A culture is a network of responsibilities."

"If it sells underwear. If it sells tickets. There's no rule that can't be broken. No stereotype not turned upside down, pulled inside out."

"That statistics of inequality don't demonstrate a 'Black crisis'—that perspective confuses cause and victim, solutions and responsibility."

"Is it still news that some people's bad times (slavery, colonial subjugation, racial oppression, despair) have underwritten other people's good times (prosperity, luxury, imperial domination, complacency)."

"A state proclaiming itself besieged by terrorists asserts its total innocence."

"Then again, if we think a little deeper, we might ask ourselves— who isn't on death row?"

As I'm sure you sussed from the cover, his name is John Edgar Wideman.

John has been publishing longer than I've been alive, but I didn't hear of him until the early 2000s, when I was a grad student studying creative writing in New York. My professor assigned a short story John had written titled "Weight," a story which begins "My mother is a weightlifter. You know what I mean?"

Two sentences—that's all it took for me to judge John kindred in a crucial way. The very next summer, I fortuned a chance to study with him in an "intensive" fiction workshop and set to the task of acquainting myself with more of his work. That was over twenty years ago.

In the more than two decades since, I've come to understand John's prose as avant-garde. Which is to say, learned how apt he is to "employ every new trick and technology I'm able to muster in whatever kind of writing I'm attempting" as he writes in this collection—or in other words, how his style has evolved in content and form; in language and point of view; in the use of rhetorical tools like a superlong sentence or a stream-of-consciousness passage or a meta narrative. Reading John across the years has been to witness what obtains from him perceiving the "lines between fiction and nonfiction" as "more and more arbitrary, blurred, problematic" (for fact, the lyric essay and autofiction wouldn't look the same without him); has been to discover how much he's favored the psychic exploration of a bildungsroman over the what-comes-next imperative of plot; has been to glean the way his desire to explore the human interior spans genres. And of course, John's willingness to expand himself as intellectual and artist has also had the effect of challenging his readers.

Nobody nowhere never should call his work a light read.

There were several essays (what ain't an essay?) in this collected that I'd never read, and even the ones I'd read several times offered fresh insight (a hallmark of enduring work, no?) in my reread. In these pieces, John probes the murder of Emmett Till, the Watts Rebellion, the 1992 LA Revolt, the September 11 attacks and "War on Terror," and the Black Lives Matter movement (moment?). He uses his extraordinary gifts to interrogate the work/ and or lives of Charles Chesnutt, W. E. B. Du Bois, Ralph Ellison, Richard Wright, Louis Till, Thelonious Monk, Albert Murray, Malcolm X, Zora Neale Hurston, Gayl Jones, Rodney King, Jesse Jackson, Michael Jordan, Denzel Washington, and Spike Lee.

Du Bois, a model and hero of John's, proclaimed that the problem of the twentieth century was the problem of the color line, and one of the most remarkable aspects of this collection is how, in the main, John makes clear that the problem of the twenty-first century is *still* at heart the color line. There's also the way the work gathered forges ligatures from one of John's ideas to the next (he sometimes introduces an idea in one decade that he expands or complicates in a whole other decade); how he links the collective thought of one era to another, him shining light on how a current historical figure echoes a past one. Another strength is how John avoids hagiographizing the people he writes about, how no matter the stature of his subject, he sees sober-eyed their humanness. Plus, the way he's able to drop from the perch of his pedigree (more on this) to disassemble on the page. Like in "The Language of Home," when he describes a boyhood memory of hanging with white friends after he'd transferred to a "better" school. John and his cut buddies call a cigarette a "nigarette" and admonish one another for "nigger-lipping" while they puff and pass. "Speaking out, identifying myself with the group being slurred by these expressions, was impossible," writes John. "I had neither the words nor the heart."

But of course, the collection, *Languages of Home*, takes its title from that essay, and for good reason, given that another of its immense virtues is how John charts the evolution of his voice—its inimitable quality most drew me to his work—his movement away from the often exclusionary language of the King's English/the academy, to the speechifying, signifying, colloquial tongues of where and who and what he comes from.

Pittsburgh, Pennsylvania.

Homewood.

I put that on Homewood, John might've sworn way back when if some young punk put to question his word.

That pedigree. Homewood's finest was the second Black man to win a prestigious Rhodes Scholarship. He is also the recipient of a MacArthur "Genius" Award and the Pen/Faulkner Award (twice). He is a professor emeritus at Brown University. Beyond this collected nonfiction, he's the author of several books of nonfiction as well as novels and short story collections, as well as countless stand-alone short stories—all-told incontrovertible proof of his sustained brilliance.

Robust oeuvre—check!

Universal respect—check!

Cataract of international acclaim—check!

Still yet, my wish for John is a wider audience. Is a readership that's nothing short of the luminaries (none worthier of luminescence) of his time: Morrison, Baldwin, Wilson, Achebe, Brooks, Márquez, Walcott—go ahead, name the somebody.

The more readers, the more voices, voices, voices, to resound truths into an emphatic Greek chorus: for upwards of fifty years, John Edgar Wideman has been essential to world literature, a paradigmatic writer's writer, one of, if not the greatest, of my people to ever make art from words.

And I put that on whatever you want.

Mitchell S. Jackson

LANGUAGES OF HOME

FEAR IN THE STREETS

1971

. . . he saw himself—all that for which he had lived—and saw clearly that it was not real at all, but a terrible and huge deception which had hidden both life and death.

—Tolstoy, "The Death of Ivan Ilych"

We fear what we don't understand. We fear night and death, those dark layers of ourselves that rise to scuttle our well-intentioned efforts to become the better person we sometimes think we want to be. I have a fear of madness, of self-willed destruction that I don't believe is unique in me.

When I was a boy growing up in the city, I was afraid to walk the streets after dark. Then came years in which I was fearless. I was part of the night. It could hide me, change me, free parts of me that didn't come to life while the sun shone. Now, as close to a man as thirty years have teased me, I feel the old fears returning. I listen. I read. I am convinced the night streets are unsafe. Full circle the darkness is inhabited by a bestiary of threatening shapes that daylight only partially dispels. I sleep with a bayonet under my bed.

Whistling was my magic as a child. If I made noise, if I filled my consciousness with noisy proof of my existence, I could somehow navigate the three-block gauntlet from Liberty Elementary School playground to our house on Copeland Street. A whistled melody was good company, a totem to charm the phantoms stalking me silently behind tall shrubbery or lurking in shadowed recesses between buildings. What was always just beyond the reach of my eyes or fingertips subdued me. Everything was too large, too overgrown with layers of mystery, and night intensified the contrast between what little I could see and all those intimidating forces, invisible but controlling my destiny.

I was wiser then. I understood how the city betrayed me; I could continually sense the disproportionate scale. I knew I walked on water, that the same voices that calmed the sea could whip it into a murderous froth. The modern city has made man obsolete. It is not built for men. Supermetropolis serves conglomerates, masses. It serves the disposable, homogenized citizen I do not wish to be—nor do you, nor any man, unless the city has its way and generates a new version of man conforming to its scale.

The urban environment has spawned paradoxes. Although technology indulges our illusions of control—we run as fast as four hundred horses, stand on a star and see the far side of the earth—our bodies have deteriorated shamefully. While its machines grow in numbers and sophistication, the city as a setting for human growth has evolved or reverted to a state of threatening primitiveness in which all man's physical endowments are required for survival.

The life of the native was never safe. Personal danger was the universal fact of life. There was an almost complete lack of control of natural forces. The forests and rivers were full of dangerous animals, and dangerous human enemies were always close at hand. The insect pests and the tropical diseases made the conditions of life hard and its duration brief. To the real dangers were added an abundance of malignant spirits. An ever-present fear of the natural and supernatural enemies was the normal condition of daily life and protection was the ever-present need.

This anthropologist's re-creation of the bush natives' fear-ridden environment is undoubtably an exaggeration, but for today's city-dweller the description is more than metaphorically true. The reliance on drugs to change what we see and what we are, the appeal of occultism, astrology, demon worship, parapsychology, and exotic diets indicate that for many the traditional "enlightened" modes of defense—doctors, lawyers, the Reason of scientists—are no longer adequate. The pervasive violence enshrined in so many aspects of our culture is further proof of the need to externalize our fear of personal annihilation. Experiencing vicariously through electronic antennae the deaths of others—whether bulls or men—reassures us of the reality of our lives. But worship of violence even from afar is double-edged. Regardless of the individual city-dweller's personal exposure to violence, the media function as an extension of his senses, and a larger-than-life city is created, a Supermetropolis in which the timid resident of West Philadelphia can poke his head from the second-story window of his row house and find his nostrils twitching from the acrid smoke of Watts burning. "It can't happen here" is an anachronistic statement. Instant communication makes it happen here all the time. "Here" becomes synonymous with everywhere, and, in the case of the city, fear in the streets is ubiquitous.

At night the city-dweller is perhaps most vulnerable. The instincts nature provided for his safety in dark, alien surroundings have decayed to inadequacy; he can't see or hear enough, he can't fight or run well enough. When I see joggers in the city parks or skulking flat-footed through the quiet morning streets, I find myself asking what they are running from. From death? From obsolescence? What panic are they acting out? Compartmentalized, hemmed in by the towering city, reminded on every side of the place from which they must not stray, do they escape for twenty minutes? Can they recall in the exercise of taut muscles and rhythmic breathing the freedom they have compromised? Given the restrictions placed upon his basic human drives, the repression of his animal energy, does the city-dweller share the frustration, the subconscious reservoirs of violence Frantz Fanon found in his study of colonized, oppressed natives: "His dreams are of actions and of aggression . . . jumping, swimming, climbing . . . I burst out laughing . . . I span a river in one stride . . . I am followed by a flood of motorcars which never catch up with me"?

We fear ghosts. Ghosts are real.

The editor of this magazine commissioned me to write a piece on fear in the streets. That was eleven months ago. Since then his summer tenants were robbed, he has been shot at through his kitchen window, the rear window of his car was smashed while parked outside his home, his stereo set was stolen, and finally he lost a prospective buyer of his house when, after a final purchase-consummating tour, buyer and real estate agent, descending the front steps at 12:30 p.m., witnessed a mugging barely eighty feet from where they stood.

On a bright, brisk February afternoon my wife decided to roll our new baby carriage and new baby to a friend's house six blocks away: a Sunday stroll on a route well-traveled, residential, with houses for the most part sitting well back from the pavement, giving the streets a broad, spacious feeling. At her destination, as she prepared to unravel the baby from his mound of blankets, she was assaulted. Hands went over her eyes, but she wrenched free and her screams frightened the assailant away.

A birthday present from my in-laws, a portable television set, was stolen from our kitchen by thieves who entered a back window and gathered up everything that looked valuable while we slept peacefully above. We traveled three hundred miles to another city carrying with us a new set, compliments of the insurance company. At our destination, my parents' home in Pittsburgh, a robbery occurred, and among the casualties was our second TV set.

Barricaded from traffic during the summer, our street (called a square because it is cut off at each end by a "T" junction) is a playground for our children, and traditionally the adults partake of its sanctuary for annual block parties. I am the only black man on the block, although directly to the west in the adjacent neighborhood, eighty percent of the residents are black. The May Day party was a collective enterprise giving the young professionals—teachers, architects, students, blue-collar families—a sense of community identification with the square.

Then black children trickle in from the "forest." One. Three. Several small groups silent at the periphery of the merrymaking. Residents of the block became nervous. Unity is gone. We are political creatures and we scuttle to the rightness or leftness of our beliefs. And even if you side with the children, or even if you are black yourself, the sudden self-consciousness, the sense of being other, is electric. The weatherman had promised a clear day, but here were sure-enough clouds massing above the vulnerable picnic spread. A sense of being betrayed. Some begin to whisper, to retreat to the shadows of the porches they own.

"Hey, I paid for those rolls." "Look at them grab." "Give to one and in five minutes they'll all be here with their hands out." Gradually the whispers solidify to flat statements of outrage. The black children become not casual, curious intruders but outriders, scouts for a larger, plotted invasion. That one keeps staring at us. The older one with all the hair. Whose steps is he sitting on? Do you think she should ask him to move? He may be signaling the others. It will begin to rain any moment. Flood. Inundation. One more outpost in the city overwhelmed by barbarians.

"Youth Slain on North Philadelphia Doorstep," the headline read. The shooting, his mother said, was the third time he had been the victim of a gang attack. In the spring of 1969 he was stabbed, and, working in West Chester, he was jumped and beaten here, while getting off a bus.

She said her son had had nightmares that he was being killed, and once told her: "I hope they shoot me and get it over with so I won't have to suffer."

According to a recruiting brochure issued by the Philadelphia Police Department, Philadelphia, the scene of all the items noted above, is, of America's ten largest cities, the safest, therefore, the best policed.

We fear most in others the evils we see in ourselves. Comparing theater to the plague, Antonin Artaud suggests that plague symptoms may be generated by spiritual disorders, that cultural failure and collapse may attack the "very organs of the body, the particular physical sites where human will, consciousness, and thought are imminent and apt to occur." What he says of the essential theater may be true of fear in the streets:

"Like the plague, it is the revelation, the bringing forth, the exteriorization of a depth of latent cruelty by means of which all the perverse possibilities of the mind, whether of an individual or a people, are localized."

It is cathartic, facile, and seldom justifiable to blame our misfortunes on immediate circumstances, to castigate the shortcomings of present political leaders and political programs, when we fear walking the city streets at night and hesitate to venture on some streets even in broad daylight. We can curse the moon and the billions spent to stage a golfing exhibition there; we can hate the yellow people or the black people who sap the strength of our economy. We myopically scan the bland middle distance while resisting the look inward.

But if the expressive possibilities of body and imagination are inhibited, the organism cannot be healthy. Fear is the grossest reaction of an animal. A kind of ironic paralysis both alerts the nerve endings, bringing them to a throbbing pitch of awareness, and simultaneously dulls their capacity to discriminate. Tied to a chair in a dark room, the fraternity initiate who has been promised a bath of scalding water to test his mettle will delight his potential brothers with a shriek of pain when they pour ice water over his flesh.

The Vietnam War, no more or less than the violence essential to the way we raise and educate our children, is not sufficient cause for the epidemic of fear, but, like any external circumstance, must be scrupulously measured within the context of that highly personal vision we have of ourselves. This personal vision is necessarily opaque to others, and we use its opacity as a screen behind which, we assure those who bother to ask, resides a fundamentally good man whose honorable intentions and humane disposition are a counterpoise to the sometimes hedonistic irrationality of his acts.

Yet we can judge the quality of our collective inner lives by the kinds of diseases that plague us. How the very cells run wild, how the hearts rot, the nerves quiver to madness. We recognize the urge toward self-destruction—fast driving, cigarettes, drugs, alcohol—made glamorous and acceptable. See the moral chaos just as doggedly cultivated by our head-in-the-sand disregard for the lives of others who happen to be an inch outside the network of relationships we perceive as necessary to gratify our immediate needs. How we deceive ourselves by sending twenty dollars to Pakistan or writing indignant magazine articles while the body counts, the crime counts, the bereaved statements of victims and survivors remain as routine to us each morning as that first cup of coffee.

Where is the fine line between the pilot's thumb on his rocket-launcher napalming suspicious movement two thousand feet below him in the jungle, and the finger of the dogface hooked in the trigger of his automatic weapon firing into a mass of civilians? And if we countenance these acts by burrowing even deeper into business-as-usual routines, if when the six thousand miles between us and the shooting shrinks to a few city blocks and the "jungle" is a ghetto where black boys are killing other black boys almost daily in gang wars that viciously celebrate the only kind of manhood our society allows them, if we are standing under a streetlamp praying for a bus or taxi to whisk us away from the threatening darkness, and if, finally, after the doors are locked, the windows shuttered, the alarms set, the weapons checked, the extra cigarette smoked as waves of resentment, aggression, and fright shudder over our bodies and seem to recede only as they are drawn off by the tides of sleep, what will we dream? We must pay our dues. The city rises with us each morning.

Some days there's so much city you can't hide. You step out of the subway mole-blind, and the city is there, stinking, loud, switching its wide behind, brushing its wino shoulders against your chest. Other days— or rather mostly nights—it disappears, a blue haze collaring the tallest buildings, but, beneath that, planes of thick darkness either too close or too far away. You see nothing. You are walking down a narrow hallway in a strange house, just you and the echo of you. All the cardboard scenery has been collapsed. If there is a city, it sleeps, it is profoundly imperturbable.

A kind of womb sometimes. On occasion a plastic dome, a lid beneath which you are pressure-cooked and displayed. Hot. Cold. Hawk's gonna get you. Monumental architecture, wide boulevards, good for pomp-and-circumstance parades, bad for people with few clothes. Broad avenues straight and uncluttered in the best Napoleonic tradition for cannoneers to sight down. Burning. Because in its environs and grimy enclaves the factories belch, because in its guts are victims mortally wounded, stopped furnaces, Bigger Thomases watching Cadillacs mince past.

If you want really to talk about fear in the streets, you must begin by dividing the subject matter into black and white. White fear. Black fear. Conditions of the common soul, proceeding from the same gut roots, but channeled brutally by the divisive lies with which Americans have chosen to understand themselves. White fear in the streets is fear of black. Black fear in the streets is fear of white. So it seems. Whites fear the burly, black brute, that bugaboo hulking gorilla-legged across the Western imagination since Europe's first encounter with Africa, that beast first chained, then trained, then chained again in institutionalized fetters. Blacks fear the treacherous white keeper of the keys with his guns and whips, his forked tongue and false gods.

If cultures generate men and cities, they just as surely produce myths. Historically, the black man has been the beast of burden onto which have been loaded all those dark truths about Everyman that the American Everyman didn't want to believe about himself. In the popular imagination zoological metaphors were most appropriate for describing the Negro. His smell, his speech, his physical appearance, his morality, his intelligence were poetized with unpleasant metaphors drawn from the beast kingdom. The American colonists in the eighteenth and nineteenth centuries, blind as Melville's Captain Delano to the slave's urge to be free, saw rebellion as a diseased lust within the black breast for white woman, white land, white blood. That distortion of the black man's desire for freedom and independence persists even now; it feeds the myth of the burly, black brute, the archrapist, arsonist, jack-of-all-crimes cartoon figure that haunts the white city-dweller.

The black city-dweller is not untouched by the myth of the black brute. Internally and externally, he struggles with the sordid images of himself and their dehumanizing effects. In this struggle the decaying city is a metaphysical cage. Its filth, violence, and brutality—the streets lined with uncollected garbage, the bloody emergency wards, the derelicts and addicts—are an epiphany validating the worst things the black man has heard about himself. The city is an elaborate *I told you so*, proof that the beast fouls his lair. If not, why doesn't he do better? Why doesn't he clean up or join the exodus to the suburbs? Why can't he melt like other immigrants into the collective stew? Reams of statistics describe the black city-dweller; he is the Urban Problem, the Plight of Our Cities. Words employed gingerly like tongs handle him without touching his foreign black flesh. When the newscaster intones, "Urban Inner-City Schools," we all know what kind of school he's talking about, whom we'll find sitting numbly in its classrooms.

The crime rate among poor blacks is high, so blacks fear other blacks, the predatory attacks of their fellows who have internalized the brute image and prowl the streets of the city. Ironically, the policeman, white or black, is equally feared. In protecting black from black, he is notoriously inept. But the cop as intermediary between black and white has an unambiguous role; he knows which hand feeds him, and he pursues his task with zeal. For the black city-dweller the cop is the most immediate, concrete evidence that the larger, white world wishes to cordon him off. Along with the decadent, violent fantasies of the media, the policeman enters the black home and defines the nature of the white world. Embodied in his protection of society, his maintenance of law and order, are assumptions concerning black men; the cop carries a gun, uses dogs, employs chains and cages, sanctions in his stare the beast image. He fears the beast in blacks, and beasts only respond to force, therefore, unremitting force is used to instill permanent fear, fear that will lock the black man in his beast place. Whatever else the policeman is, he is also a further validation of the cage. The success of these relationships is apparent in the frightened black men preying on one another, in the compensatory intransigence of gun-carrying blacks as they engage police in Wild West shoot-outs, in the iron bars barricading city apartments and crowded jails.

The black city-dweller sees in the confrontation of Black Panther and policeman a dramatization of his personal desire for self-determination. The Panther's particular solution—"Yes, I am an animal, but I choose which one, one which is sleek, fast, and deadly, one who is bigger and badder than the pig beast I now crown you"—may not be his answer, but he can identify wholeheartedly with the process of redefinition, the imperatives that drive the Panthers. Fear of tainted blackness within and fear of white external control must be scuttled before any kind of liberation, physical or spiritual, can begin.

As a society we seem to be systematically eliminating the middle ground between extremes. We are winners or losers, black or white, haves or have-nots, young or old, radical or conservative. What Fanon called Manicheanism, that vision of the world that entertains only absolutes and sees change coming only after violent reversal ("The first shall be last and the last first"), is the product of fear, fear that has reached the proportions of a debilitating psychic plague. In our collective consciousness the sons of light must forever do battle with the sons of darkness. It's never clear who's going to win, so when we walk the streets or glance into the sky, we sense palpable threats. Will the towers of steel and concrete crash down on us at the first note of some clarion trumpet, will the cracking pavements open to swallow us?

I was not quite six months old when Pearl Harbor was bombed. Fighting has never really stopped since then. So I can date myself by the anniversaries of the Pacific war, an antique war from the distance of thirty years. Plenty of bloodshed (we did the best we could), but a storm in a teacup compared to how we can kill each other now. Some constants: massacre, atrocity, My Lai, Song May. Slaughter of the innocents. On the six o'clock nationwide news, an interviewer, almost appalled, almost incredulous, asked the young ex-G.I., "How could you, the father of two young children yourself, shoot down defenseless mothers and babies?" The question was rhetorical, the reporter's voice hovering over an unsounded void, seeking that within himself that would admit the potential of committing the same crime. But with proper respect for the media, with no sense of drama, humor, or irony, with deference to any reporter invested with the wealth and sophistication of a major network in his voice, his manners, his clothes—the way he walked into the soldier's living room, the ease with which he lifted from nonentity the soldier's quiet suburban life, even to its nylon carpets and slip-covered furniture—with deference and the proper bland submission due such an emissary of power, the soldier (crippled now by what he stolidly believed was a God-sent land mine whose hot metal canceled out transgression and guilt by kindling his legs) answered haltingly, "The situation occurred over two years ago . . . March '68 . . . and I only had one baby then."

Clarity. Knowledge is overwhelming. Déjà vu. Film clips from Nazi Germany: an analogy the participants in the My Lai massacre themselves exhume. Ditches and the bowling pin people topple backward, disappear, are registered in red lights on some neon tote board. A pattern asserts itself. The score. The numbers are digested, interpreted, explained. Bodies—mostly women and children—alongside the ditch. "Like they had bright red paint poured over them." A Paris newspaper says the American regime of Richard Nixon is certainly not the Germany of Adolf Hitler. There are some comforts in the analyses—the running river of time into which you can never step twice at the same place. But blood runs also. Brings deeper, inconsolable fears, knowledge.

In a society that thrives on the fruits of war, on domestic oppression and economic exploitation of the weak, in a society that has perverted its basic moral, ethical code into something like "Do unto others before they do unto you," in a nation where truth is an adjunct of power and power is brute force, is it any wonder that the dreams of its citizenry are filled with fear of retaliation, with images of bloody confrontation, a reversal of roles in which the assailant finds himself nakedly helpless before the rage of his former victim?

Cobbs Creek divides Upper Darby, a largely white suburban township, from the southwestern tip of Philadelphia, a neighborhood that is predominantly black.

A fifteen-year-old boy was shot and killed in Cobbs Creek Park. He was struck in the heart by a single shot. The dead boy's mother spoke to a reporter: *"My son or any of the kids can't even play in this neighborhood. The Negroes just keep coming across the Creek and they keep breaking windows and aerials off cars. Kids can't even take their bikes to the park or play at the ballfield. That's how bad things are.*

"We were supposed to take Stephen down to the shore Friday for the whole summer, to get him away from all this mess.

"I'm very bitter. I hope they catch my son's killer and I hope he gets first degree . . ."

In the period of April ninth to June fifteenth this boy was the third to die in the park. The other victims were black.

Air. Water. Fire. Earth. In our cities we know each element is dangerous and steadily growing more corrupt. The human deterioration is perhaps more precipitate. Threatened on all sides, unable to face or name the most profound source of our fears, we stunt imaginative, spiritual seeking and call symptom cause. Crime in the streets is only one troubled surface, one more miasma exhaled by the cities' rotten innards. Brute niggers, dope fiends, sadistic pot-bellied cops, hippies—these cartoons are as close to reality as we come in externalizing the needs, force, and direction of our culture. At some level we realize that the city has trapped us, that it has evolved into a kind of procrustean couch, stretching our human shape unrecognizably. The city as a vision of community, of mutual interdependence and cooperation, as a base of material comfort and security, has failed. Instead our cities are blandly symbolic of spiritual death. Neon lights tell us that there is no darkness, crowds tell us there is no loneliness, the monstrous architecture of our town halls tells us there is no injustice, the vast stretches of run-down housing and the teeming black poor tell us we have come far, that progress is real. We have schools so that ignorance will disappear; we have hospitals and doctors to conquer pain.

The city glistens, a reassuring, vast grid of lights, nebulas and comet tails, when you approach it, flying at night. We jet so quickly from city to city that perhaps distance and time will become superfluous. The plane circles closer. Wings tilt right and left, the vista changes, pinpoints of light twinkle in every direction. Like an astronomer, you can find the forms of heroes outlined in the stars below you. You wonder where home is as you dip closer to the luminescent seas. You sense the thrill, the miracle of it all. A man flying. A broad plain mystically glowing in the darkness. Wonder. Beauty. Awe. A fleeting pride.

For a few seconds you disbelieve the locked doors, the rooms, the bed and the bayonet beneath it.

REVIEW:
THE MARROW OF TRADITION
BY CHARLES W. CHESNUTT

1972

The fiction of Charles Waddell Chesnutt has suffered from the lack of serious readers and serious critical attention. The period in which the main body of his work was published (1899–1905) was a time when North and South had reconciled their differences over the Negro problem and cemented a prosperous, commercial partnership, an epoch that saw the European nations in a mad rush for the resources and cheap labor of the nonwhite world, when the doctrine of white supremacy was the essential ingredient harmonizing the economic, social and political philosophies that justified the thrust of European industrialized societies toward global control and domination. Given such a period, it is not surprising that the work of a nonwhite author who took as his dominant theme the dehumanizing, destructive consequences of racial prejudice was ignored by the reading public. The continued neglect of Chesnutt is perhaps an indication of the persistence of those racist attitudes so pompously rationalized by civilized men at the dawning of the twentieth century.

To honor its part of the political compromise that allowed Rutherford B. Hayes to be elected president in 1876, the Hayes administration rapidly abdicated responsibility for the newly freed Negro slaves. Titling his book *The Negro: The Southerner's Problem*, Thomas Nelson

Page was not so much arguing for a point of view as he was accurately describing the relationship between the federal government and the black man at the turn of the century. The political abandonment of the Negro to the good judgment of the reconstructed slavocracy was paralleled in literature by the ascendancy of white, southern writers (the plantation school) who attempted to sustain through their portrayal of black characters that myth of Negro inferiority that had long served the apologists of slavery.

A Chesnutt character such as Doctor Miller can be viewed simply as a reaction against prevailing stereotypes, a well-intentioned but predictably flat black knight created to do battle with the defamers of his race. But Chesnutt's innovations, as well as his importance as a novelist, have been seen too often in a narrow historical sense (he is remembered as a pioneer, the first black author published in *The Atlantic*), and then dismissed as a curiosity, quaint, genteel, worth at best a footnote in the mainstream anthologies. Examining his most complex and successful work, *The Marrow of Tradition*, I hope to demonstrate the broader historical and artistic implications of his imagination.

The Marrow of Tradition divides into two distinct sections. In the larger section, chapters one through twenty-six, Chesnutt wishes to render on a broad canvas a panoramic view of southern society. For Chesnutt, the truth of the South can be encompassed only by a comprehensive overview that includes all classes, both races, and a variety of perspectives—social, economic, and political. To examine life in the South, he creates the town of Wellington and its inhabitants as a focus for his novel. The narrative unfolds through a series of set pieces: a birth, a christening, scenes in a nursery, a segregated train, a small-town newspaper office. Many characters, black and white, are introduced, and through their manner of speaking as well as their positions in the town we begin to gain a sense of familiarity with Wellington. The casual pace of the narrative and the seemingly arbitrary selection of detail are belied by the tension, self-deception, and dishonesty that eventually culminate in a violent crime. Sandy, a black servant, is accused of robbery, rape, and murder.

Mammy Jane's dialect version of the Carteret family history had warned the reader at the beginning of the novel that at least two Wellingtons exist. Two sets of chroniclers, one black, the other white, have recorded the history of Wellington. The blacks remember the hypocrisy and violence of the slaveholding past because the caste system of the town demands an observance of rituals in their daily lives—rituals that perpetuate the master-slave relationship. The whites forget, because they must believe that the supremacy of white over black in Wellington is not the result of the criminal abuse of power but is sanctioned by an abiding supernatural order that justifies and protects the town.

A fresh instance of murder and robbery exposes the fragile truce between these antagonistic versions of reality. Violence kept alive in the continued oppression of black by white explodes in all its ugliness when a dissolute young white man, Tom Delamere, disguises himself as a black and robs his aunt in order to pay off his gambling debts. She dies of the shock, and Sandy is accused of the crime. A lynching is barely averted as the citizens of Wellington discard their veneer of civilization and collectively act out the ritual drama of outraged white purity versus the "burly, black brute." Even when Sandy's innocence is established, and the identity of the murderer known, the leaders of Wellington cannot alter the time-honored script. Evidence is suppressed and the town slowly returns to "normalcy," a normalcy paid for by a series of rationalizations and falsifications whose intent is to deny the town's guilt:

> They must not lynch the Negro, and yet, for the credit of the town, its aristocracy, and the race, the truth of this ghastly story must not see the light.

Two transitional chapters, "The Vagaries of the Higher Law" and "In Season and Out," summarize the events that have transpired in Wellington. The essay style of these chapters should not suggest lack of artistry. Their documentary tone adds to the realism cultivated by Chesnutt throughout the Wellington section and supplies the global perspective that reminds us that Wellington's crime did not occur accidentally or in a vacuum. The reader has witnessed the conscious distortion of history; he has seen how a society can willfully turn its back on the truth, choosing instead to wear the emperor's clothes. The fabric of the social order can become a lie, a self-imposed delusion that flies apart at the slightest challenge.

Chesnutt balances his straightforward expository prose with highly dramatic cameos that not only illustrate the morality and logic of his argument but subtly render, as all good fiction must, the word into flesh. "In Season and Out" concludes with a close-up of Mammy Jane's son Jerry and a group of Wellington's white civic leaders. Their interaction epitomizes the meaning of the novel's first 247 pages. Truth, frank disclosure, an acknowledgment of mutual humanity, are impossible. In a perverse display of subterfuge and imagination, Jerry and the white men literally create one another each time they meet.

> "This stuff [skin lightener] is rank poison, Jerry," continued the general with a mock solemnity which did not impose upon Jerry, who nevertheless listened with an air of great alarm. He suspected that the general was making fun of him; but also knew that the general would like to think that Jerry believed him in earnest; and to please the white folks was Jerry's consistent aim in life.

The second, shorter section of Marrow (chapters twenty-nine through thirty-seven) measures on an intimate human scale the cost of a social order built on lies. Dr. Miller, his wife, and Olivia Carteret are the characters who dominate. Dr. Miller is Wellington's most successful Negro in the sense that he is as close to white as the town's written and unwritten laws will allow any black to be. His "white" appearance, his superior education, deportment, speech, wealth, and social standing seem to place Miller in a class by himself, making him the classic "middle man," neither fish nor fowl, whose existence both dramatizes the arbitrariness of distinctions based on race and simultaneously reinforces the absolute force of such distinctions.

The wealth of incidents and details contained in Helen Chesnutt's biography of her father indicates that much of Miller's personality was a projection of Charles Waddell Chesnutt. Chesnutt was a man who seemed extraordinarily in control of himself, stable, disciplined, capable of enormous sustained effort, a self-taught intellectual whose strivings for knowledge, culture, and a career brought him into line with the Anglo-Saxon success model of his age. Like Miller, Chesnutt had learned to compartmentalize; the roles of professional man, father of a family, member of an oppressed minority, could be separated so that success in one area would not be undercut by insult or frustration in another. Chesnutt could view his writing as a business and give up a full-time commitment to it because the income from his books did not support his family in the style they were accustomed to. On one hand such compartmentalization is admirable and healthy, but taken to the extreme sanctioned by Western industrialized culture at the turn of the century, such an aptitude allowed Christian gentlemen to butcher and rob the nonwhite peoples of the earth. By forestalling an honest appraisal of the whole man, by resisting that long, hard look at the stresses and contradictions inherent in the multiplicity of "faces" he presented to Wellington, Miller was committing a perilous blunder. Chesnutt was serious enough, insightful enough, to realize that the individual will someday, somehow, be called upon to account for the arbitrary divisions by which he has shaped his life.

The accounting, the paying of dues, is anticipated by sensitive men and seldom without dread. Chesnutt perceived himself as securely part of the mainstream of American society, yet his race and its reflection in the perspective and content of his writing gradually alienated him from complete participation. Although it first seemed only a subtle wedge, the color line as it existed in the literary sphere made writing unprofitable for Chesnutt, and eventually, as a vocation, impossible. His literarily stagnant later life, with its compulsive, artificial distractions, was the eventual toll. As a foreshadowing epiphany of Chesnutt's suppressed dread, Miller is not allowed to sink slowly into oblivion but is cut down abruptly, absolutely. Racial awareness must be maintained by a Negro in American society no matter how many other roles he plays or how well he plays them. Ironically, there is no other means of transcending race. The cost of remembering blackness may be annoying, painful, an insupportable burden, or a heightened consciousness of self that is integrative and toughening, but the cost of forgetting is annihilation, sudden or subtle.

Miller's wife, Janet, is the half sister of Olivia Carteret, yet the sisters, although sharing an uncanny likeness ("Dey ce't'nly does favor one annuder—anybody mought low dey wuz twins, if dey did n' know better") and the same father, have never spoken. The sordid details of the Carteret family history, which Mammy Jane unfolds at the opening of *Marrow*, have robbed Janet and Olivia of the possibility of human communication. Instead of sisterly affection, their relationship is defined by gothically distorted expectations and apprehensions.

> Olivia felt a violent wave of antipathy sweep over her toward this baseborn sister who had thus thrust herself beneath her eyes. If she had not cast her brazen glance toward the window, she herself would not have turned away and lost sight of her child. To this shameless intrusion, linked with Clara's carelessness, had been due the catastrophe, so narrowly averted, which might have darkened her own life forever.

The chaos that nearly engulfed Wellington earlier in the novel never recedes far below the surface of events. When Olivia Carteret burns the last written record of her sister's rightful inheritance, she is acting as an individual, but her act parallels the town's attempt to tamper with the truth of history. In a situation that demanded that she act as a moral woman, she acted as a "white" woman, which meant that she could set aside all consideration of Janet's rights simply because Janet was black.

> If the woman had been white—but the woman had not been white, and the same rule of moral conduct did not, could not, in the very

nature of things, apply, as between white people! For, if this were not so, slavery had been, not merely an economic mistake, but a great crime against humanity.

By focusing on a series of individual acts which grew out of a collective, systematized distortion of the slaveholding past, Chesnutt forces the reader to perceive the inevitability of violence—and to recognize the responsibility that all the citizens of Wellington must bear for living a lie.

In the spring and summer of 1901, at the height of his fame as a fiction writer, Chesnutt was working on the novel, originally based on a race riot in the state where he had grown up and taught school. During a lecture tour of the South that year, he assiduously gathered firsthand accounts of the Wilmington, North Carolina, massacre. Although his reflections on the riot, together with his impressions of the South, were profoundly dispiriting, Chesnutt felt he had begun a "much better book than I have heretofore written."

Since two books of short stories, a novel, and a biography had brought much acclaim but only a fraction of the income he had earned from his previous jobs, Chesnutt needed more than aesthetic satisfaction from his new book: "Upon its reception will depend in some measure whether I shall write, for the present, any more 'Afro-American' novels; for a man must live and consider his family." Unfortunately, the publication of *The Marrow of Tradition* occasioned more controversy than sales. As has been so often the case, a handful of aggressive critics will use a new novel by a black writer as an excuse to air their sentiments on the "Negro question," and since the majority of the reading public already have their minds made up about Negroes, they either agree wholeheartedly with the critic or stop reading the review after its ideological stance becomes apparent. In either case the novel as an imaginative experience to be shared arouses no more curiosity for the reader of the review than it did for the reviewer.

The complex attitude Chesnutt developed toward the disaster in Wilmington is embodied in his characterization of Dr. Miller. Present throughout the novel, Miller seems to stand as an ideal character, one of Du Bois's "talented tenth" of Negro intellectuals who could absorb the highest values and professional skills of Western culture and use those for the uplift and betterment of their race. A reader as acute as Leroi Jones, in reaction to what he mistakenly perceives as Chesnutt's elitist, accommodationist point of view, chides both author and hero:

> This kind of hideous attitude in a Negro (and most of the Negro novelists of the time were quite close to Chesnutt in their social attitudes) could only stem from an acceptance of the idea of the superiority of the white man, or at least the proposition that the Negro, somehow, must completely lose himself within the culture and social order of the ex-master. It is another aspect of the slave mentality.

The problem with Jones's assessment is that he makes a total identification between Chesnutt the author and Miller the character. Although Chesnutt the man shares many traits with the "refined Afro-American doctor" he has created, Chesnutt the author builds distance between the narrative voice of *Marrow* and Miller's point of view. It is instructive to observe the sentiments on accommodationists that Chesnutt recorded at another occasion.

> If to live is the first duty of man, as perhaps it is the first instinct, then those who thus stoop to conquer may be right. But is it needful to stoop so low, and if so, where lies the ultimate responsibility for this debasement?

Does *Marrow* endorse the position of Miller? Does Chesnutt stand or fall with the norms that govern Miller's stance toward the whites and blacks of Wellington? If, as I have suggested, the strongest effects of the novel are achieved through accumulation, if its structure is dynamic and requires the reader to keep in mind that history is not simply progressive but cyclical, and that personal, family, communal, national, and finally global history are part of the same spiraling process, then one would refrain from categorizing Miller until all the evidence is in.

Instead of offering more biographical, psychological analysis of Chesnutt and thereby falling into that large category of critics who describe the black writer as *created rather than creator*, I wish to examine the evidence supplied by Chesnutt's storytelling art. The reader must look at all the elements of that art, from Chesnutt's comprehension of national and international politics, which provides the organizing theme of the novel, to stylistic details such as the sustained leitmotiv of disguise and masquerade warning the reader never to accept appearance for reality in Wellington. Further, the reader should take into account the variety of narrative tones, which range from intrusive essay-commentary to dramatic presentation. The book is further enriched with dialect, folk maxims, and parodies of newspaper verbiage, all providing a fascinating cross section of language styles written and spoken at the turn of the century.

Chapters one through twenty-six, which I have designated as part one, have a distinctive set of characteristics that distinguish their narrative mode from that of the second section. A large cast of characters, numerous changes of scene, abrupt transition of mood, place, and time, all contribute to the panoramic effect of part one. The leisurely pace of the early chapters is set by the voice of a narrator who does not hesitate to intrude himself into the action to make authorial judgments or asides. Although at times crudely manipulative or redundant, for the most part the voice is knowledgeable and humane, rising and falling to control the rhythm of the novel.

By chapter twenty-seven the action that centered on the crime of young Delamere seemingly has been closed. The reader has been exposed to the inner workings of Wellington as well as to the voice and values of the narrator who has acted as anatomist. Chesnutt can assume now that the reader has a basic working knowledge of the town and its inhabitants; therefore, as the climactic massacre of the blacks unfolds, the storyteller can take a different stance toward his audience—he can come closer to Joyce's third mode of artistic creation, the dramatic, in which the artist is invisible behind his artifact, silently paring his fingernails.

In his presentation of the massacre, Chesnutt is less chatty, his style is tighter, leaner, he allows characters and events to speak for themselves. The steadfast loyalty of Mammy Jane to the Carterets is rewarded by violent death in the streets. Jerry's record of sycophancy and slavishness does not protect his hide as he is caught in the fusillade of bullets that a white mob aims at Josh Green's supporters. Ellis, the young, white liberal from the North, is traumatized into inaction as he wanders through the bloody streets, his zombielike trance echoing Dr. Miller's shocked numbness when he drives his buggy through the chaos. Josh Green, with his cry of an eye for an eye, goes down in a hail of bullets, but not before he fulfills the self-avowed purpose of his life: vengeance on the enemy who ruined his family. Is it more than coincidental that Josh dies defending the hospital Miller has built? Was Miller correct in refusing the plea of Josh and the other blacks to lead them in self-defense? By single-mindedly searching for his family during the disaster, was Miller defining his responsibility too narrowly? Mammy Jane, Jerry, Josh, and finally Miller's wife, Janet, must be considered individually, but also as personifications of the turmoil within Miller and the whole black community. In this light it becomes apparent that Miller's primary focus for self-identification, his immediate family and his professional life, is not being dramatized as the ideal resolution of the conflicts a black man in Miller's position must face.

By the end of the novel Miller has undergone a literal and symbolic descent. He has been brutally "leveled" to the status of the town's lowliest nigger. His hospital has been burned down, his son is dead, his very existence as a physical body has been undermined as Chesnutt uses the metaphor of invisibility to characterize him during his descent into "The Valley of the Shadow." Ordered down from his buggy by a white man, Miller asks, "Why?" The man's answer is simple: "Because we've ordered you to come down! This is the white people's day, and when they order, a nigger must obey. We're going to search you for weapons." The paragraph following this exchange is notable because it includes many features of Chesnutt's style: repetition, symbolic action, sustained imagery.

> Miller stepped down from his buggy. His interlocutor, who made no effort at disguise, was a clerk in a dry goods store where Miller bought most of his family and hospital supplies. He made no sign of recognition, however, and Miller claimed no acquaintance. This man, who had for several years emptied Miller's pockets in the course of more or less legitimate trade, now went through them, aided by another man, more rapidly than ever before, the searchers convincing themselves that Miller carried no deadly weapon upon his person. Meanwhile, a third ransacked the buggy with like result. Miller recognized several others of the party, who made not the slightest attempt at disguise, though no names were called by any one.

Miller is mistaken for their enemy as he rides past black peasants in his white man's buggy. He is invisible to Old Sally the nurse, "Are you *sho* dat's you, doctuh?" and Mrs. Butler, "Is it really you, Dr. Miller?" Miller is neither white nor black, but a shadowy ghost slipping through the streets and fields of Wellington: "In the dusk his own color, slight in the daytime, would not attract attention, and by dodging in the shadows he might avoid those who might wish to intercept him." The social order is exposed as chaos. The truth of the riot forces Wellington to recognize in itself the Marrow of Tradition, the bone-deep knowledge that men are either black or white and that nothing can occur between them that does not first take into account that dichotomy. This truth has stripped away the margin that Miller had believed supported his special kind of life.

His life's work in ruins, his future snatched away by the murder of his son, Miller is morally as well as physically invisible. He cannot make a choice. Rather than answering the pleas of Mrs. Carteret to save her son's life, he equivocates, finally deferring to his wife, asking her to decide for him. The sisters, then, are left to sort out accounts. Desperate because of the peril to her child, Olivia Carteret had gone to her knees to beg Miller's assistance. "The next moment, with a sudden revulsion of feeling, she had thrown herself at his feet—at the feet of a Negro, this proud white woman—and was clasping his knees wildly." She is even prepared to recognize Janet as her sister and to bestow upon the daughter of a slave the share of the inheritance that is rightfully hers.

> Whether the truth would still further incense Janet, or move her to mercy, she could not tell; she would leave the issue to God. "Listen, sister!" she said. "I have a confession to make. You are my lawful sister. My father was married to your mother. You are entitled to his name, and to half the estate."

Janet attempts to spare the life of the Carteret child by sending her husband to tend him, but Chesnutt makes clear the sources of her motivation. In her grief she has come to the conscious recognition of the past and its cost. She understands how foolish she was to place in another's hands the right to legitimize her identity.

> You imagined that the shame of being a Negro swallowed up every other ignominy,—and in your eyes I am a Negro, though I am your sister, and you are white, and people have taken me for you on the streets,—and you, therefore, left me nameless all my life! Now, when an honest man has given me a name of which I can be proud, you offer me the one of which you robbed me, and of which I can make no use. For twenty-five years I, poor, despicable fool, would have kissed your feet for a word, a nod, a smile. Now, when this tardy recognition comes, for which I have waited so long, it is tainted with fraud and crime and blood, and I must pay for it with my child's life!

The last sentence of the novel is: "There's time enough, but none to spare." The meaning of this sentence, just as the meaning of Miller's attempt to resolve the question of his blackness in Wellington at the turn of the twentieth century, must be seen in the total context of the novel, a context that is subtle, complex, and suggestive far beyond the treatment traditionally accorded it.

REVIEW:
THE UNFINISHED QUEST OF RICHARD WRIGHT BY MICHEL FABRE

1973

Michel Fabre's critical biography, *The Unfinished Quest of Richard Wright*, provides the kind of information that is indispensable for the serious study of any literature and culture. It is symptomatic of our times and our confusions that I did not say indispensable for the study of "Afro-American" or "American" literature. Fabre's approach and method transcend the mysticism, racism, and polemic that have marred discussions of black writers throughout our national history. His book is a model for the kind of scholarship that might initiate constructive dialogue about the writing of black Americans and its relationship to American literature and culture.

Although Richard Wright has received much more critical attention than any other Afro-American author, evaluation of his writing has been based upon an incomplete, often fanciful picture of his life. In Wright's case a little knowledge of his life has proved an irresistible temptation to potential biographers. Constance Webb's *Richard Wright*, the most serious book-length biography before Fabre, though readable, full of fascinating detail, and loyal to its subject, was marred by the author's attempt at a "you are there" intimacy; employing a disconcerting omniscience more permissible in a fiction writer, she reconstructed dinner parties and train rides, not hesitating to enter into the consciousness of the people she described.

Since many of Miss Webb's reconstructions are based upon conversations with Richard Wright, the reader finds himself relying too much upon the authority and accuracy of the biographer's memory. Fabre promises a subsequent volume that would contain fuller analyses of Wright's fiction than it was possible to include in the present study, yet the commentaries and judgments he renders here far surpass the plot summaries of Webb's study. We are thus clearly welcoming the most important book to date on one of America's most important writers.

As numerous as the articles and books on Wright have been they have failed to question a simplistic view of the man and his career. Wright has been seen as a lean, hungry, angry young man who spit out *Native Son* and *Black Boy* as a protest against the racism that crippled his early life. Misled by communism and hypersensitive to racial prejudice, Wright ungenerously bolted the country that had given him fame, fortune, and the subject matter for his writing. In exile, flirtation with European intellectuals, Third World politics, and nonfiction could not replace the native roots that had nourished his literary expression; he suffered a gradual decline in expressive powers and health, becoming in his isolation a rather sad figure, out of date, eclipsed by other, hipper, brighter black writers who were competing for the mantle he had once worn as America's Number 1 Author.

This mythical version of Wright was created by many forces, among them the peculiar traditions of the literary establishment that foster propositions such as that black writers can be explained by examining the circumstances of their lives rather than by examining what they wrote, or there can be only one important black writer at a time. More specific factors responsible for the negative image of Wright have evolved from the tendency among critics to divide Wright's life into segments. Based on a broad outline of his life and treatment of each segment separately, the major phases of Wright's career—his espousal of communism, the spectacular success of *Native Son* and *Black Boy*, the move to France, the American reception of his later writing, his growing identification with an international rather than an American perspective—are used as proof of a disintegrating rather than an evolving art and personality.

Fabre's research and his central thesis are a corrective to the fragmented version of Wright's career. "Literature and politics were two equally indispensable tools in the service of humanism. This is why I insist upon judging Wright's work as a whole, not separating his writing from its ideological framework, and not making a split, only artificially justified by his exile, in the unfolding of his career. It is only by respecting this unity in its ideological, racial, and historical context that Wright's importance can be fairly evaluated."

Wright's motives for joining the Communist Party, for example, are shown to be complex and personal, organically connected to his Mississippi childhood, less the wholehearted endorsement of an ideological position than an effort to find a coherent intellectual and emotional context that would allow him to see himself and have others see him as a black man who was a writer. On another level, communism with its emphasis on the social responsibility of the writer coincided with Wright's desire to alter radically the course of Negro writing.

Wright had no patience with literature that was "external to the lives of educated Negroes. That the productions of their writers should have been something of a guide in their daily living is a matter which seems never to have been raised seriously. Negro writing became a sort of conspicuous ornamentation." These judgments are from Wright's "Blueprint for Negro Writing" (1937), an article in which the priority of a racial, "nationalist" perspective is already in subtle conflict with the standard Marxist line.

Fabre convincingly documents how Wright's enthusiasm for the party line waxed in proportion to the latitude it permitted for his primary definition of himself as black and a writer. After the natural stage of infatuation with Marxist thought, especially its call for liberation of the oppressed and the warmth of fellowship to be found in the John Reed

Clubs, Wright's basic wariness, his lifelong passion for independence and artistic freedom caused him to regard communism as at best a tool.

Wright's reactions to communism, to the existential philosophies of Sartre and Camus, to the political and cultural awakening of Africa and the rest of the Third World, were essentially experimental, or what might be called "warm blooded." The self-educated man's profound respect for books and ideas never turned Wright into an ideologue, a cold theorist who could separate the evidence of his personal feelings, the reality of his past suffering, his likes and dislikes of individuals from what seemed to be the imperatives of reason or the dictates of a philosophical position. Wright could immerse himself in a program of study, could devote his time and his writing energy mercilessly to the service of a particular cause or preoccupation, but as he grappled some part of him was always questioning.

Though consumed by the desire to know, not only first principles but how those first principles would affect what was human in him, Wright never denied the burden and reality of individual consciousness: "When the feeling of the fact of being a Negro is accepted fully into the consciousness of a Negro there's something universal about it and something that lifts it above being a Negro in America. Oh, will I ever have the strength and courage to tell what I feel and think; and do I know it well enough to tell it?"

A sense of mission propelled Wright throughout his life. In his writing he wanted to create the reality of Negro life. Only in a narrow sense was this task exclusively an artistic goal, since he felt he must remove simultaneously the emptiness from the center of his own life, an emptiness he saw reflected in the core of Negro experience. Finally, as he participated in the gradual awakening of the "wretched of the earth," whose cultural dependence and economic exploitation mirrored his experiences, he began to sense those "supporting minds" and "kindred feelings" he had been seeking that could corroborate the authenticity of his own inner life. Fabre demonstrates how Wright's emotional and intellectual identification with the Third World was not a desperate groping for a new source of inspiration to replace his lost American roots but rather a logical development of his continuous investigation of the meaning of Negro culture and character.

Fabre establishes the integrity of Wright's quest so effectively that the reader is forced to reconsider the meaning of his exile. Was Wright, as countless critics and even his agent Paul Reynolds charged, missing out on what was happening in America? Were his attitudes and knowledge of the American scene dated? From Wright's point of view it was America that had become static. He saw post–World War II American society as unresponsive to the international currents of intellectual, political, even moral awakening. America between 1945 and 1959 was a backwater, mired in the race problem, the cold war, screening its backwardness, its hypocrisy and provincialism behind a facade of material progress, economic and military might.

Wright meanwhile was expanding outward, involving himself in the ferment of European intellectual life, the problems of the newly created African and Asian states; in short the international context which would eventually intrude itself upon the American consciousness in the form of Asian wars and the new militancy of disaffected minorities and the young. Are Americans now prepared to do more than cry over Bigger Thomas and their scarified black boys? Are we ready to deal with the entirety of Wright's vision, the connections he made between the fate of American Negroes and the fate of the Western World?

When Fabre notes that at the beginning of his research he was grateful "no legend had sprung up" about Wright because it would be "easier to break the silence than destroy an established myth," he is not taking into account the myth of Richard Wright which justified the conspiracy of silence Fabre encountered in 1961. Yet as he assiduously supplies the details of Wright's life, Fabre implicitly demolishes the superficial unity imposed upon Wright's career.

What are the grounds for considering a book or an author "great"? Who designates the contents of that shelf of books called classics and how and why do critics generate from these works the rules and standards used to judge other books? Far from being academic, such questions are raised stridently and persistently as writers and critics challenge the assumptions that have made American Literature a synonym for White American Literature. One of the values of Michel Fabre's study is that it makes a case for the stature of Richard Wright through scrupulous documentation, a case that challenges many traditional notions of Wright, as well as traditional ways of looking at Afro-American literature. It is not that Fabre is always right, but rather that the level of argument and his high standards of scholarship invite a continuing discourse in their terms rather than the all-too-familiar impassioned rhetoric that has obscured the work of black American writers.

DEFINING THE
BLACK VOICE IN FICTION

1977

> The fact is, of course, that there is no such thing as Negro dialect; that what we call by that name is the attempt to express, with such a degree of phonetic correctness as to suggest the sound, English pronounced as an ignorant old southern Negro would be supposed to speak it, and at the same time to preserve a sufficient approximation to the correct spelling to make it easy reading.

—Charles Chesnutt

Negro dialect as it was conventionalized in American literature of the eighteenth and nineteenth centuries was not black speech but the colonial interface of two language cultures—one written, literary, and the other oral, traditional. The resources of the black oral folk tradition were expropriated for the enrichment of the dominant culture, and the existence of the colony depended on its usefulness to its exploiters. The literary frame in which Negro dialect appeared was a natural extension of the colonial relationship, assuring that the interface would be rendered in the terms of the literature culture. These terms led to an undervaluing of the oral tradition and its subordination within the literary frame because much of what was essentially expressive in oral performance did not "translate" into writing. A kind of emasculation of oral culture occurred; it was streamlined, censored so it appeared infantile beside the matured mode of literary expression.[1] Specifically the oral tradition lost the spontaniety of improvisation, gesture, intonation, song, dance, mime effects, metrical and rhythmic structures.[2] In addition to the loss of performance effects (the immediate, "hot" impact), oral literature rendered in print lost its depth in time, the link with the ancestors and sources of vitality. In the case of black speech the literary frame cut off its allusiveness, the sources of moral and aesthetic authority, the organic system which energized the words and word structures. The traditional fabric was rent and destroyed. Black speech was reduced in print to the arbitrary shorthand of Negro dialect.[3]

Against this background one can view the evolution of the black voice in American literature as the attempts of various writers to free themselves from a frame which a priori devalues black speech. Certain continuities and problems shared by black American writers can be moved out of the context of political ideology and analyzed in terms of language and literary style.

> *Some view our sable race with scornful eye,*
> *"Their colour is a diabolic die."*
> *Remember, Christians, Negroes, black as Cain,*
> *May be refin'd, and join th' angelic train.*[4]

These lines are from "On Being Brought from Africa to America" by Phillis Wheatley, an African girl who was brought as a slave to America in 1761 and learned English so quickly and thoroughly that she was writing poetry in her new language within a few years.

> She was crying, not from anything I said, but she must have skinned her ass when she hit the floor. I turned on the light and she was sucking her arm and getting the blanket and crying. I kept calling her a goddamn bull, but I didn't like what I was wondering. I was wondering how Cat Lawson got her to mind. Because that wasn't the kind of kid that would respect anybody on account of age.[5]

Gayl Jones, a young black woman, is the author of the second passage, a moment in her novel *Corregidora* (1975), written while she was a graduate student at Brown University. Are there connections to be made between these two examples of black writing? Shouldn't a critic of black writing be able to define areas of continuity, devise strategies, suggest logical categories for handling these widely different styles if in fact the critic argues for a black tradition in American literature? Not that these two young female writers need to be alike because they are black; rather, are there signs of unity in diversity which we may draw from their examples? And where might Chesnutt's or Dunbar's use of dialect fit? In order to unite these writers, one of the central problems in the study of black literature must be confronted: the task of charting the evolution of black speech into a self-sufficient, independent literary code.[6]

For an African brought to America as a slave in the seventeenth and eighteenth centuries the literary code of English was at least thrice removed: by the initial language barrier of his African tongue, by the discrepancy between the oral and literate traditions in English, and finally by the African tradition in which verbal art was an oral rather than a written mode. Wheatley transcended two barriers—she learned to speak English and she learned a literary code of that language. Since the norms of eighteenth-century poetry reflected little of the language she heard spoken around her, her notion of poetry would be that it was a closed system, derived from imitation of earlier written works. No place existed in this variety of poetry for the rough-and-ready Americanized English she might hear in the streets, or the speech of other Afro-Americans with whom she might come into contact, and of course there was no room for Africanisms she might recall. The conventions of neoclassical poetry ruled out casual talk; her voice and feelings had to be generalized according to rules of poetic diction and characterization; the particulars of her African past, if they were acceptable at all, had to be subordinated to the reigning conventions she absorbed. Wheatley was affected by specific facts of the literary historical environment into which she was transplanted. Her experience of poetry in Africa just wouldn't count as poetry in her new situation. The aesthetic canons which she might have internalized were irrelevant to the new context because no language or social framework existed to reinforce them. This barrier was too great to surmount. Wheatley is absorbing a foreign literary tradition just as she learns a foreign language; they are not an extension of her past experiences with language but are meant to replace what came before. In terms of the evolutionary framework I'm attempting to sketch, Wheatley represents the meeting of oral and literate cultures, and, therefore, the potential for interpenetration, a potential her writing does not exploit.

For the oral poet or folk artist a different situation obtained. In work songs, dancing, field hollers, religious music, the use of the drum, and the perpetuation of drum effects after drums were forbidden, the aesthetic canons of African oral tradition survived the middle passage. African languages and the functions of language in African societies not only facilitated for Africans the learning of a new language but exerted demonstrable effects on the manner in which other Americans spoke English. The folk artist could employ in his creations a mature, familiar style whose general features would be recognizable to the majority of African peoples being brought as slaves from West Africa. Wheatley eschews this "captive audience" and does not attempt to render the distinctiveness of black speech in her poetry: artistic expression for her is defined by the eighteenth-century literary code of English, a code doubly foreign, a tradition in which her achievements seem both miraculous and pedestrian.

In most western European countries where there are traces of a change from an oral to a literary tradition, the development seems to have come about through those trained in some degree in a foreign literary tradition that has itself entered from foreign sources. At some point someone applies the ideas of written literature to native oral tradition.[7] This pattern characterizes the development of black literature in America. The ideas of written literature (Anglo-American) are gradually applied to the native oral cultures (Afro-American), forming, in the New World, a process which later becomes a matter of cross-fertilization and fusion in the hands of black artists. Since exposure to both written and oral cultures and an opportunity to publish were unlikely for a black during the eighteenth and nineteenth centuries, it is not surprising that southern white men of letters were instrumental in the incorporation of black speech and folklore into written literature. Neither is it surprising that since southern white males were most influential in applying the ideas of written to oral literature, the form and content of black speech were conditioned to serve special interests.

A distinction must be made here between what counts and doesn't count in the official version of American literary history. Many writers black and white used Negro dialect in their work before dialect was exploited by white southern writers in the last quarter of the nineteenth century. The slave narrative is an example of a genre where the development of black speech as a literary language might fruitfully be investigated, but the narratives factual and fictional have been traditionally perceived as extraliterary, and the work of black writers such as William Wells Brown has been noted strictly from a historical/chronological perspective rather than subjected to literary analysis. The narratives, the fiction of Brown and Delaney, did not count as literary facts. A new question needs to be asked—how does black speech evolve into a literary language?—before these "extraliterary" facts can be "discovered" in Ejxenbaum's sense: "the incorporation of a new set of facts (under the sign of some particular correlation) strikes us as being the discovery of those facts, since their existence outside a system (their 'contingent' status) had been from a scientific point of view equivalent to their non-existence."[8]

From the point of view of American literature, then, the fact of black speech (and the oral roots of a distinct literary tradition—ultimately the tradition itself) existed only when it was properly "framed" within works which had status in the dominant literary system. For black speech the frame was the means of entering the literate culture, and the frame also defined the purposes or ends for which black speech could be employed. The frame conferred reality on black speech; the literary frame was a mediator, a legitimizer. What was outside the frame chaotic, marginal, not worthy of the reader's attention becomes, once inside, conventionalized into respectability.

The frame can inhere in the structure of a work (the dialect stories of Chesnutt's Uncle Julius are tales within tales, seemingly subordinate to the voice of John, a narrator who speaks literary English)[9]; in the subjective "voice-over" of a third-person omniscient (Irwin Russell's "Christmas Night in the Quarters"); in objective, depersonalized descriptive adjectives and stage directions ("befo de wah," said the gnarled, old slave, gazing nostalgically at the sumptuous oaks shading the spacious veranda of the big house). Or the frame can be implicit: conventions of Negro speech, manners, dress, once firmly established, can upon their appearance trigger automatic responses in an audience. James Weldon Johnson in the preface to *The Book of American Negro Poetry* yearns for the day when a "colored poet of the United States may sit down to write in dialect without feeling that his first line will put the general reader in a frame of mind which demands that the poem be humorous or pathetic."[10] The frame implies a linguistic hierarchy, the dominance of one language variety over all others. This linguistic subordination extends naturally to the dominance of one version of reality over others.

If the lines from Wheatley's "On Being Brought from Africa to America" are at one end of the continuum representing the evolution of black speech to a self-sufficient literary language, the narrator of *Corregidora* demonstrates how far other writers have moved out of the frame. Wheatley's poem illustrates almost total dependence on a foreign literary tradition, foreign to African languages, to American speech, to the traditions of African verbal art. Transition—the application of the ideas of the written literature to a native oral tradition—exists potentially, but has not begun. Gayl Jones also exhibits her debt to a literary tradition, but it is a tradition including Wheatley and Pope, Faulkner and Ellison, a tradition richer in models and less foreign to American speech. The salient issue here is not the throng of influences on *Corregidora* which may be mustered from other works of literature, but rather the relationship between literate and oral traditions in Jones's novel. Gayl Jones is a member of a black speech community, and this membership implicates a significant dimension of her literary style. In contrast to Wheatley, for whom oral traditions black or white are negligible, the fluency of Jones in two language cultures permits her to create a considerable dramatic tension between them, a tension responsible for much of the novel's impact and uniqueness. One critic's comment, "The book is written with almost embarrassing power,"[11] is evidence of how difficult this tension is to resolve. In the quoted passage from *Corregidora* there is no hierarchical relationship between black speech and a separate literary language, no implicit dependency. The norms of black oral tradition exist full-bodied in the verbal style of the novel: lexicon, syntax, grammar, attitudes toward speech; moral and aesthetic judgments are rendered in the terms of the universe they reflect and reinforce. The entire novel flows through the filter of the narrator's sensibility, and Corregidora's sensibility is constructed of blocks of black speech, her own, her men's, the speech of the people who patronize Happy's bar, the voices of her mother and the dead black women keeping alive the memories of slavery. Black speech is allowed to do (the author insists that it can) everything any other variety of literary language can do. The message comes through loud and clear to the reader: there is no privileged position from which to view this fictional world, no terms into which it asks to be translated; its rawness is not incidental, not local color or exoticism from which other, more familiar voices will relieve you. A black woman's voice creates the only valid terms for Corregidora's world; the authority of her language is not subordinated to other codes; the frame has disappeared.

In this novel and others black speech as a literary language has become *creolized*; that is, it has moved from being a *pidgin* at an earlier historical stage, and has become the only (or principal) language of a speech community. A pidgin has no native speakers. It exists as a *lingua franca*, a language used for purposes of wider communication, especially in a group in which the native language of no member of the group will suffice.[12] Negro dialect as it was conventionalized in nineteenth-century American literature fits perfectly the definition of a pidgin. But *dialect* or *pidgin* are no longer accurate words when speaking about the black language of contemporary Afro-American fiction. An independent literary language has developed from the halting pidgin of dialect. Verbal structures, grammar, and vocabulary are related to but not explicable solely by the logic of standard English. Black writers have created their own code of discourse from the resources of the black oral tradition and the models of American literature.

Wright viewed racial conflict in American society as a struggle over the nature of reality. Chesnutt anticipated him when he juxtaposed the dialect voice with standard literary discourse (a code for the real), dramatizing the inadequacy of the assumptions (encoded in literary discourse as part of the real) that locked the black voice and black character into conventionalized, formulaic molds. Uncle Julius, like Kilroy, peeks around the frame, uses it for his own purposes, ultimately demolishing its restrictions. In order to move closer to *Corregidora*, we must look to writers other than Chesnutt for literary transformations of the outward forms of black folk speech.

Zora Neale Hurston's *Their Eyes Were Watching God* (1937) is begun in conventional literary discourse, but as Janie's voice takes over the narration, Hurston returns dialect to its roots in black folk speech, elaborating the context in which black speech is the independent expression of a speech community rather than a shorthand for indicating Negro inferiority. Hurston depicts the form and functioning of black speech within a specific cultural setting, and because this setting is a totally black community, any external frame is minimized. The language reflects the lives of rural black folk and is adequate as any peoples' language is adequate for a full range of communicative needs. This is not to suggest a lack of aesthetic dimensions in black speech. These in fact are emphasized in Hurston through the sustained metaphor of "talk"—talk as ritual, talk as play, talk as prop of institutions and values in the community, and, embracing all its other functions, talk as an instrument for validating experience and vice versa, experience as the confirming ground of talk. Authenticity of character, of experience are related by Hurston to the connection between word and act. ". . . you got to *go* there, to *know* there,"[13] a connection embodied by black speech in its various artistic modes—boasts, courtship speech, the dozens, preaching, singing the blues, etc. Because Hurston focuses on black speech as it functions in a specific community setting, the reader's attention is drawn away from the external form of dialect—the comic orthography, the elisions, preposterous words, the "eye dialect"—in short, the stylistic stock-in-trade of nineteenth- and early twentieth-century writers of Negro dialect, stylistic tricks that were subversive because they suggested invidious comparisons between the written and spoken, divergence or deviancy from the "norm." The question of technical accuracy in rendering dialect is also put in proper perspective by Hurston's approach. Whether Chesnutt or Cable or Harris came closest in approximating the *actual* speech of southern rural blacks is a specialist's concern, which may be sorted out with tape recorders and statistical analysis, but a question that leaves literary evaluation untouched. Once a convention for dramatizing black speech appears in fiction, the literary critic should be concerned not with matters of phonetic accuracy, but with tracing the evolution of a written code and determining how that code refers to the spoken language in suggestive, artful, creative ways. How does Hurston's or Chesnutt's rendering of black speech make available to the reader those elements of language which manifest the full range of Afro-American experience in the southern rural United States? In the sense that Dell Hymes develops for the concept, blacks form speech communities, and their speech acts must be viewed as phenomena rooted in distinct cultural settings. To understand what a person is saying one must learn to recognize not only the culturally variable nature of words themselves, but of the social situations that occasion speech acts.[14]

Black speech like any other variety of language defines reality for its users. Black speech in American literature could not perform this function until it divested itself of the frame, those elements in a literary tradition which resolve in favor of the literate, conflicting versions of reality codified into written and oral modes of expression. In the same sense that the French New Novel could not totally dispense with all "realistic" conventions of fiction, black speech cannot escape entirely the frame of American literary language. Barthes in S/Z discusses the code of realism in "readerly" fiction, arguing that the code of novelistic realism refers to a pictorial code which is itself not "reality" but a set of conventions for depicting reality within the frame of a classical painting.[15] As long as the depiction of black reality was dependent for its verification on the conventions of another code (mainstream American literature) and the conventions of that code were not examined as Barthes examines the relationship of fictive and pictorial realism, the black voice in American fiction could never become a distinct, independent index to reality. The New Novelists had to explode in their fiction a dependence on pictorial conventions to deprive the traditional novelists' "realism" of its arbitrary authority, and in a similar fashion Chesnutt, Hurston, and Jones each attack the authority of the literary frame which mediates between black speech and reality. Such attacks and counterstatements embodied in the writing of black American writers form one of the unities in diversity which substantiate a Black Tradition in American Literature.

NOTES

1. Albert B. Lord, *The Singer of Tales* (New York: Atheneum, 1970), ch. 6.

2. Ruth H. Finnegan, *Oral Literature in Africa* (London: Clarendon Press, 1970), pp. 3–15.

3. Tremaine McDowell, "Notes on Negro Dialect in the American Novel to 1821," *American Speech* 5 (1929–30), 291–96; Richard Walser, "Negro Dialect in Eighteenth-Century Drama," *American Speech* 30 (1955), 269–76.

4. Phillis Wheatley, "On Being Brought from Africa to America," in *Early Black American Poets*, ed. William H. Robinson, Jr. (Dubuque: Wm. C. Brown Co., 1971), p. 100.

5. Gayl Jones, *Corregidora* (New York: Random House, 1975), p. 39.

6. "Code" is used here and *passim* in the sense developed by Roland Barthes in *S/Z*, trans. Richard Miller (New York: Hill and Wang, 1974): see pp. 18–20 on the five codes, pp. 54–56 on the code of pictorial realism in literary mimesis, and pp. 80–81 on the code of "realistic" novels.

7. Lord, p. 133.

8. B. M. Ejxenbaum, "Literary Environment," in *Readings in Russian Poetics: Formalist and Structuralist Views*, ed. Ladislav Matejka and Krystyna Pomorska (Cambridge: MIT Press, 1971), p. 56.

9. Charles W. Chesnutt, *The Conjure Woman* (1899; rpt. Ann Arbor: Univ. of Michigan Press, 1969).

10. James Weldon Johnson, "The Preface to the First Edition of *The Book of American Negro Poetry*" (1922; rpt. in *Black American Literature in America*, ed. Houston A. Baker [New York: McGraw Hill, 1971]), p. 191.

11. *Corregidora*, book jacket copy.

12. J. L. Dillard, *Black English* (New York: Random House, 1972), pp. 73–138.

13. *Their Eyes Were Watching God* (1937; rpt. Greenwich: Fawcett Publications, 1969), p. 158.

14. Dell Hymes, "Models of the Interaction of Language and Social Life," in *Directions in Sociolinguistics*, ed. John J. Gunaperz and Dell Hymes (New York: Holt, Rinehart and Winston, 1972), pp. 35–71.

15. Barthes, p. 41 ff.

REVIEW:
STOMPING THE BLUES:
RITUAL IN BLACK MUSIC
AND SPEECH

1978

All page numbers in parentheses refer to
Stomping the Blues *(McGraw-Hill, 1976).*

Stomping the Blues is full of messages. For those of you who haven't
heard, blues music and by implication Afro-American art in general are
not created by spontaneous, uninhibited, natural outpouring of emotion.
Rather, the dues that must be paid in order to play the blues involve the
same self-restraint, discipline, and grounding in idiomatic tradition to
which any artist must submit. And critics of blues whose first obligation
is increasing "the accessibility of the aesthetic presentation" must come to
terms with the peculiarities of a "given process of stylization" (196). And
further, that dance antedates music and all other art forms, since much
evidence suggests dance was the "first means by which human consciousness objectified, symbolized, and stylized its perceptions, conceptions
and feelings" (189). And also that the idea of defining a special state of
feeling with the color "blue" dates back at least to Middle English ("bla"),
and that anyone wishing to understand blues music and its seminal role

in Afro-American culture must acquaint themselves with the distinction between the emotional mood "blues" (the property of no particular nation or race) and the blues (native to the U.S.), "a magical combination of idiomatic incantation and percussion that creates the dance-oriented good time music" (16). And also this blues music which is a ritual for dispersing gloom and spreading glee has both African and European roots but an essence understandable only in terms of the experience of American blacks.

And so on and so on the messages instruct those who know very little about blues music and those who thought they knew a lot. Which is not to suggest the messages become tendentious or tedious. The message form, the medium constantly delights the reader. This is a book Produced and Art Directed by Harry Lewine. Scores of photographs complement and extend the text. The lavish illustrations, the artful arrangement and choice of pictures in Albert Murray's *Stomping the Blues* are part of the ritual celebrating and evocating black music.

The incantatory qualities of Murray's prose work just as effectively as the pictures to bring the musicians and music to life. Like Pater on Renaissance painters or Hemingway on bull fighting, the art of Murray's prose style becomes as interesting, absorbing as the subject matter. A subtle reciprocity occurs: as the writer unravels the mysteries, the formal aesthetic core of the activity being investigated (blues, painting, bull fighting), its rules and rituals become a guide, a standard of conduct informing the way the subject is written about. Without minimizing Murray's insights on the blues (this essay, after all, begins with a sampling), I would like to leave for experts on blues music an evaluation of what Murray has said and how his comments relate to other major statements about the blues, and focus this essay on two other issues: Do the structure and technique of Murray's essay parallel devices employed by blues musicians, and if Murray's prose can be seen as an extension, refinement, modification of the same tradition nourishing blues music, what are the implications of this relationship between music and writing for a definition of Afro-American culture?

Examining such questions raises the issue of metaphor as a form of analysis. Harold Courlander in his study *American Negro Folk Music* argues that blues and Afro-American religious songs get their point across through innuendo, repetition, hints, allusion rather than telling of explicit, chronological, developed stories. Bruce Jackson asserts that the structural units of folk songs are typically metaphor and line rather than plot and that the songs don't weave narrative elements together to create a story but instead accumulate images to create a feeling. Murray's examination of the blues fits squarely into this tradition. The net he casts to trap the meaning of blues music is itself an artifact carefully wrought with the devices similar to those employed in making blues music. Murray's central metaphor in *Stomping the Blues* is language. In a good poem or a convincing essay objects linked, compared and contrasted by simile or metaphor, go beyond the stage of having a logical, analogous relationship to one another and assume a temporary, magical equivalency. The reader feels that he or she is understanding something basic about the intrinsic nature of the objects compared, not simply the inevitable circularity and overlap of the meaning of words. When Murray talks repeatedly about vernacular, idiom, accent, voice, voicing, speech, phrase, and fluency he is not only extending the metaphoric relationship between language and music but establishing a continuity along which "language" and "music" are two rather arbitrary signposts.

The power of words to clarify, order, and arrange is the tip of an iceberg, the foundation of the power is out of sight, below the surface. It has to do with preconscious recognition of order, design, necessity, the cycles and rhythms of nature. Incantatory language, magic formulas attempt to give form to this level of sound, relating directly rather than referentially to the meaning and force of things. Music plunges downward for its force, words are the force distilled, lightened, tamed, and domesticated for convenience. But words can plunge downward, can seek revitalizations. When they do this they lose their hard, brittle outlines, they bend, merge, glow as the arbitrary sheath containing them disintegrates and their auras of force are released. The words of a Church of God in Christ preacher as they stretch and mutate and go on back home and *down home* where the congregation needs them to be, and needs to be itself, change in register from spoken to chanted to sung. When the gospel chorus and the congregation respond, the world is being made over because the world is being made over. This remaking and renaming is a ritual at the core of Old Time Religion and Afro-American speech styles. The congregation by translating the word to song has reclaimed its right to understand the world in its own terms. No longer strangers in a strange land, struggling to master the foreign speech of strangers, the chanting and singing is a God-Spirit granted fluency (singing became a form of speaking in tongues). Listening to the Reverend C. L. Franklin or the sermons of Martin Luther King one will hear that the implicit subject is nearly always language, the word. If not in the content of the speech, then in the form of the preacher's language as he stretches, personalizes, mocks, parodies standard English, when he bounces backward and forward from standard to biblical to black vernacular cadences, when he repeats a single word or phrase, hammering at it again and again till it is forged with the assent of the congregation into just the shape that can bear some archetype of the communal experience, when words are heightened rhythmically and tonally and merge into the lines of a hymn or a moan, a shout or cry, the message of the preacher's language is clear. *Let's get down.* Let's get on down and see what this thing is we're feeling and talking about. Let's get on down and tell it like it is. Shout it out. Sing it out. Tell the truth. Bring down the spirit.

This is the fundamental ritual of Afro-American speech: evocative, incantatory, transforming. The word seeking to return to its origin in song, approaching song (as the work, play movements of a dance-beat-oriented people approach dance movements) to validate the truth of the experience the word seeks to celebrate. *Stomping the Blues* is an important book in a variety of ways, but nothing it accomplishes is more effective than its enactment of this primal ritual.

From its beginnings in the pidgin spoken along the slaving coasts of West Africa, Afro-American speech has served ritualistic as well as more mundane communicative functions. In the New World the stage of Afro-American speech known as Plantation Creole was a repository of black insight, survival techniques, and expressive strategies. The language of the slaves functioned to restore and maintain the sense of dignity denied them within the social, political, and linguistic bondage forced upon them by their "Masters." In songs, stories, the names they bestowed on one another and upon whites, in the use of black speech as a code whites could not decipher, slaves were performing emancipatory rites. Formal structures imprinted by these rites upon black speech remain intact in the language spoken by substantial numbers of contemporary Afro-Americans. The call-and-response pattern, heightened rhythmic and tonal effects, metaphors and imagery drawn from archytypal communal experiences, the dozens, signifying, jiving, obscenity, copping a plea, fancy talk, indirection, innuendo, figurative speech, the reliance on affective qualities of speech (tone, repetition, kinesics, rhythm) as much or more than intellection to persuade, all have their roots in the ritual functions of Afro-American speech.

The same point that Murray makes about the blues, that they are essentially the embodiment of a ritual and that Afro-American musical tradition maintains its force and coherency through a recapitulation of these ritualistic elements in various forms and combinations—from field cries to avant-garde Jazz—can be made about the narrative voice of *Stomping the Blues*. Begin with the elegance of the book. Like the jazz musician's clothing the book is consciously styled to make a calculated impression: it is itself an artifact expressing definite ideas about what is proper and together. The book even in paperback is well made and expensive. Its pages are compositions in black and white. A bold, assertive typeface, milky white paper, frequent italics and decorative initial letters, ornate borders designed around musical motifs, the cascades of photos—half page and full page and spreading over two pages at a time—all contribute to an image of sophistication, of casual contrivance and the cool of absolute control. And image speaking as clearly as the photo of Duke Ellington (p. 235). Duke in formal dress, his face full front to the camera, shaded so his pencil-thin mustache and eyebrows slightly raised (a rake's leer, a Beg your pardon, Madame, a neophyte's smoldering innocence, Daddy-O-Try-Me If You Dare) complement the angle of the top hat slanting across his brow.

The narrative voice of *Stomping the Blues* is just as stylized and laid-back as the image of Duke. Variations in tone give the voice both its authority—a requisite for narrative continuity—and its unpredictability, the quality enhancing our word-by-word, sentence-by-sentence delight in each moment. The voice Murray creates speaks down-home southern idiom ("the actual voices of which all blues instrumentation is an extension speak primarily and definitively as well as the idiomatic accents and tonalities of U.S. Negroes down south," 118), urban street talk, academese, the argot of musicians, formal preaching, teaching rhetoric of the blues people who *know there* because they've *been there.* Not only does the voice command numerous varieties of language, it also has the musical sense of timing necessary for quick changes, shifts, and counterpoint. The narrator creates verbal equivalencies of the strategies he identifies with the blues tradition in Afro-American music: improvisation, call-and-response interaction with the audience, riffing, breaks, parody and stylized quotation of a variety of sources.

"Playing the Blues" is a section about technique containing definitions of riff, break, tonal coloration, syncopation, and other devices essential to the blues tradition. Take Murray's definition of a blues riff as "a brief musical phrase that is repeated, sometimes with very subtle variations, over the length of a stanza as the chordal pattern follows its normal progression" and change the word *stanza* to *section* and *chordal pattern* to *narrative exposition* and you have a description of a rhetorical device Murray employs throughout *Stomping the Blues.* Playing with his definition of the break as "a very special kind of ad-lib bridge passage or cadenza-like interlude between two musical phrases that are separated by an interruption or interval in the established cadence," in a similar way you arrive at another characteristic prose strategy structuring Murray's analysis of the blues. "Playing the Blues" begins with a paragraph that is a break; the railroading train imagery of the same section is a riff rising to a dominant role in the composition with the six-page photo essay on mighty trains and black railroad men.

> But even no old pro that you have become, sometimes all you have to hear is the also and also of the drummer signifying on the high-hat cymbal, even in the distance land it is as if it were the also and also of time itself whispering red alert as if in blue italical, and all you have to do to keep them in their proper place, which in deep in the dozens, is to pet your feet and soap your fingers (258).

In this passage the words *signifying* and *dozens* provide tonal coloration (black speech), the *also and also* and *all* are riffs punctuating the exposition, and *which is deep in the dozens* is an ad-lib break in the breathing space provided by the established cadence of the sentence.

The structure of *Stomping the Blues* preserves the ritualistic qualities of black speech and sustains the parallels between the playing of Afro-American music and writing. Each section of the book ("The Blues as Such," "Singing the Blues," "The Blues as Statement," etc.) is an interlude, a rap, a seeming improvisation on some aspect of the blues. The method inside each section is associative: a general concept or insight is stated then changes are rung in a theme-and-variations fashion. Murray's evocation of the blues is neither linear nor exhaustive. A single word, *play*, or concept—instruments played in a drumlike fashion, or pattern of imagery—trains and railroading—becomes a point of departure and the reader is treated to a series of factual, metaphoric, provocative, evocative excursions into the territory these ideas suggest to Murray's imagination. The manner in which Murray's text and the photos reinforce one another is significant. There is no predictable, hierarchical arrangement of words and pictures. Rather, the blocks of prose meander through the photos. Or vice versa. The reader may be initially disconcerted by the seemingly haphazard arrangement, but once he relaxes and stops treating the pictures as interruptions, once he realizes he is on his own time, that the repetitive, compulsive left-to-right eye scanning across lines of print has been purposely short-circuited, and that the reader is being encouraged to turn pages slowly to get into and round the pictures, that the captions beneath the pictures are another worthwhile digression, a different mode of word painting within and around the continuous (?) narrative, he is ready to enjoy the music. Pictures are a commentary on words and words comment on the pictures but together they point to another dimension, the space created by Visual Poetry where media converge and evolve a new experience. The reader is being invited to share the pictures, to discover and reminisce simultaneously, to orchestrate the expressive media of the book and proceed at his own pace.

Incantatory rituals are often marked by the repetition of magic formulas. Abbra Cadabra. Enny Meeny Minny Mo. Shazam. A Tisket a Tasket or Hi do hi do hi de ho or scat singing or the repeated shout of a sanctified gospel chorus are translations of this formulaic incantation into black music. In Baraka's story "Screamers" (*Tales*, 1967) the saxman Lynn Hope "got his riff, that rhythmic figure we knew he would repeat, the honked note that would be his personal evaluation of the world. And he screamed it so the veins in his face stood out like neon. 'Uhh, yeh. Uhh, yeh, Uhh, yeh,' we all screamed to push him further." Lynn's honked riff drives "Five or six hundred hopped up woogies" from the dance hall right out into the middle of Belmont Avenue. The "form of the secret communal expression," the "sweetest revolution," which Baraka's short story describes are what Murray attempts to capture in his study of the blues. Both writers are emphasizing the magical, evocative, transforming qualities of black expressive culture and experimenting with ways of enacting these qualities in writing. A magic formula precedes the epilogue of *Stomping the Blues*: "*And one and two and three and four and another one and a two and a three and a four and also and also and also.*" The italics here or embodying other formulas, *getting with it, taking care of business, let the good times roll, one more time* are not accidental. Italics mark the words as special, heighten them, make you see them, even hear them if you've been around the places where somebody is always shouting out such encouragement, always urging the music higher and higher and themselves higher and higher till the music is where it's at and the music is what's happening and you are flying there where it's all happening.

Murray's prose, like the pictures, invites the reader to actively partic-ipate. Like the verbal art *signifying* much of the success of Murray's style depends on a body of information shared by the reader and writer, on experiences not indicated by the dictionary meaning of Murray's words. The words and images of *Stomping the Blues* must be metaphorically reprocessed after their literal significance has been absorbed. Murray tells us how and when such reprocessing should occur by embedding "keys" in the narrative. The subtlety of the introduction of these keys into his discourse and the humor, irony or insight of the *double-entendres* sug-gested by the keys are measures of Murray's art. The facility with which the reader can catch and decipher keys depends upon his familiarity with Afro-American language and culture. Which is not to suggest racially determined critical acumen or exclusivity or political separateness, but to acknowledge for black writing what Murray asserts about Afro-American music: its special combination of spontaneity, improvisation, and control depends upon grounding in a specific cultural setting, and idiomatic flu-ency comes only after saturation in the experiences of which the musical stylization is one distillation.

"Stomping the blues" is whipping gloom and misery, is gaining a tempo-rary victory over the blue devils always there pecking around and through and under the fabric of our lives. "Stomping the blues" is also dancing with the get-down style of dance-beat-oriented people, people who "refine all movement in the direction of dance-beat elegance . . . work movements become dance movements and so do their play movements; and so, indeed, do all the movements they use every day, including the way they walk, stand, turn, wave, shake hands, reach, or make any gesture at all" (189). To say someone or something is "stomped down" is to employ a figure of speech from the repetoire of Afro-American oral tradition. The phrase can be an intensifier, like "stone," of either positive or negative qualities. It can also mean "whipped" in the sense of "beaten down," "bedraggled," "bereft of possibility and promise," but all of these with a slightly comic inflection that derives from exaggeration and the recognition that pathos when it is extreme grows perilously close to the ridiculous. "Stomped down" derives various shades of meaning from its verbal context, from tonal and rhythmic subtleties of pronunciation. It is recorded in the narratives of ex-slaves, and, I've heard it as recently as yesterday in a story my seventy-six-year-old aunt told at a wake. The resonances of stomp, stomping, and stomped down (and I have mentioned only a few) key the reader to dimensions of the ritual embodied in blues dancing. To fully appreciate Murray's word magic one must sort through the peculiarities, the specifics of Afro-American culture to identify such resonances, just as Murray rescues from dictionaries this history in the English language of associating a feeling state with the color blue. Murray is explicit about the responsibilities of the music critic who would write about blues or jazz:

> The most fundamental requisite for mediating between the work of art and the audience, spectators or readers . . . is not reverence for the so-called classics but rather an understanding of what is being stylized plus an accurate insight into how it is being stylized. Each masterwork of art, it must be remembered, is always first of all a comprehensive synthesis of all the aspects of its idiom. Thus to ignore its idiomatic roots is to miss the essential nature of its statement, and art is nothing if not stylized statement. (196)

The way *Stomping the Blues* is put together—the rhythmic counterpoint between words and images; its rhetorical strategies, the stylized intimacy of the narrative voice, the voice's wide range of speech and literary styles, its incantatory use of exhortation and magic formula; the embodiment of black speech rituals (i.e., *signifying, dozens*): the constant metaphorical links between language and music, dance movement and speech—point to structural continuities in the various media of Afro-American expressive culture. Murray's book literally evokes the Good Time atmosphere of the Saturday Nite Function. How we learn about the blues is part of what we learn.

In *South to a Very Old Place, The Omni-Americans*, and to some extent in his novel *Train Whistle Guitar*, Murray acted as a kind of cultural guardian attacking the fakelorists who had erected an ideology based on distortions of Afro-American culture. While he goes after those responsible for the myths about black life prevailing in the larger society, he supplies corrective interpretations, challenging not only specific myths but the general culture framework which harbors the myths. We have learned "black" history can not be written by simply inserting the names and numbers of black folk into a conventional version of the American past. Murray is making a parallel argument in regard to the Arts. Students of Afro-American culture need to examine the assumptions behind received notions of what constitutes art. The expressive arts produced by black Americans are informed by rituals one of whose prime purposes is to transcend the limits and boundaries imposed by the power of the majority society. Bursting categories as basic as time and space, an alternate version of reality is formed as black people live their lives outside of the "mainstream" of American culture. What Murray attests to is the power of these alternative versions, how they shatter the complacencies of a mainstream, how the notion of a placid, separate, abiding mainstream is a fiction once you go below the surface—whether of language or music—and ask a few of the right questions:

"What counts in a work of art, which after all must achieve such universality as it can through the particulars of the experience most native to it, is not the degree to which it conforms to theories, formulas and rules that are best regarded as being, like Aristotle's *Poetics*, generalizations after the fact, but how adequately it fulfills the requirements of the circumstances for which it was created" (196).

Murray is challenging critic and layman, black people and white; he is asking why you walk, talk, dance, sing, dream, style the way you do. He is signifying, transposing James Baldwin's famous phrase so it reads: "If you don't know my name, you don't know your Mama's."

THE LANGUAGE OF HOME

1985

Why do writers write about the same place over and over again? There are probably as many answers to this question as there are writers obsessed with a city, a county, a village, or a community. Rather than try to speak for others whose one certified virtue is speaking well for themselves, I'll focus my thoughts on the turn my own work has taken, my excursions home again, home again in fiction and nonfiction, to Homewood, a black neighborhood in Pittsburgh.

In the green woods of Maine, beside a lake, 2,200 miles from my present home in Wyoming, even farther in most ways from the cityscapes of my imagination, there is a gray wooden lawn chair perched on the edge of a dock. The setting is crucial. Like most writers, I observe rituals. A meticulously arranged scenario, certain pens, paper, a time of day, an alignment of furniture, particular clothing, coffee cooled to a precise temperature—the variations are infinite, but each writer knows his or her version of the preparatory ritual must be exactly duplicated if writing is to begin, prosper.

Repetition dignifies these rituals. My return home begins with a ceremony. Early morning is my time. Bundled in a hooded sweatsuit, more a protection against mosquitoes than weather, I slouch in my gray chair at the end of the dock facing Long Lake. The morning play of water, wind, and light has never been the same once in the eighteen summers I've watched. From where I sit, it's almost two miles to the opposite shore.

59

Picture a long, dark, ominous spine, low-hanging mist, white birches leaning over the water, a stillness so profound you can hear fish breaking the surface to catch insects. Whatever kind of weather they happen to be producing, the elements are always perfectly harmonized, synchronized.

The trick is to borrow, to internalize for a few quiet instants, the peace of the elements at play. Whatever mood or scene I'm attempting to capture, the first condition is inner calm, a simultaneous grasping and letting go that allows me to be a witness, a mirror. This state has gradually become more accessible to me only after fighting for years to believe again in my primal perceptions, my primal language, the words, gestures, and feelings of my earliest memories. At some point I taught myself to stop translating from one language to another. I've learned I can say the things I want to say using the words and telling the stories of Homewood people. The blackness of my writing inheres in its history, its bilingual, Creole, maroon, bastardized, miscegenated, cross-cultural acceptance of itself in the mirror only it can manufacture.

I was once a paperboy. To deliver the *Pittsburgh Post-Gazette*, I had to climb Negley Avenue Hill. On bad days, with a sack of newspapers slung over my back, the cobbled hill seemed almost vertical, and I mounted it hand over hand with the help of an invisible rope anchored at the crest. Because rich white people resided at the top of Negley, the climb was almost worthwhile. They tipped royally, compensating me for the rigors of the ascent, the enormous distances separating their houses. I whistled a lot as I made my rounds. The turf atop Negley Hill remained foreign. Immense houses of stone and brick, long curving driveways, sculpted trees and shrubberies, lawns cleaner than most people's living-room floors. If I wasn't whistling, I was singing inside my head. The music of the Drifters, Dells, Turbans, Spaniels, Miracles, Flamingos, Louis Berry, Jerry Butler, all the quartets and stars in whose songs I could imagine a shape for my feelings.

On those lily-white streets bordering the Squirrel Hill section of Pittsburgh, I knew I was an intruder. Would I be discovered, punished? The songs were protection, a talisman, but they also could betray me.

If anybody ever heard the music inside my head, I'd be in real trouble. Though I couldn't have articulated it at the time, I sensed that my music wove an alternate version of reality, one that included me and incriminated me, one that could sweep away the stones. Some evenings I was buoyed by the danger, the trespass I was committing, walking those sleepy streets, carrying doo-wop and "Oh, What a Night" and "For Your Precious Love," contraband in my skull.

Thirty years later, and things haven't changed much. I return to Pittsburgh again and again in my writing. Three books of fiction, a nonfiction narrative, *Brothers and Keepers*, a pair of new novels in the works, all rooted in Homewood, the actual black community where I was raised, the imaginary landscape I dream up as I go along. Every book a voyage home, each a struggle up a steep incline whose familiarity makes it more rather than less difficult. I find myself, each time a book is finished, in an alien place, whistling, singing to keep away the strangers who own the hilltop and everything else.

On our way back and forth to Peabody High School, my partner Scott Payne and I crossed Penn Avenue, the main drag of East Liberty, which was in those days a thriving pocket of stores, theaters, banks, and restaurants. On Penn Avenue was a confectioner's we liked to ogle. One day as we stared at the windowload of fanciful sweets, I said to Scott in my best stuck-up, siddity white folks' voice, "The prices here are exorbitant," emphasizing the final exotic word, precisely chopping it into four syllables, the orotund "or" deep in my throat the way I'd heard somebody somewhere say it. A nicely dressed white lady who would have been quite at home on Negley Hill laying that extra 25 or 50 cents on me when I collected at the end of the week heard me say "exorbitant" and did a wide-eyed double take. If I'd yelled an obscenity at her, she couldn't have looked more shocked, outraged. She regarded her companion, another middle-aged, coifed-for-shopping matron, and the two of them wagged their heads in dismay.

Did you hear that? Did you hear what he said? . . .

Not until years later did I begin to guess at the nature of my offense.

I'd stolen a piece of their language. Not only was it in my possession, I also had the nerve to flaunt it in a public place, in their righteous faces. To them a colored kid with a big word instead of a watermelon in his mouth wasn't even funny. I was peeking under their clothes, maybe even shouting that they, like the emperor, weren't wearing any.

Language is power. I was fighting skirmishes in a battle still engaging me—legitimizing the language of my tribe. The songs in my head on Negley Hill, the fancy word I appropriated and mocked surveying in a shop window sweets I couldn't afford, were means I had developed to create sense in a world that insistently denied me. When my family moved to Shadyside so I could attend "better" schools and we were one of only three or four black families in the neighborhood, I learned to laugh with the white guys when we hid in a stairwell outside Liberty School gym and passed around a "nigarette." I hated it when a buddy took a greedy, wet puff, "nigger-lipping" a butt before he passed it on to me.

Speaking out, identifying myself with the group being slurred by these expressions, was impossible. I had neither the words nor the heart. I talked the talk and walked the walk of the rest of my companions.

When Lavinia, my first love, on leave one summer from Harlem to visit her grandfather, who boarded in my grandparents' house, urged me to wear my jeans slung low on my hips like the black boys and Spanish boys she'd left behind on Convent Avenue, her distaste for the white kids' style, her assertion that another way was both possible and better, struck me with the force of revelation. At thirteen Lavinia possessed a woman's body, and the fact that she would let me, only thirteen myself, touch it kept me in a constant state of agitation and awe. She was larger than life and grew more fascinating, more like a goddess as she described Harlem's black ways, its authority to be what it wished to be. Lavinia didn't exactly hate whites; they were beneath her contempt. It dawned on me that there was a Negley Hill where my white buddies, those unconscious kings of the earth, would be scared to deliver papers.

I've taught Ralph Ellison's *Invisible Man* to many classes, lots of people, including Lois, a fundamentalist Christian from Wyoming who was so shocked by the language and situations dramatized in the books of my Afro-American literature class that she threatened to report me to my chairman unless I allowed her to skip the readings her husband, a one-man board of censors, found objectionable. There was also David Bradley, who sat through one of my first fumbling attempts to teach black writing at the University of Pennsylvania and went on to produce a prizewinning novel, *The Chaneysville Incident*, which absorbed and extended the traditions Mr. Ellison affirms. I return to *Invisible Man* not because of a scarcity of good books by black authors but because without Mr. Ellison's work in the mix—monumental, prophetic, bristling with flashes of light—something necessary has been left unsaid, something's missing no matter what combination of books and authors I select for a course.

Mr. Ellison's vision is indispensable because it makes tangible so much of the fiber, the nuance, connecting other Afro-American writers to him and one another. *Invisible Man* is a home, and Afro-American writers predictably return to it.

Although its faults—a protagonist whose abstractness inhibits a reader's emotional identification with him, episodes brilliant in themselves but too long, too allegorical, too distracting from the narrative sequence, minor, stereotypical roles for its female characters—cause the novel to be like any home, less than perfect, it also has the incalculable advantages of home cooking. For many of us, *Invisible Man* came first, educating our palates, defining what's good, stamping our tastes for a lifetime.

My wife, Judy, has spent almost every summer of her life in Maine. For her the lake and pinewoods of Camp Takajo are a special place. She's found no other spot on earth that duplicates the haunting dance of sunlight as it seeps down through the dark trunks of the pine trees. Because she taught me to see this indwelling spirit that animates the green woods, it lives now, not only in trees but in her. Certain affinities, constellations of meaning are triggered for me by arrangements and rearrangements of green, light, and shadow. A green robe Judy wears, a path fringed with greenery winding from cabin to lake, feathery pine branches a hundred feet up that crackle with light when wind stirs them, all these images connect, permeate each other.

Words, objects, rituals have the power to shine forth. They accumulate this power, this endless string of associations presiding Januslike backward and forward in time, because by circumstance or choice we must return to them. We live many lives, and the confusion, the chaos of a splintered existence is lessened a bit by the riveting flashes that connect our multiple selves to one another and to other lives. When I write I want to show how simple acts, simple words can be transformed to release their spiritual force. This is less a conscious aesthetic to be argued or analyzed than a determination to draw from the unique voices of Homewood's people the means for documenting the reality of their attitudes and emotions. I want to trace the comings and goings of my people on the invisible plane of existence where so much of the substance of black life resides.

Everyone lives a significant portion of life below the surface. Art records and elaborates this unseen dimension. A minority culture systematically prevented from outward expression of its dreams, wishes, and aspirations must evolve ways for both individuals and the group to sustain its underground life. Afro-Americans have become experts at living in at least two places simultaneously, cultivating a sensitivity to the distance—comic, ironic, tragic—between our outer and inner lives. For us music, speech, and body movement are repositories for preserving history, values, dignity, a sense of ourselves as separate, whole. Double-entendre, signifying, mimicry, call-and-response patterns of storytelling, oratory and song, style as cutting edge, as a weapon against enforced anonymity have been honed to display and protect our secrets.

One of the earliest lessons I learned as a child was that if you looked away from something, it might not be there when you looked back. I feared loss, feared turning to speak to someone and finding no one there. Being black and poor reinforced the wisdom of a tentative purchase on experience. Don't get too close, doubt what you think you see. Need, commitment set you up for a fall, create the conditions for disaster. If you let your eyes touch lightly, rely on an impressionistic touch and go, then you may achieve the emotional economy of faint gains, faint losses. Writing forces me to risk ignoring the logic of this lesson. Another legacy from Mr. Ellison, the implicit challenge he poses—who will write our history?—has helped turn me around. The stance, the habit of looking long and hard, especially at those things—a face, a hand, a home—that matter, makes them matter more and more. I examine minutely the place I come from, repeat its stories, sing its songs, preserve its language and values, because they make me what I am and because if I don't, who will?

PREFACE:

CHARLES W. CHESNUTT AND THE WPA NARRATIVES: THE ORAL AND LITERATE ROOTS OF AFRO-AMERICAN LITERATURE

1985

Charles Waddell Chesnutt was a man who straddled two worlds. A rigorous program of self-education acquainted him with books. He studied Latin, German, French, and read the classic English writers. Like so many men of his time he sought to school himself in the Anglo-Saxon literary tradition; also, just as studiously, he absorbed the black folk culture of the rural South where he was raised and taught school. In his fiction Chesnutt drew from both worlds, the literate and oral, but what has endured as an original element in his work and as a model for other Afro-American writers in his use of the black oral tradition.

From the drama of the colonial period through the late nineteenth century when Chesnutt began to write, Negroes in American literature had been characterized in a special fashion by their speech. Negro dialect in drama, fiction, and poetry was a way of pointing to the difference between blacks and whites; the form and function of black speech as it was represented was to indicate black inferiority. Black speech, the mirror of black people's mind and character, was codified by dialect into a deviant variety of good English. Negro dialect lacked proper grammar, its comic orthography suggested ignorance, its "dats" and "dems" and "possums" implied lazy, slovenly pronunciation if not the downright physical impossibility of getting thick lips around the King's English. Malapropisms, far-fetched words, the preoccupation with telling children's stories, with talk about eating, drinking, and dancing, the rampant displays of superstition and fear of the supernatural expressed in black talk were all proof positive of the infantilism, carnality, instability, and illogicality of black folk. *Difference* in the dialect tradition clearly signaled *deficiency*. Afro-American speech had been devalued, robbed of those mature aesthetic and functional dimensions it had developed in the New World.

One strategy for a black writer who wished to be taken seriously was to avoid altogether the incriminating dialect tradition. Phillis Wheatley is an early example of this tact. Chesnutt's contemporary Paul Laurence Dunbar experienced acutely the schizophrenia enforced upon the black writer. He lamented the neglect of his "straight" poetry and complained that he had no choice but to write in dialect if he wanted people to listen to him. Chesnutt chose another strategy, one for which he is seldom given credit as a major innovator. Employing a tale-within-a-tale technique he "framed" black speech so that in his best stories Chesnutt blends the literary and oral traditions without implying that the black storyteller's mode of perceiving and re-creating reality is any less valid than the written word. Black speech in the form of Negro dialect entered American literature as a curiosity, a comic interlude, a shorthand for perpetuating myths and prejudices about black people. Chesnutt's frame displays the written and spoken word on equal terms or at least as legitimate contenders for the reader's sympathy.

"As de storm tale come to me from my wife, who git it from her mammy, Nancy, it bout like this."

"Dat de blessed truth, too, cause dat exactly what I hear bout dem."

"Does I 'member much bout slavery times? Well, dere is no way for me to disremember, unless I die."

"I 'spects knowin' bout things is just 'bout good and true as seein' them."

These are the voices of ex-slaves recorded by Works Progress Administration workers during the late 1930s. They are from the South Carolina volumes, part of George P. Rawick's monumental collection of ex-slave narratives. Dozens of similar citations could be mustered from the narratives, testifying to the authority and tenacity of oral tradition in Afro-American culture. From 1866 to 1883, Chesnutt lived in the South. He was a contemporary of the former slaves who were interviewed during the 1930s. In his fiction he drew from the common stock of stories, memories, and experiences which appear later in these reminiscences. The former slaves were young men and women when Chesnutt began writing; most of them could not read, they were bearers of an oral rather than literate tradition. In a sense Chesnutt wrote the stories they told thirty years later. The ramifications of this situation are fascinating. For historians Chesnutt's fiction and the WPA narratives offer a double focus on the period that both attempt to reconstruct. Two views of slavery and reconstruction can be consulted for verification, contradiction, and for the light they shed on each other and upon the customs and facts of the times they reflect. Linguists have the rare opportunity to compare a fiction writer's stylization of a speech community with transcriptions of speech from that community. The literary scholar can look for points of confirmation, influence, continuity, and synthesis between the oral and literate roots of Afro-American fiction.

Chesnutt's story "A Deep Sleeper" was first published in 1892, one of the *Two Tales* bound together and issued in a small printing by the Boston publisher Arthur Ware. "A Deep Sleeper" was included in the list of twenty stories Chesnutt hoped might make a book and submitted with that end in mind to Houghton Mifflin on October 22, 1897. The story was not one of those eventually selected to be part of Chesnutt's first book, *The Conjure Woman* (1899), and was not reprinted until the publication of *The Short Fiction of Charles W. Chesnutt* in 1974. It is safe to say the story has had few readers. However, it is Chesnutt at his best. Uncle Julius stands at the center of the story and its form embodies the tale-within-a-tale structure of all the stories in *The Conjure Woman*. Chesnutt frees the narrative of Uncle Julius so the old ex-slave can stand as a witness, a source of truth about black life during slavery. The voice of Uncle Julius in "A Deep Sleeper" anticipates the voices of the thousands of former slaves who will be interviewed nearly half a century later. The remainder of this essay will examine (1) how Chesnutt altered the traditional frame which emasculated black speech; (2) how the art of the ex-slave narratives can be approached and defined; and (3) how Uncle Julius's narrative shares formal, stylistic features with the narratives of ex-slaves transcribed by the WPA workers.

II

"A Deep Sleeper" begins on a soporific July afternoon in the rural South during Reconstruction. The first-person narrator, a transplanted northerner who owns the plantation upon which the action occurs, decides that the eating of a watermelon might break the monotony of the sultry July day so he commandeers the aid of Uncle Julius, a relic from the days of slavery inherited when the plantation was purchased. Julius complains of "rheumatiz" and instead of fetching the watermelon himself goes off to waken Tom and instruct him to bring a wheelbarrow to the piazza. When Julius returns to the whites sitting on the piazza he mentions that Tom is one of the "Seben Sleepers" and that the boy's grandfather had once slept a month. The curiosity of the whites is aroused and Julius complies with the women's clamor for a story. Julius's tale takes place during slavery days and concerns the deep sleeper Skundus, his courting of Cindy, their enforced separation, Skundus's "deep sleep" which caused him to disappear for a month, and the eventual marriage of the slaves Cindy and Skundus. Julius's dialect narrative is the centerpiece of Chesnutt's story, taking up nearly five of its seven pages. When Tom finally arrives with the wheelbarrow, the group from the piazza stroll out to the watermelon patch and find the prize melon they intended to harvest is gone.

The title "A Deep Sleeper" is enigmatic, becoming more so after several readings of the text it commands. Does the title refer to a quality of the tale that follows? Is this story "a sleeper"? Are its form and message cunning, sly, crafty? Is the tale difficult to fathom or understand, is it obscure? Or do these meanings of the word *deep* describe Skundus, the sleeper whose tale Julius narrates? Or is it Uncle Julius himself who is deep-learned, understanding, wise? Who is sleeping? Skundus? His grandson Tom? All black people? All whites who continue to delude themselves about the depth, the humanity of the black folk over whom they wield lethal power? To whom is the title addressed? To a white audience which accepts the archetype of the sleepy, lethargic black and for whom Skundus and progeny would be humorous examples? Or instead of holding up the black clown (and watermelon thief) for derision, is the butt of the story's joke the self-enforced gullibility of the master class, the masters who must accept the pilfering of their property, the tall tales of their slaves, accept "deep sleeps" which last for a month? However the title is construed, the words *deep* and *sleep* alert a reader to look below the surface and to be on the watch for someone asleep. The action of the story becomes a gloss on the multiple significations of these words.

"A Deep Sleeper" is composed of a number of movements, internal and external, and these movements can be understood as the result of exercises of power. The exercise of power is being dramatized in the tale. The movement of the words of the story, their linear progress from the title to last word, is a comment on the exercise of power. The first-person narrator (who for convenience will be called "John" as he is in subsequent stories) is compromised by the structure of the story he is relating; what he wishes to say is conditioned by how he must say it. A large part of his story is delivered by Uncle Julius's voice. The convention of labeling or titling a story allows another voice, not necessarily the first-person narrator's, to have the first word, or words, to set the scene and qualify all that comes after. The action of a story, the events portrayed, can have meaning that arises independent of the significance alleged by the narrator; so in fact "A Deep Sleeper" is bracketed by a first "word" (the title) and a last "word" (the disappearance of the popular watermelon), signifiers not controlled by the voice of the plantation-owner/narrator. What seems on the surface to be John's story is rather a demonstration of authorial control over the voice of a first-person narrator. The reader has no way of knowing how John would react to having his story called "A Deep Sleeper." The reader can only guess at the depth of John's understanding of the function or meaning of the story Julius tells. The reader's questions about such matters must be referred to someone outside the story, to an implied author as he is manifested in the weave of voices and events that constitute the story.

That we should be prepared to hear other voices and add their testimony to John's is emphasized by Uncle Julius's "tale within a tale." When the dialect voice of Julius takes over, the first-person narrator, John, disappears and is forgotten; he and the world he described in the opening "literary" paragraphs of "A Deep Sleeper" return only when Julius has finished his narration, only when, to put the matter another way, Julius permits him to speak again. An action has been completed that is a statement about power and authority. The literate narrator's role as proprietor of the story and owner of the watermelon, as master of words and property, has been undermined. The reader is left at the conclusion of the story to sort out his or her own conclusions rather than accept the words of the single, stable guide who seemed to be on hand in the story's first paragraphs.

If the movement of the story, its linear progression from beginning to end, expresses the tension between apparent power and power not so apparent, then one might expect to find parallel movements within the story illustrative of hidden versus apparent power. Like buckets to catch rain from a leaky roof, blacks are moved around in the story according to the needs, wills, and whims of whites. Cindy's removal to Kunnel Wash'n'ton McAdoo's place a hundred miles away from Skundus, her intended husband, is an obvious case. That black people had no control over such removals is made clear by Julius; "Skundus didn' lack ter hab Cindy go, but he couldn' do nuthin.'" Cindy "didn' hab no mo' ter say 'bout comin' dan she did 'bout goin!" The balance of power seems clear. The master class is absolutely in control. Promises made to blacks are not binding. When Marse Dugal's wife reminds him that niggers have no rights a white man need respect, he breaks his word to Cindy and Skundus, salving his conscience with a few little white lies, to them and to himself. John, Julius's employer, seems to have the same command over Julius's movements as masters had over their slaves. After all, the story occurs on a Sunday afternoon and Julius is on his way home from the church he serves as a deacon, but John does not hesitate to mobilize the old man into his watermelon-fetching scheme.

These apparent exercises of power describe only the surface of black-white relationships. Below the surface, other kinds of power affect other kinds of movement. Though the slaves Cindy and Skundus appear to be pawns, they make adjustments, and these 'justments allow them to subvert the power of the master class over their lives. Skundus can "steal himself" by running away from the plantation to the swamp. Cindy can pretend her health is dependent on certain elusive roots which she must gather each day from the swamp, a dependency providing a daily excuse for being away from the Big House. Julius and his extended family work for the narrator and must follow his orders, yet Julius is a magician, a trickster, who enchants the whites lounging on the piazza, capturing them in his tale about other times and places so he controls their movements in the present. Julius contrives a fiction to entertain his listeners, to distract them from interfering with his plans. Marse Dugal manufactures a fiction to smooth over Cindy's removal from Skundus. The parallel loses its symmetry when one recalls that at stake in one deception was a watermelon, while in the other are the lives, love, and happiness of two human beings.

A series of confrontations between the powerful and powerless are enacted in the story and in each case an obvious kind of power is balanced by an unexpected force wielded by the supposed powerless. The pairs brought into opposition—Julius and the narrator, Skundus and Marse Dugal, Cindy and her mistress on the McAdoo plantation—reflect a larger system of black-white power relationships in the South, the struggle to establish personal space and territorial rights. Because of its persistence over time, its pervasiveness in people's lives, this struggle has assumed the formal coherence, the stability and predictability of a ritual dance.

The elements of this dance provide a structural unity in "A Deep Sleeper" and are exhibited in the WPA narratives gathered in the 1930s. First the separation of black from white, a formal assumption paralleling the segregation of the sexes in many traditional African dances. The two groups regard each other over a broad, hard-packed dirt floor, a stage, arena, threshing ground where encounters will be choreographed. An individual dancer sallies out of each group of participants. The dancer's movements are strictly patterned. Facial expression, posture, tone of voice—all are predetermined by ancient canons of behavior. The object of the dance is complex. The whites, who have the advantage of establishing the outward forms of the dance, design the ritual to display their superiority, their dominance; the dance is a metaphor of their power. For the blacks who, like the whites, must perform for two audiences at once, the objective is to find room for maneuver within the rigid forms dictated by the whites, maneuver which allows space for private communication with the other black participants. This communication coded into the space disciplined by the whites becomes another version of the action in the exposed center of the floor. Like a good boxer, the white dancer crowds the black into a corner, cutting off the ring, systematically diminishing room for black display and maneuver, but of course such a strategy also defines the area in which the white must perform. Each pair that enacts the ritual embodies both individual norms of behavior and archetypal relationships. Though these confrontations occur within the framework sanctioned by white power, their inevitability can be turned to the advantage of blacks, can be incorporated into black routines. (Recall Muhammad Ali's "rope-a-dope" tactics vs. George Foreman.) An observer wishing to understand any movement of the dance must visualize it from the dual perspective of the two groups which are its audience.

The separation of black from white and the consequent rituals produce, among other things, two distinct types of speech which may be exemplified by the narrator, John's literary English and Julius's dialect. These varieties of speech describe two different worlds; each speech form (speech community) represents a version of reality. At some levels the languages of blacks and whites are mutually intelligible, or at least *seem* to allow a variety of exchanges. Chesnutt explores the forms and uses of language where the *seams* of mutual intelligibility burst. What Chesnutt's characters are saying cannot be understood unless the reader has an awareness of the total version of reality which a particular utterance signifies. Dell Hymes's discussion of the socio-linguistic concept *key* is useful here. In speech acts, *key* provides the tone, manner, or spirit of the words spoken. Speech acts, often the same as regards setting, participants, form of message, etc., may differ in *key*, that is, may be serious or mocking, painstaking or perfunctory depending on a signal (verbal or otherwise, i.e., wink, gesture) which is part of the speech act. *How* something is said (the "how" being defined by the speech community of a speaker) is part of *what* is said. The more a way of speaking has become shared and meaningful within a group, the more likely that crucial cues will be efficient or small in scale. Chesnutt employs numerous subtle keys, often drawn from the repertoire of Afro-American oral tradition, to achieve density of meaning in "A Deep Sleeper."

Manipulation of key can call attention to playful or artistic dimensions of speech. Satire, irony, ridicule, as Sylvia Render points out in her introduction to *Chesnutt's Short Fiction*, are called into play by *signifying*, a traditional resource of black speech communities signaled by key. Signifying is verbal art. Claudia Mitchell-Kernan has succinctly described the dynamics of signifying: the apparent meaning of an utterance is canceled by the introduction of a key that signals to those who recognize the key that the utterance should not be taken "straight." The speaker who is signifying depends upon a body of experience he shares with the audience to whom the signifying is addressed. The signifier expects his audience to process his utterance metaphorically, because their shared experience allows them to recognize the key and supplies the material for re-interpreting the utterance. In the street a skillful signifier can talk behind a victim's back while looking him in the face. Manipulation of key, employed as a rhetorical device in fiction, permits the writer to address several audiences simultaneously by appealing to pools of knowledge only segments of his readers share with him. In effect, the writer can profit from the diversity among his readers rather than be limited by it. Chesnutt took full advantage of this possibility by playing to multiple audiences, designing his "A Deep Sleeper" in layers, layers corresponding to the conflicting versions of reality perceived by blacks and whites.

"Tom's gran'daddy wuz name' Skundus," he began. "He had a brudder name' Tushus en' ernudder name' Cottus en' ernudder name' Squinchus." The old man paused a moment and gave his leg another hitch.

My sister-in-law was shaking with laughter. "What remarkable names!" she exclaimed. "Where in the world did they get them?"

Uncle Julius is speaking, *sho nuff*, like an old ignorant southern darky is supposed to speak in Negro dialect. And sho nuff he gets his laugh, the laughter Chesnutt could count on from the majority of his readers, the ones who enjoyed Joel Chandler Harris, Sidney Lanier, and Irwin Russell, the ones who turned, as Mabel and Annie and John on the piazza, to Uncle Julius for an entertaining interlude. The laughter of such readers is

encouraged, sanctioned by Mabel's. Julius's performance is that of a vir-
tuoso dialect storyteller; he is rhyming *brudder* and *enudder* so they fall
as syncopated beats in his narration. He is probably twisting his mouth
in absurd ways to pronounce the strange names Skundus, Tushus, Squinchus. That his performance for the piazza is conscious and calculated is
keyed by the "hitch" he gives his leg. One of the roles Julius is projecting
for the whites is an old, feeble man whose ailments prevent him from
fetching a watermelon. With sighs, grimaces, and explicit references,
Julius sustains this role throughout the story. Given Julius's intentions
and the successful working-out of his plan for appropriating the melon,
his comments on his pain and the mannerisms by which he pantomimes
its effects become a source of humor for those readers who appreciate the
art of fooling Master.

The source of the "remarkable names" turns out to be Marse Dugal
McAdoo, who named all the babies "wat wuz bawn on de plantation."
The absolute power of the master licensed him to name his chattel. For
some readers who share with Chesnutt a knowledge of Latin, the humor
of the names is enriched because the slaves' names correspond to the
Latin words for second, third, fourth, and fifth. Recognizing the Latin
key, certain readers have their classical learning rewarded, their vanity
touched, and their prejudice confirmed since Julius exhibits the Negro's
darned comical funny habit of muddling words when he reaches above
his proper sphere of ignorance. Within the small class that recognized
the Latin key, a smaller grouping might respond with indignation toward
the old regime which allowed such abuses of power. Some of this group
might even feel slightly ashamed that human beings were given numbers
for names, numbers for the master's convenience, numbers that reverberate ironically since they are disguised in Latin, one of the classical
languages and cultures which are the oft-exalted and extolled sources of
Western Civilization. But some readers may be keyed to other kinds of
power at work here. Julius calls the names "Hebrew," suggesting that their
source, like the source of so many other mysterious indignities the master
class imposes on its slaves, is the Bible, the Bible Julius admits he cannot

read. Uncle Julius makes it clear, "Hit ain' my fault I ain't able ter read," so his confession of illiteracy is also an indictment of the ignorance enforced upon the slave by his master. In this light, the source of the remarkable names might as well be Hebrew as Greek since, for Julius, access to this kind of knowledge has been systematically withheld. Chesnutt rightfully, ironically dismisses the question of origin and points to another kind of meaning the names contain. When the Latin words are translated into Blackspeech and given their unique pronunciation, an identity is created for the brothers apart from the dehumanizing numerical designations. Skundus is "Skundus," not *Secundus*. He is baptised by the slave community and becomes a distinct individual. His distinction, his individuality is defined and preserved in the tale Julius narrates. Marse Dugal's joke (like so many kinds of humor, a sadistic exercise of power) is turned back on him and the culture he represents. Originally named for the convenience of a white man, Secundus has been transformed by Blackspeech and oral tradition into Skundus, a legendary Deep Sleeper. The source of his name is as much of an enigma for Mabel as his behavior is an embarrassment and thorn in the side of Marse Dugal. While Mabel laughs at the remarkable names, some readers are laughing at her. When Marse Dugal threatens Skundus: "I'm gwine ter hang yer up by yer thumbs en take ev'y bit er yer black hide off'n yer," he is declaiming the literal power of the master over his slaves. But Julius also states that "evey'body knowed Marse Dugal' bark uz wuss'n his bite," and this knowledge shared by the slave community is the key for interpreting Dugal's empty words, as well as the absurd actions he has no choice but to perform when Skundus returns from his deep sleep.

In his fiction, Chesnutt is cleaning up Negro dialect, tinkering not so much with its outward form, which he inherited and felt was hopelessly artificial at best, but with its validity to carry a message apart from the demeaning one with which it was traditionally burdened. Chesnutt's illiterate speakers from Uncle Julius to Mammy Jane are distinctive not only because of the form (Negro dialect) of their speech, but because what they say is true. Oral history in Chesnutt is a vehicle for reconstructing the past so that the lies and misrepresentations of the master class become part of the written record. Negro dialect has come full circle. Rather than being an instrument of power in the hands of the enemy (Blackspeech framed in an inimical literary tradition), it is turned against the oppressor.

Can I get a witness! Chesnutt's answer is yes. He allows Julius to speak for himself. The point of view of the slave can be understood apart from and in spite of the voice of the white plantation owner. The Works Progress Administration oral history project nearly half a century later is another kind of attempt to record the black man's version of slavery and reconstruction. What Julius and the former slaves have to say is of crucial importance if one wishes a rounded view of the "peculiar institution," and scholars have begun to incorporate the slaves' view into the historiography of the period. But how the former slaves told their stories, the notions of style and form, the values embodied in the narratives have been neglected by scholars even though studying the narratives from this perspective perhaps could illuminate fundamental elements of Afro-American culture, the incredible inner sense of purpose and worth, the integrity and resiliency which enabled a people to survive their time on the cross.

III

In her study *African Oral Literature*, Ruth Finnegan lists some elements to consider in the analysis of oral literature. She points out that any accurate analysis of oral poetry, epic, etc., must take into account nonverbal as well as verbal dimensions of oral performance. To ignore matters such as audience, occasion, details of performance in an oral work is to "risk missing much of the subtlety, flexibility, and individual originality of its creator and, furthermore, to fail to give consideration to the aesthetic canons of those intimately concerned in the production and reception of this form of literature." Unfortunately, in the case of the WPA collection, we have minimal data on the actual conditions of oral performance, but some facts about the scenarios are retrievable. The speaker is most often performing for an audience of one, usually a white interviewer. The reader of the narratives is dependent on the skill of the interviewers in recording the interviewees' speech. The speaker cannot employ the full range of nonverbal effects, nor can he or she depend upon a responsiveness to the verbal interplay and overtones that would enrich his performance if his audience consisted of members of his speech community. The socio-economic context of the Jim Crow South, the expectations and role playing of blacks and whites, obviously restrict the spontaneity of oral performance. The interviewers were often inexperienced and often armed with a list of questions and instructions tending to make all interviews structurally similar. These facts have the cumulative effect of making the interviews conservative in terms of representing the full range of Afro-American oral tradition. Obscenity, bitterness, and anger toward whites, sexual references (especially to miscegenation), the contribution of music or balletic elements to the narratives, the audience's active, creative, participatory role are minimized by the circumstances of the interviews. Just as Chesnutt was fenced in by the dialect tradition, by the literary sensibilities, the morality, ethics, and mores of his turn-of-the-century American audience, the ex-slaves who told their tales to the WPA interviewers had to censure themselves, had to talk between the lines, had to protect themselves and protect the corner of truth they wished to preserve by being selective about what they said and how they said it. This strategy is typical of Afro-American culture and is manifested in African religious practices, in the syncretism of black churches in the New World, in the politics of Booker T. Washington. It is a survival technique, exemplifying an archetypal configuration, the practical accommodation of the weak who must in some fashion give in or seem to give in to the strong in order to shift the locus of combat from external, physical tests of strength to internal, imaginative competition.

In spite of the circumstances suggested above, the WPA narratives are rich and exciting, more so in many ways than the more familiar written narratives dating from the antebellum Battle of Books. Enough of the style of Afro-American oral performance has survived in the WPA narratives to allow us to analyze some of the aesthetic canons underlying each speaker's story. Since the structure of the total interview as it is printed was not controlled by the person being interviewed, one must look at smaller segments within the interviews to gain a sense of how the ex-slaves thought a story should be told. The ideal kind of segment for analysis is the self-contained story, or anecdote, which the speaker initiates and shapes. The narratives abound in such set pieces. They are usually clearly delineated within the narratives and they possess distinct beginnings, middles, and ends. The economy, pungency, and precision characteristic of so many of these tales within tales suggest that they have been told before, that given the age and experience of the narrators, the set pieces have had the benefit of numerous previous exposures to an audience. The unique interplay between performer and audience, the fact that an audience actively participates in shaping a song or story, means the form of an oft-told tale is a product of tradition and individual sensibility. When Frank Adamson begins telling about his "tribulation," he brings to the telling a conception of what a good story is and how it should be told. He shares these conceptions with the other witnesses quoted in Rawick.

Because we have texts and only minimal, if any, descriptive material bearing on nonverbal elements of transmission, the analysis of the following set piece within a narrative will treat the narrative primarily as one might treat a story or poem. This points to obvious limitations in the analysis, but has the advantage of placing the narratives in a relatively familiar evaluative frame. In spite of the interference of the interview format and the inherent limits of traditional literary analysis for describing oral performance, a strong case can be made for the distinctiveness and coherence of narrative segments.

[1.]"I's been 'possum huntin' wid your pappy, when he lived on de Wateree, just after de war. [2.]One night us got into tribulation, I tells you! [3.]'Twas 'bout midnight when de dogs make a tree. [4.]Your pappy climb up de tree, git 'bout halfway up, heard sumpin' dat once you hears it you never forgits, and dats de rattlin' of de rattles on a rattle snake's tail. [5.]Us both 'stinctly hear dat sound! [6.]What us do? [7.]Me on de ground, him up de tree, but where de snake? [8.]Dat was de misery, us didn't know. [9.]Dat snake give us fair warnin' though! [10.]Marster Sam (dat your pa) 'low: 'Frank, ease down on de ground; I'll just stay up here for a while.' [11.]I lay on them leaves, skeered to make a russle. [12.]Your pa up de tree skeered to go up or down! [13.]Broad daylight didn't move us. [14.]Sun come up, he look all 'round from his vantage up de tree, then come down, not 'til then, do I gits on my foots.

[15.]"Then I laugh and laugh and laugh, and ask Marster Sam how he felt. [16.]Marster Sam kinda frown and say: 'Damn I feels like hell! [17.]Git up dat tree! [18.]Don't you see dat 'possum up dere?' [19.]I say: 'But where de snake, Marster?' [20.]He say: 'Dat rattler done gone home, where me and you and dat 'possum gonna be pretty soon!'"

Frank Adamson's narrative is strikingly immediate and affecting. He was eighty-two years old when interviewed, but age seems to have diminished neither the clarity of his memory nor the energy of his language. His story is vivid, concrete, actual. The speaker strikes out to involve his audience personally. *It's not just me I'm talking about, it's your pappy.* The first sentence locates the time and place of the story. The next sentence states the subject of the story—tribulation—and encourages the listener's involvement with the collective pronoun *us.* The phatic *I tells you* establishes the narrator's voice as a kind of chorus. Here, as in the blues, the call-and-response pattern is embodied in a single voice; the teller or singer asserts his authority, his right to echo and *amen* his own pronouncements. The narrator/singer is both inside and outside his story, inside and outside of his experience. In sentence three, time is focused both more concretely—a precise hour is noted—and more abstractly—the hour, midnight, is the witching hour, a symbolic time of reversals, trial and tribulation, of darkness and mystery, a time like "once upon a time" that is the common property of countless stories. A specific event "when the dogs make a tree" limits the abstract, symbolic quality of midnight and returns the storyline to its actual, factual base. The idiomatic quality of the phrase is also a kind of self-description, identifying the speaker as one whose voice comes from the exact center of a specific speech community.

Sentence four is the longest in the narrative. It is balanced rhythmically by two short sentences preceding and two following it. It is musical in another sense. The tail of the sentence rattles with the repetition of *rattlin', rattles, rattle*. The phrase is difficult to say without a syncopated, cadenced, chanted inflection. The phrase is onomatopoeic, the words and the thing they describe become one. Logically, the "tribulation" of sentence one becomes identified with the snake's rattle. The word *tribulation* is onomatopoeic in a less obvious way than *rattling*, but *tribulation's* quality as a sound image (echoing the tremor and shakiness of fear) is reinforced by the logical identity between trouble and snake. Sentence five once more asserts the involvement of the teller, his participation in the story and thus his authority. It is also the teller speaking in his own voice, a person (opposed to a disembodied voice of an "author") speaking to other people. Six emphasizes and sustains the unity (affectively heightens the identification) among speaker and audience and characters in the story since all are contained in the *us*. Tribulation affects everyone. The speaker is asking for help. The narrative device is a rhetorical question whose objective is closer listener identification and active involvement. Six is also the shortest sentence in the narrative and the one that conceivably was delivered in the most emotional tone of voice.

In the two balanced, symmetrical phrases that begin sentence seven, the narrator turns back to the objective facts of his story. The narration moves from aural (a question) to visual (a scene) imagery and back again as sentence seven ends with another rhetorical question demanding the reader's attention. The master and the slave are both in trouble, one up in a tree, the other on the ground, and the snake, invisible now, is a generalized tribulation. In sentence eight, the meaning of tribulation is defined, extended. It equals "misery," uncertainty. Uncertainty means loss of control; no decision can be made on rational grounds because the snake's location is a mystery. The story pauses, its narrative thrust slows in the next two sentences as the condition of being in tribulation is explored. The snake isn't to blame for tribulation. *Dat snake give us fair warnin'.* "Marster Sam (dat's your pa)" resigns himself to the situation. His words are as casual as possible; he speaks as master but is not in control and simply voices in the form of an order to his slave a course of action dictated by the mutual predicament of the two men. The storyteller uses dialogue in this sentence, giving himself an opportunity to impersonate his former marster. Depending upon how Marster Sam's words are dramatized, the narrator can speak volumes about his character. Is the master afraid, pompous, humble, imperious, silly? The narrator has various masks to choose from and his impersonation of the master is limited only by consideration of audience, and his own mimetic abilities.

If we try to listen to Frank Adamson's story as we read it, we will hear the onomatopoeic word *russle* in sentence eleven and hear the alliteration of *lay* and *leaves*. Words that sound like the thing they describe can be performed just as dialogue can be dramatized by an expert storyteller. We can share the fear of the storyteller when he whispers a hushed *russle* just as we are engaged by the syncopated rattling above. The word *skeered* is repeated in sentences eleven and twelve. The action of the story is recapitulated in these sentences; *skeered* links the men and the sentences, and the visual image of sentence seven, "Me on de ground, him up de tree," is restated. In this predicament, master and slave are equals. *Skeered* tells us so even though one man is down and the other up. "Broad daylight" of sentence thirteen doesn't change this equality; it doesn't illuminate two separate men, but *us*. The sun is personified, made a character in the story by sentence fourteen. Entering the story, the sun repeats the visual motif of up and down. The tribulation begins to be resolved, not by the voice of a master, but by a natural force to which the speaker cautiously attends. The sun dispells uncertainty, midnight, the fears at the heart of tribulation.

It's a new day. The final five sentences dramatize this new day, rounding the tale of tribulation with a moral. Dialogue is the dominant mode. The scene acted out at the foot of the tree gives the narrator maximum opportunity to play the role of Marster Sam and to use drama's inherent capacity for indirect, satirical comment on the players. Released by the sun, on his feet again, Frank can "laugh and laugh and laugh." The repetition of the word *laugh* gives the narrator ample chance to smile or chuckle as he utters sentence fifteen. But Marster Sam is frowning. He curses, then shouts, "Git up dat tree!" The period of enforced equality ends abruptly. Since both men have shared the same tribulation, the slave's laughter at himself and the situation is also laughter directed at the master. A master's powerlessness is never a laughing matter to the master, especially when a slave is witness, and Marster Sam reasserts his authority by ordering Frank up the tree for the possum. The narrator speaks *with* the lines (his manner of dramatizing the voices of his characters) and *between* the lines (talking about the players while the players are talking by making their behavior emblematic). The slave inquires after the master's health; the slave laughs at the silliness of the night tribulation. The master is disgruntled, coarse and imperious. When Frank asks, "But where de snake, Marster?" even in his anxiety he uses a polite form of address. Marster Sam answers with a statement that reorders the world into the familiar pattern of the Slavocracy. His resumption of the Bossman tone of voice would be immediately recognized by the southern black and probably mimicked by the narrator. Tribulation is gone, and with it goes the "us," the pronoun uniting master and slave when both were threatened by the rattler. Now it's "you and me and dat 'possum," each creature in its proper sphere, each subject to the master's will. Everybody's going home.

The high density of "sound effects" in Adamson's narrative is striking. By "sound effects" in this context I mean narrative devices that lend themselves to performance as a tale is orally transmitted to an audience. Onomatopoeic words, dialogue, syncopation, phatic phrases, rhetorical questions, call-and-response patterns, repetitions of words and phrases, rhyme (the end-words of sentences eight and nine) are examples. The level of sound or aural imagery is complemented by both the rhythmic organization of the sentences and by the *percussive delivery* employed by the narrative voice.

There is, intriguingly, a correspondence between the number of words and the number of syllables in each sentence. (In the twenty sentences, four are exactly equal in number of syllables and words, eight differ only by one measure, four by only two.) What this suggests is a one-word, one-beat sentence rhythm, a pattern that allows maximum flexibility. Unencumbered by "correct" pronunciations which would determine the stress pattern in a multisyllabic word, the narrator can emphasize (tone, intensity, length) any word in a sentence; the words are unfettered notes he can arrange in patterns of his choice. Perhaps the close correspondence between number of words and number of syllables also suggests the words as things, a preference in the oral tradition for the concrete monosyllable over the less trustworthy (in terms of pronunciation, rhythm, meaning) polysyllable. An exception would be proper names, whose unique attraction to a teller of tales is their high potential as an aural image and their specificity in regard to a distinct person or place. The elision of syllables ('possum, 'stinctly,) may be partially accounted for as an accommodation to this percussive, striking-one-note-for-each-word style of delivery. If one discounts proper names as inevitable exceptions and grammatical inflections '*ed*, '*ing*, *un*' as less inevitable but occasionally compelling exceptions that give a word more than one syllable (beat), then the correlation between number of words and number of syllables in the storytelling style of the narrative would be even higher.

The use of parallel phrases is also part of the aural imagery, or sound effects, in Adamson's story. They tie together ideas, repeat rhythms, balance contrasts. *Me on the ground, him up de tree.* Repetition of other kinds echo through the story: the same word repeated: *laugh, laugh, laugh*; the same word slightly inflected, with each repetition: *rattlin', rattles, rattle* (ringing the changes); a word repeated in different sentences in order to connect a thought or image the sentences share: *skeered*; visual patterns repeated (up and down) to sustain an idea. If monosyllables and repetition seem unpromisingly monotonous as basic elements in percussive storytelling style, one should recall Albert Murray's remarks on the storytelling of Jo Jones in *Stomping the Blues*. "Nothing is more down-to-earth or more obvious than the ever-steady but somehow also ever flexible Kansas City Four/Four dance beat. Nor is anything more subtle or less monotonous. Jo Jones, the most masterful, influential, and enduring of Kansas City percussionists, is as widely celebrated for the way he signifies with his sticks and wire brushes as for the way he testifies, bears witness, exhorts, annotates, approves or otherwise comments—not only with his sticks and his foot pedals, but also with his mallets and sometimes with his bare hands. Moreover, musicians and dancers alike almost always seem to respond as readily to his most offhand insinuations as to his most forthright declarations and most authorative decrees."

Little has been said about the form of the words in Adamson's narrative because the conventions used by interviewers for transcribing the speech of the ex-slaves are arbitrary. That the former slaves dropped some letters (sounds) and added others is a fact, but the WPA narratives share with the Dialect Tradition conventionalized approximations of standard written English that unfortunately suggest deficiency rather than the maturity and sophistication of Afro-American speech styles. For the student of linguistics, there is evidence in the narratives of enduring syntactical and grammatical habits such as the durative modes of *to be*, but evaluating the evidence of African cultural and linguistic continuities is beyond the scope of the present essay.

Though aural imagery dominates the set piece quoted, just before launching into the story quoted, Frank reminisces with W. W. Dixon, his interviewer: "I 'members when you was barefoot at de bottom; now I see you a settin' dere, gittin' bare at de top, as bare as de palm of my hand." The language is powerful and evocative, "poetic" in the traditional sense; its simplicity, concreteness, and immediacy are illustrative of the kind of beauty usually attributed to the naturally poetic "folk." Such linguistic creativity, common in the narratives, is best called Magic. But if one is discussing stories which have been told and retold, sometimes for generations, one can also argue that the stories exhibit a high degree of artistic self-consciousness, particularly because the audience of the stories has participated in their shaping, exercising collectively perhaps greater demands on a piece and achieving a finer sense of when it's right and finished than an individual author ever gains on his own work. Eliot argues in "Tradition and the Individual talent," "we shall often find that not only the best, but the most individual parts of [a poet's] work may be those in which the dead poets, his ancestors, assert their immortality most vigorously." The folk tradition reflects an aggregate sensibility, a potential, a range of possibilities which manifest themselves if and only if an individual embued with this sensibility performs. The idiomatic fluency of the individual performer is a form of consciousness, a consciousness brimming with ideas and ways of depicting those ideas. It is this consciousness, refined and critiqued by so many, that the individual draws from. The paradoxical beauty of tradition is that it shapes but does not narrow consciousness; choices are made by the artist at a level usually conceived of as preconscious, but these choices enrich and complement rather than limit the choices he or she "consciously" makes. Frank Adamson did not have to "think through" every step of his story, but the depth and resonance of oral tradition inform his narrative with a sense of purpose usually attributed to conscious artistry.

IV

Turning again briefly to Chesnutt's "A Deep Sleeper," we can locate a setpiece parallel to Adamson's.

> [1.]"De only fault he had wuz his sleep'ness. [2.]He'd hafter be woke up ev'y mawnin' ter go ter his wuk, en' w'enever he got a chance he'd fall ersleep. [3.]He wuz might'ly high gittin' inter trouble mo' d'n once for gwine ter sleep in de fiel'. [4.]I never seed his beat fer sleepin'. [5.]He could sleep in de sun er sleep in de shade. [6.]He could lean

upon his hoe en' sleep. [7.]He went ter sleep walk'n 'long de road oncet, en' mighty nigh bust his head open 'gin a tree he run inter. [8.]I did heah he oncet went ter sleep while he wuz in swimmin'. [9.]He wuz floatin' at de time, en' come mighty nigh gittin' drowned befo' he work up. [10.]Ole Marse heared 'bout it, en' ferbid his gwine in swimmin' enny mo', fer he said he couldn't 'ford ter lose 'im."

The word *sleep'ness*, like *tribulation* in Adamson's story, is the subject of this narrative. Instead of transformations of his subject word (*tribulation-snake*, *tribulation-rattle*), Chesnutt elaborates the concept of sleep'ness, giving his reader concrete examples of when, where, and how sleep'ness effected (defined) Skundus. Chesnutt's narrator Julius is less involved than Adamson with the events of the story; Julius's voice engages the reader less directly than Frank's. The personal pronoun *I* appears only twice and *us* never. Most sentences (six) begin with *He* so that the narrator's energy is used in piling up descriptive details about Skundus. The elaborations of the word *sleep'ness* do not unravel a plot line but rather, attached to Skundus, release the word from its ordinary meaning. Sleep'ness is stretched until it becomes preposterous and comic. Julius blends realistic details into his special definition of sleep'ness, rendering the realistic touches in a plain matter-of-fact voice so that the reader is bounced from the fantastic to the commonplace and back again. The process is calculated. Julius's intent is to unsettle his audience, to humor them into suspending their disbelief so he can substitute for a moment his vision for theirs. If his listeners play his game, Julius will entertain them, he will transport them from the piazza to a much more interesting world where anything can happen.

Chesnutt's narrative, since it is written, is structured less by sound effects than it is by a theme and variations spinning out of humorous examples of sleep'ness. But Chesnutt does draw upon many devices employed by Adamson's oral narrative. Repetition of key words such as *sleep* to establish patterns of meaning and sound; rhythmic repetition in balanced phrases, "He could sleep in de sun er sleep in de shade"; the "I" voice as a chorus, as a witness to the facts of the story, "I never seed his beat fer sleepin'!" Chesnutt captures the one-syllable-per-word percussive beat in Uncle Julius's voice. The word count and syllable count highly correlate, especially if one discounts proper names and the necessary grammatical inflections. Chesnutt does not employ dialogue in this passage, but reports the master's speech in sentence ten. Though the quote is indirect, its form would allow Julius to imitate his master's voice: "he said he couldn't 'ford ter lose 'im." Like Adamson, Julius allows the master to have the last word, but both narrators are signifying, are rounding their tales with a moral. The master in "A Deep Sleeper" is concerned about Skundus the piece of property, not Skundus the human being. Julius reveals this fact, not by editorializing in his own voice, but by letting Marse Dugal speak for himself.

Julius's narrative about Skundus continues for approximately four pages after the passage quoted above. The entire story as discussed earlier functions in a fashion similar to Adamson's narrative, making its point through indirection, humor, satire. In the extended story, Chesnutt dramatizes the Afro-American propensity for word and image-making. *Fittified* and *catacornered fits* are two of Julius's coinages. The Latin names bestowed by Marse Dugal (as well as Dugal's own name) are translated into the language of the black folk on the plantation. Chesnutt parallels the inventiveness of the oral tradition and illustrates the rich possibilities of this tradition when it is transmitted into written word. Newspapers advertising rewards for runaway slaves become *noospapers*, a punning, Joycean conflation of *news* and *noose*, evoking the lynch rope and the conspiracy of public institutions to keep the black man in bondage.

The oral tradition experienced firsthand during his youth in North Carolina is evidenced in Chesnutt's use of dialect, but it is dialect with roots in the black speech of ex-slaves like Frank Adamson rather than the Negro dialect tradition which by Chesnutt's time was mainly a literary convention for mocking black life.

WHAT IS AFRO,
WHAT IS AMERICAN?

1986

Unfortunately for scholars and serious fans of Ralph Ellison, there is little in this volume that has not been published before. In fact, at first glance *Going to the Territory*—a mix of occasional pieces, essays, speeches, interviews and reviews, many of them two decades old—bears a disquieting resemblance to *Shadow and Act*, a collection of Ralph Ellison's nonfiction writings published in 1964. Both books evaluate Richard Wright's stature as a writer, elaborate the intricate interplay between Afro-American fiction and folklore, explore the novel as a vehicle for moral and ethical truth, worry the notion of American identity and consider the craft of fiction as discipline and vocation. *Going to the Territory* is best viewed as a continuation of the project begun when Mr. Ellison introduced *Shadow and Act* as "an attempt to transform some of the themes, the problems, the enigmas, the contradictions of character and culture native to my predicament, into what Andre Malraux has described as 'conscious thought.'"

What captures the reader of *Going to the Territory*, then, is not novelty, not outrageous theories and claims, but the subtle, jazzlike changes Mr. Ellison rings against the steady backbeat of his abiding concerns as artist and critic. The rapid, almost casual allusions that occur in "Hidden Name and Complex Fate," an often-quoted essay from *Shadow and Act*, reappear in the title essay of the present volume. On this second go-round we learn more about Johnson Chestnut Whittaker, a principal at Mr. Ellison's high school in Oklahoma. Whittaker, a "white" (fair-skinned) black man, was mutilated by his classmates at West Point in order to deny him a commission. We get frequent glimpses of Hazel Harrison, the music teacher at Tuskegee Institute who possessed manuscripts presented to her by Prokofiev. Mr. Ellison's Oklahoma boyhood and his aspiration to become a renaissance man are given context by his recollection of Bessie Smith singing "Goin' to the Nation, Going to the Terr'tor," a lyrical rendering of the impulse of blacks and other Americans to push toward the frontier and its promise of freedom.

The reader is impressed and delighted by the integrity of Mr. Ellison's vision. His voice is assured, calm, wise. The first-person mode, the transcriptions of talk, give a relaxed, intimate tone to many of these essays. Mr. Ellison is remembering; he's lived more than thirty years with his classic, *Invisible Man*, towering over his shoulder. But fame must have its compensations, not least the quiet power and authority he displays here.

On the other hand, this collection is anything but mellow. Mr. Ellison instructs literary people to "keep a sharp eye on what's happening in the unintellectualized areas of our experience. Our peripheral vision had better be damned good. Because while baseball, basketball and football players cannot really tell us how to write our books, they do demonstrate where much of the significant action is taking place." Mr. Ellison can assume a boxer's stance, aggressive, wary, on his toes. Much to fight with and fight about—Lyndon B. Johnson's role in the civil rights struggle, the melting pot as a valid metaphor for American culture, a discussion of the relative weights of "Afro" and "American" in the expression "Afro-American." All of this, with the highly abstract, ponderously intellectual language of scattered passages, makes Mr. Ellison's writing challenging. If you're not prepared to debate vigorously the point in question, if your knowledge of the facts is spotty and you don't have a personal stake in your point of view, you'll find your arguments swatted away.

In a tribute to Erskine Caldwell, Mr. Ellison quotes Baudelaire: "The wise man never laughs but that he trembles." One of the funniest moments in this book—one that causes me to tremble—confirms why the writer, like the fighter, must maintain constant vigilance. It follows an eloquent exposition of the creative process that produced *Invisible Man*. From the author's audience of West Point cadets this question arises: "Sir, was it your intention to include any protest in the novel?" LUCK-ILY, Mr. Ellison is a connoisseur of irony and dissonance. From them he fashions a personal angle of vision. Speaking at Brown during a cere-mony dedicated to Inman E. Page, who in 1877 became that university's first black graduate and later succeeded Johnson Chestnut Whittaker as principal of Mr. Ellison's high school in Oklahoma City, the author revels in the unexpected twists and turns of history, the lofty intentions and tragic cross-purposes of the democratic process that brought Page's old student Ralph Ellison to a rostrum at Brown. The underground his-tory that both creates and is created by men like Page and Mr. Ellison explodes into visibility when Mr. Ellison writes: "By pushing significant details of our experience into the underground of unwritten history, we not only overlook much which is positive, but we blur our conceptions of where and who we are. . . . It is as though we dread to acknowledge the complex, pluralistic nature of our society, and as a result we find our-selves stumbling upon our true national identity under circumstances in which we least expect to do so."

Great writers are always teaching us how to read them. One measure of greatness is how much we need the lessons, how much we appreci-ate them and then take them for granted. In a master's fiction there are implicit instructions and when he or she writes about writing, the mes-sages become insistent. Change the word *visual* to *verbal* and Mr. Ellison's depiction of Romare Bearden's paintings becomes a lucid summary of *Invisible Man*: "Through an act of creative will, he has blended strange visual harmonies out of the shrill, indigenous dichotomies of Ameri-can life, and in doing so, reflected the irrepressible thrust of a people to endure and keep its intimate sense of its own identity."

Mr. Ellison goes a step further in "The Little Man at Chehaw Station," describing the ideal reader of his fiction. The little man, this Kilroy who is always listening and to whom the true artist must always defer by playing his best no matter where or when—even in a tiny railroad station in Chehaw, Alabama—is no more or less than the spirit of our American place, not the marketplace, mind you, but the vernacular, always-up-for-grabs agency of cultural change, creativity, and possibility. No American performs better for this audience than Ralph Waldo Ellison.

On a squallish, ice-glazed November day in 1967, Ralph and Fanny Ellison stood near their two-hundred-year-old home in the Berkshires and watched it burn. The building slipped easily into flames driven by high winds.

"We just managed to get our Labrador retriever out," Mr. Ellison recalls. The couple could not rescue a goodly chunk of his still-uncompleted novel. The first was, of course, *Invisible Man*, the classic that won the National Book Award in 1953. "For a long time after the fire, I was scrambling around not knowing what was going on," Mr. Ellison said.

When there is news of Mr. Ellison, most people sort through it for clues about the second novel. Speaking with him about his latest essay collection, *Going to the Territory*, it seemed natural to mention it. "Until the recent stir about my new book of essays, the novel has been coming very well," he said by phone from his Manhattan apartment. When will it be done? "I don't know."

Is it like the first one? "It's quite different . . . a broader canvas. Though I think it will have some of the wildness of *Invisible Man*." Will it be a multivolume affair? (In 1982, the manuscript was reported to be nearly 20 inches thick.) "No, it's not, I know that's gotten around, though."

Does it bother him that people always ask about it? "I don't feel particularly uncomfortable with it. I know I have become something of a joke on this subject. One of the things I've tried to do is not let the publicity surrounding a book get out of hand. When I was writing *Invisible Man*, no one was hanging around saying 'when, when.' I have made my peace with my slow tempo of creation."

In contrast, *Going to the Territory* seems to have pulled itself together. "These pieces were not conceived of as a collection," the seventy-two-year-old author said. "They were written as they were called for and they may have some thematic continuity of which I am not aware."

These days Mr. Ellison has set his course for the Berkshires—and work.

THE BLACK WRITER AND
THE MAGIC OF THE WORD

1988

At a certain point in my writing career, after I had done three books, I made a decision. I wanted to reach out to readers that the earlier works had perhaps excluded. I wanted to get everybody's ear. I had in mind a book for people familiar with America, with the technique and history of the novel—a book that audience could appreciate and applaud and relate to the Great Traditions, if there really are such things. But at the same time a book my brothers, sister, aunts, uncles, cousins, mother, and father would want to read. And in my mind it became quite clear that I wouldn't be writing down to a black audience. My people's lives embrace the whole range of human experience. In fact, the language they speak, refined and tested by centuries of racial oppression and racial assertion, offers a unique vision of America. So it wasn't a question of condescending to a less educated set of readers, but of becoming more ambitious.

My goal has always been to write as well as anybody has ever written, but I am sure now that for a long time I didn't know what really counted as legitimate subject matter, legitimate language, for such an enterprise. To write the very best, didn't you have to cheat on your past a little, didn't you have to "transcend Blackness"? Didn't you have to prove yourself by grounding yourself outside a black environment like Homewood, the community in Pittsburgh where I was raised?

I was university educated, and as you go through schools like the University of Pennsylvania and Oxford University, you get a value system imposed on you. You don't just guess what the best is; people tell you what the best is. Lessons, styles seep in. As I had grown up, a value system had formed; college attempted to put another in place, and so I was not consciously turning my back on blackness, I was just becoming acculturated, and the acculturation pushed my writing in predictable directions.

When I began to teach literature in college, I taught what I'd learned: books by white authors. Then, about 1967 or 1968, I took a summer and part of a year to develop a course in Afro-American literature. I went from a very superficial acquaintance to an absolute immersion in black literature. Afro-American literature courses have become a special love. And my writing has absolutely been transformed by my study of Afro-American writing and culture.

For seven years between books, I was exploring voice, doing a lot of practicing, studying, "woodshedding," as the musicians would say—catching up. I was learning—relearning may be more accurate—a new language with which to talk about my experience, a language I used in my novel *Damballah*: "Hey man, what's to it? . . . ain't nothing to it something to it I wouldn't be out here in all this sun you looking good you into something go on man you got it all you know you the Man hey now that was a stone fox you know what I'm talking about you don't be creeping past me."

Afro-Americans must communicate in a written language which in varying degrees is foreign to our oral traditions. You learn the language of power, learn it well enough to read and write but its forms and logic cut you off, separate you from the primal authenticity of your experience, experience whose meaning resides in the first language you speak, the language not only of words but gestures, movements, rules of silence and expressive possibilities, of facial and tactile understanding, a language of immediate, sensual, intimate reciprocity, of communal and self-definition.

Houston A. Baker, Jr., in *The Journey Back*, a study of Afro-American writers and culture, speculates on the ex-slave Frederick Douglass's autobiographical narrative: "The voice of the unwritten self, once it is subjected to the linguistic codes, literary conventions, and audience expectations of a literate population, is perhaps never again the authentic voice of black American slavery. It is, rather, the voice of a self transformed by an autobiographical act into a sharer in the general public discourse about slavery." He goes on to ask, "Where in Douglass's narrative does a prototypical black American self reside?"

Does an Afro-American necessarily lose contact with an authentic self if he or she decides to tell a story in print, in a second acquired tongue? Are the only options silence or fatal compromise?

For hundreds of years black people have been speaking English. Beginning as a pidgin or trade language on the west coast of Africa, then transformed to a creole as a second generation of Africans was born on American soil, the English that black people speak has a distinct history, intertwined but always systematically in tension with the standard or mainstream variety of English spoken by newscasters and other imaginary Americans. The key word is *systematically*. Since language and culture are symbiotic, if we can begin to describe systematically the kinds and quantity of distance between speech patterns and standard norms, we also will be defining the roots of Afro-American culture. And if we can identify the means Afro-American writers employ to keep the oral roots of black culture alive and kicking in our fiction, we can perhaps find that place in our writing where Houston Baker's prototypical black American self resides.

In simple terms, the "inside" of black speech is just as important as its outside. One highly developed aspect of black speech and Afro-American oral tradition is the means by which its users can signify how they feel about what they're saying. Dual messages are transmitted in a single speech act. Distance between black speech and standard speech always exists, but under various circumstances black speakers acknowledge and use this distance differently. At one end of the continuum measuring this distance between black speech and standard English is bilingual fluency; at the other, silence. Play is the aesthetic, functional manipulation of standard English to mock, to create irony or satire or double-entendre, to signify meanings accessible only to a special segment of the audience. Play creates a distinctly Afro-American version of English; the speaker acknowledges to himself and announces to his audience that he's not taking the language of the slavemaster altogether seriously. But the play is serious business. A survival technique, an art form reproducing English in a nonrepresentational fashion, or, if you will, employing what Robert Ferris Thompson, in *African Art in Motion*, called the "mid-point mimesis" characteristic of West African sculpture and other arts.

Think of the massive forehead of a Benin mask, how the exaggerated, dominant brow projects cool intelligence, or the elongated, swanlike necks of carved Yoruba female figures, which embody grace, elegance, and balance through the calculated distortion of natural proportions. Think of kidnapped Africans learning English during slavery days, improvising, stylizing the master's speech, using it, abusing it, treating it as real, but not too real. If we conceive of the context in which kidnapped Africans learned English during slavery days, clearly the new language would be tainted by the master/slave relationship.

Learning English to survive would have been necessary, but inside the slave's mind a natural resistance, a balkiness, fear, suspicion, even hatred of the new language would condition the learning process. A deep intuitive understanding of the fact that there's no place, no room for me inside this thing, this language that is one more cruel weapon my captors wield against me. Recall Caliban's plight. Recall the numb black children nodding in schoolrooms today. The structure of an English pidgin reflects laws of linguistic change, but it also mirrors the dynamics of the social context in which it evolved. The language created in this crucible must not be viewed simply as a clumsy attempt to master the sounds and syntax of English; it should also be seen as a record of the harsh circumstances of its birth, a vehicle captive Africans employed to express their feelings toward English, which is not so much spoken as played with.

The goal of a particular pronunciation is only partially to represent an English sound. The discrepancy between a word in black speech and the same word in standard English can function symbolically to stylize, personalize, to appropriate a word. In Charles Waddell Chesnutt's story "A Deep Sleeper," originally published in 1887, a character named by his master Secundus after the second Latin ordinal number is known on the plantation as Skundus. If pushed, Skundus's fellow slaves could have learned to enunciate "Secundus" in spite of their inherent laziness, big lips, and mental inferiority. The point is they chose not to. They rebaptized Skundus to secure his identity in the black speech community, an identity that slips the yoke and turns the joke back on the pretentious white owner and the dehumanizing number-label he attached to his property.

This process of symbolic abstraction, of creating verbal icons, is basic to black versions of English. Africans took English sounds and with variation in tempo, rhythm, tone, and timbre transformed them. Pushing English in the direction of their more tonal African languages, new sense evolved as well as new sounds. Play reinforced a tendency to draw out the music buried within English—rhyme, interpolation of African syllables and words, or just plain scat-singing nonsense marked this African stylization of the speech of their captors. The process parallels the magic Billie Holiday performed on the banal tunes and lyrics of Tin Pan Alley.

The testimony of contemporary Africans who speak Wes Cos or Kriol or pidgin, West Indian fancy talk, the oral narratives of ex-slaves, contemporary narratives collected from prisons, bars, street corners, and the workingplace, as well as rap records and the folk-derived forms of Afro-American music, all testify to the fact that black speech is not simply faulty English but a witness to a much deeper fault, a crack running below the surface, a fatal flaw in the forms and pretensions of so-called civilized language.

The historical, outside approach to defining Afro-American speech emphasizes the capacity to speak a second, new language, but what is just as important as capacity is desire and will. And will resides inside an individual. Slaves spoke as much or as little as they chose to speak. In this sense, silence is a logical extreme of play, deadly serious play with standard English, signifying that we ain't playing no more. Pretense is ended. There's nothing more to say. The distance between your version of reality and mine admits no possibility of mutual intelligibility. (Perhaps that's why a black person who's quiet in the company of whites is often perceived by whites as stupid or sullen or dangerous.) Obviously it would not have been to the slave's advantage to reveal to his master his full capacity, whether of language, intelligence, or ability to work. The exercise of will, then as today, is a variable difficult to determine from the outside, yet clearly significant if one wishes to understand how, why, and when blacks use different registers of English.

A fiction writer is not a slave; he or she is a participant in a literary as well as an oral culture. Most black writers are impressively fluent in a variety of dialects: black, white, genteel, literate, and many registers in between. Yet just as the slave's oral pidgin English was English transformed by his original African language and the master-slave relationship, the black writer's English, if examined closely, will reveal its sources in Afro-American culture, a culture that has been generated partly as a response to racism. If he wished to survive, the slave was forced to learn the sounds and syntax of English. If black writers wish to publish, we have to learn the grammars of twentieth-century American culture and adjust our literate speech to their constraints: economic, political, moral, aesthetic. Whatever individuality, whatever freedom of expression either writer or slave achieves can be illuminated by viewing what they say against the systemic net of restrictions designed to inhibit their voices.

Recall that Billie Holiday's genius flourished in spite of the fact she received only third-rate songs to record, in spite of the fact that her style didn't fit audience expectations, in spite of the simplistic, sentimental lyrics of American popular music, in spite of racism and sexism. The deep structures of African languages survived in the slaves' version of the new language enforced upon them. So too, in the case of Afro-American writing, an authentic prototypical back American self can shine forth in spite of the restrictions imposed upon this voice when it breaks into print.

The terrible thing is that as writers or critics we are forced into certain kinds of choices, choices laden with values the writer doesn't necessarily hold. A critic can argue, "Wideman is a good writer; he uses Afro-American folklore, he knows this or that about his heritage and culture." The critic can make that argument, show it in the work and pat me on the back, but that doesn't get me out of the ghetto. Even if I've accomplished what the critic ascribes to me—and surely that is enough—there is still an implied, invidious comparison: "Okay. Wideman does fine with Afro-American stuff, but on the other hand back at headquarters, the real writers are doing thus and so. . . ." To protect ourselves as critics and artists, we are forced to jump back and forth, measure ourselves against an imaginary mainstream, define what we are doing in somebody else's terms. One thing for sure: it is a terrible bind.

The historical problem is unavoidably there, and how you solve it creates a sort of "out of the frying pan into the fire" dilemma. There is an Afro-American tradition. There are Afro-American writers working right now; it makes sense to talk about us as a group. It is natural, enlightening, intelligent to approach the work that way, but at the same time, to do so perpetuates the whole wrongheaded notion of looking at things in terms of black and white, and in our culture this implies not simply a distinction, but black inferiority. In academia, Mr. Dewy-Eyed Optimistic (who is really Mr. Turn-Them-Back in disguise) believes that the purpose of Afro-American literature classes is remedial, a fine-tuning of the curriculum, and argues that the millennium will arrive when American literature classes include *Invisible Man*. The real challenge of Afro-American culture gets lost. It's not a question of making a little more room in the inn but tearing the old building down, letting the tenants know their losses are such that no one is assured of a place, that the notion of permanently owning a place is as defunct as the inn.

When someone asks if I like being called an Afro-American writer, it's almost like asking which of my names I prefer. When I play basketball, some of the young guys at the university gym call me Doc, and I like that. Back in Pittsburgh at Mellon Park playground, some of the old guys call me Spanky; that's okay too. But I don't want other people to call me those names. Names are contextual. They make sense in certain situations, but the same names are insulting in others. Various literary labels are okay with me, as long as people don't get confused and call me out of my name; that's the important thing.

In the fiction I have published during the last several years, I have been trying to recover some lost experience, to reeducate myself about some of the things I missed because the world was moving so fast. My books returned to Homewood and settled in. I am trying to listen again. Fortunately, my people are kind, compassionate, patient. In contrast to Thomas Wolfe, I can go home again, listen again. There is a basic conservatism in any folk life. Little sayings and phrases that I read in the WPA ex-slave narratives, I'd heard before in my living room. For instance, "Stomp down ugly." When I found that phrase in a slave narrative I cracked up because I had been hearing that my whole life. Afro-American culture is conservative; and it gives you a chance to go back. Writing is a means of preservation for the community, the ethnic group, as well as the individual artist.

Cultures, ethnic groups, nations are fragile, mortal. A whole way of life can disappear. For a long time I'd entertained a secret fear about black people, black culture in the United States. Not the stark '60s paranoia about genocide, but a creeping, exhausting sense that a link was being severed, a connection lost. The main currents of black life had little to do with whatever was unique, special about Africans who had been transplanted to the New World, Africans who'd experienced their Time on the Cross but who'd never lost touch with the old ways, the ancestral spirits that animated Afro-American prayers, music and motion. I had a sense that after all the suffering and struggle, we were losing with a whimper what no one had been able to steal, crush or beat out of us. The melting pot would have its way. Slowly, surely the monoculture would claim us. Black Kens and Barbies would be free at last. I seldom spoke this fear, both because I didn't want to believe it could happen and because I didn't know exactly how to express what caused me to feel it might happen. Plus, I have a superstition. Naming things can give them life. A former slave being questioned about illness and mortality on slave plantations before emancipation declared that people were healthier back then because back then folks didn't know the names of all these diseases they know nowadays. When James Baldwin protested, "Nobody Knows My Name," he was complaining about invisibility, the status of nonexistence his color had relegated him to. Of course he was right and wrong. Everybody knew his name. And when they called him "nigger" they tried to manufacture and own him in the same breath.

N. Scott Momaday has pointed out the precariousness of any oral culture, how the tales and ways of Native American people have always been just one generation from extinction. If each generation doesn't learn and pass on the stories and customs, the vitality of ethnic traditions ends. As a fiction writer, a critic, and a teacher I am trying to forge bulwarks and bridges, protect and share what is uniquely mine and yours. I depend upon the magic of the word.

MICHAEL JORDAN LEAPS
THE GREAT DIVIDE

1990

This old woman told me she went to visit this old retired bullfighter who raised bulls for the ring. She had told him about this record that had been made by a black American musician, and he didn't believe that a foreigner, an American—and especially a black American—could make such a record. He sat there and listened to it. After it was finished, he rose from his chair and put on his bullfighting equipment and outfit, went out and fought one of his bulls for the first time since he had retired, and killed the bull. When she asked him why he had done it, he said he had been so moved by the music that he just had to fight the bull.

—Miles: The Autobiography

When it's played the way it's spozed to be played, basketball happens in the air, the pure air; flying, floating, elevated above the floor, levitating the way oppressed peoples of this earth imagine themselves in their dreams, as I do in my lifelong fantasies of escape and power, finally, at last, once and for all, free. For glimpses of this ideal future game we should thank, among others, Elgin Baylor, Connie Hawkins, David Thompson, Helicopter Knowings, and of course, Julius Erving, Dr. J. Some venerate Larry Bird for reminding us how close a man can come to a perfect gravity-free game and still keep his head, his feet firmly planted on terra firma. Or love Magic Johnson for confounding boundaries, conjuring new space, passing lanes, fast-break and break-down lanes neither above the court nor exactly on it, but somehow whittling and expanding simultaneously the territory in which the game is enacted. But really, as we envision soaring and swooping, extending, refining the combat zone of basketball into a fourth, outer, other dimension, the dreamy ozone of flight without wings, of going up and not coming down till we're good and ready, then it's Michael Jordan we must recognize as the truest prophet of what might be possible.

A great artist transforms our world, removes scales from our eyes, plugs from our ears, gloves from our fingertips, teaches us to perceive reality differently. Proust said of his countryman and contemporary, the late-nineteenth-century Impressionist Auguste Renoir: "Before Renoir painted there were no Renoir women in Paris, now you see them everywhere." Tex Winters, a veteran Chicago Bulls coach, a traditionalist who came up preaching the conventional wisdom that a lay-up is the highest-percentage shot, enjoys Michael Jordan's dunks, but, says MJ, "Every time I make one, he says, 'So whatever happened to the simple lay-up?' 'I don't know, Tex, this is how I've been playing my whole career.' You know, this stuff here and this stuff here [the hands are rocking, cradling, stuffing an imaginary ball] is like a lay-up to me. You know I've been doing that and that's the creativity of the game now. But it drives him nuts . . . and he says, 'Well, why don't you draw the foul?' I say I never have. The defense alters many of my shots, so I create. I've always been able to create in those situations, and I guess that's the Afro-American game I have, that's just natural to me. And even though it may not be the traditional game that Americans have been taught, it works for me. Why not?"

The lady is gaudy as Carnival. Magenta, sky blue, lime, scarlet, orange swirl in the dress that balloons between her sashed waist and bare knees.

Somebody's grandmother, gift-wrapped and wobbly on Madison Street, toreadoring through four lanes of traffic converging on Chicago Stadium. Out for a party. Taxi driver says this is where they stand at night. Whore women, he calls them, a disgusted judgmental swipe in his voice, which until now has been a mellow tour-guide patter, pointing out the Sears Tower, Ditka's, asking me how tall is Michael Jordan. The tallest in basketball? Laughing at his memory of a photo of Manute Bol beside Muggsy Bogues. Claiming to have seen Michael Jordan at Shelter, a West Side club late on Wednesday, the night of Game Four after the Bulls beat Detroit last spring to even the best-of-seven NBA championship semifinal at two games apiece. Yes, with two other fellas. Tall like him. Lots of people asking him to sign his name. Autographs, you know. A slightly chopped, guttural, Middle Eastern–flavored Chicagoese, patched together in the two and a half years he's resided in the States. "I came here as student. My family sent me three thousand dinars a year, and I could have apartment, pay my bills, drive a car. Then hard times at home. Dinar worth much less in dollars. Four people, all of them, must work a month to earn one thousand dinars. No school now. I must work now. American wife and new baby, man."

The driver's from Jordan, but the joke doesn't strike me until I'm mumbling out the cab in front of Chicago Stadium. JORDAN, the country. Appearing in the same column, just above JORDAN, MICHAEL, in *Readers' Guide to Periodical Literature*, where I researched Michael Jordan's career. Usually more entries in each volume under JORDAN, MICHAEL, than any other JORDAN.

The other passenger sharing a cab from O'Hare to downtown Chicago is a young German from Hamburg, in the city with about one hundred thousand fellow conventioneers for the Consumer Electronics Show. It's while he's calculating exchange rates to answer the driver's question about the cost of a Mercedes in Germany that the lady stumbles backward from the curb into the street, blocking strings of cars pulled up at a light. She pirouettes. Curtsies. The puffy dress of many colors glows brighter, wilder against grays and browns of ravaged cityscape.

Partially demolished or burnt-out or abandoned warehouses and storefronts line both sides of Madison. Interspersed between buildings are jerry-rigged parking lots where you'd leave your car overnight only if you had a serious grudge against it. I think of a mouth rotten with decay, gaps where teeth have fallen out. Competing for the rush of ball-game traffic, squads of shills and barkers hip-hop into the stalled traffic, shucking and jiving with anyone who'll pay attention. One looms at the window of our cab, sandwiched in, a hand-lettered sign tapping the windshield, begging us to park in his oasis, until the woman impeding our progress decides to attempt the curb again and mounts it this time, Minnie Mouse high heels firmly planted as she gives the honking cars a flounce of Technicolor behind and a high-fived middle finger.

The woman's black, and so are most of the faces on Madison as we cruise toward the stadium in a tide of cars carrying white faces. Closer, still plenty of black faces mix into the crowd—vendors, scalpers, guys in sneakers and silky sweat suits doing whatever they're out there doing—but when the cab stops and deposits me into a thin crust of dark people who aren't going in, I cut through quickly to join the mob of whites who are.

I forget I am supposed to stop at the press trailer for my credentials but slip inside the building without showing a pass or a ticket because mass confusion reigns at the gate. Then I discover why people are buzzing and shoving, why the gate crew is overwhelmed and defeated: Jesse Jackson. Even if it belongs to Michael Jordan this evening, Chicago's still Jackson's town too. And everyone wants to touch or be touched by this man who is instantly recognized, not only here in Chicago but all over the world. Casually dressed tonight, black slacks, matching black short-sleeved shirt that displays his powerful shoulders and arms. He could be a ballplayer. A running back, a tight end. But the eyes, the bearing are a quarterback's. Head high, he scans the whole field, checks out many things at once, smiles, and presses the flesh of the one he's greeting but stays alert to the bigger picture. When a hassled ticket-taker stares suspiciously at me, I nod toward Jesse, as if to say, I'm with him, he's the reason I'm here, and that's enough to chase the red-faced gatekeeper's scrutiny to easier prey. This minute exchange, insignificant as it may be, raises my spirits. Not because Jesse Jackson's presence enabled me to get away with anything—after all, I'm legit, certified, qualified to enter the arena—but because the respect, the recognizability he's earned reflects on me, empowers me, subtly alters others' perceptions of who I am, what I can do. When I hug the Reverend Jesse Jackson I try to impart a little of my appreciation to the broad shoulders I grip. By just being out there, being heard and seen, by standing for something—for instance, an African-American man's right, duty, and ability to aim for the stars—he's saved us all a lot of grief, bought us, black men, white, the entire rainbow of sexes and colors, more time to get our sorry act together. *Thank you* is what I always feel the need to say when I encounter the deep light of his smile.

Your town, man.

Brother Wideman, what are you doing here?

Writing about Michael Jordan.

We don't get any further. Somebody else needs a piece of him, a word, a touch from our Blarney stone, our Somebody.

In Michael's house the PA system is cranked to a sirenlike, earsplitting pitch, many decibels higher than a humane health code should permit. The Luvabulls, Chicago's aerobicized version of the Dallas Cowboy Cheerleaders, shake that fine, sculpted booty to pump up the fans. Very basic here. Primal-scream time. The incredible uproar enters your pores, your blood, your brain. Your nervous system becomes an extension of the overwhelming assault upon it. In simplest terms, you're ready for total war, transformed into a weapon poised to be unleashed upon the enemy.

From my third-row-end-zone folding chair, depth perception is nil. The game is played on a flat, two-dimensional screen. Under the opposite basket the players appear as they would crowded into the wrong end of a telescope.

Then, as the ball moves toward the near goal, action explodes, a zoom lens hurtles bodies at you larger, more intense than life. Middle ground doesn't exist. You're surprised when a ref holds up both arms to indicate a three-point goal scored from beyond the twenty-three-foot line. But your inability to gauge the distance of jump shots or measure the swift, subtle penetration, step by step, yard by yard as guards dribble between their legs, behind the back, spinning, dipping, shouldering, teasing their way upcourt, is compensated for by your power to watch the glacial increments achieved by big men muscling each other for position under your basket, the intimacy of those instants when the ball is in the air at your end of the court and just about everybody on both teams seems driven to converge into a space not larger than two telephone booths. Then it's grapple, grunt, and groan only forty feet away. You can read the effort, the fear, the focus in a player's eyes. For a few seconds you're on the court, sweating, absorbing the impact, the crash of big bodies into one another, wood buckling underfoot, some- one's elbow in your ribs, shouts in your ear, the wheezes, sighs, curses, hearing a language spoken here and nowhere else except when people are fighting or making love.

MJ: What do I like about basketball? *Hmmm.* That's a good ques- tion. I started when I was twelve. And I enjoyed it to the point that I started to do things other people couldn't do. And that intrigued me more. Now I still enjoy it because of the excitement I get from fans, from the people, and still having the same ability to do things that other people can't do but want to do and they can do only through you. They watch you do it, then they think that they can do it. Or maybe they know it's something they can't do and iron-ically, that's why they feel good watching me. That drives me. I'm able to do something that no one else can do.

And I love competition. I've earned respect thanks to basket-ball. And I'm not here just to hand it to the next person. Day in and day out I see people take on that challenge, to take what I have earned. Joe Dumars, for one—I mean, I respect him, don't get me wrong. It's his job. I've got something that people want. The ability to gain respect for my basketball skills. And I don't ever want to give it away. Whenever the time comes when I'm not able to do that, then I'll just back away from the game.

JW: We've always been given credit for our athletic skill, our bod-ies. You've been blessed with exceptional physical gifts, and all your mastery of the game gets lost in the rush. But I believe your mind, the way you conceive the game, plays as large a role as your physical abilities. As much as any other player I've seen, you seem to play the game with your mind.

MJ: The mental aspect of the game came when I got into college. After winning the national championship at North Carolina in 1982, I knew I had the ability to play on that level, but there were a lot of players who had that ability. What distinguishes certain players from others is the mental aspect. You've got to approach the game strong, in a mental sense. So from my sophomore year on, I took it as a challenge to try and outthink the defense, out-think the next player. He might have similar skills, but if I can be very strong mentally and really determined mentally, I can rise above most opponents. As you know, I went through college ball with Coach Dean Smith, and he's [a] very good psychological-type coach. He doesn't yell at you. He says one line and you think within yourself and know that you've done something wrong. . . . When I face a challenger, I've got to watch him, watch what he loves to do, watch things that I've done that haven't worked. . . . How can I come up with some weapon, some other surprises to overpower them?

JW: You don't just use someone on your team to work two-on-two. Your plan seems to involve all ten players on the court. A chesslike plan for all four quarters.

MJ: I think I have a good habit of evaluating situations on the floor, offensively, defensively, teammate or opponent. And somehow filling in the right puzzle pieces to click. To get myself in a certain mode or mood to open a game or get a roll going. For instance, the last game we lost to Detroit in the playoffs last spring: We're down twenty, eighteen, twenty-two points at the half. Came back to eleven or ten down. I became a point guard. Somehow I sensed it, sensed no one else wanted to do it or no one else was going to do it until I did it. You could see once I started pushing, started doing these things, everybody else seemed like they got a little bit higher, the game started to go higher, and that pushes my game a little higher, higher, higher. I kept pulling them up, trying to get them to a level where we could win.

Then, you know, I got tired, I had to sit out and rest. Let Detroit come all the way back. It hurts a little bit, but then again I feel good about the fact that I mean so much to those guys, in a sense that if I don't play, if I don't do certain things, then they're not going to play well. It's like when people say it's a one-man gang in Chicago. I take it as a compliment, but then it's unfair that I would have to do all that.

I can dictate what I want to do in the course of the game. I can say to my friends, Well, I'll score twelve points in the first quarter . . . then I can relax in the second quarter and score maybe six, eight. Not take as many shots, but in the second half I can go fifteen, sixteen, quick. That's how much confidence I have in my ability to dictate how many points I can score and be effective and give the team an opportunity to win.

I don't mind taking a beating or scoring just a few points in the first half, because I feel the second half I'm going to have the mental advantage. My man is going to relax. He feels he's got an advantage, he's got me controlled, that means he's going to let down his guard just a little bit. If I can get past that guard one time I feel that I've got the confidence to break him down.

On the same night in July that Michael Jordan slipped on a damp outdoor court at his basketball camp on the Elmhurst College campus, jamming his wrist and elbow, on a court in a park called Mill River in North Amherst, Massachusetts, my elbow cracked against something hard that was moving fast, so when I talked with Michael Jordan the next morning in Elmhurst, Illinois, on the outskirts of Chicago, my elbow was sore and puffy, his wrapped and packed in ice.

We'd won two straight in our pickup, playground run, pretty ordinary, local, tacky hoop that's fine if you're inside the game, but nothing to merit a spectator's attention. Ten on the court, nine or ten on the sidelines hanging out or waiting to take on the winners, a small band of witnesses, then, for something extraordinary that happened next. On a breakaway dribble Sekou beats everybody to the hoop except two opponents who hadn't bothered to run back to their offensive end. It was that kind of game, spurts of hustle, lunch breaks while somebody else did the work. Sekou solo, racing for the hoop, two defenders converging to cut him off, slapping at the ball, bodying him into a vise to stop his momentum. What happens next is almost too quick to follow. Sekou picks up his dribble about eight feet from the basket, turns his back to the goal, to the two guys who are clamping him, as if, outnumbered, he's looking downcourt for help. A quick feint, shoulders and head dipped one way, and then he brings the ball across his body, slamming it hard against the asphalt, *blam*, in the space his fake has cleared. Ball bounds higher than the basket and for an instant I think he's trying a trick shot, bouncing the ball into the basket, a jive shot that's missing badly as the ball zooms way over the rim toward the far side of the backboard. While I'm thinking this and thinking Sekou's getting outrageous, throwing up a silly, wasteful, selfish shot even for the playground, even in a game he can dominate because he's by far the best athlete, while I'm thinking this and feeling a little pissed off at his hotdogging and ball hogging, the ball's still in the air, and Sekou spins and rises, a pivot off his back foot so he's facing the hoop, one short step gathering himself, one long stride carrying him around the frozen defenders and then another step in the air, rising till he catches the rock in flight and crams it one-handed down, *down* through the iron.

Hoop, poles, and backboard shudder. A moment of stunned silence, then the joint erupts. Nobody can believe what they've seen. The two players guarding Sekou kind of slink off. But it wasn't about turning people into chumps or making anybody feel bad. It was Sekou's glory. Glory reflected instantly on all of us because he was one of us out there in the game and he'd suddenly lifted the game to a higher plane. We were all larger and better. Hell, none of us could rise like Sekou, but he carried us up there with him. He needed us now to amen and goddamn and high-five and time-out. Time out, stop this shit right here. Nate, the griot, style-point judge, and resident master of ceremonies, begins to perform his job of putting into words what everybody's thinking. *Time out.* We all wander onto the court, to the basket that's still vibrating, including the two guys Sekou had rocked. Sekou is hugged, patted, praised. Skin smacks skin, slaps skin. Did you see that? Did you see that? I ain't never seen nothing like that. Damn, Sekou. Where'd you learn that shit? Learned it sitting right here. Right here when I was coming up. My boy Patrick. Puerto Rican dude, you know Patrick. He used to do it. Hey man, Patrick could play but Patrick didn't have no serious rise like that, man. Right. He'd bounce it, go get it, shoot it off the board. Seen him do it more than once. Sitting right here on this bench I seen him do it. Yeah, well, cool, I can believe it. But man that shit you did. One hand and shit . . . damn . . . damn, Sekou.

I almost told Michael Jordan about Sekou's move. Asked Michael if he'd ever attempted it, seen it done. Maybe, I thought, someday when I'm watching the Bulls on the tube Michael will do a Sekou for a national audience and I won't exactly take credit, but deep inside I'll be saying, Uh-huh, uh-huh. Because we all need it, the sense of connection, the feeling we can be better than we are, even if better only through someone else, an agent, a representative, Mother Teresa, Mandela, one of us ourselves taken to a higher power, altered for a moment, alive in another's body and mind. One reason we need games, sports, the heroes they produce. To rise. To fly.

I didn't have to tell Michael Jordan Sekou's story. MJ earns a living by performing nearly on a regular basis similar magical feats for an audience of millions across the globe. I told him instead about my elbow. Tuesday night had been a bad night for elbows all over North America. Commiserating, solicitous about his injury, but also hopelessly vain, proud of mine, as if our sore elbows matched us, blood brothers meeting at last, a whole lifetime of news, gossip, and stuff to catch up on. Since we couldn't very well engage in that one-on-one game I'd been fantasizing, not with him handicapped by a fat elbow, we might as well get on with the interview I'd been seeking since the end of the NBA playoffs. Relax and get it on in this borrowed office at Elmhurst, my tape recorder on the desk between us, Michael Jordan settled back in a borrowed swivel chair, alert, accommodating. Mellow, remarkably fresh after a protracted autograph session, signing one item apiece for each of the 350 or so campers who'd been sitting transfixed in a circle around him earlier that morning as he shared some of his glory with them in a luminous exchange that masked itself as a simple lesson in basketball basics from Michael Jordan.

JW: Your style of play comes from the playground, comes from tradition, the African-American way of playing basketball.

MJ: Can't teach it.

JW: When I was coming up, if a coach yelled "playground move" at you it meant there was something wrong with it, which also meant in a funny way there was something wrong with the playground, and since the playground was a black world, there was something wrong with you, a black player out there doing something your way rather than their way.

MJ: I've been doing it my way. When you come out of high school, you have natural, raw ability. No one coaches it; I mean, maybe nowadays, but when I was coming out of high school, it was all natural ability. The jumping, quickness. When I went to North Carolina, it was a different phase of my life. Knowledge of basketball from Naismith on . . . rebounds, defense, free-throw shooting, techniques. Then, when I got to the pros, what people saw was the raw talent I'd worked on myself for eleven, twelve years *and* the knowledge I'd learned at the University of North Carolina. Unity of both. That's what makes up Michael Jordan's all-around basketball skills.

JW: It seems to me we have to keep asserting the factors that make us unique. We can't let coaches or myths about body types take credit for achievements that are a synthesis of our intelligence, physical gifts, our tradition of playing the game a special way.

MJ: We were born to play like we do.

JW: Players like you and Magic have transformed the game. Made it more of a player's game, returned it closer to its African-American roots on the playground.

MJ: You know, when you think about it, passing like Magic's is as natural, as freewheeling, as creative as you can be. You can call it playground if you want, but the guy is great. And certainly he's transcended the old idea of point guard. You never saw a six-eight, six-nine point guard before he came around. No coach would ever put a six-eight guy back there.

JW: If you were big, you were told to go rebound, especially if you were big and black.

MJ: Rebound. Go do a jump lay-up, be a center, a forward. A man six-eight started playing, dribbling in his backyard. Said, I can do these things. Now look. Everybody's trying to get a six-nine point guard.

JW: For me, the real creativity of the game begins with the playground. Like last night, watching young guys play, playing with them, that's where the new stuff is coming from. Then the basketball establishment names it and claims it.

MJ: They claim it. But they can't. The game today is going away from the big guy, the old idea everybody's got to have a Jabbar, Chamberlain. Game today is going toward a versatile game. Players who rebound, steal, block, run the court, score, the versatile player who can play more than one position. Which Magic started. Or maybe he didn't start it, but he made it famous. This is where the game's going now.

JW: Other people name it and claim it. That kind of appropriation's been a problem for African-American culture from the beginning. Music's an obvious example. What kind of music do you like?

MJ: I love jazz. I love mellow music. I love David Sanborn. Love Grover Washington, Jr. Rap . . . it's okay for some people. But huh-uh. Not in my house.

JW: Do you listen to Miles Davis?

MJ: Yeah.

JW: He talks about his art in a new biography he wrote with Quincy Troupe. When Miles relates jazz to boxing, I also hear him talking about writing, my art, and basketball, yours.

MJ: I know what you're saying.

JW: Right. There's a core of improvisation, spontaneity in all African-American arts.

MJ: I'm always working to put surprises, something new in my game. Improvisation, spontaneity, all that stuff.

What's in a name: *Michael*—archangel, conqueror of Satan. "Now war arose in heaven. Michael and his angels fighting against the dragon; and the dragon and his angels fought, but they were defeated" (Revelation 12:7); *Jordan*—the foremost river in Palestine, runs from the Lebanon to the Dead Sea, 125 miles, though its meanderings double that length. "Jordan water's bitter and cold . . . chills the body, don't hurt the soul . . ." (African-American traditional spiritual). *Michael Jordan*—a name worth many millions per annum. What's in that name that makes it so incredibly valuable to the people who have millions to spend for advertising what they sell, who compete for the privilege of owning, possessing Michael Jordan's name to adorn or endorse their products? In a country where Willie Horton's name and image helped win (or lose) a presidential election, a country in which one out of every four young black males is in prison, on parole or probation, a country where serious academics convene to consider whether the black male is an endangered species, how can we account for Michael Jordan's enormous popularity? Because MJ is an American of African descent, isn't he? Maybe we're more mixed up about race than we already know we are. Perhaps MJ is proof there are no rules about race, no limits to what a black man can accomplish in our society. Or maybe he's the exception that proves the rule, the absence of rules. The bedrock chaos and confusion that dogs us. At some level we must desire the ambiguity of our racial thinking. It must work for us, serve us. When one group wants something bad enough from the other, we reserve the right to ignore or insist upon the inherent similarities among all races, whichever side of the coin suits our purposes. One moment color-blind, the next proclaiming one group's whiteness, the other's blackness, to justify whatever mischief we're up to. It's this flip-flopping that defines and perpetuates our race problem. Our national schizophrenia and disgrace. It's also the door that allows MJ entry to superstardom, to become a national hero, our new DiMaggio, permits him to earn his small fraction of the billions we spend to escape rather than confront the liabilities of our society.

Sports Illustrated offers a free Michael Jordan video if you subscribe right away. Call today. In this ad, which saturates prime time on the national sports network, a gallery of young people, male and female, express their wonder, admiration, awe, and identification with Michael Jordan's supernatural basketball prowess. He can truly fly. The chorus is all white, good-looking, clean cut, casually but hiply dressed. An audience of consumers the ad both targets and embodies. A very calculated kind of wish fulfillment at work. A premeditated attempt to bond MJ with these middle-class white kids with highly disposable incomes.

In other ads, black kids wear fancy sneakers, play ball, compete to be a future Michael Jordan. There's a good chance lots of TV viewers who are white will enter the work force and become dutiful, conspicuous consumers, maybe even buy themselves some vicarious flight time by owning stuff MJ endorses. But what future is in store for those who intend to *be* the next MJ? Buy Jordan or be Jordan. Very different messages. Different futures, white and black. Who's zooming who?

In another national ad, why do we need the mediating figure of an old, distinguished-looking, white-haired, Caucasian gentleman in charge, giving instructions, leading MJ into a roomful of kids clamoring for MJ's magic power?

The Palace at Auburn Hills, the Detroit Pistons' home, contrasts starkly with Chicago Stadium. Chicago, the oldest NBA arena; the Palace one of the newest. Chicago Stadium is gritty, the Palace plush. In the Auburn Hills crowd an even greater absence of dark faces than in Chicago Stadium. But they share some of the same fight songs. *We will, we will, rock you.* And the Isley Brothers' classic "Shout." On a massive screen in the center of the Palace, cuts from the old John Belushi flick *Animal House* drive the Detroit fans wild. "Shout" is background music for an archetypal late-'50s, early-'60s frat party. White college kids in togas twist and shout and knock themselves out. Pre-Vietnam American Empire PG-rated version of a Roman orgy. A riot of sloppy boozing, making out, sophomoric antics to the beat of a jackleg, black rhythm-and-blues band that features a frenzied, conk-haired singer, sweating, eyes rolling, gate-mouthed, screaming, "Hey-ay, hey-ay. Hey-ay, hey-ay, shout! C'mon now, shout." Minstrel auctioneer steering the action higher, higher. Musicians on the screen performing for their audience of hopped-up, pampered students fuse with the present excitement, black gladiators on the hardwood floor of the Palace revving up their whooping fans. Nothing is an accident. Or is it? Do race relations progress, or are we doomed to a series of reruns?

JW: What's the biggest misconception that is part of your public image? What's out there, supposedly a mirror, but doesn't reflect your features?

MJ: I'm fortunate that there are no big misunderstandings. My biggest concern is that people view me as being some kind of a god, but I'm not. I make mistakes, have faults. I'm moody, I've got many negative things about me. Everybody has negative things about them. But from the image that's been projected of me, I can't do any wrong. Which is scary. And it's probably one of the biggest fears I have. And I don't know how to open people's eyes. I mean, I'm not going to go out and make a mistake so that people can see I make mistakes. Hey, you know, I try to live a positive life, love to live a positive life, but I do have negative things about me and I do make mistakes. And I'm so worried that if I make a mistake today, it can ruin the positive things I try to project. It's a day-in, day-out, nine-to-five job.

JW: A lot of pressure.

MJ: Pressure I didn't ask for, but it was given to me and I've been living, living with it.

JW: A kind of trap, isn't it, because you say, "I don't want everybody to think I'm a paragon of virtue. I'm a real person." But you also know in the back of your mind being a paragon is worth X number of dollars a day. So you don't like it but you profit from it.

MJ: Right. It has its advantages as well as disadvantages. Advantages financially. I'm asked to endorse corporations that are very prestigious as well as very wealthy. I have the respect of many, many kids as well as parents, their admiration. So it's not *just* the financial part. You said the financial part, but the respect that I earn from the 350 kids in this camp and their parents, friends, equals the financial part of it. The respect I get from those people—that's the pressure.

JW: Not to let them down.

MJ: Not to let them down.

Postgame Chicago Stadium. Oldest arena in the league. Old-fashioned bandbox. Exterior built on monumental, muscle-flexing scale. Inside you have to duck your head to negotiate a landing that leads to steep steps descending to locker rooms. Red-painted walls, rough, unfinished. Overhead a confusion of pipes, wires—the arteries of the beast exposed. Ranks of folding chairs set up for postgame interviews. MJ breaks a two-day silence with the media. Annoyed that the press misinterpreted some animated exchanges between teammates and himself.

None of the usual question-and-answer interplay. MJ says his piece and splits, flanked by yellow-nylon-jacketed security men, three of them, polite but firm, benign sheep dogs guarding him, discouraging the wolves.

In MJ's cubicle near the door hangs a greenish suit, a bright tropical-print shirt, yellows, black, beige, oranges, et cetera. He's played magnificently, admonished the press, clearly weary, but the effort of the game's still in his eyes, distracting, distancing him, part of him still in another gear; maybe remembering, maybe savoring, maybe just unable to cut it loose, the flow, the purity, the high of the game when every moment counts, registers, so as he undresses, the yellow jacket assigned to his corner has to remind him not to get naked, other people are in the room.

A man chatting up the security person screening MJ's cubicle holds a basketball for MJ to sign. As MJ undresses he's invited to a reporter's wedding. The soon-to-be groom is jiving with another member of the press, saying something about maybe having a kid will help him settle down, improve his sense of responsibility. MJ, proud father of two-year-old Jeffrey Michael, interrupts. "You got to earn the respect of kids. Responsibility and respect, huh-uh. You don't just get it when you have a kid. Or a couple kids."

Word's sent in that Whitney Houston and her entourage are waiting next door for a photo session. Celebrity hugging and mugging. I say hi to a man hovering near MJ's corner. Thought he might be MJ's cut buddy or an older brother. Turns out to be MJ's father. Same dark, tight skin. Same compact, defined physique. "Yes, I think I'm Mister Jordan. Hold on a minute, let me check my social security card." A kidder like his son. Like his son, he gives you friendly pats. Or maybe it's son like father. In the father's face, a quality of youthfulness and age combined, not chronological age but the timeless serenity of a tribal elder, a man with position, authority, an earned place in a community. In the locker room of the Spectrum in Philly, I'd been struck by the same mix in MJ's face as he addressed reporters. Unperturbed by lights, cameras, mikes, the patent buzz and jostle of media rudeness swarming around him, he sits poised on a shelf in a dressing stall, his posture unmistakably that immemorial high-kneed, flex-thighed, legs-widespread, weight-on-the-buttocks squat of rural Africans. Long hands dangling between his knees, head erect, occasionally bowing as he retreats into a private, inner realm to consider a question, an answer before he spoke. Dignified, respectful. A disposition of body learned how many grandfathers ago, in what faraway place. Passed on, surviving in this strange land.

From the shower MJ calls for slip-ons. Emerges wrapped in a towel. A man, an African-American man in a suit of dark skin, tall, broad-shouldered, long-limbed, narrow-waisted, bony ankles and wrists, his body lean-muscled, sleek, race cars, cheetahs, a computer-designed body for someone intended to sprint and leap, loose and tautly strung simultaneously, but also, like your body and mine, a cage. MJ is trapped within boundaries he cannot cross, you cannot cross. No candid camera needs to strip him any further. Why should it? Whose interests would be served? Some of his business is not ours. Are there skeletons in his closet? Letters buried in a trunk, sealed correspondence? What are we seeking with our demands for outtakes, for what's X-rated in public figures' lives? In the crush of the locker room, one reporter (a female) whispers to another; we build these guys up so we can be around to sell the story when they fall.

Naked MJ. A price on his head. He pays it. We pay it. Hundreds of thousands of fans plunk down the price of a ticket to catch his act live. Millions of dollars are spent to connect products with the way this body performs on a basketball court. What about feedback? If body sells products, how do products affect body? Do they commodify it, place a price on it? Flesh and blood linked symbiotically with products whose value is their ability to create profit. If profit's what it's all about—body, game, product—does profit-making displace ballplaying? Are there inevitable moments when what's required of MJ the ballplayer is different from what's required of the PR Jordan created by corporate interests for media consumption?

The PR Michael Jordan doesn't need to win a ring. He's already everything he needs to be without a ring. Greatest pressure on him from this perspective is to maintain, replicate, duplicate whatever it is that works, sells. It's an unfunny joke when MJ says wryly, "Fans come to see me score fifty and the home team win." The PR Jordan doesn't really lose when he has a spectacular game and his teammates are mediocre. He's still MJ. But if he puts forth a kamikaze, all-or-nothing, individual effort and fails by forcing or missing shots, by coming up short, the blame falls squarely on his shoulders. If he plays that tune too often, will the public continue to buy it?

Can a player be bigger than the game? Is Jordan that good? Does he risk making a mockery of the game? (Recall John Lennon. His lament that the Beatles' early, extraordinary success pressured them to repeat themselves, blunted artistic innovation, eventually pushed them into self-parody, the songs they'd written taking over, consuming them.)

The young man from Mississippi, baby of eleven children, speaks with a slow, muddy, down-home drawl. We're both relaxing in the unseasonably warm sun, outside Hartford, the Bradley International Airport B Terminal. My destination: Chicago, Game Six of last spring's NBA Eastern Championship. He's headed for his sister's home in Indiana. A nice place, he hopes. Time to settle down after five, six years of roaming, but decent work's hard to find. "I sure hope Michael wins him a ring. Boy, I want to see that. 'Cause my man Michael's the best. Been the best awhile. He's getting up there a little bit in age, you know. Ain't old yet but you know, he can't do like he used to. Used to be he could go out anytime and bust sixty-three. He's still good, still the best now but he better go on and get him his ring."

JW: I'm jumping way back on you now. Laney High School, Wilmington, N.C., the late seventies, early eighties. How did it feel to sit on the bench?

MJ: I hated it . . . you can't help anybody sitting on the bench. I mean, it's great to cheer, but I'm not that type of person. I'm not a cheerleader.

JW: You couldn't make the team?

MJ: I was pissed. Because my best friend, he was about six-six, he made the team. He wasn't good but he was six-six and that's tall in high school. He made the team and I felt I was better. . . . They went into the playoffs and I was sitting at the end of the bench and I couldn't cheer them on because I felt I should have been on the team. This is the only time that I didn't actually cheer for them. I wanted them to lose. Ironically, I wanted them to lose to prove to them that I could help them. This is what I was thinking at the time: You made a mistake by not putting me on the team and you're going to see it because you're going to lose. Which isn't the way you want to raise your kids . . . but many kids now do think that way, only because of their desire to get out and show that they can help or they can give something.

I think to be successful, I think you have to be selfish, or else you never achieve. And once you get to your highest level, then you have to be unselfish. When I first came to the league, I was a very selfish person in the sense I thought for myself first, the team second . . . and I still think that way in a sense. But at the same time, individual accolades piled up for me and were very soothing to the selfishness that I'd had in myself. They taught me how, you know, to finally forget about the self and help out the team, which is where I am now. I always wanted the team to be successful but I felt, selfishly, I wanted to be the main cause.

Phi Gamma Delta was assailed Monday with charges of racism, becoming the second fraternity to face such accusations stemming from activities during Round-Up last weekend.

At the root of the newest charges is a T-shirt sold and distributed by the fraternity—often known as the Fijis—during its annual "low-hoop" basketball tournament Saturday. On the T-shirt is the face of a "Sambo" caricature atop the body of professional basketball player Michael Jordan.

Meanwhile, Delta Tau Delta continued its internal investigation into Friday's incident in which FUCK COONS and FUCK YOU NIGS DIE were spray-painted on a car destroyed with sledgehammers on fraternity property. . . .

—*The Daily Texan*, University of Texas, Austin, 4/10/90.

We're slightly lost. My wife and I in a rental car on the edge of Shreveport, Louisiana, leading two rented vans carrying the Central Massachusetts Cougars. We're looking for the Centenary College Gold Dome, where soon, quite soon, opening ceremonies of the AAU Junior Olympic Girls Basketball national tourney will commence. Suddenly we cross Jordan Street, and I know we'll find the Gold Dome, be on time for the festivities, that my daughter, Jamila, and her Cougar teammates will do just fine, whatever. Renoir women everywhere, Jordans everywhere.

Next day, while girls of every size, shape, color, creed, and ethnic background, from nearly every state in the Union, are playing hoop in local high school gyms, about three miles from the Cougars' motel, at the Bossier City Civic Center, Klansmen in hoods and robes distribute leaflets at a rally for the former Klan leader David Duke, who's running for the U.S. Senate.

MJ: Well, I think real often in terms of role models, in terms of positive leaders in this world . . . Nelson Mandela, Bill Cosby. . . . We're trying to show there are outlets, there are guidelines, there are positive things you can look for and achieve. I mean, we're trying to give them an example to go for. I think that's the reason I try to maintain the position I have in the corporate world as well as in the community. That we can do this, prove that success is not limited to certain people, it's not limited to a certain color. . . . Grab a hand and pull someone up. Be a guide or a role model. Give some type of guidelines for other people to follow.

JW: What ways do you have of controlling this tidal wave of public attention? How do you remain separate from the Michael Jordan created "out there"?

MJ: Stay reachable. Stay in touch. Don't isolate. I don't try to isolate myself from anybody. I think if people can feel that they can touch or come up and talk to you, you're going to have a relationship and have some influence on them. My old friends, who I try to stay in touch with at all times, I think they always keep me close to earth.

About six years ago I was only forty-three, so I couldn't understand why the jumper was falling short every time, banging harmlessly off the front of the iron. After a summer-camp game my wife, Judy, had watched mainly because our sons, Dan and Jake, were also playing, I asked her if she'd noticed anything unusual about my jump shot. "Well, not exactly," she offered, "except when you jumped your feet never left the ground."

JW: When you're playing, what part of the audience is most important to you?

MJ: Kids. I can notice a kid enjoying himself. On the free-throw line, *bing*, that quick, I'll wink at him, smile, lick a tongue at him, and keep going and still maintain the concentration that I need for the game. That's my personality. I've always done it. I can catch eye-to-eye a mother, a father, anybody . . . kid around with them as I'm playing in a serious and very intense game. That's the way I relax, that's the way I get my enjoyment from playing the game of basketball. Seeing people enjoying themselves and relating to them like I'm enjoying myself. Certainly letting them know they're part of the game.

The game. I am being introduced to a group of young African-American men, fifteen or so high school city kids from Springfield, Massachusetts, who are attending the first-ever sessions of a summer camp at Hampshire College, an experiment intended to improve both their basketball skills and SAT scores. My host, Dennis Jackson (a coach, coincidentally, at Five-Star hoop camp back when Michael Jordan, still a high schooler, made his debut into the national spotlight), is generously extolling my credentials. Author, professor, college ballplayer, Rhodes scholar, but it isn't till Dennis Jackson says this man is working on an article about MJ that I know I have everybody's attention. I tell them that I haven't received an interview with MJ yet, he's cooling out after the long season, but they're eager to hear any detail of any MJ moment I've been privy to so far. An anecdote or two and then I ask them to free-associate. When I say *MJ* what comes to mind first? *Air, jam, slam-dunk, greatest, wow* are some of the words I catch, but the real action is in faces and bodies. No one can sit still. Suddenly it's Christmas morning and they're little boys humping down the stairs into a living room full of all they've been wishing for. Body English, *ohhs* and *ahhs.* Hey man, he can do anything, anything. DJ assures me that if Mike promised, I'll get my interview. *As good a player as MJ is, he's ten times the person.* We're all in a good mood, and I preach a little. Dreams. The importance of believing in yourself. My luck in having a family that supported me, instilled the notion I was special, that I could do anything, be anything. Dreams, goals. Treasuring, respecting the family that loves you and stands behind you.

What if you don't have no family?

The question stops me in my tracks. Silences me. I study each face pointed toward me, see the guys I grew up with, my sons, brothers, Sekou, MJ, myself, the faces of South African kids *toi-toing* in joy and defiance down a dirt street in Crossroads. I'd believed the young men were listening, and because I'd felt them open up, I'd been giving everything I had, trying to string together many years, many moments, my fear, anger, frustration, the hungers that had driven me, the drumbeat of a basketball on asphalt a rhythm under everything else, patterning the crazy-quilt chaos of images I was trying to make real, to connect with their lives. What if there's no family, no person, no community out there returning, substantiating the fragile dream a young man spins of himself? Silenced.

Michael said he didn't like politics. I'll always stand up for what I think is right, but. . . . Politics, he said, was about making choices. And then you get into: This side's right and that side's wrong. Then you got a fight on your hands. Michael's friends say he naturally shies away from controversy. He's mellow. Middle-of-the-road. Even when the guys are just sitting around and start arguing about something, Michael doesn't like it. He won't take sides, tries to smooth things out. That's Michael.

Finally I respond to the young man at the circle's edge leaning back on his arms. He doesn't possess an NBA body. He may be very smart, but that can be trouble as easily as salvation. You have me, I want to say. I support you, love you, you are part of me, we're in this together. But I know damn well he's asking for more. Needs more. Really, he's asking for nothing while he's asking everything.

Find a friend. I bet you have a cut buddy already. Someone to hang with and depend on. One person who won't let you fall. And you won't let him fall. Lean on each other. It's hard, hard, but just one person can make a difference sometimes.

They look at the books I've written. Ask more questions. Mostly about Michael again. Some eyes are drifting back to the court. This rap's been nice, but it's also only a kind of intermission. The game. I should have brought my sneakers. Should be thirty years younger. But why, seeing the perils besetting these kids, would anyone want to be thirty years younger? And why, if you're Peter Pan playing a game you love and getting paid a fortune for it and adored and you can fly too, why would you ever want to grow a minute older?

The young men from Springfield say hello.

Nate, the historian from the court at Mill River, said: "Tell the Michael I say hello."

PREFACE:
BREAKING ICE,
ED. TERRY MacMILLAN

1990

Dear Terry,

Congratulations. It's time we had a new anthology of African-American fiction. I don't know what you've gathered, but I'm sure your sample will be enjoyable and instructive. The notes that follow are wishes, cautions, play with the issues and ideas that could/should, in my view, surface in a collection of contemporary Afro-American writing.

> The African artist allows wide scope to his fantasy in the mask. . . . With colors, feathers, and horns he accomplishes some astonishingly lively effects. In a slow creative process he brings to life a work which constitutes a new unit, a new being. If the sculpture proves to be a success, a helpful medium, the tribe adheres to this form and passes it on from generation to generation. . . . Thus we have a style, a firmly established formal canon, which may not be lightly discarded. . . . For this reason a style retains its specific character for decades, even centuries. It stands and falls with the faith to which it is linked.

—*The Art of Black Africa*, Elsy Leuzinger

Since we're seen as marginal politically, economically, and culturally, African-American writers have a special, vexing stake in reforming, revitalizing the American imagination. History is a cage, a conundrum we must escape or resolve before our art can go freely about its business. As has always been the case, in order to break into print we must be prepared to deal with the extraliterary forces that have conspired to keep us silent, or our stories, novels, and poems will continue to be treated as marginally as our lives, unhinged, unattached to the everyday reality of "mainstream," majority readers. Magazine editors know that their jobs depend upon purveying images the public recognizes and approves, so they seldom include our fictions, and almost never choose those which transcend stereotypes and threaten to expose the fantasies of superiority, the bedrock lies and brute force that sustain the majority's power over the *other.* Framed in foreign, inimical contexts, minority stories appear at best as exotic slices of life and local color, at worst as ghettorized irrelevancies.

However, as the assumptions of the monoculture are challenged, overrun, defrock themselves daily in full view of the shameless media, more and more of the best fiction gravitates toward the category of "minority." The truth that each of us starts out alone, a minority of one, each in a slightly different place (no place), resides somewhere in the lower frequencies of our communal consciousness. New worlds, alternative versions of reality are burgeoning. In spite of enormous, overwhelming societal pressures to conform, to standardize the shape and meaning of individual lives, voices like Ralph Ellison's reach us, impelling us to attend to the *chaos which lives within the pattern* of our certainties.

Good stories transport us to these extraordinarily diverse regions where individual lives are enacted. For a few minutes we can climb inside another's skin. Mysteriously, the dissolution of ego also sharpens the sense of self, reinforces independence and relativity of point of view. People's lives resist a simple telling, cannot be understood safely, reductively from some static still point, some universally acknowledged center around which all other lives orbit. Narrative is a reciprocal process, regressive and progressive, dynamic. When a culture hardens into helio-centricity, fancies itself the star of creation, when otherness is imagined as a great darkness except for what the star illuminates, it's only a matter of time until the center collapses in upon itself, imploding with sigh and whimper.

Minority writers hold certain peculiar advantages in circumstances of cultural breakdown, reorientation, transition. We've accumulated centuries of experience dealing with problems of marginality, problems that are suddenly on center stage for the whole society: inadequacy of language, failure of institutions, a disintegrating metropolitan vision that denies us or swallows us, that attracts and repels, that promises salvation and extinction. We've always been outsiders, orphans, bastard children, hard-pressed to make our claims heard. In order to endure slavery and oppression it's been necessary to cultivate the double-consciousness of sere, artist, mother. Beaten down by countless assertions of the inade-quacy, the repugnance of our own skin, we've been forced to enter the skins of others, to see, as a condition of survival, the world and ourselves through the eyes of others. Our stories can place us back at the center, at the controls; they can offer alternative realities, access to the sanctuary we carry around inside our skulls. The African-American imagination has evolved as discipline, defense, coping mechanism, counterweight to the galling facts of life. We've learned to confer upon ourselves the power of making up our lives, changing them as we go along.

Marginality has also refined our awareness, our proficiency in non-literary modes of storytelling. Folk culture preserves and expresses an identity, a history, a self-evaluation apart from those destructive, incar-cerating images proliferated by the mainline culture. Consciously and unconsciously we've integrated these resources of folk culture into our writing. Our songs, dreams, dances, styles of walk and talk, dressing, cooking, sport, our heroes and heroines provide a record of how a par-ticular group has lived in the world, in it, but not of it. A record so dis-tinctive and abiding that its origins in culture have been misconstrued as rooted in biology. A long-tested view of history is incorporated in the art of African-American people, and our history can be derived from careful study of forms and influences that enter our cultural performances and rituals. In spite of and because of marginal status, a powerful, indigenous vernacular tradition has survived, not unbroken, but unbowed, a magnet, a focused energy, something with its own logic, rules, and integrity connecting current developments to the past. An articulate, syncretizing force our best artists have drawn upon, a force sustaining both individual talent and tradition. Though minstrel shows were popularized as a parody of black life, these musical reviews were also a vehicle for preserving authentic African-derived elements of black American culture. Today rap, for all its excesses and commercialization, reasserts the African core of black music: polyrhythmic dance beat, improvisational spontaneity, incantatory use of the word to name, blame, shame, and summon power, the obligation of ritual to instruct and enthuse. It's no coincidence that rap exploded as the big business of music was luring many black artists into "crossing over." Huge sums were paid to black recording artists; then a kind of lobotomy was performed on their work, homogenizing, commodifying, pacifying it by removing large portions of what made the music think and be. Like angry ancestral spirits, the imperatives of tradition rose up, reanimated themselves, mounted the corner chanters and hip hoppers. As soul diminished to a category on the pop charts, the beat from the street said no-no-no, you're too sweet. Try some of this instead. Stomp your feet. Don't admit defeat. Put your hands together. Hit it. Hit. Boom. Crank up the volume. Bare bones percussion and chant holler scream. Our loud selves, our angry selves. Our flying feet and words and raunchy dreams. Instruments not possessed mimicked by our voices. Electronics appropriated. Recording tricknology explored and deconstructed, techniques reversed, foregrounded, parodied. Chaboom. Boom. Sounds of city, of machines of inner space and outer space merge. Boom boxes. Doom boxes. Call the roll of the ancestors. Every god from Jah, Isis, Jehovah, Allah, and Shango to James Brown and the Famous Flames. Say the names. Let them strut the earth again. Get right, children. Rap burst forth precisely where it did, when it did because that's where the long, long night of poverty and discrimination, of violent marginality remained a hurting truth nobody else was telling. That's where the creative energies of a subject people were being choked and channeled into self-destruction.

When an aesthetic tradition remembers its roots, the social conditions (slavery, oppression, marginality) and the expressive resources it employed to cope with these conditions, the counterversion of these conditions it elaborated through art, when it doesn't allow itself to be distracted, that is, keeps telling the truth which brought it into being—the necessity of remaining human, defining human in its own terms, resisting those destructive definitions in the Master's tongue, attitudes and art—then that tradition remains alive, a referent, a repository of value, money we can take to the bank. Afro-American traditions contain the memory of a hard, unclean break. This partially accounts for key postures that are subversive, disruptive, disjunctive. To the brutality that once ripped us away and now tries to rip us apart, we turn a stylized mask of indifference, of malleability, a core of iron, silent refusal. Boom. Chaboom. Boom. While our feet, feet, feet, dance to another beat.

I look for, cherish this in our fiction.

On the other hand—or should I say other face, since the shield I'm raising has two sides and one cannot be lifted without the other—what about the future? Is there any difference between sitting in at an all-white lunch counter and a minority writer composing a story in English? What's the fate of a black story in a white world of white stories? What can we accomplish with our *colors, feathers, and horns*, how can we fruitfully extend our tradition? How do we break out of the circle of majority-controlled publishing houses, distributors, critics, editors, readers? Vernacular language is not enough. Integration is not enough, unless one views mathematical, proportional representation as a goal instead of a step. If what a writer wants is freedom of expression, then somehow that larger goal must be addressed implicitly/explicitly in our fictions. A story should somehow contain clues that align it with tradition and critique tradition, establish the new space it requires, demands, appropriates, hint at how it may bring forth other things like itself, where these others have, will, and are coming from. This does not mean defining criteria for admitting stories into some ideologically sound, privileged category, but seeking conditions, mining territory that maximizes the possibility of free, original expression. We must continue inventing our stories, sustaining, not sacrificing, the double consciousness that is a necessity for any writing with the ambition of forging its own place.

Black music again illuminates glories and pitfalls, the possibility of integrity, how artists nourished by shared cultural roots can prove again and again that, even though they are moving through raindrops, they don't have to get soaked. Their art signifies they are in the storm but not of it, black music is a movable feast, fluid in time, space, modality, exhibiting in theme and variations multiple relationships with the politically, socially, aesthetically dominant order, the fullest possible range of relationships, including the power and independence to change places, reverse the hierarchy, *be* the dominant order.

What lessons are transferable to the realm of literature? Is musical language freer, less inscribed with the historical baggage of European hegemony, exploitation, racism? Is it practical within the forms and frequencies of this instrument (written English) to roll back history, those negative accretions, those iron bars and "White Only" signs that steal one's voice, one's breath away?

Are there ways fiction can express the dialectic, the tension, the conversation, the warfare of competing versions of reality English contains? One crucial first step may be recognizing that black/white, either/or perceptions of the tensions within language are woefully inadequate. Start by taking nothing for granted, giving nothing away. Study the language. The way we've begun to comb the past. Rehistoricize. Contest. Contest. Return junk mail to sender. Call into question the language's complacencies about itself. At the level of spelling, grammar, how it's taught, but also deeper, its sounds, their mamas, its coded pretensions to legitimacy, gentility, exclusivity, seniority, logic. Unveil chaos within the patterns of certainty. Restate issues and paradigms so they are not simply the old race problem relexified. Whose language is it, anyway?

Martin Bernal in *Black Athena* has traced the link between European theories of race and language. How nineteenth-century theories of language development parallel, buttress, and reinforce hierarchical concepts of race and culture. How social "sciences," the soft core posing as the hard core of academic humanities curricula, were tainted at their inception by racist assumptions and agendas. How romantic linguistic theory was used as a tool to prove the superiority of the West. How uncritical absorption of certain hallowed tenets of Western thought is like participating in your own lynching. Be prepared to critique any call for "back to basics" in light of the research Bernal gathers and summarizes. The great lie that systems of thought are pure, universal, uncontaminated by cultural bias is once more being gussied up for public consumption. Whose Great Books in whose interest must be read? Whose stories should be told? By whom? To what ends?

How does language grow, change? What are the dynamics that allow individual speakers to learn a language, adapt it to the infinite geography of their inner imaginative worlds, the outer social play, the constant intercourse of both? Can the writer love language and also keep it at arm's length as material, a medium, foregrounding its arbitrariness, its treacherousness, never calling it his/her own, never completely identifying with it but making intimate claims by exploring what it can do, what it could do if the writer has patience, luck, skill, and practices, practices, practices?

In it, but not of it. And that stance produces bodies of enabling legislation, a grammar of nuanced tensions, incompatibilities, doors and windows that not only dramatize the stance itself but implicate the medium. A reciprocal unraveling below whose surface is always the unquiet recognition that this language we're using constantly pulls many directions at once and unless we keep alert, keep fighting the undertow, acknowledge the currents going our way and every other damned way, we drown. We are not alone but not separate either; any voice we accomplish is really many voices, and the most powerful voices are always steeped in unutterable silences. A story is a formula for extracting meaning from chaos, a handful of water we scoop up to recall an ocean. Nothing really stands still for this reduction, this abstraction. We need readers who are willing to be coconspirators. It's at this level of primal encounter that we must operate in order to reclaim the language for our expressive purposes. The hidden subject remains: what is our situation with respect to this language? Where does it come from? Where do I come from? Where do we meet and how shall I name this meeting place? What is *food*? What is *eating*? Why do people go to lunch counters? Black music offers a counter integrative model because it poses this species of question about music and fills us with the thrill of knowing yes, yes, the answers, if there are any, and it probably doesn't matter whether there are or not, yay or nay, the answers and the questions are still up for grabs.

INTRODUCTION:
THE SOULS OF BLACK FOLK BY W. E. B. DU BOIS

1990

If I could put one and only one book into the hands of students to whom I was teaching post–Civil War American history, I would choose without hesitation *The Souls of Black Folk*. Both because of what the book *does* and for what it *is*. Du Bois is quite explicit about his intentions: "Herein lie buried many things which if read with patience may show the strange meaning of being black here at the dawning of the Twentieth Century." Rather than contracting the relevance of *Souls*, the author's blackness becomes a prism that focuses and radiates light in all colors of the spectrum. Born in 1868, only a few years after slavery was outlawed in this nation, Du Bois died on August 27, 1963, the day before the historic civil rights march on Washington, D.C. From the double perspective of conqueror and victim he witnessed the tumultuous growth of America into a world power: two global wars, the Korean conflict, our open and covert forays into Europe's last mad scramble for colonial territory and Empire. In 1958 he would proclaim the dubious distinction conferred by our military and industrial ascendancy: "No nation threatens us. We threaten the world."

That same year Du Bois, who at ninety commenced work on a new autobiography, wrote,

I would have been hailed with approval if I had died at 50. At 75
my death was practically requested. If living does not give value,
wisdom and meaning to life, then there is no sense in living at all.
If immature and inexperienced men rule the earth, then the earth
deserves what it gets: the repetition of age-old mistakes, and wild
welcome for what men knew a thousand years ago was disaster.

An irascible man, aristocratic, arrogant, aloof, egotistical, possessed
of a tooth-jarring moral rectitude. Courageous, honorable, loyal, indom-
itable, passionate, supremely intelligent. As all of us, a mix of virtues and
vice, but also different because he was a genius. Like Freud's excavations
of the unconscious, Einstein's revelations of the physical universe, Marx's
exploration of the economic foundations of social organization, Du Bois's
insights have profoundly altered the way we look at ourselves. *The problem of the twentieth century is the problem of the color line.* With this utterance the unconscious, relativity, class warfare are all implicated. Du Bois
posits a shift of cataclysmic proportions, demanding a reorientation of
consciousness as radical as that required by physics at the atomic level.
What is the color line? How important would it be to man's destiny?

To the powerful and privileged Du Bois's message was simple: you are
not alone. Those whom you have ruled, treated as inferior, as another
species whose purpose on earth is to serve you or remain invisible until
called, those creatures have souls and inevitably you must encounter
them, and the encounter will be on their terms as well as yours because
the globe is shrinking and races and cultures will collide. Myths of superiority, the literal dominance of arms, numbers, or technological advantage can only maintain the old world order for a limited time.

For the oppressed, *Souls* is a beacon, a rallying cry. Du Bois redraws
the map of the world's peoples, venturing into unknown territory, sup-
plying detail, shape, and substance to what had been designated impenetrable swamp and desert. He locates us, sketches our features, gives us
names. *Us* turns out to be most people on the earth, people of color, emi-
grants, refugees, mixed bloods, exiles, the poor and dispossessed, women

and men who didn't count, who were unseen and unheard. When I read about *two-ness*, "two souls, two thoughts, two unreconciled strivings; two warring ideals in one dark body," I felt a great sense of relief. My experience was being validated. What I felt as a black person in America counted, deserved to be on the record. It wasn't simply my personality, my overwrought imagination that created the alienation and ambivalence dogging me, my seesawing emotions as I negotiated the unspoken, unwritten iron rules of racial etiquette with their violent sanctions always simmering just below the surface. Such matters could and should be hauled into the light of day. And understanding how to chart my life would connect me with millions of other lives. The color line raises the issue of identity. Theirs. Yours. Mine. Will we blend, change, survive, or is the color line one more measure of the limits of our collective imagination, our cultural graveyard of either/or terminal distinctions: black/white, male/female, young/old, good/bad, rich/poor, spirit/flesh? Is it possible to imagine ourselves other than we are, better? These are the monumental questions reverberating in *The Souls of Black Folk*, matters unresolved by the last one hundred years, which have tumbled us, bloody and confused, onto the threshold of the twenty-first century.

Souls demonstrates unequivocally how the race problem is forever linked to the American Dream, that our pretensions to greatness will remain just pretensions until the benefits of freedom, democracy, and opportunity are enjoyed by all citizens. What's at stake, Du Bois reminds us, always, in the American experiment is not simply sharing material wealth, but maintaining spiritual health. Du Bois's acute exposition of the sources and cures of racial conflict impels us to admit that race problems are not perpetuated because we lack answers. Answers, solutions abound. What's missing is the will to implement solutions, the courage to look inside ourselves, where any fundamental change must begin. Du Bois tells us that answers, absurdly intricate and simple, have always been available; we carry them around in our hearts.

Given the level of "thinking" about race in the early 1900s—when white supremacy was the unquestioned credo of civilized men, when

Europe was dividing Africa, Asia, and the islands of the sea into colonial preserves, ruthlessly crushing indigenous political opposition, subduing or eradicating surplus native populations, when blacks in the United States possessed no rights a white man was bound to respect—it's a miracle that Du Bois could conceive, let alone publish, the positive vision *Souls* distilled from this chaos.

To narrate his story Du Bois invents a magical structure. Incidentally, along the way he creates an enduring model for the emerging field of Afro-American studies, one that is cross-disciplinary, cross-cultural, politically engaged, humanistic. Humanistic because always at the center of *Souls* is an individual human voice, a record of intellectual and spiritual strivings, the felt texture of Du Bois's experience, which is, he acknowledges, the only measure any one of us can take of this awakening we call life: "I seem to see a way of elucidating the inner meaning and significance of that race problem by explaining it in terms of the one human life that I know best."

Although *Souls* consists of essays written at various times, with various styles and purposes, it is vastly more than the sum of its parts. Empirical studies of rural poverty in the cotton-growing Black Belt of the South, a minihistory of Reconstruction and the Freedmen's Bureau, metaphysical reflections on black identity, polemical outcries against racial violence, an ethnomusicological treatise, personal essay, elegy, short fiction, allegory, poetry—the ingredients of *Souls* combine and fuse genres. An allusive richness, a plenitude and multiplicity of voice and texture are achieved, suggestively avant-garde, dauntingly postmodern. Master metaphors and tropes—the Veil, the prison house, twoness, song as spirit voice, dawn as light and illumination, beginning and revelation—unify the essays.

For the minority writer wishing to break into print, Du Bois, like his contemporary Charles Waddell Chesnutt and later Zora Neale Hurston in their pioneering efforts to legitimize black vernacular in serious fiction, offers a storehouse of techniques and tactics for overcoming a hostile literary environment. For example, the phrases from slave songs that precede each section of *Souls* seem to be a relatively conventional means of providing structural coherence and unity. But consider these framing devices in terms of the continuing historic struggle for black voices to make themselves heard in a white literary tradition. Slave narratives, one of the earliest forms embodying this *determination to be heard,* were customarily framed by testimony from white editors or spokespersons from the dominant community whose presence authenticated the slave's witness. The frame was ironically a sign of both independence and dependence. Du Bois recapitulates and revises this custom by framing his essays with double epigraphs, one from black oral tradition, one from the literate, one a culturally marginal voice, one from mainstream Western literature, anonymous slave composers paired with Lord Byron, Omar Khayyam, Elizabeth Barrett Browning, Algernon Charles Swinburne, Alfred, Lord Tennyson. The frame is reinterpreted and rendered as a sign of cultural parity, interpenetration, of the black voice asserting equality as Du Bois claims authority to establish new relationships among the cultural items he appropriates.

Souls is finally a work of art whose existence creates a resounding response to the critics, detractors, and destroyers of black life Du Bois attacks. Neither Du Bois nor *Souls* stands hat in hand looking for charity, articulating any special pleading, representing any special interests. We're being taught, urged to rethink, reevaluate our American experience. Not to see it whole—no one could abide that much reality—but to begin to imagine the multiple perspectives any thoughtful vision must include.

Your country? How came it yours? Before the Pilgrim landed we were here. Here we have brought our three gifts and mingled them with yours: a gift of story and song . . . the gift of sweat and brawn to beat back the wilderness, conquer the soil and lay the foundations of this vast economic empire . . . a gift of the Spirit. Around us the history of the land has centered for thrice a hundred years; out of the nation's heart we have called all that was best to throttle and subdue all that was worst.

I've read and taught *Souls* many times. And each time when I close the book, beauty and pain linger.

The clarity of Du Bois's vision, the precision and evocative lyric power of his language touch me. In some quiet part of myself—a place where I first learned forty years ago, in the AME Zion church, versions of what Du Bois called "Sorrow Songs," versions still sung today; a place that recalls Sundays and my best clothes and shoes shined, dark, familiar, adult faces transformed by prayer and meditation into strangers; a place where I would always be a child cowed by awesome, thundering sermons that Reverend Felder danced and the gospel chorus chanted, words and music that taught me the world was a straight and narrow opening and time the faint light in that tiny opening and you were always pushing through, always squeezed through and crowds at my back and crowds gone on before me, but I could only glimpse them from this precious place, this place that roars and is quiet in myself—now, when I think amen after reading Du Bois, it is the same amen I whispered as a child by my bedside saying my prayers.

And pain. The disquieting thought that okay, all right, give the man credit for crystal-clear analysis, prescience, prophecy, whatever, but isn't it also possible his understanding of what was wrong *then* remains so relevant, so perceptive, so uncannily clairvoyant of what's wrong *now* because nothing has changed? Nothing has changed, and perhaps never will. I'm chilled and angered by that thought. Anger fades into fear, fear for my children, yours. I'm left with little hope, echo the sentiment Du Bois weaves into the *Afterthought* of *Souls*, a wish conveying more longing than conviction: "in Thy good time may infinite reason turn the tangle straight."

DEAD BLACK MEN AND OTHER FALLOUT FROM THE AMERICAN DREAM

1992

NAKED TRUTH

Airports are white again. In the past few years, I've been traveling far too much, but traveling is a teacher, too, and I've noticed how few black people fly, fewer even than the few in the sixties.

Even into metro hubs like Detroit or Atlanta, often no black faces on a plane. Except, now that stewing is no longer a glamorous job, there are more stewards and stewardesses of color. Three sisters in charge of a lily-white flight into Salt Lake City (was the assignment coincidence, choice, punishment?), black-vernacular *Ladies and Gentlemens* over the inter-com, one sister telling a smiling, suntanned gentleman in his pinstripe shirt and spotted suspenders who requested the whole can of sparkling water after she'd served him his cupful, "I'm not giving you this because I want to."

Somebody coming or going left a *Hartford Courant* on a seat. "L.A. Is a City Under Siege." Watching TV's coverage of the stricken city, I'd resisted the sense of déjà vu the images and voices were insinuating. This city burning was not Watts all over again, not 1943 or the uprising in

Tulsa in 1921 or East St. Louis in 1918. I'm thirty years older than I was in the sixties, and so is my country, and that much closer to death. So if nothing else, and there's much, much else, what's different, what's diminishing is the possibility that change, the change that's gotta come, will occur in my lifetime. Or the lifetime of the USA.

Look out. Here we come. Black men still mean trouble. Means we ain't dead yet. Means the old, unfinished battles drag on. Young men are the future, the fighters. If they're around, trouble's around. Young men have the power, the potential to make babies and knock you down and seize tomorrow. From the ranks of young men, as Jesse Jackson once reminded me, the warriors come. Any country fears the warrior-age men of its rivals and enemies. Wars are organized to exterminate them. But here we come, our hats turned around or christened with Xs, your cross, your worst nightmare. XXX equals many times, many kisses or blows, crisscross, crucifixion, crossroads, unknown, convergence, focus, bull's-eye. X the spot X marks. Living bodies of dead men. Naked truth. In your face.

A CHOICE, MY BROTHERS

Michael speaks and carries himself like one of the national leaders we wish we had. He's a black man whose mind and body stir fantasies about ancient kingdoms, royalty, what might have been accomplished in some other, better country, my friend Michael stops me. C'mon upstairs a minute. Something I want you to see. Mike's minutes have been known to last days, and I was in a hurry as usual to get away from campus, back home to prepare for a weekend trip to Marygrove College in Detroit later that afternoon, but Mike's tone of challenge and conspiracy diverted me up the back steps of Herter Hall, into the miniauditorium where his class on the civil-rights movement was meeting. I sat in the front row. Behind me fifty or so students, and wonder of wonders on the UMass campus, perhaps a third of them something other than white. Mike stalked to the stage, impatient with his Indian grad assistant, K.G., who'd neglected to bring the episode of *Eyes on the Prize* Mike planned on showing to his class.

Squinting through professorial half-glasses, Michael read to us from an article that surveyed the activities of the KKK in electoral politics over the past fifty years. The names of presidents, Supreme Court justices, and senators with public Klan affiliations were cited, a testimony to the fact that the Klan was once a respectable American institution. "Today Klan membership is a political liability . . . politicians with that connection deny it, the Klan is generally seen as aberrant. That surely must be progress." Michael finishes, stares out at his audience. Yes, somebody replies. In this day and age the country would not tolerate overt Klan language or sentiments from the White House or any other public official on a national level. A bearded white kid pops up his hand. He's certain the Klan was becoming less visible only because Klan ideology, instead of being driven underground, had been mainstreamed into the average white American's thinking about race by the precepts and practice of the last two occupants of the White House. More was said, and Mike was pushing the discussion to its ramifications for the current presidential campaign, barely concealing his delight at the prospect of a wild card being introduced into the boring, adolescent bickering and mutual masturbation of the two-party system when the lights went out, K.G.'s not-too-subtle method of telling Michael the film he'd been sent to fetch had arrived.

I had to split before the documentary ended, so I never learned that morning exactly what Mike had hijacked me up the steps to see, but what I took with me to Detroit that weekend and soon after into L.A. was the image of a long line of Black Panthers in Oakland, California, in 1968 at the funeral of little Bobby Hutton. Black berets, black leather jackets, military dignity and severity in each face. The brothers were strong, ready. One face after another in line, similar, even exactly alike, slant of beret, puff of Afro beneath, leather shiny as armor, alike until the camera panned closer, then you saw, even though the film was black and white, how the faces were different colors, wore different lips and noses, were not a phalanx of threatening darkness but young men, some boyish in spite of facial hair, masks of mourning and menace, individuals each of whom had lost a friend, a comrade, a fellow soldier and had come together to honor the fallen one, gathered in solidarity to grieve. I understood in the fraction of a second in which the lens framed each face that grief also contained the will to survive, and the will to survive was everywhere, explained everything, black leather, black berets, the military formation, guns in their cars parked around the funeral chapel, marches on the Legislature in the state capitol, confrontations with Oakland police who cruised the Panthers' neighborhoods like an occupying army. Rituals of survival, indelible evidence of how seriously the young men treated their lives, Bobby Hutton's life. They meant business. Surviving as black men was serious, deadly business to which they had committed themselves, work they must do themselves because nobody else cared, except perhaps their mothers and lovers, except their enemies, building cells and digging graves, enemies who counted them as dead already.

Arrayed in their colors and attitudes, the Panthers sent a chill through the nation then and shook me up again as I sat in a UMass classroom, knowing they were gone gone gone, and in their place gangs of young black men full of self-destructive, unfocused rage, crack and chaos, hustling drugs, spouting obscene, race-baiting, woman-hating rap, slam-dunk ideology as rude and crude as the Klan's. But what did I know really? Weren't the young men taking to the L.A. streets my brothers, sons, fathers, me? In their day, the Panthers, Malcolm X, the black-power radicals had been called hatemongers, apostles of violence, reverse racists, un-American criminals. I'd been bombarded like other Americans by this negative publicity, images of guns, anger, mayhem, and murder. I couldn't help being confused, suspicious. Could America be as bad as the Panthers claimed? Were there actually dirty wars, secret wars raging daily in black urban communities across the land? Were the Panthers thugs, or could they be the kid nobody had invited to the parade, shouting that the strutting emperor is naked?

The Panthers were black men rebelling against an America whose interests were best served by their silence, submission, extinction. No room in the inn. Sixties integration was a vision of change, all right, but not white people changing, not white people giving up one iota of their power and dominion. Spare change, maybe. Education, haircuts, keeping your dick in your pants, your pants with your behind in them on your side of the tracks, talking and walking in ways that don't disturb or offend white people, ignoring the stunning economic inequities between your communities and theirs, leaving behind the security of the wolf packs you travel in, the families that love you unconditionally, venturing out on your own, one or two at a time to the Wonderland in pursuit of those carrot-and-stick opportunities doled out to a handful of chosen ones, none of that mess would change the basic power relationships between whites and blacks but might get you one inch closer to the ever-receding horizon of the Promised Land, certainly steal you far, far from home, exiled miles from the ones you've deserted.

Curtis Mayfield sang in the sixties: *If you had a choice of colors, which one would you choose, my brothers?* This choice was made easy for the Panthers. They had no choice. They were unacceptable to society in their present form. Even if they beat the hundred-to-one odds and attained economic self-sufficiency or middle-class status, a black face would still stare back at them in the mirror. So they began treating that face as salvation instead of stigma. In the smoke and fire of rebellion, choices become narrow and harsh as the circumstances locking you down. Middle ground disappears. Smash windows, mark walls with your name, terrorize dark Asian eyes to erase the image of your ugliness etched in them. You take back the night. Your color, the truth they said you couldn't know. *If you had a choice, my brothers.*

If the Panthers are gone, the righteous truth of their insight remains, twenty-seven years later, articulated, amended this time by a brick through a window, a torch through the doorway of a ransacked video store. Perhaps the abiding result of the fires in L.A. is the rebirth of Panther militant self-assertion, its potential to be organized, conscious, purposeful, as warring gangs of Crips and Bloods learn to truce, reason together, forge a space for collective survival on terms they dictate. Perhaps the taste of unity, the possibility of alliances across racial lines—graffiti everywhere in South Central L.A. celebrated: CRIPS AND BLOODS FOREVER TOGETHER, CRIPS AND BLOODS AND MEX—was so exhilarating that a few hours of it, a few nights of bullets flying, fast cars racing through the streets, dealing with the enemy directly, brutally, cauterizing old, open wounds, liberating the taunting goods stored behind lock and key in your communities so your people can walk in and take what they want, maybe the bloodshed and satisfaction enough to nullify years of fratricidal gang-banging, blaze the possibility of a different future. How's it feel, the purity of fury, of chaos, nobody running the show, not even you, just going with the flow, down and dirty?

At one stage, freedom does feel like the devastation of nothing else to lose. Power can follow from that perception, power freeing you to act. Imagine yourself taking over. Claiming, performing your life on your terms. The thrill and risk and possibility of change, real change, the exciting, heady passion preparing you for the actual dawn of freedom, freedom's weight and responsibility, the realization that you pay with your life for each choice you make.

For America, African-American expressive culture has always embodied the possibility of choice and change, the radical alternative, good news or bad news, depending on your point of view, of being something other than a white person. Whether it's boogieing or walking on air like Michael Jordan or dancing like Michael Jackson, or singing the blues or participating in the good-time communal rituals of church, picnics, storytelling, or escaping into the forbidden, dangerous darkness whites project into the sexual lives of the other, African-American culture has served as an antidote to the materialistic culture of the West, a last psychic frontier or a retrograde dose of fear, the nigger, slave, ghetto-burning junky, welfare queen you could become if you slip, dangerous, hostile territory, nonetheless tempting, inviting, for all that. We've heard about black kids favoring blond dolls, the pathetic, unrequited love of the black middle class for the master's ways, things, looks, but just as telling are the stories I often hear recited in private by white people who admit to childhood fantasies of being black, of yearning to cross the line to the other, forbidden side where all the good stuff seemed to be. Our dreams, our imaginations contain the seeds of health and sickness. One crucial, abiding dimension of American history can be read as our country's love/hate affair with the black body.

The black man's body, the game, basketball, bearing his body's imprint, is used to sell everything from breakfast cereal to automobiles. Our current popular culture would be incomprehensible to an outsider unless he or she understood basketball as the key to deciphering speech styles, clothing styles, metaphors employed by kids, politicians, and housewives. Yet that same iconized, commodified black man's body is beaten, incarcerated, the nightmare thief, rapist, addict that Americans arm themselves against.

If you had a choice, my brothers.

South Africans are choosing at this very moment whether to say yes or no to a nonracialized society. Yes or no. And if yes, preparing on a national level to take immediate steps toward that goal. Nonracial means one score, one way of accounting, one set of humane standards for everyone in the country becomes the new bottom line. Forget for a moment your opinion of who the lions are and who the lambs, imagine the Hollywood Hills sliding down, the flat acres of South Central Los Angeles rising.

Until that happy day, a day reachable only through protracted sacrifice and struggle, there are sides to be chosen. You can't choose both. It's either racialized privilege or justice. Inequality or peace. If all of us choose solely on the basis of color or race, I don't see how the nation will survive. If we choose to act as if race, class, and gender don't matter, act as if they haven't created separate, hostile, unequal nations warring inside one nation, we won't survive, either.

BLACK NIGHT IN THE CITY

Flying over L.A., searching for fires among the million, million lights spreading below in patterns and confusion. Black emptiness of water, giant Pac-Man jaws devour fields of lights, define the shape of the city. Could this insurrection be the beginning of the end of capitalism, the West cracking, capitulating, as dead and impotent at its core as the other evil empire whose downfall we cheered without apprehending how soon our time would come? The final test, after all, of any governmental system is its ability to govern its people, or enough of its people, to intimidate and bully those others within its borders unwilling or unable to go along with the rule of the majority. When people have no stake in following a government's rules of order, the rules can be maintained only by force. A state of war exists: People are subdued rather than governed. Violence begets violence begets anarchy until people grow weary of killing one another, demand a new government responsive to all the people.

Power's out. It's pitch-black night in the city. Thirty blocks of Western Avenue I ride down are pockmarked by smoldering ruins. Shells of buildings torched to blackened chunks of concrete foundation, ribs of scorched steel. Black people owned that. Over there was Korean. Didn't burn that one but they ran in and ramshacked it good. *Ram-shacked.* George the taxi driver grew up around here. Knows how to bypass roadblocks set up at major intersections and freeway entrances to contain the trouble where it exploded here in the South Central neighborhoods of the poor, old, blacks, Hispanics, Asian shopkeepers who service the milk, bread, gas, liquor needs of the captive population. Fires bring out cops and the truth. What George avoids by twisting and turning through back streets is here always, just not in such an aggressive, bald-faced form: red flares on the tarmac funneling traffic into a single lane, checkpoints manned by soldiers in full battle dress, armed to the teeth, Jeeps, Humvees, patrol cars, itchy fingers, fear and hate you don't see day in, day out, but if you live here you know they are always in place, the barriers between your community and theirs, your reality and theirs. You've long ago decided trying to cross over isn't worth the trouble of beating your head against brick walls, aggravating yourself, endangering yourself to get over. Now, this night, hundreds of fires are consuming the stores where you shop, threatening your homes, stripping your pretensions of inhabiting the same city they do. You don't even have to try to remember to forget the invisible walls shutting you away, because the walls glow and dance and hum in these machines and men blocking your exit. You belong where you are. No accident. Smoke seethes behind you, thick in your thick nostrils from the mini-malls and swap meets and commercial strips that were also signs of shame and humiliation and also part of your neighborhood, the parched and mean turf shrinking behind you, shrinking smaller, tighter, busting at the seams like the inferior clothing with designer labels they sell you that shrinks when you dump it in the uncheckable heat of gritty-bellied Laundromat dryers. The little you possessed is less now, rolling up behind you like a rug the sheriff's deputies are taking away to stack on the curb with the rest of your stuff because there's now no roof you own or rent to put them under. You're halfway afraid to look back because whatever it is closing down on you hot-breathed and in no mood to play is probably gaining like old Satchel Paige said and up ahead the no-exit, no-entrance, no-way signs, red, white, and blue interstate shields, the barricade, even when you can't see it clear as you see it tonight, always halting you abruptly as bayonets and bullets.

George blurts, Aw, no. Naw. Naw. What I was telling you about a while ago I wanted to show you. Club where lots of Spanish chicks go dancing. Naw. Damn. It's gone, man. Look at that. They got it too. Right there. Burned down.

And a few blocks later nearly the same words, the sigh, a groan like you've just heard bad news about an old friend. Naw. Naw. Damn. I was planning to go by there in the morning. Koreans owned it. Carried all kinds of electronic gear you couldn't get nowhere else. Dimmer like this one. See? For the back of the cab. Need a . . . you know. One of those deals change the current. Converter? No. You know what I mean. Adapter? Yeah, *adapter*. Planned on running by here tomorrow morning pick me up one. Place gone now. It's crazy. Crazy. Crazy. I saw people with their little shopping bags the morning after the first fires. Like they expected the grocery store to be here when they got up the next morning after they watched it burn. Like it's supposed to rise up overnight and they can just go in and buy what they need. Like nothing's different. Just got to show up with their shopping bags. Some these houses been without power for days. You can imagine what inside the refrigerator's like. Old people mostly all that live around in through here. Got no place to buy a bottle of milk, loaf of bread now. No cars. If they had cars, no gas. Gas stations some the first things shut down or burned. Hollywood Race Track over there. They say Mafia burned down the old one 'cause the guy owned it owed them money. Rebuilt it, theirs now. Crazy, crazy. I've never seen anything like it. People just filled with hate. Hate. Saw two guys riding around in a brand-new pickup. One had this big wrench going from water hydrant to water hydrant with a wrench cutting on the water so wouldn't be pressure in the hoses to fight the fires.

George had lost a son in Desert Storm. The next day we talked to a Desert Storm vet who dreamed of returning to the Middle East so he could visit Mecca. The vet and two buddies were drinking purple Kool-Aid laced with something quite potent. Between the lines of his garbled monologue, the story of a man puzzled, outraged by the irony of fighting for his country then betrayed by his country, belligerent, proud, lost in daydreams of a holy pilgrimage, nightmares of intense combat, the truth deeply understood but beyond his power to articulate, except in half-drugged, nearly comic, heartbreaking sputterings of loss and perplexity and bone-deep hurt, George, George, George, I'm sorry, man, about your son, man. He was a good man. Good man. Lemme tell you, man, whole lot more of us wasn't spozed to come back neither. Whole lot. None of us, really, man. Why you think we standing here? Military's a bitch, man. Coulda called our guard unit. Called us up right away. I'm a soldier. I was over there, I know. We could have been in the streets in a minute, man, but they called their cracker units, took them days to get here. We first in line going to the goddamn desert. Tell me about it.

George was a vet, too. He'd been hassled Rodney King–style while in uniform after 'Nam. Knew the Korean woman, Soon Ja Du, who shot a young black girl, Latasha Harlins, from behind. He felt sorry for the woman. No reason to shoot the girl, but there's more to the story. Came to this country speaking no English. Husband watching TV while she did all the work. She couldn't speak or read, held a list you'd hand her upside down. You had to point to what you wanted. Husband started running around with young black girls. Didn't recognize her when I stopped in one day. She came here a girl. Looked sixty in a couple years.

All this is Spanish now. Yeah, but I still hang out here. Hey, this is where I grew up. Still my home, don't care who's living in the houses. You know how you'd feel no matter who moved in and took over if you grew up here. Still belongs to you, you know everything there is to know about it.

I think of all those lights on the flatness below the plane, the sheer number, the magnitude of their collective power, pretty, intricate, and dazzling as a Christmas tree and just as vulnerable as a Christmas tree, a switch could turn the lights off, a series of switches failing click, click, click, and they'd all be out, gone, gone, nothing, as if the dark ocean swept over them, a tidal surge joining black water to black water as far as any horizon. In less than a second, all the acres of sparkle and glitter disappear as if none of it ever existed.

SOME VIOLENCE

Rodney King makes me think of something white. The bulk of him on his knees, flopping over on his back, twisting, lurching; he's the great white whale, skewered by harpoons, tethered by ropes, surrounded by his tormentors, hunters who have pursued and landed him, who desperately try to subdue the mystery he represents with blows of their clubs. For the moment he's like Gulliver captured by the Lilliputians, trapped in their element, bound and helpless, but all around the blurry edges of the video images, darkness surges and seethes. Any moment it will erase the flickering scene.

As we listened to responsible Americans from the president on down condemning the violence of rioters and looters, we might have asked: What would be a reasonable response to centuries of murderous physical and mental abuse? Even if it was your great-great-granddaddy or your daddy who locked a man and his family in a cage, how forgiving do you expect the man should be when he finally bursts free and finds you standing beside the cage with the key in your pocket?

As early as D. W. Griffith's *Birth of a Nation* (1915), filmic depictions of black liberation forged explicit links between freedom and chaos, riot, and rape. William Styron's novel *The Confessions of Nat Turner*, perhaps unwittingly but quite explicitly, perpetuates the misguided notion that a black man's lust for freedom is really his lust for white women. Though initial TV coverage of the riots fell short of Griffith's lurid, suggestive cartoons, it reinforced the venerable tradition he fathered. Buried not so deeply in the images of flames, of property stolen, ruined, of crowds scattering, fleeing like rabbits from police, grinning looters, Sambo looters made to appear ridiculous as monkeys in tuxedos by the unmanageability of the booty they'd seized, the outraged, fatherly voices describing looters as criminal, barbaric, promising vengeance, et cetera, et cetera—beneath this comic/tragic surface of civilization gone awry lies the unspeakable fear of rape, miscegenation, the chaos of social disorder in which racial purity, and therefore racial boundaries and privilege, no longer exists. Property is white and rioters are black, and property in the patriarchal lexicon of course includes white women, so black demands for equal opportunity and equal access become symbolic assaults, rapes. Doesn't this uppityness, these demands and threats from people who just yesterday were themselves things owned by whites, justify the blows applied to Rodney King? Isn't King's body the locus of sin, of chaos, past, present, and future?

One could tabulate the baleful statistics, concretize the everyday violence pervading many neighborhoods in South Central Los Angeles. Homicide, suicide, infant mortality, muggings, malnutrition, domestic abuse, homelessness, arson, rape, robbery, the scale of violence would be appalling, as dramatic as the atrocities associated with the "riots." What is more elusive and finally more disturbing than either the violence condemned by the president or the violence he condoned until it blew up in his face is our steadfast determination to reside in Beverly Hills or reside in Amherst, Massachusetts, as if what we know about South Central Los Angeles is not connected to our lives.

Americans have an obsession with facts, and we know far too many facts about our fellow countrymen, facts that have eroded other kinds of knowledge, withered our imaginative faculty, our power to emotionally identify, magically transport ourselves as art does beneath another person's skin. As obsessive as the concern with facts is our compulsion to express them in racial terms: one column for blacks, one for whites. While this practice may serve some useful purpose, it is also an admission of defeat. It feeds the notion that a shamefully high mortality rate among black babies is not the entire nation's problem but a black problem. Since the victims are black, things aren't as bad as they might seem. It's them, not us. And this false comfort, this sense of difference and immunity, has nurtured a pathological separation from reality. What goes around, comes around. The meanest self-interest should teach white people they cannot afford the fiction of immunity. In the past century, every major social cataclysm, every man-made or natural disaster that's ravaged the black community, gradually, inevitably, sometimes instantly, rocks us all. Problems seemingly race-specific only appear that way because the defective legal-political, social, and moral climates of the nation situate black communities in a position of extreme vulnerability. For better or worse we've always been point men, the canaries in cages that miners tote deep underground.

The peculiar and perhaps fatal American violence is the refusal to connect. We simplify the world with categorical divisions—black/white, male/female, old/young—and then cling to these in spite of the evidence of our intellects, our senses. A violence so disruptive and irrational it blinds us to our self-interests. A violence epitomized by a juror who sympathizes with the fear of a dozen armed policemen as they beat a black man to his knees but can't acknowledge Rodney King's pain as the blows were inflicted. The violence that allows a luxury car wash on La Cienega Boulevard in Hollywood to flourish while fires still smolder only blocks away, violence perpetrated by a blond woman, coiffed, miniskirted, bred to bone and sleekness, who squats down at the bumper of her BMW convertible, orders one of the half-dozen Hispanic men in coveralls scrubbing, polishing, buffing, wiping, to crawl underneath the vehicle and remove dirt she's spied there.

Were the outraged voices condemning the violence of rioters reading from the double-columned, white-reality-here, black-reality-over-there book forgetting the violence that permits whole cities to fester? Were those voices promising to stop violence with violence attempting to close the racial divide or preparing us to plunge deeper into the chasm?

WHEN FEAR PITCHES A TENT

I stay in Los Angeles four days, accumulating a notebook full of impressions, two tapes of voices, pounds of newspapers, a frustrating sense of inadequacy as the media put a lid on the pot they've been furiously stirring, begin closing down the story, diffusing, fragmenting it into human-interest subplots that are neat and predictable, reducing the meaning of what's happened into formulaic clichés that are the language of television, trivializing, tidying the story as if closure has been achieved, as if events actually follow the pattern the media impose upon them, as if leaving L.A. is justified because something with a beginning, middle, and end has run its course. Leaving L.A. as if there's a reason other than the media's own insatiable need to fill time with "new" stories, leaving as if a reason other than serving their own interests and the interests of their sponsors brought the cameras and commentators to L.A. in the first place. The carpetbagging presence of press and TV is as dangerous and aggressive as the military occupation of black and Hispanic neighborhoods, perhaps more dangerous because we've been conditioned not to see the press, treat it as an invisible fly on the wall even when its legions outnumber the troops.

My anger at the media is of course directed partly at myself, my mission, and is also part envy. I'm overwhelmed, marginalized. Television's power to create reality is literally incomprehensible because it infiltrates and usurps the space of comprehension, replaces our eyes and ears, and feeds us the data we process into meaning. But the data aren't raw. Images, sound bites, are framed, organized not so much by one ideological stance or another, though that happens often enough, but by the nature of the beast, collecting, omitting, selecting sights and sounds. A beast with a history, personality, limits, habits that determine what it can and will pass on to us. Processed information with all the risks, shortcuts, shortcomings, and deceptions of processed food. We're only beginning to learn how to put warning labels on processed information, how to regulate what's unhealthy, addicting, how to identify additives that cheat or contain poisons. We've fallen into the lazy habit of making no distinction between what the screen brings us and what we gather from the natural exercise of our eyes, ears, noses out in the street.

Have we witnessed a riot or revolt? Should we react with compassion or force? Are the cops who beat King guilty or not guilty? Issues are not so much raised as erased. Either/or, yes or no. As if stating two opposing sides of an issue, presenting buzz words that frame a controversy, is a way of resolving it. As the media close down the Los Angeles story, the presentation of adversarial voices is a means of copping out on issues. A stage where antagonists scream and hoot at one another à la *Donahue* or *Geraldo* is the real action, the entertainment, what sells soap. Four days of cloying overload in Los Angeles and the media are on their way out, covering their tracks, effectively squashing any desire to think and/or feel. How many times can you watch the infamous video before you and King become patients etherized upon a table?

My last day in L.A., Stan picks me up at my hotel. (Talk about lack of connection—my hotel's in Beverly Hills, and between forays into the battle zones of South Central, I recline in a lounge chair beside the rooftop pool, enjoying birdsong, peace and quiet, aware every so often of sirens, police choppers battering the air overhead.) I'd last seen Stan twenty-seven years ago in England at Oxford University, where we were Rhodes scholars. Big news in 1963, when we were elected, two black student-athletes off to compete with the best and brightest at Oxford, one from the East, one from the West, bicoastal proof in an era of sit-ins, freedom rides, picketing, and marches that things were getting better, the system worked.

I described to Stan my first night in town, arriving at LAX more than two hours late, my plane delayed in Pittsburgh, forced to swing far out over the ocean to avoid smoke and gunfire as it landed, how driving through South Central with George the cabdriver I had to keep pinching myself to remember I was still in the continental U.S., not the latest foreign hellhole of the moment, still in my own country, home and not home in a way, because everything left standing, and most buildings remained intact, was reminiscent of Homewood, East Liberty, the Northside, black communities in Pittsburgh where I'd grown up. The cityscape flatter, yes, and larger in scale, but a familiar stage set, though no people were visible and the insides of numerous buildings had been charred to ashes, and red-lighted barricades pulsed at major intersections.

Not scared on that first night. Scared wouldn't come until the last day, the evening of the day Stan picked me up at Le Parc is when scared arrived and carved out a dwelling place. Monday, the day Mayor Bradley lifted curfew and the city resumed its normal face, pedestrians and traffic reappeared in the streets, bars and restaurants reopened, then fear pitched its tent in my gut because I knew how thin and arbitrary normal was, the thrashing angers it screened, the scores to be settled still seething in far too many citizens' hearts, the inevitability of spontaneous bursts of violence, somewhere, anywhere, anytime under the cover of this normalcy. I was a black man walking in an overwhelmingly white neighborhood, a target, a lightning rod, and the clouds, the storm surely hadn't passed. What was this "normal," anyway, for whose return people prayed? For whites, normal meant not having to worry about the violence and desperation endemic to areas of the city like South Central. For residents of such areas, normal meant hunkering down again and accepting again the degrading portion of life in South Central allotted them.

Fear and unease came later, fueled perhaps by what Stan told me as he chauffeured me on a daylight tour of his city. The week he returned from Oxford in 1965, the Watts rebellion greeted him like a welcome-home banner. Since then, Stan had developed a successful law practice, served the city as an appointed commissioner. Prosperous, looking good, a family man, he drives us by his handsome home in the high cotton of the Crenshaw district, an oasis of substantial, occasionally stately dwellings girded by lawns, flower gardens, the lavender lace of jacaranda trees blooming, only a few brisk steps from the devastation of Crenshaw Center I'd visited Sunday, one side of the multilane, divided Crenshaw Boulevard a two-block-long barbecued ruin, the other the epicenter of what seemed a spontaneous street fair, crowds out celebrating the end of a war, liberation from an enemy occupation.

SURPLUS PEOPLE

As Stan shared his knowledge of the city with me, he spoke both as native son and university-trained political scientist. Our conversation had begun decades before; maybe it had continued over the years, despite distance and silence. Here's the corner where black L.A. began, back when my parents, who are old enough really to be my grandparents, arrived here from Texas after World War I. Central Avenue, the main drag. Eventually it ran all the way from around Twentieth Street well into the Hundreds. When entertainers came to town in the forties and fifties, downtown L.A. was segregated, so they stayed in places like the Dunbar Hotel. Dunbar's seen better days, but it's still standing. Show you when we pass. Louis Armstrong, Count Basie, Ella, the Duke, they all stayed in hotels on Central like the Dunbar. This is old Watts. Almost entirely Spanish now. Just a few elderly blacks left. In the last ten years or so, he tells me, a new wave of immigrants, Latinos from Central America—Salvadorans, Guatemalans—settled here. Mexican nationals who've been in L.A. a long time tended to live in East L.A. Fortunes were made by Hispanic realtors.

Five or six people would sign a lease. Evidence of tradition, communal spirit, communal living, also the necessity forced upon poor people to pool funds, share cooking and living space, many inhabitants occupying a dwelling in shifts. I recalled my grandfather telling me about barracks-like rooming houses in the Hill District of Pittsburgh where black men fresh up from the South boarded in the early decades of the century. You pulled your shift in the mill and another man rented your bed till you returned to sleep while he fed the screaming furnaces. I thought of South Africa, where the impossibly close quarters of migrant-worker dormitories are a staging ground and accelerant of tribal animosity, the so-called black-on-black violence that apartheid breeds.

Many of L.A.'s traditionally black areas became brown areas. Latino immigrants invested in homes and Hispanic entrepreneurs invested in real estate, so a vacuum existed, and another wave of immigrants, Korean this time, moved in and bought stores abandoned by whites and the black merchant class. Consequently, few businesses in Latino neighborhoods owned by Latinos. Damage generally much more wholesale in Hispanic neighborhoods. Whole blocks burned down, because they're all Korean-owned. In the black communities a checkerboard pattern reflecting the fact that most black-owned businesses were spared.

Korean merchants took risks, Stan explains. Not because Koreans like risks, but prices were low in depressed Hispanic and black neighborhoods and the Koreans themselves were recent immigrants and immigrants of color and learned the hard lesson that opportunities available to them were restricted. Large Anglo firms had decided even before the Watts rebellion to move out of the city to the suburbs or to go international. Post-Watts, the trickle turned to a stampede. It's that defection by major financial institutions, the cold-blooded logic of profit-taking, of writing off, redlining certain segments of Los Angeles, the bottom-line concept that business exists to earn money, period. Forget making friends or serving the public or civic obligations; those are trimmings, luxuries. Decisions arrived on high by banks, insurance companies, corporations to desert the inner city are the seeds of the present troubles, the key to sorting out what seems to be racial antagonism between blacks and Koreans, Koreans and Hispanics.

Each immigrant group came to L.A. in pursuit of the American Dream, and the Dream failed each group in distinct but related ways. Blacks and Mexicans were first to arrive in large numbers, and classic racism thwarted them. You can view the remains of their dreams in the ghettos of South Central and East L.A. The black population in L.A. is shrinking in total numbers and as a percentage of the whole. The black middle class is following whites to the suburbs, but there's a catch. To find available, affordable land for housing, blacks are winding up in the desert. To relieve the burdens and stresses of heavy mortgages, demanding jobs, hours of commuting, the pressure of competing in a predominantly white, often hostile, workplace, some of these black strivers, like their white counterparts, have become a bullish market for the cocaine trade.

Latinos fleeing poverty and political oppression arrived in a flood during the flush seventies and eighties. Sharing resources, pooling, and saving enabled them to improve their living conditions. They took over the low-paying jobs once held by blacks—domestics, gardeners, janitors, hospital workers, laborers, childcare. Stan says the building where his law offices are located used to turn black after 6:00 with the exit of professionals, the influx of janitors, watchmen, and office cleaners. Now he never sees a black face when he works late. Recession hit this class of Latino working poor severely. No jobs, no money, no prospects; they were trapped by lack of training and education, large families, terrorism of the immigration service, drugs, prejudice, their foreign culture and language. The dream died; they were an untouchable caste, frozen on the bottom rung of the economic ladder.

Koreans arrived determined to be merchants, buying failing businesses in Hispanic and black neighborhoods. The function of such businesses in the larger economic picture is to snatch back the few dollars that trickle down into the hands of the working poor, the unemployed, mothers on welfare, the elderly on social security, exploiting segments of the public that big business no longer deems worth the trouble to service.

Since labor is expensive, Korean businesses tended to be family concerns. Long hours, hard work, minimal overhead, streamlined services were survival strategies. Korean businesses monopolized the cash coming into the community and eventually turned a profit, prospering and expanding while the neighborhoods supporting them languished. An explosion was inevitable, a systemic failure whose symptom, not cause, was racial animosity between Koreans and other people of color. Overpricing, inferior goods, poor service, no stake in the community as long as it continued to be a cash cow, inevitable friction and paranoia generated between outsiders (whom insiders view as taking everything) and insiders (whom outsiders view as wanting something for nothing)—these factors that had ignited the Watts rebellion and countless other outbreaks of urban unrest, in short the white man's burden in his dealings with colonized peoples, were part of what Koreans unwittingly inherited as they buckled themselves up for a ride on the American Dream machine.

Race fear is the public face of economic war. And economic war hides race fear. The pyramidal structure of American society rests on the great mass of people at its base. During a large portion of our history, slaves seemed to define the bottom of the pyramid. But that turns out to be only partially true, a clever and convenient fiction to disguise, then and now, the fact that down on the bottom, shoulder to shoulder, backside to backside, were whole lots of people, black, white, all colors in this country and in other countries, who weren't called slaves or niggers but nonetheless performed the function of a captive, exploited, expendable source of labor and resources, colonized, sweatshopped, indentured, commandeered, apprenticed, the labor that built our country into a world power. Technology, monopoly capitalism, the disappearing middle class have steadily diminished the number of individuals we need to draw from the pool to keep the wheels of society turning. But the pool steadily grows larger, and that's the problem of our cities, our nation, the century. The very American address to this problem has been to ignore it or label it with words like *underclass* or *homeless*. Labels divide us, the problems remain. The very notion of "home," containing as it does visions of white picket fences, Dick, Jane, and Spot, Mom and Daddy, trivializes and sentimentalizes the plight of huge segments of the population for whom such homes never have and never will exist. The problem is not that people don't have homes, they have no country, no government willing to claim them, assist them. They are the leading edge, visible now on America's city streets, of a vast sea of displaced, surplus people, refugees, immigrants, the unemployed, unskilled, political or racial undesirables, utopian dreamers, the alienated and oppressed, those who want radical change, who are change, the by-products of a failing industrialized global society, unwanted, as unassimilable as nuclear waste. They'll knock, then pound, eventually kick in the door. At what point will we respond? *A choice, my brothers.*

THE DREAM WASN'T WORKING

Although we've turned our backs, these folk won't go away. Not in South Central L.A. Not in Amherst or London. Ask imperial Rome, France in the eighteenth century, China, Russia, or South Africa today. The South Central ghettos, brutally cordoned and policed, and the barred, burglar-alarmed, security-patrolled enclaves of Hollywood Hills mirror one another obscenely, grotesquely. Who's locked in? Who's locked out? Who's free? We incarcerate a larger percentage of our population than any other nation, private citizens have armed themselves to the teeth, we license policemen like Daryl Gates and the ones who beat up Rodney King to use any means necessary to maintain a thin blue line of protection, yet the mania for security rages unabated.

Trouble with turning one's back on trouble is that you lose sight of what's behind you. You know you've done something wrong, your back shouldn't be exposed, you're vulnerable, the menace swells larger than life as your imagination works overtime.

But after all the analysis, accounting, assessment of property smashed and burned, things destroyed, who are the dead? Predictably, always and always young men of color. Of the dead, nearly 80 percent are men of color. And let no fool imagine I'm valuing some lives over others based on color. But who are the dead? Men of color. Not innocent, not even young. Old when they die, lives cut off prematurely, everything crammed into a few years—torn from the nest, wings clipped, tired and desperate too soon. Lives foreshortened, old, dead too soon. Who are the dead? Black or brown men who for good reasons and bad were driven to take back what's been taken from them, give back what's been done unto them. Not Black Panthers yet, not revolutionary suicides yet, but blood-letting with a message nonetheless. Unless you're prepared to kill us all, we won't go away and if you come for us we won't go easy and won't go alone. BLOODS CRIPS MEX TOGETHER. 5/3/92

It was time to go. We'd cruised in Stan's Isuzu Trooper nearly two hours, from Beverly Hills to South Central and now downtown where Stan pointed out his building and the torched shell of a structure in a shopping plaza just across the street. No. Not Watts again. Some things never change—the visible reality of urban decay, the inner reality of America's apartheid mind-set and convictions. But this time the fires hadn't been confined to black neighborhoods, the people killing, burning, and looting, the ones looted and burned and dead were of all races. The Dream wasn't working for anybody, not as comforting illusion, not as a means of social control. The antagonists this time weren't black versus white, the problem's not even strictly American. The Dream's demise is tied to a new world order dawning, the end of America's global domination; no longer would a startlingly disproportionate share of the world's resources continue to magically appear on our doorsteps. These changes permitted a few Americans to become obscenely rich, created misery for millions.

What kind of world was this? Two successful black men, trained, privileged, empowered, yet at any intersection we could be pulled over and Rodney Kinged. A sad story, one you could shed a tear over, but not the real deal. The real deal is millions and millions of Americans walking around in a carefully constructed daze, full of hurt, hate, anger, losing the capacity to love, to talk, to help one another, living the lies of separate and unequal.

Near the beginning of the ride, when we were just happy to see each other again, full of do you remember and have you seen and whatever happened to, the simple chatty bubbling joy of sentences unfinished, questions interrupted, survivor joy—more poignant because it's two black middle-age men and so many of the guys we grew up with dead, dying, or gone, gone, gone—a high always threatening to turn bittersweet like one of Smokey Robinson's old halfway-fast, halfway-slow, sad, slick, "Tracks of My Tears" kind of tunes, Stan reminded me of a moment I'd totally forgotten till he began to reminisce. Only took a few words of the story and I was there, back in England, a soft, quiet dawn unfolding on one of Oxford's residential streets. We're a quarter-century younger, returning to our college digs from a party probably. Two large American Negroes tugging on a slanted street sign, trying to wrestle it out of the ground. Like in a movie we both look up on cue and an English bobby is staring incredulously at us on this peaceful, early-morning, deserted English street. The bobby stares at two young black men, foreigners most likely, otherwise normal-appearing black men, silently, intently engrossed in attempting to rip an innocent signpost from its moorings. What in heaven's name are you blokes doing? I looked at Stan. Stan looked at me. We both stared at the bobby and for a long time nobody said a word.

MONUMENT TO MALCOLM

1992

Cairo is full of cemeteries. The poor and homeless live in sprawling ghettos among crumbling tombstones of the dead. Belowground in older quarters of Cairo, invisible cities of the dead are layered, each layer a deeper plunge into Cairo's history. Ancient monuments everywhere in the streets, the Sphinx, the pyramids just down the road, disrupt a visitor's sense of time. *Now*, the entire modern era, feels like a stage set. Tomorrow workers will strike it, build another, and you'll be gone.

A perfect city for the making of a movie. Within its fabulous profusion of ancient and modern, living and dead, you can frame and edit, construct the city you need. Wherever we are, we must construct illusions and make believers of ourselves or we fall prey to the most fragile, dangerous illusion: that our lives go on forever, that some world exists, solid, fixed, dependable, apart from the ones we create. Spike Lee knows better. He's come to Cairo because Malcolm X is here, living in these streets and mosques and open marketplaces where he once strolled in 1959 and 1964. All Spike Lee has to do is frame and edit, reconstruct the illusion. He's a moviemaker, an illusionist through and through.

Spike Lee recalls his mother screaming "they killed him, they killed him" that day in 1968 when Martin Luther King was shot, but he retains no childhood memories of Malcolm, who was assassinated in 1965 at the age of thirty-nine, when Lee was seven years old. Yet Malcolm's presence as martyr, myth, incarnation of black manhood, guide, and seer had an incalculable impact on Lee and countless other young African-Americans who grew into adulthood during the eighties. Alex Haley's *The Autobiography of Malcolm X*, Malcolm's speeches on recordings, video, and in print provided a reality check. Malcolm X told the truth, lived the truth. Truth was revealed in his shocking death and in the power of his spirit to survive the grave. Young black people recognized the oppressive America Malcolm described, drew inspiration from his uncompromising determination not to be destroyed by racism, embraced his singular example of strength, courage, dignity, intellectual rigor.

Over dinner—fish-buffet night at Cairo's Meridien Hotel—Spike Lee considers the challenges of bringing the life of Malcolm X to the screen. "Being truthful about the man and still making it a personal film. All my films are personal. Having a great love for Malcolm I don't feel was a problem at all. Rewriting the script I was able, you know, to get myself in there. Not take over but just get in there. Directing doesn't just come from words on paper. People have been trying to make the Malcolm X film for twenty years. And I don't think it's a coincidence that it happened right now. There are a lot of things in life, like timing . . . I think all that stuff works for this film to be made right now. I think that one of the reasons why Hollywood didn't make it before is they probably felt there wasn't a star, a black actor, you know, somebody who could play Malcolm X, a matinee idol with box office appeal . . . also they're scared of it."

Haraka. The headscarf is PLO *ghotra*, the satiny warm-up top Nike, jeans hippie-faded and black, round retro granny shades, cotton sweat socks by Champion; Spike Lee is dressed eclectically, layered for a full day of shooting in Cairo's changeable January weather—cold mornings, hot afternoons—but the directorial style is pure pharaoh. *Haraka.* Action. Out of a time tunnel, a parade of 1950s and 1960s vehicles crosses in front of the cameras. Behind this carefully choreographed procession of relics Jeddah Street bursts instantly into activity. Imagine all the teeming, exotic Eastern bazaars you've ever seen in the movies—an oxcart, baskets of chickens, beggars; armless, legless, handless cripples; enormous loads balanced on women's heads, merchants hawking their wares from rows of closet-sized shops, merchandise spilling, like the overstuffed cleavage of a starlet, into the narrow streets. Now envision all this commotion in an enclosed space, bordered by ropes, by large, gruff locals hired for the day to shoo back spectators, by barricades of equipment trucks and transport vehicles. Then just beyond the margin of onlookers packed around the busy street scene is the sleepy Cairo of today—shuttered shops, empty cobbled walkways, sudden mosques, the walls of a prison, everything centuries old, a museum, another stage upon which someone has plopped the tiny bubble Spike Lee rules like Rameses.

Haraka. But this morning there's too much action. A fruit and bread fight escalates and a couple hundred extras turn the first take into a Marx Brothers comedy. Spike Lee is jumping up and down, yelling stop, stop, till Samir, a distinguished Egyptian producer/director who's the major-domo of these Egyptian shoots of the *Malcolm X* movie, echoes in Arabic over his bullhorn what Spike Lee's hollering.

"Sammi, Sammi, man. I said plenty action. Give me plenty, plenty action. Lots of action. But not crazy. Your people are going crazy out there."

"Yes, yes, I agree. Too much. It is too much."

"I said stir them up. Plenty action. What'd you tell your people, Sammi? They're bugging out on me."

Spike wags his head in dismay, a tinge of disgust tightens his lips, twists his mouth. He lets everyone know in no uncertain terms he's not a happy camper. It is no mean feat to gather together the elements of this shoot. First, production designer Wynn Thomas scouts the city for a promising locale. "I like the way Spike writes. I have no trouble using his scripts as a guide. Kind of sketchy, skeletal, but they're evocative. Give me everything I need." Then the logistics of getting everybody up and out and in place by first light. Finding a space for the caterers to pitch their tent so the crew can be fed from dawn to dusk. Countless details that demand enormous expenditures of time and money.

Money has been a vexed issue from the start, when Warner Bros. refused to budget *Malcolm X* at the level Spike Lee argued the film required. "I told Warner Bros. from the beginning that this was a three-hour film, and they're still giving me a big fight about it. I told them from the beginning the scope and magnitude of what we wanted with this film and they're like, yeah, right. There's going to be a fight. They really haven't been the most supportive." Lack of money meant the cancelation of further filming in Saudi Arabia and threatened Spike Lee's creative control of the project, because once the movie runs over budget it's subject to receivership, with the insurance underwriters assuming control of the purse strings.

All that on the line, to say nothing of the original battle to obtain the right to make this *Malcolm X* movie. A string of corpses—producers, writers, directors, studio executives—litter that trail. To say nothing of the excruciating struggle black directors must endure to make any movie in Hollywood, then the nerve-racking, mettle-testing push against the odds to do *their* movies, *their* way. Everything was at stake in the Cairo intersection, in the hands, for a moment, of non-English-speaking people who somehow had gotten the impression they were being paid to throw bread and fruit at each other and have a good time.

So the director beats his hands against the scarf he'd wound round his X cap, as if he's trying to get at the hair beneath and tear it out. "Shit. Goddamnit. Did you see that shit." Then he's smiling, grins briefly, furtively, hand in front of mouth. The way the crowd had translated Samir's translation of Spike's call for plenty, plenty action would have been perfect, after all, for another movie, a zany, slapstick *Amos and Andy Meet Yo' Mummy's Ghost*. Funny if your reputation, your movie's financial solvency, the future of black filmmaking in America, the image and thus availability of Malcolm for an at-risk generation of young people weren't also riding on each frame you organized and achieved.

None of that was fair, but it was how things worked. Spike Lee grins anyway, then restores his game face, orders the cars to retreat, watches them as they pick their way in reverse back through the chaos of a blown take. He darts here and there, talking to six people at once, pointing his finger at culprits, admonishing, teaching with sign language. He scopes out the throng, notices something missing, and shouts like a shopper in a deli. "Sammi. You got any Americans?" Finally, he climbs above the fray to the shaky, gutted third floor of a building either being demolished or remodeled that offered a serendipitous perch, discovered only that morning, for aerial shots of the animated bazaar through which Denzel Washington as Malcolm would stroll for a few seconds on the arm of a supremely dignified, very weathered, very dark old man recruited from among the Egyptian extras, both men draped in the snow-white ihram of Muslim pilgrims.

The immense interior of the Muhammad Ali Mosque emptied of worshipers, acres of rugs and prayer mats temporarily stripped off its floor, daybreak, the central dome towering above you like some ideal you might aspire toward but you know you'll never reach, swallows you whole. You catch your breath the way you catch it plunging the first time each summer into a cool Maine lake. Figures clustered around cameras and lighting apparatus seem miles away across the tile floor. You wave because speaking before you need to speak would break the spell. You'd return to being who you usually are, instead of a pilgrim treading on an unknown shore.

Ernest Dickerson, director of photography; Wynn Thomas, production designer; Ruth Carter, costume designer; Preston Holmes, production supervisor, are among those you meet your first morning on location with *Malcolm X* in Cairo. (No shoes allowed inside the mosque. Everybody wears at least one pair of heavy socks. You can tell the rookie by his cold feet.) They'd helped put Spike Lee on the Hollywood map, and more important, along with him, presented on-screen versions of black life that black Americans could enjoy, argue about, identify with, claim. As Lee would tell me, "All of us have been together for at least five films:

She's Gotta Have It, School Daze, Do the Right Thing, Mo' Better Blues, Jungle Fever. We've developed, you know, a shorthand. We're all on the same wavelength. All of us love our craft, really try hard to be the best we can. And with each film, we've tried to make it better than the last. None of us want to be stagnant. You know me. World's number one Knicks fan. I draw sports analogies. On sports teams, you must constantly infuse new blood or you all get old at once. I always try and groom new people when we do films, in internships or whatever."

The crew voices—urban, hip, brightly nuanced, crackly with intelligence, the tit-for-tat verbal play, familiar registers of the African-American vernacular—are incongruous in this mosque. The talk made it feel too easy to be as far away from home as I knew I was in this cavernous space where, cupped under the arching dome, framed by its massive piers, all time was present, equal.

Then talk stops because El-Hajj Malik El-Shabazz appears in the smoky needle's eye of the door I'd entered a few minutes before. He pauses a second as if he'd disembarked from some celestial elevator and needs to check and see if he's on the correct floor, then strides past the marble, gilded, three-tiered tomb of Muhammad Ali toward us.

Yes. Malcolm's loose-limbed, rangy steps, his neat three-buttoned suit, pursed lips, out-thrust chin, reddish hair, and beard. Unmistakably him. An illusion actual in the flesh.

Later, Marietta Carter, in charge of makeup, would show me, in her loose-leaf notebook, the dozens of photos of Malcolm and of Denzel Washington becoming Malcolm at different ages, different stages of the movie, and her art, an almost mystical but also scrupulous, methodical, step-by-step superimposition of image upon actor, mask upon face, would astound me, but I didn't know yet about the work that went into achieving the likeness; all I saw was a ghost in a trim, blue gray suit, a ghost whose socks whisper across the hard, bare floor of the Muhammad Ali Mosque, who must be Malcolm and no one else, until I shook Denzel Washington's hand and said, "Excuse me for staring, man." The resemblance was eerie, disquieting almost, one more layer of make-believe to negotiate before I'd feel firmly planted on solid ground, understand the rules functioning in Cairo.

Denzel had studied Malcolm's life, played him a decade before in the Negro Ensemble Company's production of *When the Chickens Come Home to Roost*. But the meshing of images, this morning's startling result, required more than conscious effort and practice. Michelangelo said the *David* was already in the stone. His job was to release him.

As Carter explains to me, when they were shooting in New York, the crew barely survived the day they killed Malcolm. Harlem's Audubon Ballroom, where the actual assassination occurred, was unavailable, so Malcolm's murder was reenacted in a similar building nearby. Some actors were in awful shape already when they met Marietta Carter for their makeup session that morning, already beginning to shift mind and body backward to the actual event, forward into the long day ahead of them, a day of grief, shock, hyperintensity, living and reliving the horror of El-Hajj Malik El-Shabazz gunned down in front of his wife and children. One of those mornings Marietta dons surgical gloves to protect herself from the bad karma seeping through her clients' hair and skin. You can feel it, smell it. You don't want to touch it. The actress playing Betty Shabazz was in particularly bad shape when Marietta greeted her that morning and by the end of the day, exhausted, nearly hysterical. When blanks fired by the assassins exploded in the make-believe Audubon, they set off real fear, an actual stampede for the door. Somebody got trampled. Others remember being overwhelmed by panic, anger, fear. It's happening again. Happening again. It was awful. The memories it brought back. Like an emergency ward. Betty Shabazz screaming and sobbing and shaking all day.

In a recent interview with critic Skip Gates, Spike Lee commented on the process of recovering Malcolm. "I was the director. I rewrote the script by James Baldwin and Arnold Perl, and I will take full responsibility. I will say that this is the Malcolm I see." Consider the possibilities, the problems, the audacity. At this very moment biographers and critics are disputing minute points as seemingly manageable and definitive as the color of Malcolm's eyes. The testimony of Malcolm's contemporaries (they say blue or gray or green or hazel or . . .) provides more license than direction to a filmmaker.

Malcolm Little. Detroit Red. Rhythm Red. Malcolm X. El-Hajj Malik El-Shabazz. "He was all these things and he was constantly evolving. That's what I find interesting, following the process, as he goes from one stage to another . . . he was killed in the process of changing. A very complex person with a bunch of stuff going on in his mind. And you have to somehow find a way to put it on the screen, those changes."

Without slighting their other achievements, one could describe Spike Lee movies (*School Daze* is perhaps the most self-consciously realized example) as musical revues, vehicles for presenting performances of contemporary African-American song, dance, verbal arts. Classic vaudeville, minstrel shows, the Broadway show are models. Highly skilled renditions of genres drawn from black urban street culture. Another way of saying this is that America's hierarchical, left-brain, materialistic, puritanical culture needs periodic infusions of "life," and these infusions are often derived from black culture—the Negro spirituals introduced to the North by the Fisk University choir and minstrel shows, the improvisation and spontaneity of jazz, black dance in the twenties, freedom songs, marches, oratory of the sixties, the body language of pro basketball, the percussive motion and lyrics of rap today. Part of the extraordinary impact of Spike Lee's cinema derives from this peculiar tradition of love/hate, covert/overt cultural exchange.

The typical form of a Spike Lee movie resembles the structure of a picaresque novel. Great bits, scenes, set pieces, production numbers joined together with a minimal or sporadic attention to development of character and theme, resolution of plot. Large issues raised by the movies are compromised, diffused by sudden plot twists, lost in the fast shuffle of brilliant digressions. But the weakness inherent in Lee's smorgasbord approach is balanced by virtues. Like Duke Ellington, Spike Lee has become a master at composing and orchestrating moments in which the exceptionally talented artists he gathers round him can show their stuff. A profoundly African-American jazz aesthetic of spontaneity and improvisation pulses at the core of the movies. In a tribute to the late Robin Harris, Spike Lee said, "I cast him as Sweet Dick Willie [in *Do the Right Thing*]—all the comedy was his own. I merely set up the situation, rolled the camera, and let Sweet Dick Willie be." Wesley Snipes notes, "You don't come to a Spike Lee Joint without something as an actor. If you're expecting to be coached into you character, forget it, it's not gonna happen. Spike's carrying enough hats as it is. You have to be very confident as an actor because he's going to give you free rein."

Of course, as Lee insists, improvisation that works depends on countless hours in the woodshed, discipline, mastery of technique, respect and love of craft. "You can't just come out and improvise. It takes a great, skilled musician to improvise."

An artist's greatest strengths seem always to be liabilities, vulnerabilities, and part of the audience's fascination with the artist is watching him or her dance on that razor's edge. Will we get a whole bunch of engaging, lively cameos of Malcolm X, ingredients with which we can roll our own version of the man and his times? Or will Malcolm X represent a step up, expansion of the repertoire, cultivation of a new ground?

The challenge of *Malcolm X* is to tell a good story. Telling a good story means sustaining and amplifying the character of El-Hajj Malik El-Shabazz, creating a real life, a dream, something we haven't seen before, something larger than its constituent parts, incorporating what's known, not known, guessed at, wished, into a coherent, credible whole. Like Cairo, a good story unites the visible and invisible, living and dead, layers on top of layers, employs accident, conscious stylization. New life proliferates in the ruins. Monuments infused with new vitality.

While planning *Mo' Better Blues*, Spike Lee considers the pros and cons of using an actual musician's life as the subject of his jazz movie. "I realized any film based on Charlie Parker's life would be open season for criticism. Audiences bring excess baggage to films based on the lives of real people. Folks were bound to walk out of the theater saying, 'I knew Bird, he didn't hold his horn like that.' . . . I decided to stick with fictional characters . . . knowing that it would give me more freedom as a writer."

One hopes her critical reaction to *Malcolm X* won't bog down into nit-picking, fact checking, the correctness of Lee's portrayal. A fuller measure of success will be the courage of Spike Lee's vision, how he earns this vision, his unique way of seeing, interpreting Malcolm and Malcolm's times. Do the bits and pieces hang together, reverberate, inform one another? The truth of illusion. The illusion of truth. Real toads thriving in imaginary gardens. A vision to which facts cling for their life rather than the other way around, a vision clinging for its life to facts.

So how will Spike Lee handle the controversies surrounding Malcolm's life and legacy?

I bet our curiosity draws us in droves to view what Spike Lee's made of Malcolm. What Malcolm's made of Spike Lee.

To the question, how did you come up with the idea to ask wealthy blacks to help you finance postproduction costs after the bond company sent pink slips to your staff, Lee's answer is instantaneous.

Malcolm. Do for self.

Then Spike Lee bursts into Malcolm oratory: "I'm tired of asking white folks, 'Please, Mr. White Man, do this for me.' 'Please, Mr. White Man, this.' 'Please, Mr. White Man, do that.' *Do for self.* Black folks got plenty money . . . first person I called was Bill Cosby. Then Oprah Winfrey. Michael Jordan. Prince. Tracy Chapman. Janet Jackson. A woman, Peggy Cooper Cafritz, who lives in D.C."

Any official reaction from Warner Bros.?

"No. We have a nickname for Warner Bros. The Plantation. I'm escaping. I'm sailing away on the Good Ship Jesus. I'm taking the Underground Railroad. I'm booking like old Harriet Tubman. And getting the hell out of Dodge. I'm saying let my people go. 'Cause I been 'buked and scorned. We've been 'buked and scorned."

Sail on. Sail on, Mr. Lee.

MALCOLM X:
THE ART OF AUTOBIOGRAPHY

1992

We urgently need to retrieve those past traditions that can become the source of reconciliation and wholeness, for it is more important to learn from those traditions than to dwell on pain and injustice.

—Francoise Lionnet,
Autoethnography: The An-Archic Style of Dust Tracks on a Road

Sometimes the god wears a woman's face, sometimes a man's. Both suffer the same fate. Betrayal, dismemberment, the body pieces scattered, interred in a thousand thousand unknown places. Then she comes, always she, inconsolable, her tears a frozen rain drenching the land that has not cycled past winter since her lost one disappeared. She will scour the whole wide world until she finds every fragment of her beloved. And when she has gathered them and united them and breathed life again into the body, the earth too, as if it has been kissed, will begin softly to stir again, bud, bloom, warm as she does, her outstretched arms and smile open wide as a horizon in welcome.

Malcolm Martin, Martin Malcolm, the *m*s are some ancient sister in the amen corner *mmmmmm*, they are great mountains, cloud crowned, silhouetted against red dawn, as close to sky as solid earth ever reaches. They are men, mortals, mothers' sons; they were murdered, martyred, mirror our suffering, our history—betrayed, torn apart, dispersed. They wear the masks of men, of life or death, but it is not these accidental features we mourn. We are seeking always the body of our wholeness, what we once were and could be again, the promise of redemption Malcolm Martin Mandela seem to carry in their persons, a new day close enough to touch, to bestow a name upon—Malcolm, Martin, Mandela. What is snatched always just as it appears close enough to grasp.

For me writing about Malcolm is entering a space of myth and mourning. The way you enter an intense conversation, many voices that have been speaking to, at, and through one another for a very long time. In another way you are dreaming and responsible for every word you write, the words overheard and words not heard, words you say and words dismissed, echoed, repeated, inserted, quoted, paraphrased. Nothing escapes you. Everything does. *All stories are true*, as Achebe tells us the Igbo say. Reliable and unverifiable as dreams.

What could be viewed as a rather undignified squabble, an endless wrangling over our past, over what's dead and gone, bickering over the corpse of a dead man—who gets the head, the heart, the eyes, the penis, the gold teeth—is also a struggle to constitute the present, a present self and selves inseparable from the kind and quality of remembering we empower ourselves to imagine. In dreams responsibilities are assumed. A culture is a network of responsibilities, dynamic, willed, shared, sustained over time to create meaning, shape for individual lives. Du Bois said culture begins with a lie. A more benign word than *lie*, a word retaining the sense of illusion but emphasizing illusion's creativity, not its deceptive side, is *artifice*. Artifice (dreaming) makes artifacts: a self, a culture can begin with a vision of Malcolm as both seed and the fruit it wishes to produce.

This space of mourning and myth, then, is also and also and also (as Albert Murray might say) a magical space. A language appropriate to this terrain is required, language conducive, or at least not immune, to the conjuring properties words bear. Sound and sense. Sense and sound. What comes around goes around. Words spoken or written or said inside the mind have a life of their own, a history, a sensual reality. They are events in a specific time-space continuum, sense data, things perceived but also possessing properties beyond the penumbra of the perceiver. Qualities that allow them to be said or heard by others, simultaneously shared by the living and the dead, the writer and the reader, yesterday and tomorrow. We try to conventionalize words by embedding them in our discourse, attempt to tame them, make them conform, delimit, define. But words inherit minds and bodies of their own. Keep slipping and sliding away. Contain tensions, energies within themselves, that are volatile, contagious, responsive to conditions of extreme initial sensitivity the speaker/writer cannot predict or control. So utterance is compromise, approximation, and what a word brings to the dance often confounds its partner. Correspondences, dissonances, ruptures, healing, a primal, evocative power.

Metaphor, symbol, myth, rhythm, repetition, alliteration, rhyme that alludes to music's density and precision, are appropriate here in this space conjuring Malcolm. If these registers of language are absent in discussions of Malcolm, be suspicious, and doubly suspicious of languages and points of view that claim they don't speak in tongues. Such texts are not being candid, are engaging in misrepresentation, fashioning crude allegories even as they inveigh against those ways of writing they claim are unscientific. My goal is not the truth about Malcolm, but an understanding of how he has been used, could be used, and perhaps should be used to reconsider what passes for truth about him, ourselves, our culture, our country.

You are sitting in a room listening to a man talk and you wish to tell the story of the man's life, using as far as possible the words you are hearing to tell it. As writer you have multiple allegiances: to the man revealing himself to you; to the same man who will read and judge what you write; to an editor with an editor's agenda and maddening distance; to yourself, the demands of creating a text that meets your aesthetic standards, reflects your politics; to a potential publisher and reading public, etc., etc.

You are serving many masters, and inevitably you are compromised. The man speaks and you listen but you also take notes, the first compromise and perhaps betrayal. Your notes are intended to capture the words you hear, but they are also designed to compress, select, filter, discard. A net, no matter how closely woven, holds some things and loses others. One crucial dimension lost, like water pouring through the finest seine, is the flow in time of the man's speech, the sensuous environment of orality that at best is crudely approximated by written words.

You may attempt through various stylistic conventions and devices to reconstitute for the reader your experience of hearing face-to-face the man's words. The sound of the man's narration may be represented by vocabulary, syntax, imagery, graphic devices of various sorts—quotation marks, punctuation, line breaks, visual patterning of white space and black space, markers that encode print analogs to speech—vernacular interjections, parentheses, ellipses, asterisks, footnotes, italics, dashes . . . The drama of the encounter between yourself and the man may be enhanced by "stage directions" that set the scene and cue the reader to the hows and whys of what's being said.

> Visiting the Muslim restaurant in Harlem, I asked how I could meet Minister Malcolm X, who was pointed out talking in a telephone booth right behind me. Soon he came out, a gangling, tall reddish-brown-skinned fellow, at that time thirty-five years old; when my purpose was made known, he bristled, his eyes skewering me from behind horn-rimmed glasses. "You're another one of the white man's tools sent to spy!" he accused me sharply. (*Autobiography*, 383)

Imagine yourself in a hotel room late at night listening to a man whose life story you wish to write and perhaps you'll invent other means serving the end of representing the man's voice, his presence, ultimately his *meaning* on the page. Perhaps you'll begin to appreciate how intimately truth and technique are entangled.

What's striking about Alex Haley's *Autobiography of Malcolm X* is the peculiar absence of the sorts of narrative strategies listed above. Haley presents a "talking head," first-person narration recorded from the fixed perspective of a single video camera. With a few small and one very large exception to this rule—the Epilogue from which the quote above is drawn—what we get from first to last page of the *Autobiography* is one voice addressing us, an extended monologue, sermon rap, recollection in tranquility of the awesome variety and precipitous turnabouts of Malcolm's life. The enormous popular success of the autobiography (millions of copies sold and selling), the power and persistence of the image of Malcolm it achieves, makes it worthwhile to investigate how Haley does so much with so little fuss, how an approach that appears rudimentary in fact conceals sophisticated choices, quiet mastery of a medium.

First, what does the exception tell us about the rules? Though the Epilogue was written after Malcolm's death and focuses upon his assassination and its aftermath, it remains a record of life as much as death, a concrete manifestation of how a spirit transcends the physical body's passing if the spirit's force continues to touch those who loved it, or those who didn't love but can't forget its impact, its continuing presence. Appended to the *Autobiography*, the Epilogue in many reader's minds blends with Malcolm's story, becomes part of the "as told to," a further conversation between the writer and Malcolm, Malcolm and the reader in spite of the attempt of Malcolm's enemies to silence him.

Several new, important subjects are introduced in the Epilogue: the writer of the *Autobiography*, the process of constructing the book, the relationship between writer and subject. Haley utilizes a variety of narrative modes and devices in the Epilogue. He inserts himself into the story, describes how, where, and why Malcolm is speaking, Malcolm's appearance, state of mind. Haley quotes, summarizes, cites other sources for points of view on Malcolm, ventures his own analysis and opinions explicitly in first person. This mixed form of narrative exposition is handled quite adroitly. The Epilogue becomes an eloquent extension of the *Autobiography*, a gripping, dramatically structured fugue that impels the reader toward the climax of assassination, the inevitable slow shock of recognition afterward as the world assesses the loss of Malcolm. Nearly one-sixth of the *Autobiography* (74 pages out of 456—a four-page comment by Ossie Davis, a six-page Introduction by M. S. Handler complete the volume), the Epilogue is proof positive that Haley's choice of a "talking head" for the body of his book was not chosen because he couldn't compose in another fashion.

"Nothing can be in this book's manuscript that I didn't say, and nothing can be left out that I want in" (*Autobiography*, 387). Malcolm insisted this guarantee be part of the contract between Haley and himself. In return Haley received a pledge from Malcolm to "give me a priority quota of his time for the planned 100,000 word 'as told to' book," and later Haley asked for and tells us he received from Malcolm permission to write "comments of my own about him which would not be subject to his review." How Malcolm's death affected this bargain, what kind of book his final cut of the manuscript might have produced, we can only guess. We could have posed this question to Haley, but now he's gone too. However, the nature of writing biography or autobiography or any kind of writing means that Haley's promise to Malcolm, his intent to be a "dispassionate chronicler," is a matter of disguising, not removing, his authorial presence.

Allowing Malcolm to speak for himself meant constructing a text that *seems* to have no author (in a first draft I slipped and wrote "*no other*"), that *seems* to speak for itself without mediation. I've encountered many readers who experienced the book in just such a fashion, who were surprised when reminded of Alex Haley's role. Calling the book an autobiography is of course an explicit denial of an authorial presence and encourages this reaction in readers. Yet as we should have learned from Afro-American folklore or from novelists such as James Joyce who confess the secrets of their craft, effacing the self is also a way of empowering, enabling the self. If you're skillful enough at the sleight-of-hand of storytelling (witness Charles Chesnutt's "Uncle Julius"), you can disappear, charm your audience into forgetting you're there, behind and within the tale, manipulating your audience, silently paring your fingernails. Haley performs a double-dip, disappears twice. Once into Malcolm and again with Malcolm as Malcolm the monologist, oracular teacher/preacher, the bardic blues-man who knows there because he goes there, Malcolm the storyteller collapses distance between teller and tale, tale and audience.

In the *Autobiography* Malcolm's voice issues from no particular place, no particular body, no particular time. The locus of the voice is his mind, and of course the mind can routinely accomplish what the most sophisticated experiments in written narrative can only suggest and mimic: flashback, flashforward, a seamless flow/exchange between inner and outer worlds, great leaps from location to location, lightning switches between levels of diction and discourse, switches in verb tense, grammatical person, time-space elisions, characters bursting into a scene full blown, announcing, establishing their intricate histories, their physical appearance with a single word. So it's not exactly as if Haley has narrowed his options by situating and representing the *Autobiography* as the first-person flow of Malcolm's speech and thought. Haley grants Malcolm the tyrannical authority of an author, a disembodied speaker whose implied presence blends into the reader's imagining of the tale being told.

Physical descriptions the *Autobiography's* speaker offers of himself are "time capsules" scattered through the narrative, snapshots of how he appeared at various periods in his life, the boy with "reddish brown mariny color" of skin and hair, the conked teenager in zoot suit and knobby-toed shoes. The voice presently speaking is as generic as the business suits Malcolm X wore as a minister delivering the Honorable Elijah Muhammad's message. Yet the voice also gains a larger-than-life status as it gradually usurps our attention. We make up a body to match the deeds being described, a body substantiated by our participation, identification. No actor could ever match the image of the Lone Ranger I conjured as a kid listening to the masked man's adventures on the radio (who knows, part of the attraction, part of me may have been seeing part of him as black) so I never cared much for the disappointing version of the masked rider that eventually appeared in a TV series.

Haley's disappearance into Malcolm's voice permits readers to accomplish an analogous disappearing act. We open the boundaries of our identities, we're suspended, taken up to the higher ground of Malcolm's voice as a congregation is drawn into the crystal-clear parables and anecdotes of a righteous sermon. We recognize ourselves in what's being said. We amen it. Speaking for us as well as to us, the voice attains the godlike veracity and authority conventionally attributed to the third-person omniscient mode of history texts. The story becomes our story; we manufacture a presence to fill the space Haley seems to have left undefined, unoccupied. Of course some readers, fewer and fewer now, would bring living memories of Malcolm to their reading, and many would have seen photos or films, but these fragments don't alter the rhetorical design of the book and may even enhance it because the *Autobiography*'s omnipresence, its compelling version of its subject, continues to influence images of Malcolm preserved in other media.

Haley's choice of standard English for Malcolm's voice sustains the identification, the exchange between speaker and audience. Vernacular expressions, idiomatic, traditional formulas of African-American speech, occur infrequently in the *Autobiography*, and usually appear within quotes, italics, marked explicitly to indicate that the speaker is abandoning his chosen register. Conservative as the device of a talking head, the strategy of mainstreaming Malcolm's voice is just as quietly effective. The blandness of the language of the *Autobiography* invites the reader not to perform it, but ignore it. The choice of a particular black vernacular would have raised questions of class, as well as race, potentially divisive issues. Would Malcolm be speaking only *for* and *to* those people who speak like him? Would a publisher try to sell to predominantly white readers a book in which one black man addresses other black people in terms only partially comprehensible to the white audience? (How gender is implicated raises further issues that won't be addressed here.) Haley finesses potential problems by sticking to transparent, colorless dialect. Words in the *Autobiography* are cloaked in the same sort of invisibility as the author. Haley signals us to read the text as the events of a life, directly told to us by the person who lived it. Someone is talking to us. When we listen, the writing, like the narrator, disappears into the seemingly unmediated report. Haley's genius is to convince us to hear, not read.

Another advantage Haley gains by his choice of the standard English of TV announcers, textbooks, cereal boxes, and most bestsellers is the conspicuous absence of all but the most commonplace, inert, rudimentary figurative language. Attention is drawn to action, to what's being represented, not how it's represented (unless you stubbornly, peevishly insist on asking the latter, often very relevant question). The "personality" of the narrative voice is minimalized, its role as camera eye, objective chronicler, window on reality is enhanced. (Consider the reverse of this process, TV stations juicing up the inert "facts" of weather by foregrounding the "personality" of the weatherperson.) The narrator becomes an unintrusive "voice-over" in the movie the audience constructs from his relation of incidents. If not exactly infallible, the voice Haley fashions for Malcolm has the authority of a courtroom witness, well dressed, articulate, educated, intelligent, one whose account of his experience is seductive, can't be easily discredited or ignored. Another way of saying this is that particular registers of language contain very distinct shorthands or versions of reality, and what's being activated, confirmed when a speaker skillfully manipulates a given register is the world, the assumptions that consenting adults have agreed in advance constitute what's real. Tit for tat the speaker becomes real as he or she verifies the unspoken compact.

Finally, Haley's choice of a voice for Malcolm (himself), because it's designed to transparently reveal what actually happened, can neatly accommodate an audience whose first language may not be standard English. Most African-American readers, whatever registers of English they commonly speak, can amen the familiar people, places, and events of Malcolm's story, can identify with the content of Malcolm's experience, with someone who's been down and out, 'buked and scorned. Many would understand his immersion in the fast life, prison, his religious awakening, his outrage, his simmering frustration and anger toward the American way. The structure of Malcolm's discourse complements its content. The ideological core of the *Autobiography*, the interpretation and analysis of Malcolm's life, would be familiar and convincing to African Americans whose primary mode of communication is oral, not written because in the culture of sermons, blues, street-corner raps, the speaker offers his or her life (our life) as parable, illustration, example, reasoning concretely, directly from the personal to the archetypal, from common nuggets of experience to general principles. Speakers share experiences you share with them. His or her conclusions are seldom surprises. You're taken where you've been. But because nothing is ever exactly repeated, return is not simply repetition, but sometimes often revelation.

That's me he's talking about, singing about, praying about, insulting. Yes. Yes. I was there. It happens just that way, every day. Tell the truth.

Malcolm in the *Autobiography*, like Richard Wright before him in *Black Boy* or Frederick Douglass in the *Narrative*, becomes representative in all the complex, exciting self-reflexive senses of that word. Microcosm paralleling macrocosm, laws governing the molecules in my body replicated in the movements of galaxies, ontogeny reproducing phylogeny, Picasso's art passing through stages that mirror the development of western art in the twentieth century, Du Bois embodying in *The Souls of Black Folk* a multidisciplinary, multigenre, humanistic paradigm for African-American studies, a body dancing to the phases of the moon. Richard Wright was a black man born in rural Mississippi at the turn of the century who migrated to Chicago and learned the North was not the promised land. Wright's life reflects a people's passage from south to north, rural to urban, dependency to self-determination, illiteracy to literature, silence to assertion. The witness of Malcolm's life picks up and expands Wright's story, the terrible, destructive pressure of the industrial urban north on traditional black family life, the nearly inevitable adolescent rebellion and crime, imprisonment, the phoenix rise to consciousness, black consciousness, and political activity, discovery of spirituality in forms other than Christianity, the growing awareness of a larger context in which the oppression of African Americans is symptomatic of a global struggle, the struggle of the formerly enslaved, the colonized, the outcast, the dispossessed to seize responsibility, to forge personal identity and communal consciousness that will reverse centuries of subjugation, self-hate, a consciousness capable of opening doors through which healing, healthy people might walk unbowed. Richard Wright and El-Hajj Malik El-Shabazz, representative men whose lives recapitulate the general experience. Malcolm center stage at the podium, in charge of his story, proclaiming "I remember . . . I did thus and so . . . nothing is lost." A Malcolm created and re-created in the space Alex Haley has vacated so the reader may step in, identify, become.

> I still can't quite conceive him dead. It still feels to me as if he
> has just gone into some next chapter, to be written by historians.
> (*Autobiography*, 456)

What you're reading is in a sense my autobiography: words on paper about my life I'm writing in the form of opinions, analysis, attitudes I've developed about the *Autobiography*. And you, as you read are constructing the continuing story, I almost said fiction, of your life. What I'm writing could be used as evidence against me in some book about me that most likely will never be written. But suppose it might. And suppose you too are a character in it. Maybe you're the star, the book's the story of your life, unauthorized version, and your biographer decides to reveal that on such and such a day you sat down and read a piece about Malcolm by a writer named Wideman, then goes on to quote one or two of these sentences to prove (a) they are pretty silly, (b) you were silly to read them, (c) similar instances of silliness pepper your life and characterize a significant portion of it. Suppose further that you are pissed off by these allegations (facts?) and decide to set the record straight. You engage yourself in doing what I'm doing and talking about doing. You write the story of your life.

Would you mention me in your book. Would you feel compelled to deny my influence or quote a passage or two to demonstrate how enlightening, how entertaining and accurate my portrait of Malcolm really is. Would you attack the writer who used me to make you look silly. Would your attack keep the allegations alive even if you discredited them. If you ignored the fabricated incident, would other future biographers discover it and accuse you of a coverup.

All the above, except you and me and Malcolm, of course, is a figment of my imagination. So nothing's really at stake. It's a dream. Except it's a dream that could happen, has happened already, as dreams have a funny way of happening, in spite of the fact they don't.

The words we use to express ourselves have a limited utility when it comes to distinguishing among levels of reality, between fact and fiction, because words themselves are carriers of disease as much as they are a cure. Each word has a story to tell and tells it autobiographically. Each word, like any autobiography, is an impenetrable network of commission and omission. From mist-shrouded myths of origin onward, a word, like an autobiography, is compounded of fact, fiction, dream, the product of every usage, utterance, transcription, misuse, thought, loving embrace it's been subject to. We never know a word. Only a partial collection of the uses it's been put to. Part of the story is silence. The times it wasn't said, or forgotten or censored or substituted for, the invisible, inaudible history in all the mind caves where it just might be lurking but no one will ever know for sure. Word. Malcolm.

The recent Bruce Perry biography of Malcolm needs to be read against this background. Read as a work of fiction whose every word is suspect. Word by word what Perry constructs is an autobiography, the tale of his own life fashioned from bits and pieces of Malcolm his research has uncovered, discarded, found usable. Perry does not enter my space of myth and mourning. He has no stake in closing the circle, assembling a body for Malcolm consubstantial with his own, that lives and breathes without his intervention. Perry's satisfied with grabbing a piece of Malcolm and pinning it on his wall like a trophy, the stuffed head glorifying the hunter. Perry neither acknowledges nor dreams the basic human connection between Malcolm and himself, except as one-way traffic that verifies Perry's authority, Perry's prerogatives, Malcolm's failure or success in living up to standards Perry concocts and imposes.

Not so much a matter of determining who's right and who's wrong about the facts of Malcolm's life, but asking, in response to Perry's mode of inquiry, his revisionist portrait, what are the potential benefits of his approach and who benefits? Perry uses Malcolm to authenticate a universe with Perry and others like Perry at the center. Recall the recent spate of movies that employ ostensibly "black" subjects to validate white humanity. *Cry Freedom, Mississippi Burning, A World Apart, Mean Season.* (*Dances with Wolves*, a red/white variant.)

Perry's biography is subtitled: *The Life of a Man Who Changed Black America.* You don't need to read any further to understand how Malcolm's life is going to be used—to drag him and us backward into an America that depends on discredited assumptions about race, class, and gender, a version of the world where black/white, male/female, separation/integration, and countless other either/ors act as fixed, essentialist categories into which people and experience must be sorted. Backward into the burning building. And sure enough, Perry asks if Malcolm is black or white, is he masculine or feminine, does he advocate integration or separation, love or hate, does he tell the truth or lie, are his eyes brown or green. The notion that white America and black America are separate places, the idea that a man could change one without changing the other, are variations of what Martin Bernal calls the Aryan Model, a nineteenth-century construct, romantic and racist, of the origins of Western Civilization that denies the African and Semitic roots of classic Greek culture and perpetuates the exclusion of blacks and Jews from full membership in the human family. Perry embeds Malcolm's life in historical and psychological fictions that smother felt life, reify the dead letter of theory, generate a fakelore to substantiate a cultural framework that simultaneously imprisons and excludes.

Malcolm bursts out of the frame, signals the failure of the frame to offer remedies for prejudice and oppression. Integration and segregation for instance are functionally equivalent options for Afro-American people since both concepts are hopelessly mired in, determined by bankrupt assumptions of race. Malcolm peeped the dominant group's hole card—in either a segregated or integrated society, the value of his life, African-American life, is decided by somebody else. If one group retains all political, economic, and myth-making power in its hands, those who live beside or among the dominant group have no rights the dominant group is bound to respect. In this context civil rights, equal opportunity, integration are empty formulations, illusions dependent on the same tired, twisted assumptions about race that created this mess we're in. Malcolm came to realize his life was always being measured against some other kind of life, and he understood the danger, the unmanliness, the hopelessness of such a no-win condition. So he burst the frame. Proclaimed: It's how I see them, not how they see me, that counts. I am viewer as well as viewed. Starting with myself at the center, I can generate a coherent, operative sense of being, of the world, at least as well, probably better than anybody else. I forfeit my life when I allow its value to be determined by somebody else, especially a somebody else motivated by their own interests, a somebody else (probably white) whose interests often conflict with mine, somebody not prepared to give up one iota for me to get my fair share, a somebody whose willingness to exercise any means possible, including enslavement and murder, to retain power has been conclusively documented for centuries.

What Malcolm is saying from the beginning to the end of his life, in ways progressively more conscious, humane, and sophisticated—rebel, outlaw, Muslim, Pan-Africanist, citizen of the world—is that he wants out. Out of the trick bag of dead-end ideas, a frame distorting and destroying the natural urge for self-determination, even as the urge is formulated in a language weighted to befuddle African-American aspirations. So he wants out. Forget integration or segregation. Out. And that's the freeing power of his example, its witness, its disruptive, revolutionary threat. Out. Out and gone. Malcolm delivers to the reigning elites of the sixties a message as absolute as the message runaway slaves delivered to Ole Massa. Except Malcolm wasn't running, and his direction was not "away" but toward a future, a center we're still struggling to glimpse.

The loss of Malcolm, his murder and martyrdom, our mourning clarify an emptiness at the center of my sense of myself as part of a culture. I belong to, belong with Malcolm wherever he was going. He never made it. Perhaps no one ever does. But he went on his way and left us behind. Words are one way of setting off to rediscover him, of picking up the pieces, of envisioning the myth, the mythical space engendered by identification, longing, the dream landscape the heart comprehends.

The work of Perry and others is to seal the rupture Malcolm created, restore business as usual. But the damage is past fixing, an emptiness remains in the center, an absence some of us are seeking not so much to fill as to understand. We know Malcolm is part of what we need to understand because through him we experience the bitter, bitter pain of loss, a personal loss and the hard recognition that the search for a center, for self-determination, requires a willingness to risk our lives, requires discipline, constant vigilance of body and spirit that exacts the best of us.

Bird man. Malcolm knew that much and not much more about the name. Audubon. All those years reading, reading, reading in his cell, then on the road, his briefcase stuffed with books. A hunger to know everything from *A* to *Z* and here he was, eyes bad, getting old already, and if the grim brothers and pale-faced spooks had their way, probably not going to grow much older and Audubon an *A*. Still at the beginning. Always starting over. If you knew the stories behind Harlem's place names, its people's names, you would understand its history better, yourself better. *Its.* Harlem's not an it. Surely a she. A sad-eyed, brown-skinned, big-breasted, skinny-ankled, hourglass-hipped woman who might be your elegant grandma, your tough baby sister, too much gold dangle and makeup and skirt way too tight for her own good dressed up and heading out to places where you both know she shouldn't be hanging. Would he have to rescue her. Would she come for him when he's cut down in some faraway land. In Africa would she gather you up in her arms and cradle your bloody head and sing you to the next place, *A* to *Z*. In Africa her name would not be Harlem. A blacker name like those carved in picture-writing on the jewelry of dead queens and kings, on the stones of the pyramids and temples, the statues of thick-lipped, snub-nosed gods. Would she go that far to find him and bring him home again. Home to these cities, to this wreckage of lives lost and torn apart and smoldering under tons of something too rotten, too evil to name. To this Audubon Ballroom on February 21, 1965, Harlem, New York. And if she found him and opened her arms to him would they really want to return. Here. The row of chairs he'd helped Sara Mitchell set out on stage. Empty chairs because the brothers he'd counted on to fill them had copped out. Was his brown-skinned Harlem angel already on stage, waiting invisible, occupying one of those chairs beside the microphone. Empty chairs an embarrassment, rebuke, warning, a reminder to the audience of what could have been, should be, the speaker flanked by stalwart brothers and sisters lending their weight, their support, putting their bodies on the line so he's not naked on the naked stage, so his body and theirs are one, clothing him, the flesh behind his words. But in less than a minute now, he'd leave the anteroom, face alone the ones who've come this Sunday afternoon to listen. Does he hear a whispering of wings out there. He smiles to himself thinking of the faces that will greet him on the other side of the flimsy anteroom door. He's proud and happy and gets the rise he always does, the charge of energy as he grows larger, fuller, wiser than himself, anticipating *As salaam alaikum, Wa alaikum as salaam,* the call and response, the chorus as excited as he is to begin, to transform what they feel, what they need him to say into a kind of chant, prayer, lesson, battle cry. And the bitter, galling ironic edge to his smile, the tight-lipped part that's steel and sneer and tastes like death, the knowledge that his enemies are sitting in the auditorium too, biding their time, waiting for him to slip, prepared to push him over the edge if he doesn't slip, cops in uniform, undercover cops, CIA, FBI, initials from *A* to *Z* standing for every nasty species of back alley, backstabbing surveillance and sabotage some smooth-faced, soft-handed assassin in a coat and tie in a clean office somewhere can dream up. Yes. They'll be out there to greet him too. His people. And he almost laughs out loud as he imagines the agent scared shitless who leaps out of his chair when the first shots are fired and hugs the Audubon's floorboards a million Harlem feet have danced smooth and black. The government agent who wastes the public's money filing his worm's-eye-view of what transpired on February 25, 1965:

> At this time a Negro male, wearing a three-quarter length black leather coat, pushed his chair back, stood up, and said to the Negro male sitting on his left "Get your hand out of my pocket."

> The Negro male who stood up was very dark complected, slender build, about 5'10" tall, weighing 160 pounds, age in the late twenties, lean face, with medium length straight hair.

> This man pushed his coat back and produced an object which looked to be metallic and raised his arm. At this point people from the audience, which consisted of about four hundred individuals, began jumping to their feet. Malcolm X told everyone to "take it easy."

> . . . four gunshots . . . were fired in rapid order.[1]

From that moment on the agent lying on the floor "could furnish no further information regarding the murder of Malcolm X." His view is restricted to what's below people's waists, undecipherable hieroglyphics, "the hands appeared to be those of a light-skinned Negro. This man wore brown or Cordovan-colored shoes and had medium-sized feet."[2]

The scene flashes across Malcolm's mind, consumes less than one of the seconds remaining before he leaves for the Audubon's stage. Benjamin X has primed the crowd. His voice rising and falling in those old-time religion cadences that summon spirits, harangue and levitate the congregation, a language Benjamin X will not permit his listeners to pretend they've forgotten.

Here is a man who would give his life for you.

Malcolm rubs his hands together. Color. Sweat. Blood. Pumps himself up again to answer the call. Words. Names. Audubon. Harlem. Malcolm Little. Detroit Red. Malcolm X. As he strides to the rostrum El-Hajj Malik El-Shabazz rehearses the greeting, natural to him now as the drawing in, the expelling of breath, *As salaam alaikum.*

EPILOGUE

Across the land *X*s are sprouting on people's caps. One hopes the *X* on the outside reflects activity inside the hats. When Alex Haley spoke for the time to the man who was born Malcolm Little, the man's name had become El-Hajj Malik El-Shabazz. The man had suffered the birth and death of Malcolm X, and had gone on to another name, another meta-morphosis. X, after all, signified something lost, missing, mourned. Malcolm X was an identity the man had painfully wrought for him-self and just as painfully unraveled and shed. And it's that story that Alex Haley presents to us, the story of Malcolm X who was shot dead in the Audubon Ballroom. El-Hajj Malik El-Shabazz had already split, left Malcolm X behind, was on his way somewhere else. A new story beginning . . .

Remember the movie *Viva Zapata*, the last scene when Zapata's horse, which has miraculously escaped an ambush, looks down from higher ground at the crowd gathering around its fallen rider. As govern-ment soldiers and their officers examine the rider they've shot to bloody pieces, the peasants whose rebellion Zapata led begin to quietly pass the word from mouth to ear to mouth, whispering, "That's not him, uh-uh, not our leader. No. Shit no. Not him they've shot. That bloody mess is not him."

Silhouetted against the sky the stallion rears up on its hind legs, then gallops off, bearing its invisible rider to the sanctity of the mountains, free, strong, always there when we need him, when we're ready to seek him out. El-Hajj Malik El-Shabazz.

NOTES

1. Clayborne Carson, ed., *Malcolm X: The FBI File* (New York: Carroll & Graf, 1991), 372.

2. Ibid., 373.

PREFACE:
THE HOMEWOOD BOOKS

1992

The publication of *The Homewood Books* by the University of Pittsburgh Press is a special event for me. For various reasons, including the lack of enthusiastic offers from major hardback publishers and my rather naive hope that lower prices and softcovers might entice a larger black readership, *Hiding Place* (1981), *Damballah* (1981), and *Sent for You Yesterday* (1983) were originally issued in paperback. This strategy failed to produce the explosion in sales I'd wished for, yet some pleasant surprises did occur. *Hiding Place* and *Damballah* broke ground for new fiction in paperback by being reviewed in *The New York Times Book Review*. *Sent for You Yesterday* won the PEN/Faulkner Award, surprising, even embarrassing Avon Books, since they hadn't bothered to submit my novel for the competition. Avon's attempt to cash in and catch up with the sudden notoriety of novel and novelist resulted in publication of *The Homewood Trilogy*, a fat paperback containing all three Homewood books. Editions in various formats have followed here and abroad, but none in this country in hardback.

Hard covers lend an air of permanence, as does university press publication. I welcome that illusion but appreciate much more a kind of symmetry, a sense of coming home. On elementary school trips to the natural history museum, or Shadyside Boys Club knot-hole gang excursions to

Forbes Field to watch the Pirates lose, or just trundling through the Oak-land section by trolley or bus on the way to "dahn tahn" Pittsburgh, I'd be struck by the looming silhouette of Pitt's Cathedral of Learning. Though I had passed it countless times, this gray eminence, visible on a clear day even from the heights of Brushton Hill in Homewood, remained as mys-terious, unreachable, and irrelevant to my life as the fabled churches and monuments of Europe I'd encountered only in pictures.

So it feels right that the University of Pittsburgh is now undertaking the job of presenting and preserving my fiction. We've been neighbors a long time. And it's about time to acknowledge we share a city. Whatever else that city is, it is also a project of communal imagination, a vision we are responsible for dreaming and redreaming, a project we will under-stand better as we stretch it and reshape it to embrace the views from Homewood.

Expediency was the main reason the three Homewood books were first issued in a single volume, but there are other grounds for publish-ing them together. The books are linked by shared characters, events, and, of course, locales. The fictionalized black community Homewood that grows resolutely under the uneasy eyes of its white neighbors is an embodiment of the deeds, words, ancestors, and offspring of John French. Deeper patterns of structure, theme, and language also serve as unifying devices. Music, for instance, is a dominant, organic metaphor. Albert Wilkes, of *Sent for You Yesterday*, is a piano player, and Doot, the narrator of that novel, discovers truths about himself and his history by learning to dance. Lives of individual singers such as Reba Love Jackson, song as a magical mode of storytelling, storytelling as a means by which values can be transmitted and sustained are explored in the tales of *Dam-ballah*. Tommy's music and the music of Bess, the songs they sing, hum, whistle, remember, and yearn for, the contrasting rhythms of their voices render the counterpoint of *Hiding Place*.

The three books offer a continuous investigation, from many angles, not so much of a physical location, Homewood, the actual African-American community in Pittsburgh where I was raised, but of a culture, a way of seeing and being seen. *Homewood* is an idea, a reflection of how its inhabitants act and think. The books, if successful, should mirror the characters' inner lives, their sense of themselves as spiritual beings in a world where boundaries are not defined by racial stereotypes or socioeconomic statistics.

The value of black life in America is judged, as life generally in this country is judged, by external, material signs of success. Urban ghettoes are dangerous, broken-down, economically marginal pockets of real estate infected with drugs, poverty, violence, crime, and since black life is seen as rooted in the ghetto, black people are identified with the ugliness, danger, and deterioration surrounding them. This logic is simple-minded and devastating, its hold on the American imagination as old as slavery; in fact, it recycles the classic justification for slavery, blaming the cause and consequences of oppression on the oppressed. Instead of launching a preemptive strike at the flawed assumptions that perpetuate racist thinking, blacks and whites are doomed to battle endlessly with the symptoms of racism.

In these three books again bound as one I have set myself to the task of making concrete those invisible planes of existence that bear witness to the fact that black life, for all its material impoverishment, continues to thrive, to generate alternative styles, redemptive strategies, people who hope and cope. But more than attempting to prove a "humanity," which should be self-evident anyway to those not blinded by racism, my goal is to celebrate and affirm. *Where did I come from? Who am I? Where am I going?* These unanswerable questions—the mysteries of identity and fate they address—are what I wish to investigate.

The gathering and rounding this volume represents may be clarified with a few remarks about the way these works were composed. Parts of *Damballah*, a collection of related stories, were written first. As I drafted and redrafted individual stories, I found myself not really finishing them so much as stopping work on one so I could get on with another. No matter how I tinkered and crafted the material, more needed to be said. The short story form felt too exclusive. Good stories need to stand on their own feet, and mine seemed to require their neighbors. Part of the problem was coming to terms with the vastness, the intimidating nature of the project I'd undertaken.

By 1973 I'd published three novels. It was hard to admit to myself that I'd just begun learning how to write—that whole regions of my experience, the core of African-American language and culture that nurtured me, had been barely touched by my writing up to that point. If a writer's lucky, the learning process never stops, and writing continues to be a tool for discovery. The early versions of the stories which eventually engendered *Damballah* were my way of returning to basics, my attempt to forge a new language for talking about the places I'd been, the people important to me.

My grandmother Freeda French died in 1973. I'd just begun teaching at the University of Wyoming, and the news of her death both emphasized and collapsed the two thousand miles separating Laramie from Pittsburgh. The trip home with my wife and children for my grandmother's funeral was the beginning of these three books. As family and friends sat late into the night, fueled by drink, food, talk, by sadness and bitter loss, by the healing presence of others who shared our grief and our history, the stories of Homewood's beginnings were told, stories I'd been hearing all my life without understanding, until those charged moments, their resonance, their possibilities for written literature. I've been building upon those tales ever since—not only the striking, mysterious, outrageous particulars, but the imperative suffered and passed on—that such rituals, such tellings must survive if we as a people are to survive.

It became clear to me on those nights in Pittsburgh in 1973 that I needn't look any further than the place I was born and the people who'd loved me to find what was significant and lasting in literature. My university training had both thwarted and prepared this understanding, and the tension of multiple traditions, European and African-American, the Academy and the Street, animates these texts.

That the books be read in the sequence arranged here is a suggestion, not an order. Tales in *Damballah*, "The Watermelon Story" for example, were written at the same time as late drafts of *Sent for You Yesterday*. *Hiding Place* in its first compressed essence found its way into the story collection. Sections of *Sent for You Yesterday* evolved during the period the earliest Homewood stories were being put on paper. The simple fact is that I wrote three books simultaneously. They jostled, bumped, merged, and teased each other into existence. As writer, part of the artistic problem was untangling the strands, cutting the cords so individual stories could be separated without killing the vast, unruly organism pulsing in my imagination.

I intend motion and resonance of various kinds, from the small scale of the shortest stories to the longest sustained narrative. Do not look for straightforward, linear steps from book to book. Think, rather, of circles within circles within circles, a stone dropped into a still pool, ripples and wave motion. Or imagine the Great Time of our African ancestors, a nonlinear, atemporal medium in which all things that ever *have been*, *are*, or *will be* mingle freely, the space that allows us to bump into relatives long dead or absent friends or children unborn as easily, as significantly, as we encounter the people in our daily lives. By the time I had published the first two books in this sequence, I had discovered and refined the narrative voice that creates the third. I believe I came to know that voice better, that I could be both more sure-handed and daring with it. So the careful reader can watch/listen for those kinds of stylistic progression.

Another species of movement which I hope results in a resolution of sorts is the gradual unfolding of the narrator's character, the Doot who finally essays his dance at the conclusion of the trilogy. If the books achieve unity, Doot's presence in all of them should become apparent. While he's been humming the music, writing the stories, they've been making him. His/my voice is inseparable from the Homewood voices I've been hearing since my ears and eyes opened. As the Swan Silvertones chant in their version of "Blessed Assurance," *This is my story, this is my song.*

FATHER STORIES

1994

One day neither in the past nor in the future, and not at this moment, either, all the people gathered on a high ridge that overlooked the rolling plain of earth, its forests, deserts, rivers unscrolling below them like a painting on parchment. Then the people began speaking, one by one, telling the story of a life—everything seen, heard, and felt by each soul. As the voices dreamed, a vast, bluish mist enveloped the land and the seas below. Nothing was visible. It was as if the solid earth had evaporated. Now there was nothing but the voices and the stories and the mist; and the people were afraid to stop the storytelling and afraid not to stop, because no one knew where the earth had gone.

Finally, when only a few storytellers remained to take a turn, someone shouted: Stop! Enough, enough of this talk! Enough of us have spoken! We must find the earth again!

Suddenly, the mist cleared. Below the people, the earth had changed. It had grown into the shape of the stories they'd told—a shape as wondrous and new and real as the words they'd spoken. But it was also a world unfinished, because not all the stories had been told.

Some say that death and evil entered the world because some of the people had no chance to speak. Some say that the world would be worse than it is if all the stories had been told. Some say that there are no more stories to tell. Some believe that untold stories are the only ones of value and we are lost when they are lost. Some are certain that the storytelling never stops; and this is one more story, and the earth always lies under its blanket of mist being born.

I begin again because I don't want it to end. I mean all these father stories that take us back, that bring us here, where you are, where I am, needing to make sense, to go on if we can and should.

Once, when you were five or six, all the keys to the camp vehicles disappeared. Keys for trucks, vans, rental cars, a school bus, a tractor, boats—the whole fleet necessary each summer to service the business of offering four hundred boys an eight-week escape in the Maine woods. In the innocence of the oasis that your grandfather had created—this gift of water, trees, a world apart—nobody bothered to lock things; keys were routinely left in the ignition for the next driver. Then, one day, the keys were gone. For hours, everybody searched high and low. I thought of you as I climbed into the cab of the dump truck to check for a key that might have fallen to the floor or slipped into some crevice or corner of the raw, gasoline-reeking interior. You because countless times I'd hoisted you into the cab, tucked you in the driver's seat. Nothing you enjoyed more than turning a steering wheel, roaring and vrooming engine noise while you whipped the wheel back and forth, negotiating some endless, dramatic highway only you could see. You were fascinated by that imaginary road and the wheels that rolled you there. Even before you could talk, you'd flip your toy trucks and cars on their sides or upside down so you could spin the wheels, growl motor noise.

You never admitted taking the keys, and nobody pressed you very hard after they were found, in a heap in the sand under the boat dock. But, years later, Junie, the head caretaker, mentioned that he'd seen you making your usual early-morning rounds from vehicle to vehicle the day the keys were missing, and confided to me a suspicion he had felt then but had kept to himself till you were gone and were unlikely to return for a long time. Turns out your grandfather had been suspicious, too. He didn't miss much that happened in the camp, either, and had observed what Junie had observed. I recall being rather annoyed when your grandfather suggested that I ask you if you might have noticed keys anywhere the day they disappeared. Annoyed and amazed, because you were hardly more than a baby. No reason for you to bother the keys. I'd instructed you never to touch them, and that was one of the conditions you'd promised to honor in return for the privilege of installing yourself behind steering wheels. I trusted you. Questioning my trust insulted us both. Besides, the missing keys implied a plot, a prank, sabotage, some scheme premeditated and methodically perpetrated by older campers or adults, and you were just a kid. You were my son. His grandson. So he gently hinted I might casually check with you, not because you were a suspect but because you had access and had been noticed at the scene, and so perhaps might be able to assist the searchers with a clue.

I don't remember your grandfather's ever mentioning the keys again until we'd lost you and all of us were searching once more for answers. And, since each of us had then begun to understand that answers were not around us, not in the air, and not exclusively in you, but inside us all, when your grandfather repeated ten years later his suspicions about the keys, it sounded almost like a confession, and we both understood that some searches never end.

A small army of adults, stymied, frustrated, turning the camp inside out. A couple of hours of mass confusion, pockets, drawers, memories rifled, conspiracy theories floated, paranoia blossoming, numb searches and re-searches. Minor panic when duplicate keys weren't stashed where they should be; righteous indignation and scapegoating; the buzz, the edge for weeks afterward whenever keys were mentioned, picked up, or set down in the camp office. The morning of the lost keys became one of those incidents, significant or not in themselves, that lend a name, a tone to a whole camp season: the summer of baby goats in the nature lodge, the hurricane summer, the summer a boy was lost for a night on Mount Katahdin, the summer you-remember-who bit your grandfather's finger, the summer two counselors from a boys' camp nearby were killed in a high-speed crash late at night, the summer the Israeli nurses swam topless, the summer you left and never returned.

If you'd ambled up on your short, chunky legs and handed me the lost keys, it wouldn't have convinced me you'd taken them. Nor would a confession have convinced me. Nothing you might have said or done could have solved the mystery of the keys. No accident or coincidence would have implicated you. Without a reason, with no motive, no *why*, the idea of your removing the keys remained unthinkable.

You were blond then. Huge brown eyes. Hair on your head of many kinds, a storm, a multiculture of textures: kinky, dead straight, curly, frizzy, ringlets; hair thick in places, sparse in others. All your people, on both sides of the family, ecumenically represented in the golden crown atop your head.

You cried huge tears, too. Heartbreaking, slow, sliding tears that formed gradually in the corners of your dark eyes—gleaming, shapely tears before they collapsed and inched down your cheeks. Big tears, but you cried quietly, almost privately, even though the proof of your unhappiness was smearing your face. Then again, when you needed to, you could bellow and hoot—honking Coltrane explorations of anger, temper, outrage. Most of the time, however, you cried softly, your sobs pinched off by deep, heaving sighs, with a rare, high-pitched, keening wail escaping in spite of whatever was disciplining you to wrap your sorrow so close to yourself.

I'm remembering things in no order, with no plan. These father stories. Because that's all they are.

Your mother said that the story she wishes she could write, but knows is so painful she hesitates to tell it to herself, would be about her, of course, and you, yes, but also about her father, your grandfather: what he built, who he was, his long, special life, how many other lives he touched, the place he created out of nothing, in the woods, along the lake that I'm watching this morning, and that watches me as I write.

It is her father she has returned to all these summers in Maine. What he provided, no strings attached. His gift of water, trees, weather, a world apart, full of surprise, a world unchanging. Summers in Maine were the stable, rooted part of her.

One morning, as I sit on the dock staring at the lake, a man and a boy float past in a small boat. They have turned off the putt-putt outboard motor hanging over the stern and are drifting in closer to the rocky shoreline, casting their fishing lines where the water is blackish green from shadows of tall pines lining the lake. A wake spreads languidly behind the boat, one wing plowing the dark water, its twin unfurling like a bright flag dragged across the surface. No sound except birdsong, the hiss of a fishing line arcing away from the boat, then its plopping like a coin in the bottom of a well. The weather has changed overnight. Wind from the west this morning—a cooling, drying wind lifting the mist before dawn, turning the sky unwaveringly blue at this early hour. A wind shunting away last week's mugginess and humidity, though it barely ruffles the skin of the water in this inlet. Gray bands of different shades and textures stripe the lake's center, panels of a fan lazily unfolding, closing, opening. Later, the west wind will perk up and bring chill gusts, stir a chop into the water. Smooth and quiet now for the man and the boy hunkered down in their boat. They wear baseball caps, layers of shirts and jackets, the same bulky shape twice; one form is larger than the other, and each is a slightly different color, but otherwise the two are identical, down to the way their wrists snap, their lines arc up and away from the boat. The man's lure lands farther away than the boy's each time, in scale with the hunched figures drifting past in the boat.

I will see the boat again, about an hour later, when the water is louder, when ripples driven from the west are forming scalloped waves. The boy, alone then, whips the boat full throttle in tight, spray-sluicing circles, around and around, gouging deep furrows. The nose of the boat high in the air, he hunches over the screaming engine, gunning it in short, sprinting bursts, then in sharp turns, around and around, as if he were trying to escape a swarm of hornets.

The wind is forgetting it's July. I wish for extra insulation under my hooded sweatshirt and nylon windbreaker. Trees are a baffle for the wind and conjure its sound into colder, stronger, arctic messages shuttling through the upper atmosphere. In the same way, your mother's hair when it's long and loose, catching all the colors of light, falling down around her bare shoulders, carries within itself that wind rush of surf crashing far away, the muffled roar of a crowd in a vast, distant stadium.

You'd twist thick clumps of her chestnut hair in your fist, clutch it while she held you and you sucked the thumb of your other hand. For hours. For hours if she'd let you.

Maybe all things happen, including ourselves, long before we see, hear, know they are happening. Memory, then, isn't so much archival as it is a seeking of vitality, harmony, an evocation of a truer, more nearly complete present tense. All of this, of course, relates to personality— the construction of a continuous narrative of self. Our stories. Father stories.

Do you remember your fear of leaves? Of course you do. The teasers in our family would never let you forget.

Once, in Laramie, Wyoming, after dinner, just as a full-moon night was falling and the wide, straight-arrow streets were as empty and still as Long Lake at dawn, I was riding you on my shoulders—a rare moment, the two of us together, away from your mother and brother—when, suddenly, you cried out. The street we were on had a ceiling. Branches from trees planted in people's yards hung over fences lining the sidewalk, forming a canopy overhead. I panicked. Thought I'd knocked you against a low branch or you'd got your hair tangled—or, worse, been scratched in the eye or the face. Your fingers dug into my scalp. You didn't want to let go as I tried to unseat you from my shoulders, slide you down into the light from a street lamp to see what was the matter.

You'd given me a couple of good yanks, so I was both mad and scared when I finally pulled you down, cradling you in my arms to get a clear look at your face.

No tears. No visible damage. Yet you were wild-eyed, trembling uncontrollably. The leaves had been after you. Probably not touching you but, worse, a blanket of quivering, rustling, mottled dread suddenly hovering above you. Surrounding you, rendering you speechless. Terrorized beyond words or tears, you'd gripped my hair and kicked my chest. I'd thought you were roughing me up because you wanted to play. Grabbed your wrists and squeezed them tight to hold you as I galloped down the quiet Laramie street, doing my best imitation of the bucking bronco on Wyoming license plates. You were rendered even more helpless with your hands clamped in mine, struggling to free yourself while I thought we were having fun. Your father snorting and braying, jiggedy-jig, jiggedy-jig, suddenly in league with your worst enemy, and nowhere to run, nowhere to hide—he was rushing you to your doom. No wonder your fingers tried to rip my hair out when I released your wrists. Holding on, reining me in, pounding on my skull, fighting back the only way you knew how, short of pitching yourself down from a dizzying height, down, down to the pavement, itself strewn with shadowy leaves.

When I was a kid, I harbored a morbid fear of feathers. Feathers. Not a single feather or a few loose feathers, like the ones I'd stick in my naps to play Indian, but feathers in a bunch, attached to birds who could wriggle them, flutter them, transform them into loose flesh, rotting, molting, the unnatural sign of death-in-life and life-in-death, the zombie, mummy, decaying corpses of movies and my nightmares. Feathers a kind of squirmy skin hanging off the bone, all the more horrible because feathers seemed both dry and sticky with blood. My feathers, your leaves. One afternoon at the Belmar on Homewood Avenue, in Pittsburgh, in one of those Bible-days epic movies, a man was tortured nearly to death, his bloody body flung off a fortress wall. He landed on a heap of corpses in a ditch. As the camera pans the mangled bodies, the sound of huge wings beating thumps through the Belmar's crackly speakers. After the Technicolor glare of carnage under a desert sun, the camera is blinded an instant by the black swoop of vultures. They land atop the corpses, feathers rippling, glinting as the birds begin their slow-motion, ponderously delicate lope toward the choicest morsels of meat—eyeballs, tongues, exposed guts—toward the not-quite-dead-yet man sprawled on a bed of other victims.

Then a close-up of the man's face. As he spots the vultures and screams, I scream. I know I did. Even though I couldn't hear myself, because everybody in the Belmar joined in one shrieking whoop of fear and disgust. And I never forgot the scene. Never. Never forgot, never forgave. Hated pigeons. They became my scapegoats, or scapebirds. I'd hurt them any chance I got. Trapped one in a box and tormented it. Fully intended to incinerate the crippled one who wound up on the stone steps in the hallway of my dorm freshman year until my roommate shamed me out of it when I asked to borrow his lighter and some fluid and he demanded to know for what.

Pigeons were brown and dirty. They shat everywhere. Spoiled things. Their cooing from the eaves of our roof on Finance Street could startle you awake. They sneaked around, hid in dark corners, carried disease, like rats. Far too many of the useless creatures. I focussed my fear and hate of feathers on them. Went out of my way to cause them difficulties.

Once, I was so angry at your mother's pain I thought I was angry at her. She was sharing out loud for the first time how torn apart she'd felt that summer you never came back. How she feared her father's gift had been blighted forever. Woods, lake, sky a mirror reflecting absence of father, absence of son, the presence of her grief.

I couldn't deal with the pain in her voice, so I made up another story. Presumed to tell her she was letting her pain exclude other ways of trying to make sense, with words, with stories, with the facts as given and the facts as felt, make sense of the enormity of what happens and doesn't happen, the glimmers of it we paste together trying to find peace. One different story would be the day she meets her father again in this place and what he might have to say to her and why he needed to see her and what he might remind her of and why it would need to be here, on a path through the thick pine woods where light can surprise you, penetrating in smoky shafts where it has no business being, where it sparkles, then shifts instantly, gone faster than the noises of creatures in the underbrush you never see. I make up her father, as I'm making up mine. Her father appearing to her in a suit of lights because that, too, could transpire, could redeem, could set us straight in a world where you never know what's going to happen next and often what happens is bad, is crushing, but it's never the worst thing, never the best, it's only the last thing, and not even exactly that, except once, and even then death is not exactly the last thing that happens, because you never know what's going to happen next. For better or worse, cursed and blessed by this ignorance, we invent, fill it, are born with the gift, the need, the weight of filling it with our imaginings. That are somehow as real as we are. Our mothers and fathers and children. Our stories.

I hope this is not a hard day for you. I hope you can muster peace within yourself and deal with the memories, the horrors of the past eight years. It must strike you as strange—as strange as it strikes me—that eight years have passed already. I remember a few days after hearing you were missing and a boy was found dead in the room the two of you had been sharing, I remember walking down toward the lake to be alone, because I felt myself coming apart: the mask I'd been wearing, as much for myself as for the benefit of other people, was beginning to splinter. I could hear ice cracking, great rents and seams breaking my face into pieces, carrying away chunks of numb flesh. I found myself on my knees, praying to a tree. In the middle of some absurdly compelling ritual that I'd forgotten I carried the memory of. Yet there I was on my knees, digging my fingers into the loose soil, grabbing up handfuls, sinking my face into the clawed earth as if it might heal me. Speaking to the roots of a pine tree as if its shaft might carry my message up to the sky, send it on its way to wherever I thought my anguish should be addressed.

I was praying to join you. Offering myself in exchange for you. Take me. Take me. Free my son from the terrible things happening to him. Take me in his place. Let them happen to me. I was afraid you were dying or already dead or suffering unspeakable tortures at the hands of a demon kidnapper. The tears I'd held back were flowing finally, a flood that brought none of the relief I must have believed that hoarding them would earn me when I let go at last. Just wetness burning, clouding my eyes. I couldn't will the spirit out of my body into the high branches of that tree. What felt familiar, felt like prayers beside my bed as a child, or church people moaning in the amen corner, or my mother weeping and whispering *hold on, hold on* to herself as she rocks side to side and mourns, or some naked priest chanting and climbing toward the light on a bloody ladder inside his chest—these memories of what might have been visions of holiness could not change the simple facts. I was a man who had most likely lost his son, and hugging trees and burying his face in dirt and crying for help till breath slunk out of his body wouldn't change a thing.

A desperate, private moment, one of thousands I could force myself to dredge up if I believed it might serve some purpose. I share that one example with you to say that the eight years have not passed quickly. The years are countless moments, many as intense as this one I'm describing to you, moments I conceal from myself as I've hidden them from other people. Other moments, also countless, when terrible things had to be shared, spoken aloud, in phone calls with lawyers, depositions, interviews, conferences, in the endless conversations with your mother. Literally endless, because often the other business of our lives would seem merely a digression from the dialogue with you, about you. A love story finally, love of you, your brother and sister, since no word except love makes sense of the ever-present narrative our days unfold.

Time can drag like a long string, studded and barbed, through a fresh wound, so it hasn't gone quickly. The moment-to-moment, day-by-day struggles imprint my flesh. But the eight years are also a miracle, a blink of the eye through which I watch myself wending my way from there to here. In this vast house of our fathers and mothers.

Your mother didn't need my words or images to work out her grief. She needed time. Took the time she needed to slowly, gradually, painstakingly unravel feelings knotted in what seemed for a while a hopeless tangle. No choice, really. She's who she is. Can give nothing less than her whole heart to you, to this place, inseparable from all our lives, that her father, your grandfather, provided.

For a while, I guess it must have felt impossible. And still can, I know. She may have doubted her strength, her capacity to give enough, give everything, because everything seemed to be tearing her apart, breaking her down. She needed time. Not healing time, exactly, since certain wounds never heal, but time to change and more time to learn to believe, to understand she could go on, was going on, for better or worse. She could be someone she'd never dreamed she could be. Her heart strong, whole, even as it cracks and each bit demands everything.

The fullness of time. The fullness of time. That phrase has haunted me since I first heard it or read it, though I don't know when or how the words entered my awareness, because they seem to have always been there, like certain melodies, for instance, or visual harmonies of line in your mother's body that I wondered how I'd ever lived without the first time I encountered them, although another recognition clicked in almost simultaneously, reminding me that I'd been waiting for those particular notes, those lines, a very long time. They'd been forming me before I formed my first impressions of them.

The fullness of time. Neither forward nor backward. A space capacious enough to contain your coming into and going out of the world, your consciousness of these events, the wrap of oblivion bedding them. A life, the passage of a life: the truest understanding, measure, experience of time's fullness. So many lives, and each different, each unknowable, no matter how similar to yours, your flesh and not your flesh, lives passing, like yours, into the fullness of time, where each of these lives and all of them together make no larger ripple than yours, all and each abiding in the unruffled innocence of the fullness that is time. All the things that mattered so much to you or them sinking into a dreadful, unfeatured equality that is also rest and peace, time gone: but more, always more, the hands writing, the hands snatching, hands becoming bones, then dust, then whatever comes next, what time takes and fashions of you after the possibilities, permutations, and combinations—the fullness in you—are exhausted, played out for the particular shape the fullness has assumed for a time in you, for you. You are never it but what it could be, then is not: you not lost but ventured, gained, stretched, more, until the dust is particles and the particles play unhindered, unbound, returned to the fullness of time.

I know my father's name, Edgar, and some of his fathers' names, Hannibal, Tatum, Jordan, but I can't go back any further than a certain point, except that I also know the name of a place, Greenwood, South Carolina, and an even smaller community, Promised Land, nearly abutting Greenwood, where my grandfather, who, of course, is your great-grandfather, was born, and where many of his brothers are buried, under sturdy tombstones bearing his name, our name, "Wideman," carved in stone in the place where the origins of the family name begin to dissolve into the loam of plantations owned by white men, where my grandfathers' identities dissolve, where they were boys, then men, and the men they were fade into a set of facts, sparse, ambiguous, impersonal, their intimate lives unretrievable, where what is known about a county, a region, a country and its practice of human bondage, its tradition of obscuring, stealing, or distorting black people's lives, begins to crowd out the possibility of seeing my ancestors as human beings. The powers and principalities that originally restricted our access to the life that free people naturally enjoy still rise like a shadow, a wall between my grandfathers and me, my father and me, between the two of us, father and son, son and father.

So we must speak these stories to one another.
Love.

INTRODUCTION:
LIVE FROM DEATH ROW
BY MUMIA ABU-JAMAL

1995

Recalling the horrors of African-American history, accepting the challenges our history presently places on us, is like acknowledging a difficult, unpleasant duty or debt that's been hanging over our heads a very long time, an obligation that we know in our hearts we must deal with but that we keep putting off and evading, as if one day procrastination will make the burden, the obligation we must undertake, disappear.

Mumia Abu-Jamal forces us to confront the burden of our history. In one of his columns from death row he quotes at length an 1857 ruling of the U.S. Supreme Court. The issue being determined by the Court is whether the descendants of slaves, when they shall be emancipated, are full citizens of the United States. Chief Justice Roger Taney states:

> We think they are not, and that they were not included, and were not intended to be included, under the word "citizens" in the Constitution, and can therefore claim none of the rights and privileges of the United States. . . .
>
> [A] perpetual and impossible barrier was intended to be erected between the white race and the one which they had reduced to

223

slavery, and governed as subjects with absolute and despotic power, and which they then looked upon as so far below them in the scale of created beings, that intermarriages between white persons and negroes or mulattoes were regarded as unnatural and immoral, and punished as crimes.

Justice Taney, speaking for the Court, confirms the judgment of his ancestors and articulates an attitude prevailing to this very day.

Mumia points out that Thurgood Marshall, the first person of African descent appointed to the U.S. Supreme Court, admitted, just hours after his resignation from the Court, "I'm still not free."

In another essay, Mumia calls our attention to Nelson Mandela. Released after twenty-seven years in South Africa's jails as a political prisoner, Mandela—honored, celebrated as a hero, leader, and liberator of his people, universally acknowledged to be the most powerful man in his country, its best hope for peace, possibly its next president—still didn't possess the right to vote.

Mumia Abu-Jamal's writing insists on these kinds of gut checks, reality checks. He reminds us that to move clearly in the present, we must understand the burden of our past.

Situated as he is in prison, a prison inside a prison actually, since he's confined on death row, Mumia Abu-Jamal's day-to-day life would seem to share little with ours, out here in the so-called free world. Then again, if we think a little deeper, we might ask ourselves—who isn't on death row? Perhaps one measure of humanity is our persistence in the business of attempting to construct a meaningful life in spite of the sentence of death hanging over our heads every instant of our time on earth.

Although we can't avoid our inevitable mortality, we don't need to cower in a corner, waiting for annihilation. Neither should we allow the seemingly overwhelming evil news of the day to freeze us in our tracks, nor let it become an excuse for doing nothing, for denial and avoidance, for hiding behind imaginary walls and pretending nothing can harm us.

Alternatives exist. Struggle exists. Struggle to connect, to imagine ourselves better. To imagine a better world. To take responsibility step by step, day by day, for changing the little things we can control, refusing to accept the large things that appear out of control. The life and the essays of Mumia Abu-Jamal provide us with models for struggle.

In 1981, to connect with my younger brother who was serving a life term without parole in a Pennsylvania prison, I wrote a book with him called *Brothers and Keepers*. In my research for the book I discovered a chilling fact. My country, the United States of America, ranked third among the nations of the world in the percentage of its citizens it imprisoned. Only Russia and South Africa surpassed us.

Who would have guessed that, thirteen years later, the powerful governments of two of the top three incarcerating nations would have been overturned by internal revolutions. We're number one now. And in spite of the warning implicit in the fate of governments that choose repression over reform, we're building more prisons as fast as we can.

The facile notion of incarceration as a cure for social, economic, and political problems has usurped the current national discussion of these issues. As I traveled from city to city on a book tour last fall, the dominant issue dramatized in TV campaign ads coast to coast was: Which candidate is tougher on crime.

During the same tour, a hot story in national and local newspapers, on TV news, talk shows, and radio call-ins was the IQ controversy occasioned by the publication of several books claiming that the innate intelligence of blacks was lower than that of whites. Why such widespread, excited coverage of this hoary topic?

That some people believe black folk are born inferior to whites, and thus genetically determined to occupy the lowest rung of society certainly isn't news. Neither is blaming the victim of oppression, a strategy with a history at least as ancient as Europe's slave trading in Africa. I recall sitting on college admissions committees thirty years ago and hearing many of those who are voicing the idea of black mental inferiority today singing the same song then to rationalize underrepresentation of African-Americans in higher education.

So the fact that some *experts* continue to believe in innate black inferiority (or proclaim it without truly believing, since they must know that the basic terms in the debate—race and intelligence—are problematic at best, malicious fictions at worst, and know a mountain of tables, graphs, statistics, and experiments can neither affirm nor deny premises and assumptions themselves imprecise and untestable, *how many angels can fit on the head of a pin*) is not news. Rather, the IQ controversy is an ominous sign of misinformation and repression going hand in hand. Exterminating Jews becomes easier if you're able to provide sound "scientific" reasons for pogroms.

Postulating a biologically determined IQ deficit in blacks is more than malicious mischief. It is a transparent ploy to justify (and erase from the national consciousness) thirty years of backsliding from the promise of equality exacted by the civil rights movement of the 1960s.

For African-Americans the backsliding has created a slightly larger black middle class on one hand, and on the other a growing underclass of people of color trapped on the bottom rung of an economic ladder without any more rungs. For white Americans, reneging on the promise of equality has engendered class stratification and polarization just as severe as among blacks. On the bottom, the stagnant poverty of unemployment, welfare, poor education, and transience infect more and more of those who once considered themselves working people with dignity and aspirations. In the middle a rapidly shrinking majority beset by fear, trembling, and anger. They know they are walking a tightrope—away from unforgiving poverty, toward a mirage of boundless wealth that confers immunity from hard times. A tightrope, they also know in their hearts, leads nowhere—unless they hit the lottery—except to more stressful, precarious steps along the razor's edge or a sudden, precipitous fall. Finally, at the top stands a tiny minority whose wealth is a wall protecting them from the chaos of social instability, a wall that is both a reaction to the moral chaos of inequality and dependent on it.

We face a social landscape with more (or at least as much) need for radical change than we faced in the 1960s, an era that produced, flawed though it was by lack of follow-through, a mighty impulse toward change. Yet today the opposite impulse drives us. Walls separating Americans by race, gender, class, and region are being justified and celebrated, but not in a spirit that welcomes diversity or seeks ultimate unity through mutual respect and reconciliation. Prison walls are being proposed as a final solution. They symbolize our shortsightedness, our fear of the real problems caging us all. The pity is how blindly, enthusiastically, we applaud those who are constructing the walls dooming us.

Mumia Abu-Jamal's voice is considered dangerous and subversive and thus is censored from National Public Radio, to name just one influential medium. Many books about black people, including a slew of briskly selling biographies and autobiographies—from Oprah to O.J. to Maya Angelou—are on the stands. What sets Mumia's story apart as so threatening?

It is useful to remember that the slave narrative and its progeny, the countless up-from-the-depths biographies and autobiographies of black people that repeat the form and assumptions of the slave narrative, have always been bestsellers. They encapsulate one of the master plots Americans have found acceptable for black lives. These neoslave narratives carry a message the majority of people wealthy enough to purchase books wish to hear.

The message consists of a basic *deep structure* repeated in a seemingly endless variety of packages and voices. The slave narratives of the 1800s posited and then worked themselves out in a bifurcated, either/or world. The action of the story concerns moving from one world to another. The actor is a single individual, a featured star, and we watch and listen as this protagonist undergoes his or her rite of passage. South to North, rural to urban, black environment (plantation) to white environment (everywhere, including the language in which the narrator converses with the reader), silence to literary, are some of the classic crossovers accomplished by the protagonists of such fables. If you punch in modern variants of these dichotomies—ghetto to middle class, ignorance to education, unskilled to professional, despised gangster to enlightened spokesperson, you can see how persistent and malleable the formula is.

The formula for the neoslave narrative sells because it is simple; because it accepts and maintains the categories (black/white, for instance) of the status quo; because it is about individuals, not groups, crossing boundaries; because it comforts and consoles those in power and offers a ray of hope to the powerless. Although the existing social arrangements may allow the horrors of plantations, ghettos, and prisons to exist, the narratives tell us, these arrangements also allow room for some to escape. Thus the arrangements are not absolutely evil. No one is absolutely guilty, nor are the oppressed (slave, prisoner, ghetto inhabitant) absolutely guiltless. If some overcome, why don't the others?

Vicarious identification with the narrator's harrowing adventures, particularly if the tale is told in first person "I," permits readers to have their cake and eat it too. They experience the chill and thrill of being an outsider. In the safety of an armchair, readers can root for the crafty slave as the slave pits himself against an outrageously evil system that legitimizes human bondage. Readers can ignore for a charmed moment their reliance on the same system to pay for the book, the armchair.

The neoslave narratives thus serve the ambivalent function of their ancestors. The fate of one black individual is foregrounded, removed from the network of systemic relationships connecting, defining, determining, undermining all American lives. This manner of viewing black lives at best ignores, at worst reinforces, an apartheid status quo. Divisive categories that structure the world of the narratives—slave/free, black/white, underclass/middle class, female/male—are not interrogated. The idea of a collective, intertwined fate recedes. The mechanisms of class, race, and gender we have inherited are perpetuated ironically by a genre purporting to illustrate the possibility of breaking barriers and transcending the conditions into which one is born.

Mumia Abu-Jamal's essays question matters left untouched by most of the popular stories of black lives decorating bookstores today. And therein lies much of the power, the urgency, of his writing.

His essays are important as departure and corrective. He examines the place where he is—*prison*, his status—*prisoner, black man*, but refuses to accept the notion of difference and separation these labels project. Although he yearns for freedom, demands freedom, he does not identify freedom with release from prison, does not confuse freedom with what his jailers can give or take away, does not restrict the concept of freedom to the world beyond the bars his jailers enter from each day. Although dedicated to personal liberation, he envisions that liberation as partially dependent on the collective fate of black people. He doesn't split his world down the middle to conform to the divided world prison enforces. He expresses the necessity of connection, relinquishing to no person or group the power to define him. His destiny, his manhood, is not attached to some desperate, one-way urge to cross over to a region controlled or possessed by others. What he is, who he can become, results from his daily struggle to construct an identity wherever his circumstances place him.

Isn't one of the lessons of African-American culture the reality of an unseen world, below, above, around, what is visible? Our history offers witness to the fact that our living, our art, and our spirits can prosper in the face of the most extreme physical deprivation. Aren't Mumia Abu-Jamal's words reaching us now, in spite of steel bars and a death sentence, another instance of our capacity to keep on keeping on?

The first truth Mumia tells us is that he ain't dead yet. And although his voice is vital and strong, he assures us it ain't because nobody ain't trying to kill him and shut him up. In fact, just the opposite is true. The power of his voice is rooted in his defiance of those determined to silence him. Magically, Mumia's words are clarified and purified by the toxic strata of resistance through which they must penetrate to reach us. Like the blues. Like jazz.

Remember the fairy tale about the emperor's new clothes, how a kid blurts out "He's naked" as the emperor struts past, decked out in his illusory splendor? What ever happened to the kid who spoiled the emperor's show? Consider what has happened to black men—Martin, Malcolm, Mandela—who have shouted out, "He's naked." If the fairy tale were set in an American city today and the child cast as a black boy, we know he'd be shot or locked up or both. Nobody wants to hear the bad news, the truth exposing the empire's self-delusions, especially those who profit most from the delusions.

Chinua Achebe, the great Nigerian novelist, teaches us that the poet and the king must never become too friendly because the poet's job is to bear to the people unglad tidings the king would just as soon nobody hears.

The best slave narratives and prison narratives have always asked profound questions, implicitly and explicitly, about the meaning of a life. Part of the work of blues, jazz, our best artistic endeavors, is (thank you, Mr. Ellison) *to reveal the chaos which lives within the pattern of our certainties.* In a new world where African people were transported to labor, die, and disappear, we've needed unbound voices to reformulate our destiny—voices refusing to be ensnared by somebody else's terms. We've developed the knack of finding such voices in the oddest, darkest, most unforeseen places. A chorus of them exists in Great Time, the seamless medium uniting past, present, and future. The voices are always there, if we discipline ourselves to pick them out. Listen to them, to ourselves, to the best we've managed to write and say and dance and paint and sing. African-American culture, in spite of the weight, the assaults it has endured, may contain a key to our nation's survival, a key not found simply in the goal of material prosperity, but in the force of spirit, will, communal interdependence.

Because he tells the truth, Mumia Abu-Jamal's voice can help us tear down walls—prison walls, the walls we hide behind to deny and refuse the burden of our history.

PLAYING DENNIS RODMAN

1996

. . . an attraction that has all the characteristics of breaking and entering
and of the violation of a sanctuary.

—Simulacra and Simulation *by Jean Baudrillard*

I knew the word *'tain't*. Old people used it, mainly; it was their way of contracting "it ain't" to one emphatic beat, a sound for saying "it is not" in African-American vernacular, but also for saying much more, depending on tone, timing, and inflection. But I'd never heard *'tain't* used to refer to female anatomy—not the front door or the back door but a mysteriously alluring, unclassifiable, scary region between a woman's legs ("'Tain't pussy and 'tain't asshole, it's just the *'tain't*," to quote Walter Bentley)—until a bunch of us were sitting on somebody's stoop listening to Big Walt, aka Porky, discuss with his cousin Donald some finer points of lovemaking.

I didn't understand then how part of the power of *'tain't* is that you never see it exactly. Even if your eyes gaze on that little bit of in-between skin, it's the idea that stuns, that transports to a realm where desire slips its mooring from a specific object and creates new rules, new priorities that disrupt the known and familiar. Porky's crude connoisseur's riff on *'tain't*

233

returns when I think about Dennis Rodman, the professional basketball player, and his gotta-have-it rebound jones.

Rodman embodies *'tain't*. Unclassifiable—"the most unique player in the history of the NBA," according to Chuck Daly, who coached Rodman's first pro team, the Detroit Pistons, to two consecutive NBA championships. Not exactly a forward, guard, or center, Rodman invented a role for himself which subverts the logic of traditional positions. His helter-skelter, full-court, full-time intensity blurs the line between defense and offense. He "scores" without scoring, keeping the ball in play until one of his teammates drops it through the hoop.

If you want to win basketball games, rebounding is crucial. The battle for domination of the boards is a fascinating game within the game. Rodman's relentless, no-holds-barred, kamikaze pursuit of missed shots foregrounds rebounding and frees it from subordinate status. The game's too easy, he says. What he does on the court is not about contributing his share to a team effort—not even about rebounding, when you get right down to it. "Snay" (hell, no), Rodman would say. *'Tain't* basketball and *'tain't* rebounding. It's just *'tain't*. Irreducible to anything else—a perpetual work in progress, compelling, outrageous, amoral. Rodman immerses himself in what he does, defines himself by it, stakes out new territory: percussive behavior so edgy it threatens to wreck the game that's supposed to contain it.

I didn't much care for Rodman during his early seasons in the NBA.

On the playgrounds of Pittsburgh, where I learned the game, we had a word for gawkish, all elbows and knees, one-dimensional-game, raw-boned hurry-with-no-finesse chumps who must be somebody's country cousin wetbacked into our sleek city run. The best we could say about a guy like that was "cockstrong": "the brother's cockstrong." Which meant all of the above plus the insinuation that he wasn't getting much love action, so all the energy he should be using up in some sweeter place got dropped on you. "Cockstrong" meant a guy was a load. And loaded. A pain in the butt to play against. You respected him, in a way—the strength, endurance, earnestness, hustle—but even when he was on your side he could be a liability, since he was minimally skilled, unpredictable, liable to hurt the team in a do-or-die situation, hurt you with his unsophisticated, indiscriminate flailing. Worse, sometimes a cockstrong player possessed real bad attitude. So much displaced, pent-up energy threatened to blow up, turn mean and ugly.

Playground basketball is the most democratic of games: when a court's crowded, all comers can call winners and play next. Everybody has to police himself (or herself, now that more women show up on the outdoor courts), so that each game contains ten referees or no referees, depending on how you look at it. In no other game is your just-about-naked body so constantly, helplessly, acutely vulnerable to a cheap shot. One push in the back when you're airborne and a whole season or a whole career could be lost. One ignorant, unreflective, selfish player endangers everybody. When Dennis Rodman broke into the league as the Detroit Pistons' primal piston, he worried me. No doubt about it, the boy was cockstrong, quite capable of hurting people—some of my favorite people, Michael Jordan and Scottie Pippen, for instance—and on occasion Rodman turned foolish enough, evil enough, to try.

But people change. Cocksure's not always pretty, but it's a much more benign way of being a jerk than cockstrong. And Dennis Rodman is nothing if not cocksure.

Cross-dressing, cross-naming himself (Denise), frequenting gay night clubs, going AWOL from his team, head-butting a referee, winning four rebounding titles in a row, painting his hair, dating Madonna, challenging the NBA commissioner to suspend him, badmouthing the men in suits who pay his salary, Dennis Rodman, though not voted onto this season's All-Star team, verges on media superstardom. Whether or not he acts out his fantasy of performing naked in an NBA game, his tale is on high-definition display each time he kangaroos down the court. I'm in this game, his body English says—in it, but not of it. "Show business is what I do on the court," he says.

In an age of hype, a world where simulation and appearance count as much as substance and authenticity, where appropriation and replication are viable substitutes for creativity, where show biz is the only business, the storm of publicity Rodman's bad-boy act generates is worth a fortune. He's *large*, large, and soon to be larger if his new autobiography lives up to its prerelease teases. Into this "Tempest" enters David Stern, politic lawyer, urbane huckster, commissioner of the NBA: Prospero to Rodman's Caliban. In our end-of-the-century remake of Shakespeare's play, the names of the characters are too corny to be true: Stern, Apollonian administrator/accountant; Rod Man, Dionysian up-and-down, in-and-out pogo stick. Follow the bouncing balls, the ones inside the scrotum with the silver loop attached.

Shakespeare's drama predicts the dynamic of colonialism. The play also births Caliban, the archetypal victim-product of colonial inter-course, part man, part fish, part devil, whose island Prospero steals and rules. Prospero despises and fears Caliban—"this thing of darkness I / Acknowledge mine." He's plagued by images of Caliban raping his daughter. But Prospero needs Caliban's labor, his skills, his knowledge of the island, so he enslaves him and enlists Ariel and other invisible spirits of the air to keep him in line.

Like Prospero, the contemporary sports czar rules by illusion, deploys spirits of the air (the media) to police his domain. Caliban, Frankenstein's monster, the Rogue Cyborg, and the Rod Man are kin, *'tain't*, tainted, neither one thing or another; hybrids, mutants, half-breeds, crossbreeds, hyperreal mulattoes, bad seeds, the worst nightmare of rulers whose greed and fantasies of control drive them to forge Faustian bargains with the Devil. The czar and his minions can *make* these syncretic outlaw creatures, but can't *break* them. Somewhere just out of sight, Dennis the Menace, the Worm, the Gangsta Rapper, the Rebel Robot plot their revenge.

I'm thinking about hoop; about my own playing days; about time; about my first language, the African-American vernacular that will always be the language of my feelings; about my daughter playing in the regional finals of the N.C.A.A. women's tournament. I'm thinking about the purity that's fading fast but still enhances and distinguishes the women's game. And I'm thinking about Dennis Rodman, wondering what's at stake.

Why couldn't people laugh at the TV ad in which Rodman bullies Santa Claus? Why does Rodman's refusal to allow his identity to be totally subsumed by a game offend people? Is our sense of who we are so fragile, our defense against chaos so easily breached, that we can't bear to look when a sports celebrity reminds us that the games we play and worship are only games? The Santa game. The gender game. The race game. The Mom, apple-pie, take-me-out-to-the-ballgame game. Maybe that's what really scares, outrages, and entertains us about Dennis Rodman. He dons the uniform, takes the paycheck, but doesn't exactly go to work. He enters a zone where play is not reducible to anything else. The game we've taken for real disappears, and we're left to deal with the reality of Dennis Rodman in our faces.

JUSTICE: A PERSPECTIVE

1997

I am an old man in a white month. Snow has been falling for years. I borrow a neighbor's extension ladder and lean it against the side of my house. It's way past time for cleaning snow off my roof. Yesterday's newspaper printed a warning issued by the Department of Safety informing citizens that more snow's expected, wet, heavy snow, and roofs may begin collapsing under its weight.

So I prop Mickey's ladder over the side garage door and, shovel in hand, climb. Gingerly, terrified, excited. Wet soles of old sneakers slippery as banana peels on the aluminum rungs. Climb till the steeply pitched roof with its three-foot crest of snow fills my field of vision. Tons of snow up here, a sleeping avalanche the first blow of the shovel will awaken.

Blue sky, glaring whiteness, a few wisps of snow in the air, leftovers from the last storm or scouts of storm coming. Stillness and calm when I'm as high as I dare, flattened against the portion of the ladder that juts into thin air, toes on the last rung below the bib of gutter upon which the ladder rests.

Will I fall? Will my heart burst from overexertion? This scraping and heaving the last thing I'll do with my life? What's going to happen really doesn't worry me. This silliness of clearing snow from a roof when more snow is imminent as good as any way to die. Nothing morbid about my mood, the moment. In fact I feel exhilarated. Yes. Above it all. Reduced in scale and pretension by great white walls towering above me, I could

239

be Cortez gazing for the first time at the Pacific. In a desert two thousand miles away, yellow blooms I mistake for birds pinioned to the spiky tips of a cactus. Armies of cacti, limbs upflung in postures of despair and surrender line the ridges, the washes, gullies, hills, and buttes of a harsh landscape whose undulations are the music I make tossing and turning in my bed.

Yesterday, foolishly, in the semidark of late afternoon, when a sliver of moon hung dimly in the sky, I attacked this same spot, above the garage door where the sloping roofs of master bedroom and rec room intersect. Atop my own rickety wooden stepladder, balanced on the warning label, "Danger: Do not stand above this step," I hacked at the gutters with hatchet and crowbar. Icy shrapnel peppered my face. Tears stung my eyes when I rammed the fist gripping the hatchet into a wind-sculpted bumper of ice.

Picture me chopping and prying, wearing sunglasses that protected my eyes but also just about blinded me. Picture me in the gathering gloom, in a pricey suburban subdivision on a stepladder set beside my nice, big house, determined to free the roof of ice and snow so the roof won't cave in, so the thaw when it arrives won't force melting snow backward, perversely up and under the shingles, seeping through roof-boards, soaking insulation, pooling between rafters, penetrating Sheet-rock, finally drip, drip, dripping through textured ceilings of master bedroom, upstairs bath, and downstairs front hall as it did last time this much snow, corralled by ice, collected on my roof. Picture me picturing myself, once a poor black boy, finally, in spite of the odds, grown up, risking life and limb again to do the right thing. Picture me imagining myself on the ground, slowly regaining consciousness, attempting to explain to a passerby why I'm buried half-dead in a snowdrift.

Yesterday, on that day we're picturing—stepladder too short, darkness to thick, afraid of falling, mad at nature, mad at whatever it was inside myself rousting me outdoors in freezing weather to perform a task against my will and better judgment—the worse thing about that day was the certainty, even as I spread the stepladder's legs and humped up and down to anchor its invisible feet in thigh deep snow, the worst thing I felt was the certainty of failure.

Now, today, on this new morning, in the sunlight, on my neighbor's ladder the job feels infinitely doable—my efforts will be rewarded, justice served.

I luxuriate in the view from twenty feet up. Welcome the immensity of a brilliant blue sky that puts the ominous glare of my little snow-drowned roof in perspective. Through my neighbor's window I can see the dollhouse tranquility, the good intentions of their tastefully furnished rooms. This whole business of risking my life to clear a roof is okay because I've adjusted my perspective. Worked out a new slant on things.

Everything depends on perspective. And luckily there's a science of perspective to depend upon. A science highly developed by painters of the fifteenth century. Treatises exist on the subject. How-to manuals for aspiring artists. One essential prop in the development of this science of perspective was the camera obscura, a dark room or box in which light entered only through a pinprick in one end, causing the view through the peephole to appear as an image on the black wall opposite. Just as we apply laws to simulate justice, scientists and artists evolved rules for organizing a picture of the world as it appeared when burnt as an image on a flat surface. Not the world these scientists and artists experienced every day, but the world reduced, imprisoned, reflected inside the camera obscura. The laws of linear perspective the theorists delineated were laws for reproducing a copy of a copy. Forgotten, ignored, or undiscussed was the willed blindness within the black box, the hood over the head, the problematic relationship of camera obscura images to what a human eye and heart know even if the eye's peering from inside a box at the sea of light beyond its cage.

Infatuated by the way the scenes reproduced inside the camera obscura could be replicated by mechanical, mathematically precise coordinates, most painters junked other experiments for expressing the mystery of perception and apprenticed themselves to the technology of linear perspective, the trick of rendering three dimensions on a flat surface. They forsook the floating indeterminacy of medieval manuscript illuminations and tapestries, put on hold the continuous give-and-take between an object and its image in the mind. Painting inferred the stability and consequence of a material world, a world the spirit knew as illusion and chaos, the field of play for memory, dream, desire.

The result: a world imagined through a window, *out there*, separate from the viewer, a justly proportioned, settled thing for the artist to mirror. An unspoken pact was forged between painting and audience: The version of reality revealed by the keyhole of the camera obscura became Real. The gorgeous spectacle of Renaissance art ensued. But no gain without pain. The picture frame excludes as it includes. Television the latest blip on the wall masquerading as an equivalence for the light in us, around us, containing us, contained by us, where time, space, motion, the gods dance.

I mention all that only to say no science of perspective accounts for the desert, for the dagger I see before me, hanging in the air, the dagger's handle, the desert's punctured yellow blooms bidding me close my fingers around them.

Here is what I mean. My wife, who in middle middle age is teaching herself computers, said a couple days ago it's almost refreshing how regularly, brutally computers remind you that you learn only by committing mistakes. You type away, doing what you usually do, type, typing, and then the machine goes haywire, nothing is happening the way it should and you have no idea why, but you know you must stop and adjust, figure out the mistake you've committed and rectify it if you want to resume type, typing.

Nine years ago, a week ago, a second ago my son lost control of the howling chaos inside him he'd been struggling with fiercely, silently, alone, for most of his sixteen years to quell. He was touring the western states in a chaperoned group of sixteen-year-olds, boys who'd attended summer camp together over the years. After a long, frustrating day in a rental car, a day of minor mishaps and wrong turns, the party had stopped overnight in an Arizona motel near the Grand Canyon.

There are many versions of what happened that night. Given the consequences of whatever happened, no version is very pretty. From my perspective, the one from this desk, from the snow-smothered rooftop I'm recalling, it's enough to say the boy sleeping in a cabin with my son was killed and my son fled. After a week of running, my son phoned home, and my wife and I flew to Phoenix to accompany him when he turned himself in to the police.

To decide what occurred that terrible night in an Arizona motel, the state was obliged to construct a picture, freeze-frame, and simplify events to render them in terms of the law. Like a scene achieved by an artist copying an image focused through the camera obscura, the picture the state painted was arbitrary, omitting far more than it included, disclosing a lot about the law's blind spots, its arbitrariness, how law dismembers, tears apart living tissue. In the name of justice, the state put its fearsome weight behind the view of things stipulated by the coordinates of law. From the state of Arizona's perspective, my son deserved to be treated as a hardened criminal rather than a good kid who for unaccountable reasons had snapped one night and needed help not punishment; he was tried as an adult rather than a juvenile and sentenced to life imprisonment.

The above summary mercifully leaves out a multitude of pertinent, mind-boggling, soul-crushing details. Some of these details would come to you as no surprise. Others you'd never guess, even if you tried harder than would be wise to imagine the devastation visited upon families by the loss of one young, promising life, the blighting of another.

At sixteen my son found himself suddenly transformed from a privileged, middle-class teenager growing up in a small town, attending high school, to a caged beast, hunted, baited, condemned. This required of him, of course, a change in perspective.

Required the same of his mother, brother and sister, me. I cannot speak for other members of my family, but in the nine years since my son's been in prison, I've managed no satisfactory adjustment of perspective. No notion of justice I've been able to formulate makes sense of a boy's death in Arizona, my son's sentencing and incarceration.

There is a space I need to fill when I try to write *justice*, but the space remains. I recall what my wife said about computers and making mistakes. Only this isn't like confronting a mistake and pushing buttons until the computer stops printing out a stigmata of dots, dashes, and symbols. This emptiness is more like constant bleeding. Like typing along with continuously disturbing results, sometimes far worse than others, but never really getting it close to right. Incriminating errors, painful errors, but continuing on and on, not because time heals or familiarity dulls the ache or because I think I'm getting away with anything or believe that my story unraveling in fits and starts, with dangerous, yawning gaps, is all right. I go on because I skip the space where justice should fit. Yearn for it to be filled, but keep climbing. Like some terminally ill patients long for the peace and rest they believe follows death. Yearn for the fall. Keep climbing.

Up on the housetop, click click click / Down through the chimney with Old Saint Nick. I was one of those kids who believed in Santa Claus way past the time everybody else in the crowd had put old Santa to sleep. I was his defender. Got a tooth loosened in a fistfight once protecting his honor. Impossible not to remember him up here where I am, staring at the apex of my roof, the snow-draped stone chimney astraddle it. I loved you, you bloody, jellyroll elf. Your fluffy white beard, blue-sky eyes, your plump, alkie's cheeks, your scarlet longjohns with snowy muffs of fur decorating the cuffs. Remember the time in Kaufmann's department store I climbed on your knee and the snapshot my mom paid two of my daddy's hard-earned quarters for was nothing but a blaze of light where our heads should have been. Ha, ha. Vampire, motherfucker. No reflection in the mirror. Biting off my head so I disappear too.

Here is what I mean. In the Arizona desert where they keep him you can see forever. Flat, flat to the pale, scalloped crust of mountains that might be as far away as the farthest edge of the earth, far as the moon. So distant your eye travels once around the world and back to the very spot where you're standing wondering how far away those mountains might be. You are a point, infinitesimal on that vast loop of trying to see what's out there, trying to ascertain where you stand in relationship to the emptiness surrounding you. Think of many lines emanating from the point where you are fixed, lines like laws, like the threads artists stretched across their canvases to locate the vanishing point, visible coordinates of perspective matching the lines drawn on the image produced inside the camera obscura. Lines multiplying till they form a solid sphere, like a skein of yarn wound round and round itself. You are a smaller speck on the giant ball than the invisible point where all lines converge, melt. The busyness of your gaze seeking, casting about, tracking, scanning, trying to make sense, imaging questions and answers, alternate scenarios, the restless, hungry gasps of your eyes print the numberless lines that locate you, cage you, here, nowhere, nothing in the desert where they keep him.

Reality in this desert is what's meant to elude you. The sum of your mistakes, minus them. Why you never see things clearly. Why I fail to adjust and gain perspective. In this desert the sand is grains of justice delayed, justice denied, the long, slow, proverbial arc of justice pulverized when it touches down to earth.

When it snows in the desert those low slung silhouettes on the horizon, mottled bluish and dusk, compounds of shadow and sandstone and granite and cloud, inch closer. Hunker down, staring vigilant-eyed, as near as they dare to the campfire. They lie there just beyond what they know is the circle of your effectiveness, where even if you charged at them, no way you'd catch them. How close they seem, how tame and absent, the twin mirrors of their eyes unblinking. When it snows, the long view shrinks to this intimate sharing, sharing the last dregs of heat, scraps of food, the moon. If you howl, that too will be shared, return to you as echo, burn like red cinders in your throat.

One day in the desert snow falls, a marvel, a chance to live a different life with new rules and conclusions. Sand puckers like a textured ceiling, leaks sprout, a forest of straight, transparent stems shoot up, magnified by close-up, time-lapse trick photography that collapses seasons into seconds. The bars of rain crystallize, shatter, become white flakes falling. The floor of the desert turns over in its sleep, rises, spreads its thorny arms to receive pale blossoms.

I think of this New England spring storm as a fist. I must pry open its stiff, frozen fingers and see what it's done to my house. So I take a deep breath and get on with it, start to chip and chop, pray I don't go dancing off into the frigid air, falling up, picturing myself ridiculous and dead before I hit the ground.

The ladder tips. Oh, shit. It's the Big One, ladies and gentlemen. My neighbor's two-hundred-foot aluminum extension firetruck rescue 911 naked people from blazing skyscrapers at night in a snowstorm ladder slides sideways down the blister of ice it's resting on, a slide I precipitate by cracking with my shovel the pouting lip of ice anchoring the blister. Sliding. Slow enough for me to know what's going to happen, fast enough so I'm helpless to change it.

Amazing how rapidly the mind shuttles through alternate perspectives in this kind of crisis situation. You know what I mean. Welcoming, disregarding, inventing, recalling. Line after smoke-tailed line of possibilities propelled into space. Futile as all the harpoons chasing Moby Dick, but incredibly quick. A thousand lives you might have lived and all the ones you've lived already, all the combinations and permutations of what might come and what's gone flash through your mind as the ladder shifts, a tiny wobble just below the threshold of your awareness, then something you are remembering because it must have happened—that tilt, shift, that lean, that sly, told-you-so smile—to commence the ride you're on.

Too much weight to bear. Your big, sweat-suited body way up here, pinned to the ladder's tip. For a millisecond you understand why snow and sand are the same thing. Fire and ice indistinguishable in a blow you dealt your thumb. Justice sleeps. You will not be saved. Nothing happens next. You crash through your neighbor's roof, a visitor from another planet screaming apologies in a language no one understands because nobody's home.

THE SILENCE OF THELONIOUS MONK

1997

One night years ago in Paris trying to read myself to sleep, I discovered that Verlaine loved Rimbaud. And in his fashion Rimbaud loved Verlaine. Which led to a hip-hop farce in the rain at a train station. The Gare du Midi, I think. The two poets exchanging angry words. And like flies to buttermilk a crowd attracted to the quarrel till Verlaine pulls a pistol. People scatter and Rimbaud, wounded before, hollers for a cop. Just about then, at the moment I begin mixing up their story with mine, with the little I recall of Verlaine's poetry—*Il pleure dans mon coeur / Comme il pleut sur la ville*—lines I recited to impress you, lifetimes ago, didn't I, the first time we met—just then with the poets on hold in the silence and rain buffeting the train station's iron-roofed platform, I heard the music of Thelonious Monk playing somewhere. So softly it might have been present all along as I read about the sorry-assed ending of the poets' love affair—love offered, consumed, spit out, two people shocked speechless, lurching away like drunks, like sleepwalkers, from the mess they'd made. Monk's music just below my threshold of awareness, scoring the movie I was imagining, a soundtrack inseparable from what the actors were feeling, from what I felt watching them pantomime their melodrama.

Someone playing a Monk record in Paris in the middle of the night many years ago and the scratchy music seeping through ancient

247

boardinghouse walls a kind of silence, a ground against which the fig-ure of pitta-pattering rain was displayed, rain in the city, rain Verlaine claimed he could hear echoing in his heart, then background and ground reversed and Monk the only sound reaching me through night's quiet.

Listening to Monk, I closed the book. Let the star-crossed poets rest in peace. Gave up on sleep. Decided to devote some quality time to feeling sorry for myself. Imagining unhappy ghosts, wondering which sad sto-ries had trailed me across the ocean ready to barge into the space sleep definitely had no intention of filling. Then you arrived. Silently at first. You playing so faintly in the background it would have taken the surprise of someone whispering your name in my ear to alert me to your presence. But your name, once heard, I'd have to confess you'd been there all along.

In a way it could end there, in a place as close to silence as silence gets, the moment before silence becomes what it must be next, what's been there the whole time patiently waiting, part of the silence, what makes silence speak always, even when you can't hear it. End with me wanting to tell you everything about Monk, how strange and fitting his piano solo sounded in that foreign place and you not there to tell so it could/did end except, then as now, you lurk in the silence. I can't pretend not to hear you. So I pretend you hear me telling you what I need to tell, pretend silence is you listening, your presence confirmed word by word, the ones I say, the unspoken ones I see your lips form, that form you.

Two years before Monk's death, eight years into what the critic and record producer Orrin Keepnews characterized as Monk's "final retreat into total inactivity and seclusion," the following phone conversation between Monk and Keepnews occurred:

Thelonious, are you touching the piano at all these days?

No, I'm not.

Do you want to get back to playing?

No, I don't.

I'm only in town for a few days. Would you like to come and visit, to talk about the old days?

No, I wouldn't.

Silence one of Monk's languages, everything he says laced with it. Silence a thick brogue anybody hears when Monk speaks the other tongues he's mastered. It marks Monk as being from somewhere other than wherever he happens to be, his offbeat accent, the odd way he puts something different in what we expect him to say. An extra something not supposed to be there, or an empty space where something usually is. Like all there is to say but you don't say after you learn in a casual conversation that someone precious is dead you've just been thinking you must get around to calling one day soon and never thought a day might come when you couldn't.

I heard a story from a friend who heard it from Panama Red, a conk-haired, red-bone, geechee old-timer who played with Satchmo way back when and he's still on the scene people say sounding better and better the older he gets, Panama Red who frequented the deli on Fifty-Seventh Street Monk used for kosher.

One morning numerous years ago, story time always approximate, running precisely by grace of the benefit of the doubt, Red said:

How you doing, Monk.

Uh-huh, Monk grunts.

Good morning, Mr. Monk. How you do ink this fine morning? Sammy the butcher calls over his shoulder, busy with a takeout order or whatever it is, keeping his back turned.

If the dead lunch meat replied, it would be no surprise at all to Sammy compared with how high he'd jump, how many fingers he'd lose in the slicer, if the bearish, bearded schwartze in the knitted Kufi said good morning back. Monk stares at the white man in the white apron and T-shirt behind the white deli counter. At himself in the mirror where the man saw him. At the thin, perfect sheets that buckle off the cold slab of corned beef.

Red has his little neat white package in his hand and wants to get home and fix him a chopped-liver-and-onion sandwich and have it washed down good with a cold Heineken before his first pupil of the afternoon buzzes so he's on his way out when he hears Sammy say:

Be with you in a moment, Mr. Monk.

Leave that mess you're messing wit alone, nigger, and get me some potato knishes, the story goes and Panama Red cracking up behind Monk's habit of niggering white black brown red Jew Muslim Christian, the only distinction of color mattering the ivory or ebony keys of his instrument and Thelonious subject to fuck with that difference, too, chasing rainbows.

Heard the story on the grapevine, once, twice, and tried to retell it and couldn't get it right and thought about the bird—do you remember it— coo-cooing outside the window just as we both were waking up. In the silence after the bird's song I said, Wasn't that a dainty dish to set before the king and you said Don't forget the queen and I said *Queen* doesn't rhyme with *sing* and you said It probably wasn't a blackbird singing anyway and I said I thought it was a mourning dove and then the bird started up again trying to repeat itself, trying, trying but never quite getting it right it seemed. So it tried and tried again as if it had fallen in love with the sound it had heard itself coo once perfectly.

Rain in the city. When the rain starts to falling / my love come tumbling down / and its raining teardrops in my heart. Rain a dream lots of people are sharing and shyly Monk thinks of how it might feel to climb in naked with everybody under the covers running through green grass in a soft summer shower. Then it's windshield wipers whipping back and forth. Quick glimpses of the invisible city splashing like eggs broken against the glass. I'm speeding along, let's say the West Side Highway, a storm on top, around, and under. It feels like being trapped in one of those automatic car washes doing its best to bust your windows and doors, rapping your metal skin like drumsticks. I'm driving blind and crazed as everybody else down a flooded highway no one with good sense would be out on a night like this. Then I hit a swatch of absolute quiet under an overpass and for a split second anything is possible. I remember it has happened before, this leap over the edge into vast, unexpected silence, happened before and probably will again if I survive the furious storm, the traffic and tumult waiting to punish me instantly on the far side of the underpass. In that silence that's gone before it gets here good I recalled exactly another time, driving at night with you through a rainstorm. Still in love with you though I hadn't been with you for years, ten, fifteen, till that night of dog-and-cat rain on an expressway circling the city after our eyes had met in a crowded room. You driving, me navigating, searching for a sign to Woodside you warned me would come up all the sudden. There it is. There it is, you shouted. Shit. I missed it. We can get off the next exit, I said. But you said, No. Said you didn't know the way Didn't want to get lost in the scary storm. I missed the turn for your apartment and you said, It's late anyway Too late to go back and you'd get hopelessly lost coming off the next exit, so we continued downtown to my hotel, where you dropped me off after a goodnight, goodbye-again peck on the cheek. Monk on the radio with a whole orchestra rooty-tooty at Town Hall, as we raced away from the sign I didn't see till we passed it. Monk's music breaking the silence after we missed our turn, after we hollered to hear each other over the rain, after we flew over the edge and the roof popped off and the sides split and for a moment we were suspended in a soundless bubble where invisible roads crisscrossed going nowhere, anywhere. Airborne, the tires aquaplaning, all four hooves of a galloping horse simultaneously in the air just like Muybridge, your favorite photographer, claimed, but nobody believed the nigger, did they, till he caught it on film.

Picture five or six musicians sitting around Rudy Van Gelder's living room, which is serving as a recording studio this afternoon. Keepnews is paying for the musicians' time, for Van Gelder's know-how and equipment, and everybody ready to go but Monk. Monk's had the charts a week and Keepnews knows he's studied them from comments Monk muttered while the others sauntered in for the session. But Monk is Monk. He keeps fiddle-faddling with a simple tune, da, da, da, da, plunks the notes, stares into thin air as if he's studying a house of cards he's constructed there, waiting for it to fall apart. Maybe the stare's not long in terms of minutes (unless you're Keepnews, paying the bill) but long enough for the other musicians to be annoyed. Kenny Clarke, the drummer, picks up the Sunday funnies from a coffee table. Monk changes pace, backpedals midphrase, turns the notes into a signifying riff.

K.C., you know you can't read. You drum-drum dummy. Don't be cutting your eyes at me. Ima A B C this tune to death, Mister Kenny Clarke. Take my time wit it. Uh-huh. One and two and one and two it to death, K.C. Don't care if your eyes light up and your stomach says howdy. One anna two anna one anna we don't start till I say start. Till I go over it again. Pick it clean. All the red boogers of meat off the bone then belch and fart and suck little strings I missed out my teefs and chew them last salty, sweet gristle bits till the cows come home and then, maybe then, it might be time to start so stop bugging me with your bubble eyes like you think you got somewhere better to go.

Once I asked Monk what is this thing called love. Bebop, hip-hop, whatever's good till the last drop and you never get enough of it even when you get as much as you can handle, more than you can handle, he said, just as you'd expect from somebody who's been around such things and appreciates them connoisseurly but also with a passionate edge so it's always the first time, the only time, love's ever happened and Monk can't help but grunt uh-huh, uh-huh while he's playing even though he's been loved before and it ain't no big thing, just the only thing, the music, love, lifting me.

Monk says he thinks of narrow pantherish hips, the goateed gate to heaven, and stately, stately he slides the silky drawers down, pulls them over her steepled knees, her purple-painted toes. Tosses the panties high behind his back without looking because he knows Pippen's where he's supposed to be, trailing the play, sniffing the alley-oop dish, already slamming it through the hoop so Monk can devote full attention to sliding both his large, buoyant hands up under the curve of her buttocks. A beard down there trimmed neat as Monk trims his.

Trim, one of love's names. Poontang. Leg. Nooky Cock.

Next chorus also about love. Not so much a matter of mourning a lost love as it is wondering how and when love will happen next or if love will ever happen again because in this vale of Vaseline and tears, whatever is given is also taken away. Love opens in the exact space of wondering what my chances are, figuring the hopeless odds against love. Then, biff, bam. Just when you least expect it, Monk says. Having known love before, I'm both a lucky one, ahead of the game, and also scared to death by memories of how sweet it is, how sad something that takes only a small bit of anybody's time can't be found more copiously, falling as spring rain or sunlight these simple things remind me of you and still do do do when Monk scatters notes like he's barefoot feeding chicken feed to chickens or bleeding drop by drop precious Lord in the snow.

I believe when we're born each of us receives an invisible ladder we're meant to scale. We commence slowly, little baby shaky steps. Then bolder ones as we get the hang of it. Learn our powers, learn the curious construction of these ladders leaning on air, how the rungs are placed irregularly, almost as if they customize themselves to our stepping and when we need them they're there or seem to be there solid under our feet because we're steady climbing and everybody around us steady climbing till it seems these invisible ladders, measure by measure, are music we perform as easy as breathing, playing our song, we smile shyly, uneasily the few times we remember how high and wide we've propelled ourselves into thin air step by step on rungs we never see disappearing behind us. And you can guess the rest of that tune, Monk says.

You place your foot as you always do, do, do, one in front of the other, then risk as you always do, do, do your weight on it so the other foot can catch up. Instead of dance music you hear a silent wind in your ears, blood pounding your temples, you're inside a house swept up in a tornado and it's about to pop, you're about to come tumbling down.

Don't blame the missing rung. The ladder's still there. A bridge of sighs, of notes hanging in the air. A quicksilver run down the piano keys, each rib real as it's touched, then wiped clean, gone as Monk's hand flies glissando in the other direction.

One night trying to read myself to sleep I heard the silence of rain. You might call silence a caesura, a break in a line of verse, the line pausing naturally to breathe, right on time, on a dime. But always a chance the line will never finish because the pause that refreshes can also swallow everything to the right and left of it.

Smoke curls from a gun barrel. The old poet, dissed by his young lover, shoots him, is on his way to jail. Rimbaud recovers form the wound, heads south towards long, long silence. Standing on a steamer's deck, baseball cap backward on his head, elbows on the rail, baggy pants drooping past the crack of his ass, Rimbaud sees the sea blistered by many dreamers like himself who leap off ships when no one's looking as if the arc of their falling will never end, as if the fall can't be real because nobody hears it, as if they might return to their beginnings, receive another chance, as if the fall will heal them, a hot torch welding shut the black hole, the mouth from which silence issues thick as smoke from necklaces of burning tires.

Monk speaks many languages. The same sound may have different meanings in different languages. (To say = *tu sait* = you know.) And the same sound may also produce different silences. To say nothing is not necessarily to know nothing. The same letters can represent different sounds. Or different letters equal the same sound (pane, pain, peign, Payne). In different languages or the same. A lovers' quarrel in the rain at the train station. The budding poet seals his lips evermore. The older man trims his words to sonnets, willed silence caging sound. Their quarrel echoes over and over again, what was said and not said and unsaid returns. The heart (ancient liar/lyre) hunched on its chair watching silent reruns, lip-synching new words to old songs.

Monk's through playing and everybody in the joint happy as a congregation of seals full of fish. He sits on the piano bench, hulking, mute, his legs chopped off at the knees like a Tutsi's by his fellow countrymen, listening in the dark to their hands coming together, making no sound. Sits till kingdom come, a giant sponge or ink blotter soaking up first all the light, then the air, then sucking all sound from the darkness, from the stage, the auditorium. The entire glittering city shuts down. Everything caves in, free at last in this bone-dry house.

Silence. Monk's. Mine. Yours. I haven't delved into mine very deeply yet, have I, avoid my silence like a plague, even though the disease I'm hiding from already rampant in my blood, bones, the air.

Where are you? How far to your apartment from the Woodside exit? What color are your eyes? Is your hair long or short? I know your father's gone. I met a taxi driver who happened to be from your hometown, a friendly, talkative brother about your father's age so I asked him if he knew your dad, figuring there would have been a colored part of your town and everybody would sort of know everybody else the way they used to in the places where people like our parents were raised. Yeah, oh yeah. 'Course I knew Henry Diggs, he said. Said he'd grown up knowing your dad and matter of fact had spoken with him in the American Legion club not too long before he heard your father had died. Whatever took your father, it took him fast, the man said. Seemed fine at the club. Little thin maybe but Henry always been a neat, trim-looking fellow and the next thing I heard he was gone. Had that conversation with a cabdriver about five years ago and the way he talked about your dad I could picture him neat and trim and straight-backed, clear-eyed. Then I realized the picture out-of-date. Twenty years since I'd seen your father last and I hadn't thought much about him since. Picture wasn't actually a picture anyway. When I say picture I guess I mean the taxi driver's words made your father real again. Confirmed something about him. About me. The first time I met your father and shook his hand, I noticed your color, your cheekbones in his face. That's what I'd look for in his different face if someone pointed out an old man and whispered your father's name. You singing in his silent features.

Picturing you also seems to work till I try to really see the picture. Make it stand still, frame it. View it. Then it's not a picture. It's a wish. A yearning. Many images layered one atop the other, passing through one another, each one so fragile it begins to fade, to dance, give way to the next before I can fix you in my mind. No matter how gently I lift the veil your face comes away with it. . . .

James Brown, the hardest worker in showbiz, drops down on one knee. Please. Please. Please. Don't go. A spotlight fixes the singer on a darkened stage. You see every blister of sweat on his glistening do, each teardrop like a bedbug crawling down the black satin pillowcase of his cheeks. Please. Please. Please. But nobody answers. 'Cause nobody's home. She took his love and gone. J.B. dies a little bit onstage. Then more and more. His spangled cape shimmers where he tosses it, bright pool at the edge of the stage someone he loves dived into and never came up.

Silence a good way of listening for news. Please. Please. Is anybody out there? The singer can't see beyond the smoking cone of light raining on his shoulders, light white from outside, midnight blue if you're in it. Silence is Please. Silence is Please Please Please hollered till it hurts. Noise no one hears if no one's listening. And night after night evidently they ain't.

Who wants to hear the lost one's name? Who has the nerve to say it? Monk taps it out, depressing the keys, stitching messages his machine launches into the make-believe of hearts. Hyperspace. Monk folded over his console. Mothership. Mothership. Beam me up, motherfucker. It's cold down here.

Brother Sam Cooke squeezed into a phone booth and the girl can't help it when she catches him red-handed in the act of loving somebody else behind the glass. With a single shot she blows him away. But he's unforgettable, returns many nights. Don't cry. Don't cry. No, no, no—no. Don't cry.

My silence? Mine. My silence is, as you see, as you hear, sometimes broken by Monk's music, by the words of his stories. My silence not like Monk's, not waiting for what comes next to arrive or go on about its god-damned business. I'm missing someone. My story is about losing you. About not gripping tight enough for fear my fingers would close on air. Love, if we get it, as close to music as most of us get, and in Monk's piano solos I hear your comings and goings, tiptoeing in and out of rooms, in and out of my heart, hear you like I hear the silence there would be no music without, the silence saying the song could end at this moment, any moment silence plays around. Because it always does, if you listen closely. Before the next note plays, silence always there.

Three thirty in the a.m. I'm wide awake and alone. Both glow-in-the-dark clocks say so—the square one across the room, the watch on the table beside the bed—they agree, except for a ten-minute discrepancy, like a long-standing quarrel in an old marriage. I don't take sides. Treat them both as if there is something out there in the silence yet to be resolved, and the hands of these clocks are waiting as I am for a signal so they can align themselves perfectly with it.

I lie in my bed a thousand years. Aching silently for you. My arms crossed on my chest, heavy as stone, a burden awhile, then dust trickling through the cage of ribs, until the whole carcass collapses in upon itself, soundlessly, a heap of fine powder finally the wind scatters, each particle a note unplayed, returned perfectly intact.

When Monk finishes work it's nearly dawn. He crosses Fifty-Seventh Street, a cigarette he's forgotten to light dangles from his lower lip.

What up, Monk.

Uh-huh.

Moon shines on both sides of the street. People pour from lobbies of tall hotels, carrying umbrellas. Confetti hang-glides, glittery as tinsel. A uniformed brass band marches into view, all the players spry, wrinkled old men, the familiar hymn they toot and tap and whistle and bang thrashes and ripples like a tiger caught by its tail.

Folks form a conga line, no, it's a second line hustling to catch up to Monk, who's just now noticed all the commotion behind him. The twelve white horses pulling his coffin are high-steppers, stallions graceful, big-butted, and stylized as Rockettes. They stutter-step, freeze, raise one fore-leg bent at the knee, shake it like shaking cayenne pepper on gumbo. The horses also have the corner boys' slack-leg, drag-leg pimp-strut down pat and perform it off-time in unison to the crowd's delighted squeals down Broadway while the brass band cooks and hordes of sparrow-quick pickaninnies and rump-roast-rumped church ladies wearing hats so big you think helicopter blades or two wings to hide their faces and players so spatted and chained, ringed and polished, you mize well concede everything you own to them before the game starts, everybody out marching and dancing behind Mr. Monk's bier, smoke from the cigarette he's mercifully lit to cut the funk drifting back over them, weightless as a blessing, as a fingertip grazing a note not played.

In my dream, we're kissing goodbye when Monk arrives. First his music, and then the great man himself. All the air rushes from my lungs. Thelonious Apoplecticus, immensely enlarged in girth, his cheeks puffed out like Dizzy's. He's sputtering and stuttering, exasperated, pissed off as can be. Squeaky chipmunk voice like a record playing at the wrong speed, the way they say Big O trash-talked on the b-ball court or deep-sea divers squeak if raised too rapidly from great depths. Peepy dolphin pip-pip peeps, yet I understand exactly.

Are you crazy, boy? Telling my story. Putting mouth in my words. Speechless as my music rendered your simple ass on countless occasions what kind of bullshit payback is this? Tutti-frutti motherfucker. Speaking for me. Putting your jive woogie in my boogie.

Say what, nigger? Who said I retreated to silence? Retreat hell. I was attacking in another direction.

The neat goatee and mustache he favored a raggedy wreath now, surrounding his entire moon face. He resembles certain Hindu gods with his nappy aura, his new dready cap of afterbirth in flames to his shoulders. Monk shuffles and grunts, dismisses me with a wave of his glowing hand. When it's time, when he feels like it, he'll play the note we've been waiting for. The note we thought was lost in silence. And won't it be worth the wait.

Won't it be a wonder. And meanwhile, love, while we listen, these foolish things remind me of you.

IN PRAISE OF SILENCE

1998

On a room-sized dock beside a Maine lake where for thirty-some summers I've gone each morning to write, I often find myself thinking about silence. When I'm writing or, more likely, in the spaces between writing that are also writing—the spaces when words aren't being scratched on the page, either because one thought is finished or another won't come or because I'm having thoughts for which no words exist, no words I know yet anyway—when I'm pausing, looking out at water, trees and sky, the silence of my hideaway in the woods meets the silence inside me and forms a horizon as tangible and razor-sharp as the shoreline across the lake, dividing trees from their upside-down reflections on days when water and wind are calm.

Perhaps words lie behind this horizon, but for the moment they are utterly inaccessible and can remain so for what seems like minutes, hours, days, on and off the dock. Some mornings I'm frustrated by the pause, disquieted by a foreboding that no words exist, that even if there are words, they will always fail, that this pause might go on and on, but more often I find myself growing calmer, relaxing, spreading out, breathing deeper because I'm aware of time's motion, its capaciousness, aware of being inside it, bundled, dragged, gliding along. I never get closer to understanding time than in these moments when inner and outer silence meet: Silence, a medium I enter and feel around and inside me, an affirming vital presence always, whether or not I'm conscious of it.

The more I write, the more I realize how deeply I'm indebted to a communal experience of time and silence, an African-American language evolving from that experience, a language vernacular, visceral, sensuous, depending on the entire body's expressive repertoire, subversive, liberating, freighted with laughter, song, and sigh, burdened and energized by opposition. African-rooted, culturally descended ways and means of speaking that emerged from the dungeon and dance of silence.

For a people who have endured a long, long history of waiting—waiting at the Jordan River, waiting chained in stone forts on the west coast of Africa, waiting for slavery and discrimination to end, waiting for justice and respect as first-class citizens, waiting for prison gates to open, waiting eternities in emergency wards and clinic lines of sorry urban hospitals—silence is an old, familiar companion. Time and silence, silence and time. The silence attending waiting, waiting through times of enforced silence. Silence the ground upon which wishes are inscribed while the endless waiting continues. Silence a dreaming space where what's awaited is imagined and, when it doesn't come, the space where dreams are dismantled, dissolving again into silence. Dreams born and dying and born again in the deep womb of silence, and silence, tainted though it is by disappointment and waiting, also a reservoir of hope.

Imagine yourself disembarked on an alien shore after a long, painful voyage so harrowing you're not certain you survived it. You're sick, weak, profoundly disoriented. You fear you haven't actually arrived anywhere but are just slipping into another fold of a nightmare.

You are naked and chained to others who look like you, under the merciless control of brutal strangers who look and act nothing like you and, much worse, do not speak your language. To you their language is gibberish, the ba-ba-baaing of barbarians. They communicate their orders with blows, screams, shoves, crude pantomime. You are compelled at the peril of life and limb to make sense of verbal assault, physical abuse. You realize you're learning a new language even as you swallow the bitterness, the humiliation of learning the uselessness of your own. Much of this learning and unlearning occurs in silence inside your skull, in the sanctuary where you're simultaneously struggling to retain traces of who you are, what you were before this terrible, scouring ordeal began. In order to save your life, when you attempt to utter the first word of a new tongue, are you also violating your identity and dignity? When you break your silence, are you surrendering, acknowledging the strangers' power to own you, rule you? Are you forfeiting your chance to tell your story in your own words some day?

Silence in this context is a measure of resistance and tension. A drastic expression of difference that maintains the distinction between using a language and allowing it to use you.

That was yesterday. Yet much has not changed. Centuries have not erased the archetypal differences between people of African descent brought to the new world as slaves, and the people who claimed this new world, claimed our African bodies and minds. Tension and resistance characterize the practices African-descended peoples have employed to keep their distance from imposed tongues, imposed disciplines. Generation after generation has been compelled to negotiate—for better or worse, and with self-determination and self-realization at stake—the quicksand of a foreign language that continues by its structure, vocabulary, its deployment in social interactions, its retention of racist assumptions, expressions, and attitudes, its contamination by theories of racial hierarchy to re-create the scenario of master and slave.

Uneasiness and a kind of disbelief of this incriminating language we've been forced to adopt never go away. Some of us choose to speak very, very little or not at all. Let our actions, other parts of our bodies besides the mouth, speak for us. Lots of us refuse to change speech habits that distinguish us as southern or urban or rural or hip or poor and lacking formal education. Some glory in these habits, others can switch when convenient, necessary or enjoyable. Plenty of us have mastered the master and always wear the mask. Many, whether proficient or not in standard dialects, despise them. Mangle, distort, satirize the would-be master's tongue. Reject most of it, stigmatize the so-called mainstream language, seal it in a ghetto, a barrio, separate and unequal. Some strategies are defensive, reactionary, destructive, others outrageously healthy and creative, and the totality of these strategies make up the African-American culture.

Silence marks time, saturates and shapes African-American art. Silences structure our music, fill the spaces—point, counterpoint—of rhythm, cadence, phrasing. Think of the eloquent silences of Thelonious Monk, sometimes comic, sometimes manic and threatening. Recall gospel's wordless choruses hummed, moaned, keened, words left far behind as singers strive to reach what's unsayable, the silent pulse of Great Time abiding within the song.

Silence times our habits of speech and non-speech, choreographs the intricate dance of oral tradition, marks who speaks first, last, how long and with what authority. Silence indicates who is accorded respect, deference, modulates call-and-response, draws out the music in words and phrases. Silence a species of argument, logical and emotionally persuading, heightening what's at stake. Silence like Amen at the end of a prayer invokes the presence of invisible ancestors whose voices, though quiet now, permeate the stillness, quicken the ancient wisdom silence holds.

The sign of silence presides over my work. Characters who can't speak, won't speak, choose never to speak until this world changes. Stories and essays whose explicit subject or theme is silence. My impulse to give voice to the dead, the unborn, to outlaws and outcasts whose voices have been stolen or muted by violence. Characters who talk in tongues, riddles, prophecies, at the margins, unintelligible until it's too late. Alternate forms of speech, in my fiction, which celebrate the body's ingenuity, how it compensates the loss of one expressive sense with eloquence in another. My ongoing attempt to define African-American culture, explicate its heavy debt, its intimacy with silence. My journey back to lost African cultures, to the stories of Homewood, the Pittsburgh community where I was raised. My struggle to emulate the achievement of African-American artists in song, dance, sport; invent a language that doesn't feel secondhand, borrowed, a language rich with time and silence that animate the written word.

And thinking about that struggle takes me back to those mornings on the dock in Maine. The silence I experience there is not really silence. It's an illusion. If we hear nothing, if one ever can hear nothing, it only means we aren't listening hard enough. At a minimum, we can hear ourselves listening. The total absence of sound is never a possibility for a hearing person, is it? Unless we pretend to have God's ear and can stand aside, outside being, outside self, and listen. So silence is a metaphor. A way of thinking about how it might feel to be both creature and creator, able to experience whatever there might be to hear or not hear if the earth stopped spinning. Silence is a way of imagining such a moment outside time, imagining the possibility of pausing at ground zero and examining our lives before the buzz of the world overtakes us. Nice work if we could get it, and even though we can't, we have the power to see ourselves other than we are. Silence is proof that the decision to listen or not is ours. Proof that we are called to pay attention.

THIS MAN CAN PLAY

1998

Five largish Negro men and one small white one piled into a jalopy on January 7, 1927, and headed out of Chicago for Hinckley, Illinois, fifty miles west, to play basketball for money. Abe Saperstein's Harlem, New York, Globetrotters (they didn't actually go to Harlem until 1968, after Abe was dead) were born, and seventy-plus years later you can still catch them at your local arena.

Lots has changed, hasn't it, since that first game in Hinckley, when the Globies earned seventy-five dollars and split it seven ways, one share each for the players, two for Abe—coach, promoter, number one and only substitute off the bench. As you're no doubt aware, the team achieved phenomenal international success. Other businessmen tried to emulate the Trotter formula and launched barnstorming basketball squads. Traveling professional teams with names like badges of ethnic pride, Celtics, Germans, Swedes, formed into leagues as ephemeral as most struggling teams, leagues that waxed and waned until the NBA, arising from the ashes of the American Basketball League, developed its master plan of hype and marketing, pumping up the volume, piling up profits through commodifying the basketball skills of large black men, achieving a level of success Coach Saperstein never dreamed of, and Abe Saperstein when he died was quite a rich man.

Saperstein is not included in the chorus of famous coaches—Dean Smith of North Carolina, John Thompson of Georgetown, among others—who appear and speak in Spike Lee's new movie, *He Got Game*, playing themselves, testifying to the phenomenal skills of a fictional high school hoopster, Jesus Shuttlesworth, whose father, Jake, is played by Denzel Washington. P. J. Carlesimo, victim of a disputed assault perpetrated upon him by one of his players, Latrell Sprewell, an NBA All-Star, doesn't get a speaking role in Spike Lee's movie, either (even though he was Denzel's freshman basketball coach at Fordham). Yet the invisible presence of P.J. and Abe informs the film and this narrative. Both coaches deserve at least honorable mention for making their mark on the game, for giving us something to ponder on our way to *He Got Game* and its leading man.

When he called to say he'd walk to the restaurant to meet me, I wondered if a star of Denzel's magnitude could appear on the street and not be accosted by fans. I should have known the answer. For Denzel Washington, appearance is often disguise enough. If you're a sturdily built, youngish (forty-three), athletic-looking black guy on an urban street at night, people, especially white people, tend to pretend you're not there. The passerby, even if he or she doesn't wish Denzel away, won't hardly be getting up in his face to check him out. Movie star—unless it's Samuel L. Jackson playing his latest scary, amoral, vicious, neo-minstrel hoodlum— is the last thing on the passerby's mind as he negotiates this archetypal urban minefield, the minidrama of black menace and white vulnerability all the Denzel Washingtons in the world can't root out.

An old story. Growing up black in America, Denzel Washington got plenty of practice perfecting the art of invisibility, that peculiar state of being there and not being there, with its perks and punishments, usually a perverse mix of both, for African-Americans willing to play the roles race assigns. Who authored the original script of race, where the story's headed, who's going to win or lose at the end, if there is an end, are issues most players, black or white, don't concern themselves with. Day by day, we go along to get along. We need work, any kind of work, and take it where we can get it. But is it different for a star? Do superstars transcend race, can they truly cross over? Or is a starring role just one more tributary emptying into the rushing river of the race script that carries us all along helter-skelter, a flood washing away the ground the country stands on?

Go along to get along. Wisdom as ancient as power. Can disguise buy space, comic/tragic wiggle room, freedom? Through the roles he plays, especially the role of Hollywood superstar, how much space has Denzel Washington earned? What's he doing with it?

Denzel's billed cap is pushed back from his forehead now. On cue, some young ladies at the bar send the waiter over with an offer to buy Mr. Washington a drink. A minute later, a pretty girl dawdles at our table, cheeks flushed, just on the edge of giddy, to pay her respects.

You can't take your eyes off Denzel. The man devours attention. Grasps it, won't let go. Makes you feel almost guilty when your gaze strays from his face, his mobile hands.

Before the tape starts rolling, I ask him what he thought of *He Got Game*, in which he portrays a man incarcerated for killing his wife, and in which his character becomes an exploration of a father's obligations to his children. He's fresh from his first viewing of the nearly finished movie, so he's reluctant to say very much. Loyalty to Spike causes him to hesitate, not party-line, partisan, black-on-black loyalty that mutes criticism but the decent urge to speak first to his colleague, collaborator, and friend, the person with the greatest stake in *He Got Game*.

As a matter of fact, Denzel leads off with the bad news. Interesting. Interesting, but still too long. Quickly, he adds, I was teary a lot. It got to me. A strong movie. I was moved, teary-eyed more than once.

He asks about a few scenes he remembered shooting that were missing in the version he'd just seen. Were they in the cut I'd screened a couple weeks before?

You never know, he says. Work your butt off, think you're going great, and then you see the final cut and your scene didn't make it.

Probably why I'm ready to turn to directing, he says. Acting's like someone asking you for years to write the characters, but they write the book. Or they give you the outline of their story and say: Now what I need from you, John, is, is. Or in my case now, it's just one character, the main character; they want you to write the main character, and when you finish it, give it to them and they'll use it as they see fit. They're not out to manipulate you, necessarily. They want to use the best of what you give them.

You've played many different roles, many different kinds of men. But there's another character, isn't there, who's being constructed as you star in movie after Hollywood movie. A character named Denzel Washington. Did you have to learn to play him?

The celebrity.

Call it whatever you want to call it.

To be honest with you, I think it comes into play most in interviews. Or in ceremonies like putting my handprints in the sidewalk outside Grauman's Chinese Theater, those public moments.

When I'm coaching kids, no. When I'm in the office, no. When I'm at home, no. When I'm going to the movies and somebody recognizes me, not really. I just say, How'ya doing. The celebrity person is relevant to interviews 'cause there I can combat it, deflate it. The same way I work with my kids to help them feel their daddy's just their daddy who has a different kind of job.

I deconstruct the image. When someone goes, You're this and you're that, I say, Said who? When I get all these sex-symbol and role-model and voice-of-the-black-people questions, all that kind of stuff, I back off. Say that's not me. It's not who I am.

You don't feel the pressure of other people's expectations.

Like where? Like when? At a Little League game? My daughter's hoop games? Maybe one of the reasons I wanted to do Jake Shuttlesworth in *He Got Game* is to go against the tide. Yeah, the image stuff can affect you in the way you're trying to fight it. People saying you always play the good guy, the nice guy, whatever. I'm like, wow, I didn't think so.

You know, I didn't go into acting to be a movie star. I never thought about being a movie star, ever, ever in my life, ever. Even once I started getting roles. I figured I was gonna work in the theater, and if I ever got in movies, it would be movies like *Taxi Driver*. I didn't look at guys like De Niro as movie stars. I looked at them as great actors in movies. I wasn't into movies as a kid. As a teenager, I saw *Shaft* and whatnot, but I didn't think, I want to be the actor playing Shaft. Shaft maybe. Not the actor.

The other piece to that is there weren't lots of movies where we could see ourselves. Back when I started going, there was maybe *River Niger*, *Claudine*, maybe *Bingo Long*.

I wanted to play Shakespeare, play the great classic roles. The best black theater, white, whatever, I was more into that. I mean we were snobs. I signed with the William Morris Agency before I graduated from college. My choice was to go to study at the American Conservatory Theater, not stay in New York and start working or go to Hollywood. I never thought about going to L.A.

So you wanted to be Laurence Olivier.

Yeah, I guess so.

I wanted to be Hemingway or T. S. Eliot.

Right. Right, right, exactly.

Those were the models out there.

Exactly, wanted that diamond as big as the Ritz.

In *He Got Game*, one of the scenes that affected Washington most occurs at night on a Coney Island outdoor basketball court. A father-coaching-son scene. Jake Shuttlesworth one-on-one against Jesus, his twelve-year-old son. It turns into a raw, brutal encounter. Jake, twisted up inside with anger and frustration over his own failure to make the big time, is determined to instill in his son an unshakable core of toughness and resolve, so this go-round, in Jesus, this new, prodigiously talented version of his flesh, Jake won't fail again. The coaching, the good intentions, unravel, the game turns ugly, an excuse for physical and verbal battering, Jake beating himself up in the person of his son. Even the winos hidden on the dark margins of the court urge Jake to lighten up, chill out. Way past time for a Sprewell. You root for young Jesus. Wish he was a dozen years older, a hundred pounds heavier, so he could whip his tormentor's ass, Daddy or not.

Jesus ends the game by heaving the ball over the fence into the black, black night surrounding the court. The scene's over, but Jake can't let it go. Assaults his son again at the dinner table, and the result is the accidental death of his wife when she tries to intervene, a terrible moment that sends Jake to prison and orphans his children. Denzel says the father-son scene on the court was difficult to watch.

I coach kids, he says. I work them real hard. I'm a good motivator. A rah-rah kind of guy. Get the kids ready to go. Send them out there and we just wear the other team out. Run them to death. We're better. We're faster. We know what to do. This is our time. Let's go get 'em. I teach them they own the fourth quarter. Our time. 'Cause we've worked harder. We're in better shape. Something I learned from P. J. Carlesimo at Fordham. Owning the fourth quarter. He'd run us till our tongues hanging out. He was tough. But we believed we could go out and own the fourth quarter. Tickles me to hear my little guys going around psyching up each other. We got 'em. Got 'em. We own the fourth quarter. Run those chumps out of here.

On the other hand, I've seen some parents who go way too far. I've seen coaches mean to their kids, knocking them down. Some people might say maybe that's not a bad thing. To them maybe even the scene of Jake coaching Jesus is not a bad thing. He's playing with his kid, a one-on-one game. So what, he's pushing him and knocking him down. Maybe it's just what Jesus needs.

*One thing in the suburbs. Another in the 'hood, maybe. Is it a man's role,
our role, to bring the bad news? Toughen up the kids so they'll survive a
tough, tough world. No sentiment. No soft love.*

No soft love? To what does Jesus owe his success? Was it his mother?
Was it Jake killing his mother and Jesus having to make it on his own?

Explosive. Something bad had to happen. Jake was definitely living
through his son. There's a million guys that don't make it, and they all got
a reason, an excuse. It's mainly about Jake's frustration. In a way, he also
saw this kid as his meal ticket. You know, he wanted to get paid, to get out
of the projects.

The whole thing was headed in a bad direction. Then, *boom, bam,*
something bad does happen, totally unexpected. I don't think Jake was a
wife beater. They had their bad days, sure, but, man, suddenly she's dead.
He killed her. Spike's into some tasty stuff. And it's something different
for me. Looking rough, being a con.

Jake had to get rougher and tougher to survive in prison. He had to
grow up. And still has a long way to go. I came out the jail and the first
thing I do is buy some sneakers. Shorts on, old leg wrapped up in Ace
bandages, trying to pick up where I left off. Who's the kid and who's the
adult? Jesus says no to ten thousand dollars his high school coach offers.
He's the tough one.

What made Jesus so strong?

I remember my kids' grandmother, Pauletta's mother, the switch that
appeared in our house when she was around. As parents, we'd have "discussions" with the kids. When Grandma was around, that switch would
be over by the window, and she'd tell the kids she's going to rub it on
their legs. That was enough sometimes to straighten them out. Just touch
them with it. Just touch the children with a switch. Being on the road and
coming home and trying to catch up for all that time away, found myself
being too nice. Guilty about being gone, and I let the kids get away with
murder.

*In my house, the deterrent for us kids was, Wait till your father gets
home.*

Right. Wait till your father . . . that was one of the ways we develop our imaginations, imagining how he was going to kill us when he got home, and the longer the amount of time, the better the imagination was. I remember we were playing ball near the house and my father told us to stop and went to work, and we started up again and broke a window. Everybody suddenly had somewhere to go. All my friends gone, and I got eight hours to think about my fate.

What a country. Real Jesus Shuttlesworths still in high school signing multimillion-dollar NBA contracts. Globies, wearing the uniforms of Hawks or Bulls, riding into town, itching for a fight, archetypal American road warriors with enormous guns but corked up in blackface, a few great white hopes as sidekicks, forbidden, seductive black bodies on display for a night of G-rated fun. Indians posing as cowboys and they get paid to scalp the locals. Black over white in a country historically, fiercely, dedicated to just the opposite proposition. Michael Jordan in an ad, winking at two white girls who sit on a park bench checking him out, wishing away the emperor's trousers, speculating aloud about the style of his underdrawers as the bald, black prince strolls, struts, trots by. If it sells underwear, if it sells tickets, there's no rule that can't be broken, no stereotype not turned upside down, pulled inside out.

Free at last. No category—religion, babies, mothers (shame on you, Reggie White)—not subject to the striptease of advertising's pop pornography. As long as it sells. Free at last, as long as it sells.

I love the game of basketball. Played it forty-some years, from grade school through semipro after college, long past the time the game should have passed me by, but I wouldn't let it. Loved it too much. Play it still when I watch my son Dan follow my daughter Jamila's career with the L.A. Sparks of the WNBA. Love the game. My heart hurt more than my neck when pinched nerves at the top of my spine forced me to stop running full court last year. Anything I write about hoop automatically tends toward praise song. Words want to dribble, fast-break, crossover, throw no-look passes. Shake-and-bake words, words dancing to head music in time to the bouncing ball, words energized by spirits of ancestor movement, ancestor talk. I surely don't wish to pen an elegy.

But there's P.J. and Latrell to deal with. Smoldering memories rekindled when authority and race got entangled because some white person assumes the stance of adult to child, master to slave, and verbally abuses a black person as if no restraint is required, no payback expected, deserved, or allowed.

And then there's Len Bias and Earl Manigault and L. D. Lawson from Susquehanna Street in Homewood, Pittsburgh, Pennsylvania. L.D. six feet nine inches when six feet nine inches was as large as you needed to grow to be a big man on the court. L.D. blessed with height and gifts but up on his shoulders a head for trouble mostly and ended up in prison, where drugs and sugar diabetes stole his legs, shrinking him to a wheelchair like a Tutsi warrior chopped off at the knees by a machete. The point being not simply that some don't make it. Not everybody's supposed to make it. Many are called, few chosen, and the beat goes on, hoop, art, love, any enterprise requiring huge talent and copious good fortune. The point's not a mountain of sad stories shadowing the few outrageous successes but how necessary it is to keep your eye on the real prize, the big picture, especially when you're in love with a game, the heroes of that game.

And in the case of hoop, the game I love, the big picture includes irony, paradox, pain, poor drug-ridden communities blasted by unemployment, sudden violent death, imprisonment, the slow erosion of health and prospects, affluent communities of spenders wildly consuming, addicted to possessions, communities connected mostly by the overarching dog-eat-dog ethos reigning from top to bottom of the economic scale.

Spike Lee knows most of the big picture I've been attempting to draw, or knows all of it, probably more. *He Got Game* insists (and if an artist of Spike Lee's stature didn't insist, we should insist he insist) on being more than just another pretty commercial, exploiting basketball to sell things.

And there's no doubt about the film's ambitions. Spike Lee's a high roller in this one. He's offering basketball as a mirror for the times. The game is spectacularized, then becomes lamp as well as mirror, a surface for rendering a reflection of society that's also a light for exploration, for probing the dark recesses, destabilizing bright images of hoop, our national prosperity, Jesus Shuttlesworth's future as star and savior.

Clearly, *He Got Game* is loaded with issues. Black-father-and-son stuff, prison stuff, making-it stuff, family-violence stuff, race stuff, just plain stuffs—hooping stuffs, humping stuffs. In-your-face stuffs. Stuff. At its deepest level, the film asks, What do fathers owe their sons, sons owe their fathers? Is there honorable currency with which such debts can be paid? Paid in a fashion that creates intimacy, trust, opportunities for progress from generation to generation?

In this regard, what catches the eye are the flash cards illustrating the world Jesus is struggling to reach, a "white" world of privilege and wealth not without its own unwholesome perils—the State University of Sodom and Gomorrah, with its Stepford-wife coeds, corrupt, decadent "brothers," wraithlike "sisters" floating in the margins, blond succubi, an Elmer Gantry hoop coach.

Does Jesus have other choices? Is what's at stake the potential for Jesus to be a better person or better paid? If it's better paid, end of story. Heaven is the NBA, a seat on the stock exchange. If better person, why doesn't the movie consider or generate alternatives to leaving home? Offscreen, I can't help asking how the circumstances Jesus finds himself in parallel the crossover careers of Spike Lee, Denzel Washington, *me*.

What we witness in the film tells us the game flourishes on Coney Island. As pure self-expression, as an exciting excuse for mental and physical exercise, as a means for developing toughness of backbone, spirit, and muscle. It's the real game and still to be found on the playgrounds. Jesus doesn't have to leave home to find it. It's not confined to privileged suburbs or cloistered colleges. Some people would say the last place to look for it is Madison Square Garden.

So what's up? Why does this sharp, affecting, skywalking film low-bridge itself with a tired trope? Why is one more African-American protagonist's quest for integrity, for actualization, identity, and fulfillment, predictably enacted within the framework of escaping home? What about changing home, taking others with him or her, giving back if he must go alone? What about changing what lies beyond home?

Other stories, aren't they? Ones we desperately need to begin telling. Movies, music, dance, stars that cross over, not to reach a different side from where they started but to create and experience new territory. And when the territory's vital, original, free, of course color won't disappear, but color will mean what it means. More and less than it meant before. Different meanings. Meaning beyond the cages of black and white we've fashioned for ourselves. Will the cages open? Will there be hoop dancing in the streets?

A fan came up to Denzel once, complimenting him on *Devil in a Blue Dress*, saying it was his favorite film because of one scene in the movie he'd never forget, Denzel as Easy Rawlins in a rocking chair, napping on his front porch. The compliment not about Denzel's acting but about what the scene captured, another era, a lost world when time was more expansive, when people could sit long and safely, enjoy the bliss of doing nothing on the front stoop of a little home on property their sweat had earned. The dream of modest, urban gentryhood exported north from the Plantation South. Old rural values, house, hearth, hard work, independence, respect, and intimacy with the seasons, the abiding cycles of nature, a deep, traditional spirituality not too austere to wink nor too uptight to enjoy the greedy appetites of the senses. Another mode of being in time, suddenly concrete, epiphanized for a fan by his favorite scene in his favorite movie.

When Denzel Washington and his wife, Pauletta Pearson, travel with their kids to North Carolina, it's to recover some of that lifestyle, those values that allowed Easy to relax on his porch in *Devil*.

When I went to North Carolina the first time, he says, it was for a wedding. When my family got ready to leave, my in-laws brought us to the airport. Papa's teary-eyed, Mother's teary-eyed, a brother, he's like forty years old and he's teary-eyed, too. I said, Man, I got to have some of this, 'cause this is real and genuine and this has history, this goes way back. Pauletta's grandmother, who all our kids got to know, when they met her she must've been ninety-nine years old.

Grandma Kate. She and her husband, John, worked for Dean Acheson, assistant secretary of state, I believe. They ran his house. My father-in-law, Pauletta's dad, he was a principal at the top black school down there before desegregation, Newton-Conover. Pauletta's father said the worst thing ever happened to him was integration. He had a fine school, great debating team, symphony orchestra, and then they took his best students and best teachers. The only thing left from his school now is the gym and a place where you can come and get a state meal. Integration comes and we get the gym and some cheese.

When my father-in-law comes to California, all my friends, everybody shows up. He and his wife just sit there. They're in their late eighties now. And you know he's telling the same stories over and over, but he's got so much wisdom, so much for the kids to get. He sits them out in the yard and teaches them from the book of Proverbs. He's lived his life from the book of Proverbs.

Why don't we have that on film somewhere? It's a hell of a story. We're losing our memory of the old culture.

My kids are getting the history. I'm so glad I had a chance before my father passed away to go out with him on the land, the property we owned. Him walking and showing us the boundaries, telling us the history, who was buried where, how they got the land, going back to the times when blacks couldn't own land and my great-great-grandfather married an Indian who could own land and bought it in her name. You know, two dollars an acre, a buck and a quarter an acre.

The lack of conversation between fathers and sons is one of the biggest deficits in our culture. It's a space that needs to be filled, and if we don't fill it, all kinds of dangerous stuff gets in there, somebody else gets their evil in there, and each generation is estranged from the next. We've got to start the struggle all over again with each new generation.

The kids probably had that kind of talk more with their grandfather than with me because he knows what to say. I'm not as good at it as he is. And he's a guy that didn't really have parents around. The extended family was crucial to him.

The ceremony at Grauman's Theatre was important to me. I wanted my kids there, but I don't like to parade them out or make it seem like it's some kind of duty. So I called the old man right before the ceremony. Asked him, said, Give me a little something, Papa, before I go. Well, he did. And it was quick. Like bing, bing, bing. Something about love and family I'm not going to try to paraphrase. He's a serious guy.

Turns out the kids really wanted to go. Change your shirt, Dad, so we can be coordinated. They knew it was important to me, and they wanted to be a part of it. It was cool.

My grandfather was the one I remember carrying me around on his shoulders. He was the male who gave me physical tenderness.

I think my kids get wisdom from their grandpa. Things I don't know how to articulate. I have days with my kids, try to give everybody their special days. My youngest boy, for instance, I had a day with him where it was airport, marina. Anything flying, driving, boating. He loves fast cars, all kinds of trucks.

I'm looking for things to say to him, but the day turns out to be, Okay, let's just go on and walk and talk about boats. I'm thinking, C'mon, you got to make this great speech. The generations before were about letting things come out naturally. Evolving out of the moment as opposed to trying to make a moment, because they had more time. Time to sit on the porch, whittle wood, and the lesson, whatever, came out at the appropriate time. Maybe hours later. They didn't have to say, Sit down and have this five minutes of wisdom, I gotta run.

Your father was a preacher, a talker. Did he talk to you?

No. He was working all the time. I didn't have a close relationship with him. I can remember the one time he threw me a ball. Once. And I can remember the one time he came to a game. My senior year in high school, the championship game. I scored two touchdowns, but we got crushed 44–12. I remember yelling and screaming at everybody 'cause we were scared of the other team. They'd whomped us earlier in the season. My team was letting me down in front of the old man, the one day he came.

Which is probably why I . . . I wouldn't say overcompensate . . . why I've gotten so involved in my kids' sports.

I remember asking once, Am I hanging around too much? You know, am I, are you embarrassed by me? They said, No, Dad. No. 'Cause we wanna win. I got all this psychological stuff going on and my son breaks it down, We want to win, Dad. You help us win.

I'll tell you a funny, strange kind of story. My father had a stroke. He was in the hospital. All twisted up. He knew the family was there, recognized us, but he couldn't speak at all. I was busy, busy with Spike, working on the script for *Malcolm X*, but I flew down to Virginia. Had to see my dad. I was wrapping up, needed to get back to New York, and I said, Dad, everything's going to be taken care of. Don't worry, just get well. I leaned over and kissed him on his forehead and he started choking. Couldn't help asking myself, Did he start choking 'cause I kissed him? Like he's telling me. Just because I had a stroke, don't come in here and start kissing on me.

Always wondered if it was the kiss that started him choking. Nurse was rushing in, trying to calm him down. Wondered if he was thinking, Don't take advantage of me now, boy. If I could get up out this bed . . .

Not that he was a mean man, he was a gentle man, but, you know, from a different school. Our fathers were from a different school. I recall the one time touching my father's face with my face because I remember how rough his beard was. I don't remember bunches of hugs and kisses and goo-goo stuff, whatever.

Last time I saw him, he was shriveled up, skin blackened. Doctors sat me down and said, We're basically keeping him alive on drugs. So I knew it was about time, but again I had to leave. He was twisted to one side of the bed, so I went around there and held his hand and gave him my wrap-up speech again. You're going to make it. You're going to be all right. I got to go, Dad. You're going to be all right.

He gave me a stare. I'm talking about a stare. Like, Do I look like I'm getting better? A stare you couldn't write. Didn't say a word, hadn't moved all day, but he got this look on his face. Kind of like a double take. Boy, did I just hear you right? I'm twisted and shriveled up. I can't speak. I ain't moved all day. They got all kinds of holes in me everywhere, keeping me alive, and you think I'm going to be all right. Do I look like I'm going to be all right?

We had a wake for him in Virginia, then a wake service in Mount Vernon, New York, then we were going to bury him in White Plains. It was like a road show, like he was on tour. Everybody was about dried up from crying at wakes and services, from all the stops we made. And still, to this day, I never shed a tear, didn't and I don't know why.

Your father's son.

I don't know. It's not that I worked at staying dry-eyed. I just did.

Did you ever see him cry?

I don't think so.

My father neither. And I seldom cry. Except as I get older, tears seep out unexpectedly, sometimes for no good reason I know of.

I wasn't a crier, either, but I'm more apt to tear up now. Acting's like therapy. I guess I've become softer from acting because you tap into the emotional places.

While still in high school, Jesus must be a father to his younger sister. You can see the pain, envy, and defeat in Jake Shuttlesworth's eyes when he returns from prison too late to reclaim the job of raising his children. Too late to share the stories that might have saved his family. As father, actor, director, Denzel Washington wants to speak the stories Jake lost his chance to tell.

What needs to be passed on?

We need the warm, fuzzy stories. The problems people can work out around the table.

I wonder how those warm, fuzzy stories would fly now.

You can't dictate how people are going to react to the books you write. It depends on what they're bringing to it when they open it. Same thing with theater and film. What do they bring when they come in? I can't concern myself too much with what people are going to think. You know, I gotta write the book.

If someone asks, What do you think the audience should get from this movie? I say it depends on what they bring.

Eat your popcorn and get on outta here. Let the next group in. Clean your jujubes off the floor.

Cage and dance. The earliest pro hoop games were often contested inside literal cages of metal screening or netting to separate players and fans. Hence the word *cagers* as a synonym in sportspeak for basketball players. Dance was part of the early game, too. Nightclubs like Harlem's famous Savoy sponsored teams and offered a package of a ball game followed by a dance to entice fans.

Caging dance. Dancing in a cage. Rules and forms restrict freedom of expression. Yet there's the exhilarating, deeply satisfying compromise of a sonnet. A jazz solo. Creative tension. The eternal struggle between spirit and flesh. Sinew and will. Malcolm's mind expanding, flowering in prison. Harriet Tubman returning again and again to the burning slave ship of the South to rescue her sisters and brothers. Martin's dream rattling the iron bars of the Birmingham jail.

Michael rising, defying gravity. Cage and dance. Dance and cage. No better game.

WHAT IS A BROTHER?

1998

Bringer of chaos, protector, cute little bugger. A hedge against slipping off the world.

Perhaps you've seen the famous image that decorated everything from medallions to Wedgewood plates in the eighteenth century: a black slave bound, kneeling, eyes fixed heavenward, who asks, "Am I not a man and a brother?" Lincoln freed the slaves, so the story goes, and all men are created equal and therefore deserve equal protection of the law, but a brother . . . brother's a different matter altogether, isn't it.

I mean, if we're brothers, who's the mama? Who's the daddy? Are we talking literal brothers here or some metaphysical tarbrush staining us all just because we all wiggle through the birth canal, born of woman, born to die?

Brother. Isn't that what black guys call one another, and isn't it reverse discrimination—a watered-down, conspiratorial echo of black power? Doesn't the phrase "brotherhood of man" suggest a primal division— God's separate creation of his creatures, multiple evolutionary bloodlines of white, black, red, and yellow—that it's our duty to keep pure? *Broeder-bond.* Aryan brotherhood. The lost and found Nation of Islam.

On the other hand, don't brothers bring chaos into the world? Didn't

Cain murder Abel? Didn't Joseph's jealous brothers try to waste their younger sibling? What about Osiris and Set, Ahriman and Ahura Mazda, all those cosmic wombmates who went their separate ways, established warring kingdoms of light and dark, good and evil, the mythic Manichaean polarities that plague mankind even to this very moment?

We love our younger brothers, don't we. Cute little buggers. We hate the sight of the tattling, tagalong nuisance, the late arrival who dares claim an equal share of our parents' attention. An older brother is our first taste of tyranny. The big guy who shields us from bullies. When we're really tight with somebody, we say, I love him like a brother. Big Brother spies on us. We grow unspeakably close to, unspeakably distant from, our brothers. We lose a brother, but he never goes away, his absence as tangible as the ghost pain of an amputated limb.

When we look at a brother, do we see ourselves—similar features and faults, our shared humanity, common destiny; brothers beneath the skin in spite of our differences? Or do we see what we aren't—the dark side, the bad seed, the evil twin?

Is *brother* mired in the language and politics of male domination? *Brother* a means of extending, naturalizing patriarchal power, identifying family, passing property along the male lines? Recalling the chronicles of bloody feuds, fierce implosions of clans when women bear illegitimate heirs?

Did the revolutionary slogan *Liberté, Egalité, Fraternité* leave someone out? Inevitably spawn a militant sisterhood still clamoring for a rightful share of the power its brothers usurped from the king?

If brothers weren't raised by their parents but sent away at birth to grow up in separate households with no knowledge of one another, would there be some twilight-zone vibe of recognition if they passed each other on the street as adult strangers? If your answer is no, then wouldn't you be within your rights if you responded to the kneeling slave by pointing out that maybe you are a man and a brother, since such categories are arbitrary, socially constructed? But so what. Why does that entitle you to any special consideration? If you say yes to the possibility of some transcendent, essential connector lodged in the souls of brothers, do you also believe that connection crosses race, gender, and class lines? Neither science nor religion has been consistently helpful to the kneeling slave.

The poor brother's still stuck on his knees, damned if he does, damned if he doesn't receive an answer. He should be asking a different question. Of course he's a man and a brother. Why should he put that call in anyone else's hands? His voice is the best, only, and final authority for membership in the human family. A better question might be, What kind of man or brother stoops to peddling human flesh?

Is it possible the enslaved man is lamenting not only the particular woes of his condition but also addressing, in his desperation, a universal dilemma that truly defines him as everyone's brother: the existential loneliness and fear that comes with the knowledge that we are born alone and die alone? Isn't that the daunting price of individual consciousness, the "I"? Eternal estrangement, the eternal threat of absolute extinction never more distant than the thickness of our skin. We know the inscrutable void that spit us out will one day just as abruptly gulp us down again. Isn't this knowledge the razor's edge we dance on all the days of our lives?

Brothers and sisters are a kind of hedge against oblivion. Although death remains a certainty, although time's always running out, a brother, a sister, diverts time's attention. Our attention. Multiplies our chances. Dilates time. Gives us more skin—thicker skin sometimes, thinner sometimes, more vulnerable—more time when we share joy, pain, terror, the bounties and threats out there. Share them with someone so much like us that the line dividing us blurs, becomes more like a permeable, superglue membrane.

If you're struggling to rise off your knees, shed your chains, wouldn't it be nice to find someone in this wide, surprising world who's been where you've been and understands what you're saying, who might be prepared to do unto you as he or she would have you do unto him or her if your circumstances were reversed? Someone behaving like we dream a good brother would.

THE NIGHT I WAS NOBODY

1999

On July 4th, the fireworks day, the day for picnics and patriotic speeches, I was in Clovis, New Mexico, to watch my daughter, Jamila, and her team, the Central Massachusetts Cougars, compete in the Junior Olympics Basketball national tourney. During our ten-day visit to Clovis the weather had been bizarre. Hailstones large as golf balls. Torrents of rain flooding streets hubcap deep. Running through pelting rain from their van to a gym, Jamila and several teammates cramming through a doorway had looked back just in time to see a funnel cloud touch down a few blocks away. Continuous sheet lightning had shattered the horizon, crackling for hours night and day. Spectacular, off-the-charts weather flexing its muscles, reminding people what little control they have over their lives.

Hail rat-tat-tatting against our windshield our first day in town wasn't exactly a warm welcome, but things got better fast. Clovis people were glad to see us and the mini-spike we triggered in the local economy. Hospitable, generous, our hosts lavished upon us the same kind of hands-on affection and attention to detail that had transformed an unpromising place in the middle of nowhere into a very livable community.

On top of all that, the Cougars were kicking butt, so the night of July 3rd I wanted to celebrate with a frozen margarita. I couldn't pry anybody else away from "Bubba's," the movable feast of beer, chips and chatter the adults traveling with the Cougars improvised nightly in the King's Inn Motel parking lot, so I drove off alone to find one perfect margarita.

Inside the door of Kelley's bar and lounge I was flagged by a guy collecting a cover charge and told I couldn't enter wearing my Malcolm X hat. I asked why; the guy hesitated, conferred a moment with his partner, then declared that Malcolm X hats were against the dress code. For a split second I thought it might be that *no* caps were allowed in Kelley's. But the door crew and two or three others hanging around the entranceway all wore the billed caps ubiquitous in New Mexico, duplicates of mine, except theirs sported the logos of feedstores and truck stops instead of a silver *X*.

What careened through my mind in the next couple of minutes is essentially unsayable but included scenes from my own half century of life as a black man, clips from five hundred years of black/white meetings on slave ships, auction blocks, plantations, basketball courts, in the Supreme Court's marble halls, in beds, back alleys and back rooms, kisses and lynch ropes and contracts for millions of dollars so a black face will grace a cereal box. To tease away my anger I tried joking with folks in other places. Hey, Spike Lee. That hat you gave me on the set of the Malcolm movie in Cairo ain't legal in Clovis.

But nothing about these white guys barring my way was really funny. Part of me wanted to get down and dirty. Curse the suckers. Were they prepared to do battle to keep me and my cap out? Another voice said, Be cool. Don't sully your hands. Walk away and call the cops or a lawyer. Forget these chumps. Sue the owner. Or should I win hearts and minds? Look, fellas, I understand why the *X* on my cap might offend or scare you. You probably don't know much about Malcolm. The incredible metamorphoses of his thinking, his soul. By the time he was assassinated he wasn't a racist, didn't advocate violence. He was trying to make sense of America's impossible history, free himself, free us from the crippling legacy of race hate and oppression.

While all of the above occupied my mind, my body, on its own, had assumed a gunfighter's vigilance, hands ready at sides, head cocked, weight poised, eyes tight and hard on the doorkeeper yet alert to anything stirring on the periphery. Many other eyes, all in white faces, were checking out the entranceway, recognizing the ingredients of a racial incident. Hadn't they witnessed Los Angeles going berserk on their TV screens just a couple months ago? That truck driver beaten nearly to death in the street, those packs of black hoodlums burning and looting? Invisible lines were being drawn in the air, in the sand, invisible chips bristled on shoulders.

The weather again. Our American racial weather, turbulent, unchanging in its changeability, its power to rock us and stun us and smack us from our routines and tear us apart as if none of our cities, our pieties, our promises, our dreams, ever stood a chance of holding on. The racial weather. Outside us, then suddenly, unforgettably, unforgivingly inside, reminding us of what we've only pretended to have forgotten. Our limits, our flaws. The lies and compromises we practice to avoid dealing honestly with the contradictions of race. How dependent we are on luck to survive—*when* we survive—the racial weather.

One minute you're a person, the next moment somebody starts treating you as if you're not. Often it happens just that way, just that suddenly. Particularly if you are a black man in America. Race and racism are a force larger than individuals, more powerful than law or education or government or the church, a force able to wipe these institutions away in the charged moments, minuscule or mountainous, when black and white come face to face. In Watts in 1965, or a few less-than-glorious minutes in Clovis, New Mexico, on the eve of the day that commemorates our country's freedom, our inalienable right as a nation, as citizens, to life, liberty, equality, the pursuit of happiness, those precepts and principles that still look good on paper but are often as worthless as a sheet of newspaper to protect you in a storm if you're a black man at the wrong time in the wrong place.

None of this is news, is it? Not July 3rd in Clovis, when a tiny misfire occurred, or yesterday in your town or tomorrow in mine. But haven't we made progress? Aren't things much better than they used to be? Hasn't enough been done?

We ask the wrong questions when we look around and see a handful of fabulously wealthy black people, a few others entering the middle classes. Far more striking than the positive changes are the abiding patterns and assumptions that have not changed. Not all black people are mired in social pathology, but the bottom rung of the ladder of opportunity (and the space *beneath* the bottom rung) is still defined by the color of the people trapped there—and many *are* still trapped there, no doubt about it, because their status was inherited, determined generation after generation by blood, by color. Once, all black people were legally excluded from full participation in the mainstream. Then fewer. Now only some. But the mechanisms of disenfranchisement that originally separated African Americans from other Americans persist, if not legally, then in the apartheid mind-set, convictions and practices of the majority. The seeds sleep but don't die. Ten who suffer from exclusion today can become ten thousand tomorrow. Racial weather can change that quickly.

How would the bouncer have responded if I'd calmly declared: "This is a free country, I can wear any hat I choose"? Would he thank me for standing up for our shared birthright? Or would he have to admit, if pushed, that American rights belong only to *some* Americans, white Americans?

We didn't get that far in our conversation. We usually don't. The girls' faces pulled me from the edge, girls of all colors, sizes, shapes, gritty kids bonding through hard clean competition. Weren't these guys who didn't like my X cap kids too? Who did they think I was? What did they think they were protecting? I backed out, backed down, climbed in my car and drove away from Kelley's. After all, I didn't want Kelley's. I wanted a frozen margarita and a mellow celebration. So I bought plenty of ice and the ingredients for a margarita and rejoined the festivities at Bubba's. Everybody there volunteered to go back with me to Kelley's, but I didn't want to spoil the victory party, taint our daughters' accomplishments, erase the high marks Clovis had earned hosting us.

But I haven't forgotten what happened in Kelley's. I write about it now because this is my country, the country where my sons and daughter are growing up and your daughters and sons, and the crisis, the affliction, the same ole, same ole waste of life continues across the land, the nightmar-ish weather of racism, star bursts of misery in the dark.

The statistics of inequality don't demonstrate a "black crisis"—that perspective confuses cause and victim, solutions and responsibility. When the rain falls, it falls on us all. The bad news about black men—that they die sooner and more violently than white men, are more ravaged by unemployment and lack of opportunity, are more exposed to drugs, disease, broken families and police brutality, more likely to go to jail than college, more cheated by the inertia and callousness of a government that represents and protects the most needy the least—this is not a "black problem," but a *national* shame, affecting us all. Wrenching ourselves free from the long nightmare of racism will require collective determination, countless individual acts of will, gutsy, informed, unselfish. To imagine the terrible cost of not healing ourselves, we must first imagine how good it would feel to be healed.

FOREWORD:
EVERY TONGUE GOT TO CONFESS
BY ZORA NEALE HURSTON

2001

With the example of her vibrant, poetic style Zora Neale Hurston reminded me, instructed me that the language of fiction must never become inert, that the writer at his or her desk, page by page, line by line, word by word should animate the text, attempt to make it speak as the best storytellers speak. In her fiction, and collections of African-American narratives, Hurston provides models of good old-time tale-telling sessions. With the resources of written language, she seeks to recover, uncover, discover the techniques oral bards employed to enchant and teach their audiences. Like African-American instrumental jazz, Hurston's writing imitates the human voice. At the bottom in the gut of jazz if you listen closely you can hear—no matter how complexly, obliquely, mysteriously stylized—somebody talking, crying, growling, singing, farting, praying, stomping, voicing in all those modes through which our bodies communicate some tale about how it feels to be here on earth or leaving, or about the sweet pain of hanging on between the coming and going.

In the spring of 1968 a group of African-American students arrived at my University of Pennsylvania Department of English office and asked if I would offer a class in Black Literature. I responded in a predictable fashion, given my education, social conditioning, and status as the only tenure-track assistant professor of color in the entire College of Arts and Sciences. No, thank you, I said, citing various reasons for declining—my already crowded academic schedule, my need to keep time free for fiction writing, family obligations, and the clincher—African-American literature was not my "field." The exchange lasted only five or ten minutes and I remember being vaguely satisfied with myself for smoothly, quickly marshaling reasonable arguments for refusing the students' request, but before the office door closed behind them, I also sensed something awful had occurred. Something much more significant than wriggling out fairly gracefully from one more demand on my already stressed time, something slightly incriminating, perhaps even shameful.

I'd watched the students' eyes watching me during my brisk, precise dismissal of their proposal. I'd seen the cloud, the almost instantaneous dulling and turning away and shrinking inward of the students' eyes speaking a painful truth: I had not simply said no to a course, I'd said no to them, to who they were, who I was in my little cubicle in Bennett Hall, to the beleaguered island of us, our collective endeavor to make sense of the treacherous currents that had brought us to an Ivy League university and also threatened daily to wipe out the small footholds and handholds we fashioned to survive there.

To cut one part of a long story short, by the next day I'd changed my mind, and I did teach a Black Literature course the following semester.

No white people in my office on that spring day in 1968. On the other hand, visualizing the presence of some sweaty, ham-fisted, Caucasian version of John Henry, the steel-driving man, hammering iron wedges between the students and me, incarcerating us behind bars as invisible as he was, clarifies the encounter. Why weren't novels and poems by Americans of African descent being taught at the university? Why were so few of us attending and almost none of us teaching there? What rationales and agendas were served by dispensing knowledge through arbitrary, territorial "fields"? Why had the training I'd received in the so-called best schools alienated me from my particular cultural roots and brainwashed me into believing in some objective, universal, standard brand of culture and art—essentialist, hierarchical classifications of knowledge—that doomed people like me to marginality on the campus and worse, consigned the vast majority of us who never reach college to a stigmatized, surplus underclass.

Yes, unpacking the issues above would surely be a long story, one I've undertaken to tell in thirty years of fiction and essay. So, back to the shorter story. The class I initiated partly, I admit, to assuage my guilt, to pay dues, to erase the cloud of disappointment I've never forgotten in the students' eyes. It pains me all these years later, since the conditions brewing the cloud's ugly presence remain in place, and the scene may be replicating itself, different office, different university and victims today. But the class, let's stick to my first African-American Literature class that turned out to be a gift from the students to me rather than my offering to them, the class that leads back to Zora Neale Hurston and this folklore collection.

At the end of the first trial run of the class an appreciative student handed me *The Bluest Eye* and said, Thank you for the course, Professor Wideman. Isabel Stewart, since she was a sweet, polite, subtle young woman and didn't wish to undercut an expression of gratitude by mixing it with other, more complicated motives, didn't add, You really must teach this wonderful novel, especially since you saw fit to include only one work by a female writer in your syllabus.

The one work was *Their Eyes Were Watching God*. I had discovered it when I began teaching myself what my formal education had neglected. At the time African-American writing was dominated by males and framed intellectually by a reductive, apologetic, separate-but-equal mentality whose major critical project seemed to be asserting the point: we too have written and do write and some of our stuff deserves inclusion in the mainstream.

By coincidence the two female writers who in separate ways—one by her presence, the other by her absence—were part of my first course would help transform African-American literary studies. Toni Morrison— as writer-editor and Nobel laureate—became point person of a band of awesomely talented women who would precipitate a flip-flop in African-American letters so that women today, for better or worse, dominate the field as much as men did thirty years ago. Zora Neale Hurston's representation of the folk voice in her anthropological work, autobiography, and fiction expanded the idea of what counts as literature, reframing the relationship between spoken and written verbal art, high versus low culture, affirming folk voices, female voices. Hurston foregrounds creolized language and culture in her fiction and nonfiction, dramatizing vernacular ways of speaking that are so independent, dynamic, self-assertive and expressive they cross over, challenge and transform mainstream dialects. Creole languages refuse to remain standing, hat in hand at the back door as segregated, second-class, passive aspirants for marginal inclusion within the framework of somebody else's literary aesthetic.

Though Africanized vernaculars of the rural American South are not separate languages like the Creole of Haiti or Martinique, they are distinctively different speech varieties marked by systematic linguistic structures common to Creoles. The *difference* of these Africanized vernaculars is complicated by what could be called their "unwritability," their active resistance to being captured in print.

> I began to write, that is: to die a little. As soon as my Esternome began to supply me the words, I felt death. Each of his sentences (salvaged in my memory, inscribed in the notebook) distanced him from me. With the notebooks piling up, I felt they were burying him once again. Each written sentence coated a little of him, his Creole tongue, his words, his intonation, his eyes, his airs with formaldehyde . . . The written words, my poor French words, dissipated the echo of his words forever and imposed betrayal upon my memory . . . I was emptying my memory into immobile notebooks without having brought back the quivering of the living life. (Chamoiseau: *Texaco* [321–22])

All spoken language of course resists exact phonetic inscription. But Creole's stubborn survivalist orality, its self-preserving instinct to never stand still, to stay a step ahead, a step away, the political challenge inherent in its form and function, increases the difficulty of rendering it on the page.

The difference of vernacular speech has been represented at one extreme by blackface minstrelsy and Hollywood's perpetuation of that fiction in the porn of race showcasing for the viewer's gaze deviant clowns and outlaws whose comic, obscene, violent speech (often the embodied fantasies of white scriptwriters) stands as a barely intelligible mangling of the master tongue. At the opposite end of the spectrum of imitation is a self-aware, vital, independent, creative community that speaks in Hurston's stories and the African-American narratives she gathered for this collection: "I seen it so dry the fish came swimming up the road in dust."

How speech is represented in writing raises more than questions of aesthetics. An ongoing struggle for authority and domination is present in any speech situation interfacing former slaves with former masters, minority with majority culture, spoken with written. Such interfaces bristle with extralinguistic tensions that condition and usually diminish mutual intelligibility. Put in another way, any written form of creolized language exposes the site, evidence and necessity of struggle, mirrors America's deeply seated refusal to acknowledge its Creole identity.

Traceable in court transcriptions of African testimony (see the Salem witch trials) and eighteenth-century comic drama, then refined and conventionalized by a Plantation school of highly popular nineteenth-century white writers (Sidney Lanier, Joel Chandler Harris, George Washington Cable), the so-called eye dialects' organized graphic signs such as italics, apostrophes, underlining, quotation marks, misspellings *tuh*, *gwine*, *dere*, *dem* along with tortured syntax, malapropisms, elisions, comic orthography, signifying, Joycean portmanteau words to *show* the sound of black vernacular. Whatever else the mediating visualized scrim of eye dialect accomplished by its alleged rendering of Africanized speech, inevitably, given the means employed, it also suggested ignorant, illiterate southern darkies, a consequence bemoaned by the African-American novelist Charles Waddell Chesnutt. Ironically, because he used a conventional version of eye dialect (very similar to the look Hurston chooses for the voices of these Gulf narratives), his book *The Marrow of Tradition* was rejected out of hand by African-American students in my first Black Literature class. They found Chesnutt's picturing of black speech both embarrassing and taxing to decipher. Whether or not readers can see through the veil of eye dialects' incriminating constructions and ignore or resist the prejudice they embody remains an open question. Even here in these narratives.

So what does all the above tell us about reading this collection?

"Oral literature" is an oxymoron. Creole speech is approximated, at best, by any form of written transcription. In this context it is useful to read these folktales from the Gulf States as you would foreign poetry translated into English, grateful for a window into another culture, yet always keeping in mind that what you're consuming is vastly distanced from the original. Translation destroys and displaces as much as it restores and renders available. In the case of these oral narratives, some major missing dimensions are the immediacy and sensuousness of face-to-face encounter, the spontaneous improvisation of call and response, choral repetition and echo, the voice played as a musical instrument, the kinesics of the speaker.

Translations ask us to forget as well as imagine an original. The nature of this forgetting varies depending on the theory of translation. The inevitable awkwardness of a literal rendering, emphasizing ideas and meaning, asks the reader to forget the evocative sonorities of rhythm and rhyme or rather recall their presence in the original as a kind of ennobling excuse for what often appears on the page as a fairly bare-bones, skimpy transmission of thought. Freer translations posit themselves as admirable objects of consideration within the literary tradition of the language into which they have been kidnapped, and to that extent ask readers to forget the original, except for acknowledging the original's status as a distant relative or celebrated ancestor.

So as your eyes read these folk narratives remember and forget selectively, judiciously, in order to enhance your enjoyment, your understanding of the particular species of verbal art they manifest. Imagine the situations in which these speech acts occur, the participants' multicolored voices and faces, the eloquence of nonverbal special effects employed to elaborate and transmit the text. Recall a front stoop, juke joint, funeral, wedding, barbershop, kitchen: the music, noise, communal energy and release. Forget for a while our learned habit of privileging the written over the oral, the mainstream language's hegemony over its competitors when we think "literature." Listen as well as read. Dream. Participate the way you do when you allow a song to transport you, all kinds of songs from hip-hop rap to Bach to Monk, each bearing its different history of sounds and silences.

What's offered in this volume is finally a way of viewing the world, a version of reality constructed by language that validates a worldview, and vice versa, a view that legitimizes a language. Hurston is not curating a museum of odd, humorous negroisms. She's updating by looking backward, forward, all around, the continuous presence in America of an Africanized language that's still spoken, still going strong today. A language articulating an Africanized vision of reality: unsentimental, humorous, pantheistic, robustly visceral, syncretic, blending tradition and innovation, rooted in the body's immediate experience of pleasure and pain yet also cognizant of a long view, the slow, possibly just arc of time, the tribal as well as individual destiny.

Because Hurston is a product of that world, its language describes her and *is* her. As folklore collector she's not merely an outsider looking in, taking data away. She's both writer and subject, an insider, a cultural informant engaging in self-interrogation.

The doubleness of Hurston's stance as self-conscious subject of her writing requires the reader also to realign herself or himself. Any writer who chooses to break away, to cross over and occupy liminal turf between radically different linguistic modes, between two antagonistic ways of perceiving and naming the world, takes a great risk of betraying the integrity of his first cultural community and language. Breaking away can lead to assuming the role of guide and reporter (panderer) objectifying, introducing the exotic, erotic other to a reader's gaze. When she positions herself firmly, insistently within the language of her Africanized culture and her goal is self-knowledge, self-gratification as she recalls, reconstitutes, the pleasures of speaking and acting within the culture, Hurston accomplishes crossover with minimal damage to integrity. Her crossings are expressed through language and customs she shares with the people she interviews and invents. Hurston displays otherness to a perceptive reader not by packaging and delivering it as a commodity C.O.D. to the reader, but by remembering who she was, who she is, by listening, respecting, by staring clear-eyed at her self, her many selves past, future and present in the primal language, the language of feeling they speak.

A model for this self-conscious, self-appraising work manifests itself in the critique of language contained in these Gulf narratives. First, the folktales inhabit a pantheistic world where everything talks—peas grunt when bursting through the hard soil in which they're planted; corn gossips in a cemetery; mules, alligators, horses, dogs, flies, cows, converse or sing. Language resides in the boundless sea of Great Time. One summer words frozen during a particularly severe winter thaw and suddenly the air is filled, like the air of Prospero's enchanted island, with ghostly voices.

Language is treacherous, the tales school us. Interpretation, translation of words, leads to dangerous misapprehensions or not-so-funny comic predicaments, such as one slave bragging to another that he got away with looking at Ole Missus's drawers and the second slave receiving a painful thumping when he tries to look at Ole Missus's drawers when they're not hanging on the clothesline but wrapping her behind. The tales warn us that anyone speaking must be eternally vigilant and circumspect. For one thing, tattlers' ears are everywhere and always open. Even a prayer is liable to interception and subversion.

Once there was a Negro. Every day he went under the hill to pray. So one day a white man went to see what he was doing. He was praying for God to kill all the white people; so the white man threw a brick on his head. The Negro said, "Lord can't you tell a white man from a Negro?"

A master's penchant for extravagant metaphorical overkill in his speech is satirized by a slave who transposes the master's style into an equally fanciful rhyming vernacular version and fires it back at him, "You better git outa yo' flowery beds uh ease, an put on yo' flying trapeze, cause yo' red ball uh simmons done carried yo' flame uh flapperation tuh yo' high tall mountain."

"What you say, Jack?"

The problematic relationship between oral and written is documented playfully in a tale quoting an illiterate father who chides his educated daughter because she can't write down in the letter he's dictating a mule-calling sound he clucks.

Is you got dat down yit?

Naw sir, I aint' got it yit?

How come you ain't got it?

Cause I can't spell (clucking sound).

You mean tuh tell me you been off tuh school seven years and can't spell (clucking sound)? Well, I could almost spell dat myself.

Thus these narratives from the southern states instruct us that talk functions in African-American communities as it does in Zora Neale Hurston's fiction and life—as a means of having fun, getting serious, establishing credibility and consensus, securing identity, negotiating survival, keeping hope alive, suffering and celebrating the power language bestows.

WHOSE WAR:
THE COLOR OF TERROR

2002

Nobody asked me, but I need to say what I'm thinking in this new year in New York City, five months after the Twin Towers burned, after long stretches of fall weather eerily close to perfect—clear blue skies, shirt-sleeve warmth—through December, a bizarre hesitation, as if nature couldn't get on with its life and cycle to the next season, the city enclosed in a fragile, bell-jar calm till shattered by a siren, a plane's roar overhead.

I grew up in Homewood, an African-American community in Pitts-burgh where people passing in the street might not have known each other's names but we knew something about each other's stories, so we always exchanged a greeting. We greeted each other because it feels good but also because we share the burden of racism, understand how it hurts, scars, deforms, but yes, it can be survived, and here we are, living proof meeting on the ground zero of a neighborhood street. The burning and collapse of the World Trade Center has conferred a similar sort of imme-diate intimacy upon all Americans. We've had the good luck to survive something awful, but do we truly understand, as Homewood people are disciplined to understand by the continuing presence of racism, that it ain't over yet. There's the next precarious step, and the next down the street, and to survive we must attend to the facts of division as well as the healing wish for solidarity.

Staring up at a vast, seamless blue sky, it's hard to reckon what's missing. The city shrinks in scale as the dome of sky endlessly recedes. Piles of steel and concrete are whims, the vexed arc of the city's history a moment lasting no longer than the lives of victims consumed in the burning towers. The lives lost mirror our own fragility and vulnerability, our unpredictable passage through the mysterious flow of time that eternally surrounds us, buoys us, drowns us. Ourselves the glass where we look for the faces of those who have disappeared, those we can no longer touch, where we find them looking back at us, terrified, terrifying.

A few moments ago I was a man standing at a window, nine stories up in an apartment building on the Lower East Side of New York, staring out at a building about a hundred yards away, more or less identical to his, wondering why he can't finish a piece of writing that for days had felt frustratingly close to being complete, then not even begun. Wondering why anybody, no matter how hard they'd plugged away at articulating their little piece of the puzzle, would want to throw more words on a pile so high the thing to be written about has disappeared. A man with the bright idea that he might call his work in progress "A speech to be performed because no one's listening." Like singing in the shower: no one hears you, but don't people sing their hearts out anyway, because the singing, the act itself, is also a listening to itself, so why not do your best to please yourself.

And the man standing at the window retracts his long arms from the top of the upper pane he's lowered to rest on as he stares. Then all of him retracts. Picture him standing a few moments ago where there's emptiness now. Picture him rising from a couch where he'd been stretched out, his back cushioned against the couch's arm, then rising and walking to the window. Now visualize the film running backward, the special effect of him sucked back like red wine spilled from the lip of a jug returning to fill the jug's belly, him restored exactly, legs stretched out, back against the couch's cushioned arm. Because that's who I am. What I'm doing and did. I'm the same man, a bit older now, but still a man like him, restless, worried, trying to fashion some tolerable response with words to a situation so collapsed, so asphyxiated by words, words, it's an abomination, an affront to dead people, to toss any more words on the ruins of what happened to them.

I, too, return to the couch, return also to the thought of a person alone singing in a shower. A sad thought, because all writing pretends to be something it's not, something it can't be: something or someone other, but sooner or later the writing will be snuffed back into its jug, back where I am, a writer a step, maybe two, behind my lemming words scuffling over the edge of the abyss.

I'm sorry. I'm an American of African descent, and I can't applaud my president for doing unto foreign others what he's inflicted on me and mine. Even if he calls it ole-time religion. Even if he tells me all good Americans have nothing to fear but fear itself and promises he's gonna ride over there and kick fear's ass real good, so I don't need to worry about anything, just let him handle it his way, relax and enjoy the show on TV, pay attention to each breath I take and be careful whose letters I open and listen up for the high alerts from the high-alert guy and gwan and do something nice for a Muslim neighbor this week. Plus, be patient. Don't expect too much too soon. These things take time. Their own good time. You know. The sweet by-and-by. Trust me.

I'm sorry. It all sounds too familiar. I've heard the thunder, seen the flash of his terrible swift sword before. I wish I could be the best kind of American. Not doubt his promises. Not raise his ire. I've felt his pointy boots in my butt before. But this time I can't be Tonto to his Lone Ranger. Amos to his Andy. Tambo to his Bones. Stepin to his Fetchit. I'm sorry. It's too late. I can't be as good an American as he's telling me to be. You know what I'm saying. I must be real. Hear what I'm saying. We ain't going nowhere, as the boys in the hood be saying. Nowhere. If you promote all the surviving Afghans to the status of honorary Americans, Mr. President, where exactly on the bus does that leave me. When do I get paid. When can I expect my invitation to the ranch. I hear Mr. Putin's wearing jingle-jangle silver spurs around his dacha. Heard you fixed him up with an eight-figure advance on his memoirs. Is it true he's iced up to be the Marlboro man after he retires from Russia. Anything left under the table for me. And mine.

Like all my fellow countrymen and women, even the ones who won't admit it, the ones who choose to think of themselves as not implicated, who maintain what James Baldwin called "a willed innocence," even the ones just off boats from Russia, Dominica, Thailand, Ireland, I am an heir to centuries of legal apartheid and must negotiate daily, with just about every step I take, the foul muck of unfulfilled promises, the apparent and not so apparent effects of racism that continue to plague America (and, do I need to add, plague the rest of the Alliance as well). It's complicated muck, muck that doesn't seem to dirty Colin Powell or Oprah or Michael Jordan or the black engineer in your firm who received a bigger raise than all her white colleagues, muck so thick it obscures the presence of millions of underclass African Americans living below the poverty line, hides from public concern legions of young people of color wasting away in prison. How can I support a president whose rhetoric both denies and worsens the muck when he pitches his crusade against terror as a holy war, a war of good against evil, forces of light versus forces of darkness, a summons to arms that for colored folks chillingly echoes and resuscitates the Manichaean dualism of racism.

I remain puzzled by the shock and surprise nonblack Americans express when confronted by what they deem my *"anger"* (most would accept the friendly amendment of *"rage"* or *"bitterness"* inside the quotes). Did I see in their eyes a similar shock and surprise on September 11. Is it truly news that some people's bad times (slavery, colonial subjugation, racial oppression, despair) have underwritten other people's good times (prosperity, luxury, imperial domination, complacency). News that a systematic pattern of gross inequities still has not been corrected and that those who suffer them are desperate (*angry, bitter, enraged*) for change.

For months an acrid pall of smoke rose from smoldering ruins, and now a smokescreen of terror hovers, *terror* as the enemy, terror as the problem, terror as the excuse for denying and unleashing the darkness within ourselves.

To upstage and camouflage a real war at home the threat of terror is being employed to justify a phony war in Afghanistan. A phony war because it's being pitched to the world as righteous retaliation, as self-defense after a wicked, unwarranted sucker punch when in fact the terrible September 11 attack as well as the present military incursion into Afghanistan are episodes in a long-standing vicious competition—buses bombed in Israel, helicopters strafing Palestinian homes, economic sanctions blocking the flow of food and medicine for Iraq, no-fly zones, Desert Storms, and embassy bombings—for oil and geopolitical leverage in the Middle East.

A phony war that the press, in shameless collusion with the military, exploits daily as newsy entertainment, a self-promoting concoction of fiction, fact, propaganda, and melodrama designed to keep the public tuned in, uninformed, distracted, convinced a real war is taking place.

A phony war because its stated objective—eradicating terrorism—is impossible and serves to mask unstated, alarmingly open-ended goals, a kind of fishing expedition that provides an opportunity for America to display its intimidating arsenal and test its allies' loyalty, license them to crush internal dissent.

A phony war, finally, because it's not waged to defend America from an external foe but to homogenize and coerce its citizens under a flag of rabid nationalism.

The Afghan campaign reflects a global struggle but also reveals a crisis inside America—the attempt to construct on these shores a society willing to sacrifice democracy and individual autonomy for the promise of material security, the exchange of principles for goods and services. A society willing to trade the tumultuous uncertainty generated by a government dedicated to serving the interests of many different, unequal kinds of citizens for the certainty of a government responsive to a privileged few and their self-serving, single-minded, ubiquitous, thus invisible, ideology: profit. Such a government of the few is fabricating new versions of freedom. Freedom to exploit race, class, and gender inequities without guilt or accountability; freedom to drown in ignorance while flooded by information; freedom to be plundered by corporations. Freedom to drug ourselves and subject our children's minds to the addictive mix of fantasy and propaganda, the nonstop ads that pass for a culture.

A phony war but also a real war, because as it bumbles and rumbles along people are dying and because like all wars it's a sign of failure and chaos. When we revert to the final solution of kill or be killed, all warring parties in the name of clan tribe nation religion violate the first law of civilization—that human life is precious. In this general collapse, one of the first victims is language. Words are deployed as weapons to identify, stigmatize, eliminate, the enemy. One side boasts of inflicting casualties, excoriates the other side as cowards and murderers. One side calls civilians it kills collateral damage, labels civilian deaths by its opponents terrorism.

From their initial appearance in English to describe the bloody dismantling of royal authority during the French Revolution (Burke's "thousands of those Hell-hounds called Terrorists . . . are let loose on the people") the words *terror* and *terrorist* have signified godless savagery. Other definitions—government by a system of coercive intimidation—have almost entirely disappeared. Seldom if ever perceived neutrally as a tool, a set of practices and tactics for winning a conflict, terror instead is understood as pure evil. Terror and terrorists in this Manichaean scheme are excluded even from the problematic dignity of conventional warfare.

One side's use of *terrorist* to describe the other is never the result of a reasoned exchange between antagonists. It's a refusal of dialogue, a negation of the other. The designation *terrorist* is produced by the one-way gaze of power. Only one point of view, one vision, one story, is necessary and permissible, since what defines the gaze of power is its absolute, unquestionable authority.

To label an enemy a terrorist confers the same invisibility a colonist's gaze confers upon the native. Dismissing the possibility that the native can look back at you just as you are looking at him is a first step toward blinding him and ultimately rendering him or her invisible. Once a slave or colonized native is imagined as invisible, the business of owning him, occupying and exploiting his land, becomes more efficient, pleasant.

A state proclaiming itself besieged by terrorists asserts its total innocence, cites the unreasonableness, the outrageousness, of the assaults upon it. A holy war may be launched to root out terrorism, but its form must be a punitive crusade, an angry god's vengeance exacted upon sinners, since no proper war can exist when there is no recognition of the other's list of grievances, no awareness of the relentless dynamic binding the powerful and powerless. Perhaps that's why the monumental collapsing of the Towers delivered such a shocking double dose of reality to Americans—yes, a war's been raging and yes, here's astounding proof we may have already lost it. It's as if one brick snatched away, one sledgehammer blow, demolished our Berlin Wall.

Regimes resisting change dismiss challenges to their authority by branding them terrorist provocations. In the long bloody struggles that often follow, civil protests, car bombings, kidnappings, assassinations, guerrilla warfare in the mountains, full-scale conventional military engagements, blur one into the other. At first the media duly reports on the frightening depredations of terrorists—Algerian terror, Mau Mau terror, Palestinian terror, Israeli terror, South African terror—then bears witness as fighters from the Mau Mau, the Palmach, the PLO, emerge to become leaders of new states. George Washington, inaugurated as America's first president only a few blocks from the ruins of the World Trade Center, would have been branded a terrorist if the word had been invented in 1775. Clearly not all terrorists become prime ministers or presidents, but if and when they do they rewrite the history of their struggle to attain legitimacy. This turnabout clarifies the relationship between power and terror. Terrorists are those who have no official standing, no gaze, no voice in the established order, those determined by all means possible to usurp power in order to be seen and heard. Some former terrorists survive to accomplish precisely that. Others survive long enough to decry and denounce the terrorist threat nibbling at the edges of their own regime.

The destruction of the World Trade Center was a criminal act, the loss of life an unforgivable consequence, but it would be a crime of another order, with an even greater destructive potential, to allow the evocation of the word *terror* to descend like a veil over the event, to rob us of the opportunity to see ourselves as others see us.

The terror that arises from fear of loss, fear of pain, death, annihilation, prostrates us because it's both rational and irrational. Rational because our sense of the world's uncertainty is accurate. Rational because reason confirms the difference between what is knowable and unknowable, warns us that in certain situations we can expect no answers, no help. We are alone. Irrational because that's all we have left when reason abandons us. Our naked emotions, our overwhelmed smallness.

Terror thrives in the hour of the wolf, the hour of Gestapo raids on Jewish ghettos, of blue-coated cavalry charges on Native American villages. Those predawn hours when most of us are born or die, the hour when cops smash through doors to crack down on drugs or on dissidents, the hour of transition when sleep has transported the body furthest from its waking state, when our ability to distinguish dream from not-dream weakens. Terror manifests itself at this primal juncture between sleep and waking because there we are eternally children, outside time, beyond the protections and consolations of society, prey to fear of the dark.

To a child alone, startled from sleep by a siren, the hulking bear silhouetted in the middle of the dark room is real. The child may remember being assured that no bears live on the Lower East Side of New York, may know his parents' bed is just down the hall, may even recall tossing his bulky down parka over the back of the chair instead of hanging it neatly in the closet like he's been told a million times to do. None of this helps, because reason has deserted him. Even if things get better when his mother knocks and calls him for breakfast, the darkness has been branded once again, indelibly, by agonizing, demoralizing fear, by a return to stark terror.

For those who don't lose a child's knack for perceiving the aural archaeology within the sound of words, words carry forward fragments, sound bites that reveal a word's history, its layered onomatopoeic sources, its multiplicity of shadowed meanings. *Terror* embeds a grab bag of unsettling echoes: tear (as in rip) (as in run fast), terra (earth, ground, grave, dirt, unfamiliar turf), err (mistake), air (terra firma's opposite element), eerie (strange, unnatural), error (of our ways), roar-r-r (beasts, machines, parents, gods). Of course any word's repertoire is arbitrary and precise, but that's also the point, the power of puns, double entendre, words migrating among languages, Freudian slips, Lacan's "breaks," all calling attention to the unconscious, archaic intentionality buried in the words.

But the word *terror* also incarcerates. Like the child pinned to its bed, not moving a muscle for fear it will arouse the bear, we're immobilized, paralyzed by terror. Dreading what we might discover, we resist investigating terror's source. Terror feeds on ignorance, confines us to our inflamed, tortured imaginings. If we forget that terror, like evil, resides in us, is spawned by us no matter what name we give it, then it makes good sense to march off and destroy the enemy. But we own terror. We can't off-load it onto the back of some hooded, barbaric, shadowy other. Someone we can root out of his cave and annihilate. However, we continue to be seduced by the idea that we might be able to cleanse ourselves of terror, accomplish a final resolution of our indeterminate nature. But even if we could achieve freedom from terror, what would we gain by such a radical reconfiguration of what constitutes being human. What kind of new world order would erase the terror we're born with, the terror we chip away at but never entirely remove. What system could anticipate, translate, or diffuse the abiding principle of uncertainty governing the cosmos. Systems that promise a world based on imperishable, impregnable truth deliver societies of truncated imagination, of history and appetite denied, versions of Eden where there is no dreaming, no rebellion, no Eros, where individuality is sacrificed for inter-changeability, eternal entertainment, becalmed ego, mortality disguised as immortality by the absence of dread.

Power pales (turns white with terror—imagines its enemies black—invents race) when power confronts the inevitability of change. By promis-ing to keep things as they are, promising to freeze out or squeeze out those not already secure within the safety net of privilege, Mr. Bush won (some say stole) an election. By launching a phony war he is managing to avoid the scrutiny a first-term, skin-of-its-teeth presidency deserves. Instead he's terrorizing Americans into believing that we require a wartime leader wielding unquestioned emergency powers. Beneath the drumbeat belliger-ence of his demands for national unity, if you listen you'll hear the bullying, the self-serving, the hollowness, of his appeals to patriotism. Listen care-fully and you'll also hear what he's not saying: that we need, in a democracy full of contradictions and unresolved divisions, opposition voices.

Those who mount a challenge to established order are not the embod-iment of evil. Horrifically bloody, criminal acts may blot the humanity of the perpetrators and stimulate terror in victims and survivors, but the ones who perpetuate such deeds are not the source of the terror within us. To call these people terrorists or evil, even to maintain our absolute distinction between victims and perpetrators, exercises the blind, one-way gaze of power, perpetuates the reign of the irrational and supernatu-ral, closes down the possibility that by speaking to one another we might formulate appropriate responses, even to the unthinkable.

Although trouble may always prevail, being human offers us a chance to experience moments when trouble doesn't rule, when trouble's not totally immune to compassion and reason, when we make choices, and try to bet-ter ourselves and make other lives better.

Is war a preferable alternative. If a child's afraid of the dark, do we solve the problem by buying her a gun.

LOOKING AT EMMETT TILL

2005

A nightmare of being chased has plagued my sleep since I was a boy. The monster pursuing me assumes many shapes, but its face is too terrifying for the dream to reveal. Even now I sometimes startle myself awake, screaming, the dream's power undiminished by time, the changing circumstances of my waking life.

I've come to believe the face in the dream I can't bear to look upon is Emmett Till's. Emmett Till's face, crushed, chewed, mutilated, his gray face swollen, water dripping from holes punched in his skull.

Warm gray water on that August day in 1955 when they dragged his corpse from the Tallahatchie River. Emmett Till and I both fourteen the summer they murdered him. The nightmare an old acquaintance by then, as old as anything I can remember about myself.

Yet the fact that the nightmare predates by many years the afternoon in Pittsburgh I came across Emmett Till's photograph in *Jet* magazine seems to matter not at all. The chilling dream resides in a space years can't measure, the boundless sea of Great Time, nonlinear, ever abiding, enfolding past, present, and future.

I certainly hadn't been searching for Emmett Till's picture in *Jet*. It found me. A blurred, grayish something resembling an aerial snapshot of a landscape cratered by bombs or ravaged by natural disaster. As soon as I realized the thing in the photo was a dead black boy's face, I jerked my eyes away. But not quickly enough.

I attempted to read *Jet's* story about the murder without getting snagged again by the picture. Refusing to look, lacking the power to look at Emmett Till's face, shames me to this day. Dangerous and cowardly not to look. Turning away from his eyeless stare, I blinded myself. Denied myself denying him. He'd been fourteen, like me. How could I be alive and Emmett Till dead? Who had killed him? Why? Would I recognize him if I dared look? Could my own features be horribly altered like his? I needed answers, needed to confront what frightened me in the murdered black boy's face. But Emmett Till just too dead, too gruesomely, absolutely dead to behold.

Years afterward during college I'd recall how it felt to discover Emmett Till's picture when one of my summer jobs involved delivering towels and sheets to the city morgue, and the booze-breathed old coroner who got his kicks freaking out rookies lifted a kettle's lid to prove, yes, indeed, there was a human skull inside from which he was attempting to boil the last shreds of meat.

Now when I freeze-frame a close-up shot of Emmett Till's shattered face on my VCR, am I looking? The image on the screen still denies its flesh-and-blood origins. It's a smashed, road-killed thing, not a boy's face. I'm reminded of the so-called nail fetishes, West African wood sculptures, part mask, part freestanding head, that began appearing when slaving ships crisscrossed the Atlantic. Gouged, scarred, studded with nails, glass, cartridge shells, stones, drools of raffia, hunks of fur and bone, these horrific creatures police the boundary between human and spirit worlds. Designed to terrify and humble, they embody evil's power to transcend mere human conceptions of its force, reveal the chaos always lurking within the ordinary, remind us the gods amuse themselves by snatching away our certainties.

Whether you resided in an African-American community like Homewood, where I spent half my early years, or in white areas like Shadyside, with a few houses on a couple of streets for black people—my turf when we didn't live in my grandparents' house in Homewood—everybody colored knew what was in *Jet* magazine. *Jet*'s articles as much a part of our barbershop, pool-room, ball field, corner, before- and after-church talk as the *Courier*, Pittsburgh's once-a-week newspaper, aka the *Black Dispatch*. Everybody aware of *Jet* and the *Courier* even though not everybody approved or identified to the same degree with these publications, whose existence was rooted in an unblinking acknowledgment of the reality of racial segregation, a reality their contents celebrated as much as protested.

Jet would arrive at our house on Copeland Street, Shadyside, in batches, irregularly, when Aunt Catherine, who lived down the block and never missed an issue, finished with them and got around to dropping some off. Aunt Catherine was my father's sister, and they were Harry Wideman's kids and inherited his deep brown, South Carolina skin, while my mother's side of the family was light, bright, and almost white, like my other grandfather, Daddyjohn French, from Culpepper, Virginia.

Skin color in my family, besides being tattletale proof segregation didn't always work, was a pretty good predictor of a person's attitude toward *Jet* magazine. My mother wouldn't or couldn't buy *Jet*. I've never asked her which. In pale Shadyside, *Jet* wasn't on sale. You'd have to go a good distance to find it, and with neither car nor driver's license and five kids to care for 24/7, my mother seldom ranged very far from home. Tight as money was then, I'm sure a luxury like subscribing to *Jet* never entered her mind. If by some miracle spare change became available and Brackman's Pharmacy on Walnut Street had begun stocking *Jet*, my mother would have been too self-conscious to purchase a magazine about colored people from old, icy, freckle-fingered Brackman.

Although apartheid stipulates black and white as absolutely separate categories, people construct day by day through the choices they make and allow to be made for them what constitutes blackness and whiteness, what race means, and Mr. Brackman presided over one of the whitest businesses on Walnut Street. Clearly he didn't want folks like us in his drugstore. His chilliness, disdain, and begrudging service a nasty medicine you had to swallow while he doled out your prescriptions. White kids permitted to sit on the floor in a corner and browse through the comic-book bin, but he hurried me along if he thought I attempted to read before I bought. (I knew he believed I'd steal his comics if he turned his back, so in spite of his eagle eye, I did, with sweet, sweet satisfaction every chance I got, throwing them in a garbage can before I got home to avoid that other eagle eye, my mom's.)

Though copies reached us by a circuitous and untimely route, my mother counted on *Jet*. Read it and giggled over its silliness, fussed at its shamelessness, envied and scoffed at the airs of the "sididdy folks" who paraded through it weekly. In my grandparents' house in Homewood, when my mom got down with her sisters, Geraldine and Martha, I'd eavesdrop while they riffed on *Jet*'s contents, fascinated by how they mixed Homewood people and gossip into *Jet*'s features, improvising new stories, raps, and sermons I'd never imagined when I'd read it alone.

By the time an issue of *Jet* reached me, after it had passed through the hands of Aunt Catherine, Uncle Horton, my mother, my father when he was around, the pages were curled, ink-smeared, soft and comfortable as Daddyjohn French's tobacco-ripe flannel shirts. I could fan the pages, and the widest gaps opened automatically at the best stories.

With its spatters, spots, rings from the bottom of a coffee cup, smudges of chocolate candy or lipstick, pages with turned-down corners, pages ripped out, torn covers, *Jet* was an image of the black world as I understood it then: secondhand, beat-up, second-rate. Briar patch and rebuke.

But also often truer and better than the other world around me. Much better. *Jet*, with its incriminating, renegade, embarrassing, topsy-turvy, loud, proud focus on colored doings and faces expanded my sense of possibility. Compared to other magazines of the fifties—*Life, Look, House & Garden, Redbook*—*Jet* was like WAMO, the radio station that blasted rhythm and blues and gospel, an escape from the droning mediocrity of *Your Hit Parade*, a plunge into versions of my life unavailable elsewhere on the dial, grabbing me, shaking me up, reminding me life could move to a dance beat.

In 1955, the year Emmett Till was murdered, I, like him, had just graduated from junior high. I'm trying to remember if I, like him, carried pictures of white girls in my wallet. Can't recall whether I owned a wallet in 1955. Certainly it wouldn't have been a necessity since the little bits of cash I managed to get hold of passed rapidly through my hands. "Money burns a hole in your pocket, boy," my mom said. Wanting to feel grown up, manly, I probably stuffed some sort of hand-me-down billfold in my hip pocket, and carrying around a white girl's picture in it would have been ocular proof of sexual prowess, proof the color of my skin didn't scare white chicks away or scare me away from them. A sign of power. Proof I could handle that other world, master its opportunities and dangers. Since actual romances across the color line tended to be rare and clandestine then, a photo served as evidence of things unseen. A ticket to status in my tiny clan of Shadyside brown boys, a trophy copped in another country I could flaunt in black Homewood. So I may have owned a wallet with pictures of white girlfriends/classmates in it, and if I'd traveled to Promised Land, South Carolina, with my grandfather Harry Wideman one of those summers he offered to take me down home where he'd been born and raised, who knows? Since I was a bit of a smart-aleck like Emmett Till, I might have flashed my snapshots. I liked to brag. Take on dares like him. *Okay. Okay, Emmett Till. You so bad. You talking 'bout all those white gals you got up in Chicago. Bet you won't say boo to that white lady in the store.*

Two years before Emmett Till was beaten and murdered, when both Emmett Till and I were twelve, a stroke killed my mother's father, John French. I lapsed into a kind of semicoma, feverish, silent, sleeping away whole days, a little death to cope with losing my grandfather, my family believed. Grieving for Daddyjohn was only part of the reason I retreated into myself. Yes, I missed him. Everybody was right about that, but I couldn't confide to anyone that the instant he died, there was no room for him in my heart. Once death closed his eyes, I wanted him gone, utterly, absolutely gone. I erected a shell to keep him out, to protect myself from the touch of his ghostly hands, the smells and sounds of him still lurking in the rooms of the Homewood house where we'd lived for a year with my mother's parents and her sisters after my father left our house on Copeland Street.

Losing my grandfather stunned me. He'd been my best friend. I couldn't understand how he'd changed from Daddyjohn to some invisible, frightening presence I had no name for. He'd stopped moving, speaking, breathing. For two interminable days, his body lay inside a coffin on a spindly-legged metal stand beside the piano in the living room, the dark polished wood of one oblong box echoing the other. Until we had to sell the piano a few years later, I couldn't enter the room or touch the piano unless someone else was with me. Sitting on the spinning stool, banging away for hours on the keys had been one of my favorite solitary pastimes, as unthinkable suddenly as romping with my dead grandfather, chanting the nonsense rimes he'd taught me—"Froggy went a-courting, and he did ride / Uh-huh, uh-huh."

Stunned by how empty, how threatening the spaces of my grandfather's house had become, I fought during the daylight hours to keep him away, hid under the covers of my bed at night. Stunned by guilt. By my betrayal of him, my inability to remember, to honor the love that had bound us. Love suddenly changed to fear of everything about him. Fear that love might license him to trespass from the grave. I'd never understood the dead. Shied away from talk of death, thoughts of the dead. The transformation of my grandfather the instant he became one of the dead confirmed my dread. If I couldn't trust Daddyjohn, what horrors would the rest of the dead inflict upon me? Given the nightmare's witness, am I still running, still afraid?

Emmett Till's murder was an attempt to slay an entire generation. Push us backward to the bad old days when our lives seemed not to belong to us. When white power and racism seemed unchallengeable forces of nature, when inferiority and subserviency appeared to be our birthright, when black lives seemed cheap and expendable, when the grossest insults to pride and person, up to and including murder, had to be endured. No redress, no retaliation, no justice expected. Emmett Till's dead body, like the body of James Byrd just yesterday in Texas, reminded us that the bad old days are never farther away than the thickness of skin, skin some people still claim the prerogative to burn or cut or shoot full of holes if it's dark skin. It's no accident that Emmett Till's dead face appears inhuman. The point of inflicting the agony of his last moments, killing and mutilating him, is to prove he's not human.

And it almost works. Comes close to working every time. Demonized by hot-blooded or cold-blooded statistics of crime, addiction, disease, cartooned, minstrelized, criminalized, eroticized, commodified in stereotypical representations, the black body kidnapped and displayed by the media loses all vestiges of humanity. We are set back on our collective heels by the overwhelming evidence, the constant warning that beneath black skin something *other*, something brutal lurks. A so-called lost generation of young black men dying in the streets today points backward, the way Emmett Till's rotting corpse points backward, history and prophecy at once: This is the way things have always been, will always be, the way they're supposed to be.

The circle of racism, its perverse logic remain unbroken. Boys like Emmett Till are born violating the rules, aren't they? Therefore they forfeit any rights law-abiding citizens are bound to respect. The bad places— ghettos, prisons, morgue slabs—where most of them wind up confirm the badness of the boys. Besides, does it hurt any less if the mugger's a product of nurture, not nature? Keeping him off your streets, confining him in a world apart, is what matters, isn't it?

But what if the disproportionate numbers of African-American males in prison or caught in the net of economic marginality are not a consequence of inborn black deviancy? What if incarceration and poverty are latter-day final solutions of the problem of slavery? What if the dismal lives of so many young black people indicate an intentional, systematic closing off of access to the mainstream, justified by a mythology of race that the closing off simultaneously engenders and preserves?

Nearly five hundred years ago, European ships began transporting captive Africans to the New World. Economic exploitation of the recently "discovered" Americans provided impetus for this slave trade. Buying and selling African bodies, treating them as property, commodities, livestock, produced enormous profit and imprinted a model for ignoring the moral and ethical implications of financially successful global commerce we continue to apply today. The traffic in human bodies was also fueled by a dream, a utopian dream of escape from the poverty, disease, class, and religious warfare of Europe, a dream of transforming through European enterprise and African slave labor the wilderness across the sea into a garden of wealth and prosperity, with the European colonist cast as the New Adam exercising divinely sanctioned dominion over all he surveyed.

Racism and genocide were the underside of this Edenic dream, persist today in the determined unwillingness of the heirs of the dream to surrender advantages gained when owning slaves was legal.

During its heyday slavery's enormous profit and enormous evil sparked continuous debate. Could a true Christian own slaves? Do Africans possess souls? Because it licensed and naturalized the subjugation of "inferior" Africans by "superior" Europeans, the invention of the concept of "race"—dividing humankind into a hierarchy of groups, each possessing distinct, unchangeable traits that define the groups as eternally separate and unequal—was crucial to the slaveholder's temporary victory in these debates. Over time, as slavery gradually was abolished, a systematic network of attitudes and practices based on the concept of race evolved across all fields and activities of New World societies with a uniquely pervasive, saturating force. The primary purpose of this racialized thinking was, under the guise of different vocabularies, to rationalize and maintain in public and private spheres the power European slave owners once held over their African slaves.

Emmett Till was murdered because he violated taboos governing race relations in 1955 in Money, a rural Mississippi town, but his killers were also exercising and revalidating prerogatives in place since their ancestors imported Emmett Till's ancestors to these shores. At some level everybody in Money understood this. Our horror, our refusal to look too closely at Emmett Till reside in the same deep, incriminating knowledge.

Perhaps an apartheid mentality reigns in this country because most Americans consciously hold racist attitudes or wish ill on their neighbors of African descent. I don't think so. Emmett Till dies again and again because his murder, the conditions that ensure and perpetuate it, have not been honestly examined. Denial is more acceptable to the majority of Americans than placing themselves, their inherited dominance, at risk.

Any serious attempt to achieve economic, social, and political equal opportunity in this nation must begin not simply with opening doors to selected minorities. That impulse, that trope, that ideology has failed. The majority must decide to relinquish significant measures of power and privilege if lasting transformations of self and society are to occur. There have always been open doors of sorts for minorities (emancipation, emigration, education, economic success in sports or business, passing as white). What's missing is an unambiguous, abiding determination declared in public and private by a majority of the majority to surrender privileges that are the living legacy of slavery. Begin now. Today. Give up walls, doors, keys, the dungeons, the booty, the immunity, the false identity apartheid preserves.

A first step is acknowledging that the dangerous lies of slavery continue to be told as long as we conceive of ourselves in terms of race, as black or white.

Emmett Till and the young victims of drug and territory wars raging in African-American neighborhoods today are signs of a deeply flawed society failing its children. Why do we perceive the bodies of dead *black* boys, imprisoned *black* men, homeless *black* people, addicted *black* people as *black* problems? Why do we support cynical politicians who cite these *black* problems as evidence for more brutal policing of the racial divide?

In 1955, one year after the Supreme Court's *Brown v. Board of Education* school-desegregation decision, a great struggle for civil rights commenced. The lynching of Emmett Till should have clarified exactly what was at stake: life or death. As long as racialized thinking continues to legitimize one group's life-and-death power over another, the battered face of Emmett Till will poison the middle ground of compromise between so-called whites and so-called blacks. His face unmourned, unburied, unloved, haunting the netherworld where incompatible versions of democracy clash.

It was hard to bury Emmett Till, hard, hard to bury Carole Robertson, Addie Mae Collins, Denise McNair, and Cynthia Wesley, the four girls killed by a bomb in a Birmingham, Alabama, church. So hard an entire nation began to register the convulsions of black mourning. The deaths of our children in the civil rights campaigns changed us. The oratory of great men like Martin Luther King, Jr., pushed us to realize our grief should be collective, should stir us to unify, to clarify our thinking, roll back the rock of fear. Emmett Till's mangled face could belong to anybody's son who transgressed racial laws; anyone's little girl could be crushed in the rubble of a bombed church. We read the terrorist threat inscribed upon Emmett Till's flesh and were shaken but refused to comply with the terrorists' demands.

Martin Luther King, Jr., understood the killing of our children was an effort to murder the nation's future. We mourned the young martyrs, and a dedicated few risked life and limb fighting with ferocity and dignity in the courts, churches, and streets to stop the killing. Young people served as shock troops in the movement for social justice, battling on the front lines, the hottest, most dangerous spots in Alabama and Mississippi. And though they had most to gain or lose (their precious lives, their time on this earth), they also carried on their shoulders the hopes of older generations and generations unborn.

Now there seems to be in our rituals of mourning for our dying children no sense of communal, general loss, no larger, empowering vision. We don't connect our immediate trials—drugs, gang violence, empty schools, empty minds, empty homes, empty values—to the ongoing historical struggle to liberate ourselves from the oppressive legacies of slavery and apartheid. Funerals for our young are lonely occurrences. Daily it seems, in some ghetto or another somewhere in America, a small black congregation will gather together to try to repair the hole in a brother's or mother's soul with the balm of gospel singing, prayer, the laying on of dark hands on darkened spirits.

How many a week, how many repetitions of the same, sad, isolated ceremony, the hush afterward when the true dimensions of loss and futility begin to set in? A sense of futility, of powerlessness dogs the survivors, who are burdened not only by the sudden death of a loved one but also by the knowledge that it's going to happen again today or tomorrow and that it's supposed to happen in a world where black lives are expendable, can disappear, *click*, in a fingerpop, quick like that, without a trace, as if the son or sister was hardly here at all. Hey, maybe black people really ain't worth shit, just like you've been hearing your whole life.

Curtis Jones, a cousin who accompanied Emmett Till on the trip from Chicago, Illinois, to Money, Mississippi, in August 1955, relates how close Emmett Till came to missing their train, reminding us how close Emmett Till's story came to not happening or being another story altogether, and that in turn should remind us how any story, sad or happy, is always precariously close to being other than it is. Doesn't take much to alter a familiar scene into chaos. Difficult as it is to remember what does occur, we must also try to keep alive what doesn't—the missed trains, squandered opportunities, warnings not heeded. We carry forward these fictions because what might have been is part of what gives shape to our stories. We depend on memory's capacity to hold many lives, not just the one we appear to be leading at the moment. Memory is space for storing lives we didn't lead, room where they remain alive, room for mourning them, forgiving them. Memory, like all stories we tell, a tissue of remembering, forgetting, of *what if* and *once upon a time*, burying our dead so the dead may rise.

Curtis Jones goes on to tell us about everybody piling into Grandpa Wright's automobile and trundling down the dusty road to church. How he and his cousin Emmett Till took the car into Money that afternoon while Moses Wright preached.

A bunch of boys loafing outside Bryant's General Store on Money's main drag. Sho 'nuff country town. Wooden storefronts with wooden porches. Wooden sidewalks. Overhanging wooden signs. With its smatter of brown boys out front, its frieze of tire-sized Coca-Cola signs running around the eaves of its porch, Bryant's the only game in town, Emmett Till guessed.

Climbing out of Moses Wright's old Dodge, he sports the broad smile I recall from another photo, the one of him leaning, elbow atop a TV set, clean as a string bean in his white dress shirt and tie, his chest thrust out mannishly, baby fat in his cheeks, a softish, still-forming boy whose energy, intelligence, and expectations of life are evident in the pose he's striking for the camera, just enough in-your-face swagger that you can't help smiling back at the wary eagerness to please of his smile.

To Emmett Till the boys in Money's streets are a cluster of down-home country cousins. He sees a stage beckoning on which he can perform. Steps up on the sidewalk with his cousin Curtis, to whom he is *Bo* or *Bobo*, greets his audience. Like a magician pulling a rabbit from his hat, Emmett Till pulls a white girl from his wallet. Silences everybody. Mesmerizes them with tales of what they're missing, living down here in the Mississippi woods. If he'd been selling magic beans, all of them would have dug into their overalls and extracted their last hot penny to buy some. They watch his fingers slip into his shirt pocket. Hold their breath waiting for the next trick.

Emmett Till's on a roll, can't help rubbing it in a little. What he's saying about himself sounds real good, so good he wants to hear more. All he wants really is for these brown faces to love him. As much as he's loved by the dark faces and light faces in the junior high graduation pictures from Chicago he's showing around.

He winks at the half dozen or so boys gathered round him. Nods. Smiles like the cat swallowed the canary. Points to the prettiest girl, the fairest, longest-haired one of all you can easily see, even though the faces in the class picture are tiny and gray. Emmett Till says she is the prettiest, anyway, so why not? Why not believe he's courted and won her, and ain't you-all lucky he come down here bringing you-all the good news?

Though Emmett Till remains the center of attention, the other kids giggle, scratch their naps, stroke their chins, turn their heads this way and that around the circle, commence little conversations of eye-cutting and teeth-sucking and slack-jawed awe. Somebody pops a finger against somebody's shaved skull. Somebody's hip bumps somebody else. A tall boy whistles a blues line, and you notice someone's been humming softly the whole time. Emmett Till's the preacher, and it's Sunday morning, and the sermon is righteous. On the other hand, everybody's ready for a hymn or a responsive reading, even a collection plate circulating, so they can participate, stretch their bones, hear their own voices.

You sure is something, boy. You say you bad, Emmett Till. Got all them white gals up north, you say. Bet you won't say boo to the white lady in the store.

Curtis Jones is playing checkers with old Uncle Edmund on a barrel set in the shade around the corner from the main drag. One of the boys who sauntered into the store with Emmett Till to buy candy comes running. *He did it. Emmett Till did it. That cousin of yours crazy, boy. Said, "Bye-bye, baby," to Miss Bryant.*

The old man gets up so fast he knocks over the crate he's been sitting on. *Lor' have mercy. I know the boy didn't do nothing like that. Huhuh. No. No, he didn't. You-all better get out here. That lady come out that store blow you-all's brains off.*

Several months later, after an all-white jury in the town of Sumner, Mississippi, had deliberated an hour—*Would have been less if we hadn't took time for lunch*—and found Roy Bryant and J. W. Milam not guilty of murdering Emmett Till, the two men were paid four thousand dollars by a journalist, William Bradford Huie, to tell the story of abducting, beating, and shooting Emmett Till.

To get rid of his body, they barb-wired a fifty-pound cotton-gin fan to Emmett Till's neck and threw him in the Tallahatchie River. The journalist, in a videotaped interview, said, "It seems to a rational mind today—it seems impossible that they could have killed him."

The reporter muses for a moment, then remembers, "But J. W. Milam looked up at me, and he says, 'Well, when he told me about this white girl he had, my friend, well, that's what this war's about down here now, that's what we got to fight to protect, and I just looked at him and say, *Boy, you ain't never gone to see the sun come up again.*'"

To the very end, Emmett Till didn't believe the crackers would kill him. He was fourteen, from Chicago. He'd hurt no one. These strange, funny-talking white men were a nightmare he'd awaken from sooner or later. Milam found the boy's lack of fear shocking. Called it "belligerence." Here was this nigger should be shitting his drawers. Instead he was making J. W. Milam uncomfortable. Brave or foolhardy or ignorant or blessed to be already in another place, a place these sick, sick men could never touch, whatever enabled Emmett Till to stand his ground, to be himself until the first deadly blow landed, be himself even after it landed, I hope Emmett Till understood that Milam or Bryant, whoever struck first with the intent to kill, was the one who flinched, not him.

When such thoughts come to me, I pile them like sandbags along the levees that protect my sleep. I should know better than to waste my time.

In another dream we emerge at dawn from the tree line. Breeze into Money. Rat-tat. Rat-tat-tat. Waste the whole motherfucking ville. Nothing to it. Little hick town 'bout same today as when they lynched poor brother Emmett Till.

Some the bitches come rubbing up against us after we lined 'em up by the ditch. Thinking maybe if they fuck us they won't die. We let 'em try. You know. Wasn't bad pussy, neither. But when the time come, you know, they got to go just like the rest. Rat-tat-tat. Uh-huh.

Money gone. Burnt a hole in its pocket.

I asked a lover, a woman whose whiteness made her a flesh-and-blood embodiment of the nightmare J. W. Milam discovered in Emmett Till's wallet, what she thinks of when she hears "Emmett Till."

"A black kid whistling at a white woman somewhere down south and being killed for it, is what I think," she said.

"He didn't whistle," I reply. I've heard the wolf-whistle story all my life and another that has him not moving aside for a white woman walking down the sidewalk. Both are part of the myth, but neither's probably true. The story Till's cousin Curtis Jones tells is different. And for what it's worth, his cousin was there. Something Emmett Till said to a white woman inside a store is what started it.

She wants to know where I heard the cousin's version, and I launch into a riff on my sources—*Voices of Freedom*, an oral history of the civil rights movement; Henry Hampton's video documentary, *Eyes on the Prize*; a book, *Representations of Black Masculinity in Contemporary American Art*, organized around a museum exhibit of black male images. Then I realize I'm doing all the talking, when what I'd intended to elicit was her spontaneous witness. What her memory carried forward, what it lost.

She's busy with something of her own, and we just happened to cross paths a moment in the kitchen, and she's gone before I get what I wanted. Gone before I know what I wanted. Except standing there next to the refrigerator, in the silence released by its hum, I feel utterly defeated. All the stuff spread out on my desk isn't getting me any closer to Emmett Till or a cure. Neither will man-in-the-street, woman-in-the-kitchen interviews. Other people's facts and opinions don't matter. Only one other person's voice required for this story I'm constructing to overcome a bad dream, and they shut him up a long time ago, didn't they?

Here is what happened. Four nights after the candy-buying and "Bye-bye, baby" scene in Money, at 2 a.m. on August 21, 1955, Roy Bryant, with a pistol in one hand and a flashlight in the other, appears at Moses Wright's door. "This is Mr. Bryant," he calls into the darkness. Then demands to know if Moses Wright has two niggers from Chicago inside. He says he wants the nigger done all that talk.

When Emmett Till is delivered, Bryant marches him to a car and asks someone inside, "This the right nigger?" and somebody says, "Yes, he is."

Next time Moses Wright sees Emmett Till is three days later when the sheriff summons him to identify a corpse. The body's naked and too badly damaged to tell who it is until Moses Wright notices the initialed ring on his nephew's finger.

Where were you when JFK was shot? Where were you when a man landed on the moon? When Martin Luther King, Jr., was shot? Malcolm shot? When the Rodney King verdict announced? Where were you when Emmett Till floated up to the surface of the Tallahatchie River for *Bye-bye, baby*ing a white woman?

A white man in the darkness outside a tarpaper cabin announcing the terror of his name, gripping a flashlight in his fist, a heavy-duty flashlight stuffed with thick D batteries that will become a club for bashing Emmett Till's skull.

An old black man in the shanty crammed with bodies, instantly alert when he hears, "You got those niggers from Chicago in there with you?" An old man figuring the deadly odds, how many lives bought if one handed over. Calculating the rage of his ancient enemy, weighing the risk of saying what he wants the others in his charge to hear, Emmett Till to hear, no matter what terrible things happen next.

"Got my two grandsons and a nephew in here."

A black boy inside the cabin, a boy my age whose name I don't know yet, who will never know mine. He rubs his eyes, not sure he's awake or dreaming a scary dream, one of the tales buried deep, deep he's been hearing since before we were born about the old days in the Deep South when they cut off niggers' nuts and lynched niggers and roasted niggers over fires like marshmallows.

A man in my own warm bed, lying beside a beautiful woman rubbing my shoulder, a pale, blond woman whose presence sometimes is as strange and unaccountable to me as mine must be to her, as snow falling softly through the bedroom ceiling would be, accumulating in white drifts on the down comforter.

Why am I telling Emmett Till's story this way, attempting the miracle or cheap trick of being many people, many places at once? Will words change what happened, what's missing, what's lost? Will my nightmare dissolve if I cling to the woman almost asleep now next to me, end if I believe this loving moment together might last and last?

The name Emmett is spoiled for me. In any of its spellings. As big a kick as I get from watching Emmitt Smith rush the football for the Dallas Cowboys, there is also the moment after a bone-shattering collision and he's sprawled lifeless on the turf or the moment after he's stumbled or fumbled and slumps to the bench and lifts his helmet and I see a black mother's son, a small, dark, round face, a boy's big, wide, scared eyes. All those yards gained, all that wealth, but like O.J. he'll never run far enough or fast enough. Inches behind him the worst thing the people who hate him can imagine hounds him like a shadow.

Sometimes I think the only way to end this would be with Andy Warhol–like strips of images, the same face, Emmett Till's face, replicated twelve, twenty-four, forty-eight, ninety-six times on a wall-sized canvas. Like giant postage stamps end to end, top to bottom, each version of the face exactly like the other but different names printed below each one. Martin Luther Till. Malcolm Till. Medgar Till. Nat Till. Gabriel Till. Michael Till. Huey Till. Bigger Till. Nelson Till. Mumia Till. Colin Till. Jesse Till. Your daddy, your mama, your sister, brother, aunt, cousin, uncle, niece, nephew Till . . .

Instead of the nightmare one night, this is what I dream.

I'm marching with many, many men, a multitude, a million men of all colors in Washington, D.C., marching past the bier on which the body of Emmett Till rests. The casket, as his mother demanded, is open. *I want the world to see what they did to my baby.* One by one from an endless line, the men detach themselves, pause, peer down into the satin-lined box. Pinned inside its upright lid a snapshot of Emmett Till, young, smiling, whole, a jaunty Stetson cocked high across his brow. In the casket Emmett Till is dressed in a dark suit, jacket wings spread to expose a snowy shroud pulled up to his chin. Then the awful face, patched together with string and wire, awaits each mourner.

My turn is coming soon. I'm grateful. Will not shy away this time. Will look hard this time. The line of my brothers and fathers and sons stretches ahead of me, behind me. I am drawn by them, pushed by them, steadied as we move each other along. We are a horizon girding the earth, holding the sky down. So many of us in one place at one time it scares me. More than a million of us marching through this city of monumental buildings and dark alleys. Not very long ago, we were singing, but now we march silently, more shuffle than brisk step as we approach the bier, wait our turn.

Singing's over, but it holds silently in the air, tangible as weather, as the bright sun disintegrating marble buildings, emptying alleys of shadows, warming us on a perfect October day we had no right to expect but would have been profoundly disappointed had it fallen out otherwise.

What I say when I lean over and speak one last time to Emmett Till is *I love you. I'm sorry. I won't allow it to happen ever again.* And my voice will be small and quiet when I say the words, not nearly as humble as it should be, fearful almost to pledge any good after so much bad. My small voice and short turn, and then the next man and the next, close together, leading, following one another so the murmur of our voices beside the bier never stops. An immensity, a continuous, muted shout and chant and benediction, a river gliding past the stillness of Emmett Till. Past this city, this hour, this place. River sound of blood I'm almost close enough to hear coursing in the veins of the next man.

In the dream we do not say, *Forgive us.* We are taking, not asking for, something today. There is no time left to ask for things, even things as precious as forgiveness, only time to take one step, then the next and the next, alone in this great body of men, each one standing on his own feet, moving, our shadows linked, a coolness, a shield stretching nearly unbroken across the last bed where Emmett Till sleeps.

Where we bow and hope and pray he frees us. Ourselves seen, sinking, then rising as in a mirror, then stepping away.

And then. And then this vision fades, too. I am there and not there. Not in Washington, D.C., marching with a million other men. My son Dan, my new granddaughter Qasima's father, marched. He was a witness, and the arc of his witness includes me as mine, his. So, yes, I was there in a sense but not there to view the face of Emmett Till because Emmett Till was not there, either, not in an open casket displayed to the glory of the heavens, the glories of this republic, not there except as a shadow, a stain, a wound in the million faces of the marchers, the faces of their absent fathers, sons, and brothers.

We have yet to look upon Emmett Till's face. No apocalyptic encounter, no ritual unveiling, no epiphany has freed us. The nightmare is not cured.

I cannot wish away Emmett Till's face. The horrific death mask of his erased features marks a site I ignore at my peril. The site of a grievous wound. A wound unhealed because untended. Beneath our nation's pieties, our self-delusions, our denials and distortions of history, our professed black-and-white certainties about race, lies chaos. The whirlwind that swept Emmett Till away and brings him back.

JOHN EDGAR WIDEMAN ON "LOOKING AT EMMETT TILL"

The thoughts and feelings this essay prompted continue to grow as I add, subtract, and discover new places in my writing where the material the essay excavated and invented fits. Young black boys are still being cut down as relentlessly as Till's murderers cut short his life—nobody's fault, everybody's fault, a deep, deep fault that remains in our national psyche.

The writing, or exploration, or examination, or mourning, was precipitated by turning the pages of *Jet* magazine and being confronted by Emmett Till's face, the face that has haunted me since I was fourteen, and saw myself reflected in the dead—horribly transformed, suddenly mortal, suddenly vulnerable, mutilated by my age, my color.

The writing developed more or less like the action of a basketball game—a spontaneous call-and-response process in which anticipation and reaction are indistinguishable. Improvisation is key—improvisation that's both innocent and steeped in conscious preparation, all the practice, the games played and imagined and observed, the internalization of traditions and patterns, the work of readying the body so it rises to the occasion, forgetting the moment, the possibility (necessity) of failure, risking the flow, living it no matter the outcome.

Writing is writing and I employ every new trick and technology I'm able to muster in whatever kind of writing I'm attempting. The lines between fiction and nonfiction, for me, are more and more arbitrary, blurred, problematic. In many senses, the distinctions are nonexistent. Does a photo document or fabricate an event? Is life composed of facts or a constructed fiction? Both. Always. I think biographers and historians are fiction writers who haven't come out of the closet. It's probably important to share with readers my intentions—is this piece fact or fiction?—but those intentions may include a desire not to share my intentions—fact or fiction. Good work seizes the reader's attention, enforces its unique version of reality. The best work changes the shape, the definitions of the genre, explodes traditional codes that translate/confine reality.

Language performs functions that identify communities and cultures. The collective effort of writing should be to keep the language alive as a medium for imaginative truth-telling, for communication that gives the lie to language as fact. All information includes a point of view, intention, and author. Facts pretend this isn't so. Good writing reminds us everyone's responsible for dreaming a world, and the dream, the point of view embodied by it, within it, is as close to fact, to reality, as we ever get.

Read the classics, go back in time as far as you're able—Egyptians, Greeks, cave painting—and then creep forward, trying always to stay aware of how much you're missing. This sort of foundation should be helpful as you read yourself and read your peers, your contemporaries. Don't forget what's going on in other countries, other languages—translations are better than total ignorance—and what's happening in the margins, whether it's silence or scary babble or scorn or insult or madness. Persevere with some writing that you may not like at first—especially when the writing is highly recommended by somebody you respect. Study your own writing always against this background of ongoing reading, this project of listening and learning, this understanding that the best anybody can achieve will fail, will open rather than close doors.

AT THE ISLAND'S END

2006

Three or four times a week, usually early in the morning, I jog along the East River from my apartment on Grand Street on the Lower East Side of Manhattan to Battery Park at the end of the island and back. Obviously a good way for a sixty-five-year-old writer to stay fit, but also a project to teach myself a different, quieter intimacy, step by step, inch by inch, with a city whose terror and trauma were thrust in my face the September I arrived from Massachusetts to settle here.

While renovating the apartment for me, Marty and his crew saw both planes ram the twin towers. Later that day, through the same window, I stared with them at the dark cloud where the towers had once dominated the skyline. Still, I moved in, and have resided there the past five years, including ghost months when for days many downtown streets and stores were either closed to the public or nearly deserted and when for weeks a tide of indescribable stench seeped off the smoldering charnel pit of ground zero into my new neighborhood each evening about six.

While I run, planes, briefly banned post-9/11, crisscross New York City's airspace again, too low, too loud, probably more nuisance now than threat, complicating my project anyway. Old flight paths resumed to maximize profit. Business as usual. A new tower, tallest in the world, has been promised to replace the old ones.

Though I wasn't looking to move from Grand Street, on one of my first trips along the river I noticed an "Apartment for Rent" sign sitting in a second-story window above the Paris Cafe. Given the Paris Cafe's location (since 1873) on a street corner about twenty yards from the East River, just beyond the overarching shadows of the FDR parkway and the Brooklyn Bridge, near the eye of a foul storm of fish being loaded and unloaded in the Fulton Fish Market every morning, no wonder no one was eager to live over the restaurant. Either noise or stink enough to dissuade any sane person from renting the vacant apartment.

So why some mornings did I imagine myself its tenant, hope the sign would greet me when I passed? Would I enjoy being awakened by the clamor of trucks, vans, forklifts, the odor of rotting fish clawing at my window? Perhaps the perfect awfulness outside would sink me deeper into the nest of comfort and safety pitched inside a tiny room above the Paris.

Or maybe I was attracted by the idea of disciplining myself to be unaware, if I chose, of whatever mayhem the city produced. Proud of my acquired immunity, my eccentricity. Undisturbed by crashing pallets overloaded with boxes of iced fish, the beep-beep-beep-beep warning of trucks backing up, vendors hollering, doors slammed, tailgates banged, the braying, honking and wailing of way too many vehicles crowding a limited space, tires crunching mounds of spilled ice, hoses spraying hissing streams of slimy runoff from the tarmac into South Street. Ignoring tis chaos even if it's rife in my hair, my clothes, inside me. Body and mind impervious as the Paris apartment. Pleased to have discovered a hiding place where none exists.

When I imagined living over the Paris Cafe, I guess I was actually daydreaming about living under it. Deep where the East River licks and sucks away the fill that workmen, long dead now, dumped in to tame its flow. A soundless, etherized realm. In my mind, I'm alone, hidden from view or, if I stay lucky, with my lover beside me in bed each morning, sealed like me in our bungalow, denizens of an immortal city beneath the mortal one, marveling at the quiet, the air of our mingled breaths and flesh sour and sweet as the black water at bay just beyond the porthole.

New York didn't drown, and I continue, stride by stride, to run along the river, desiring more than a hiding place, looking for more. And the city whispers, yes, more's coming. Uncovers its secrets the way ancient maps reveal wonders: "Dragons Be Here." And, sure enough, one morning I see wiggly, many-footed sections of a fiery red dragon and drums, cymbals, baton twirlers, banners and flags of bands rehearsing for a Chinatown parade, two legless people in wheelchairs smooching, fishermen, Senegalese loaded down like Santa with sacks of trinkets for Battery Park tourists and more, more, all in the same stretch of riverfront, unfinished business, business starting anew on New York's streets surviving still above the water, beneath skyscrapers that seem so immense and stolid.

FROM THE LOUIS TILL
BLUES PROJECT

2011

On the long bus ride to Columbia, South Carolina, Marlow, bored by droning tires, boring interstate scenery, amuses himself by gently picking at the
rough stitching of the Senegalese *boubou*, a tunic-length wrapper of the
sort he favors these days, kind to his bulk, though this one's fabric a bit
heavy for surprisingly mild March weather, traces the *boubou*'s threads of
many colors, assigning names to colors, imagining lives for them, following
colors that entwine, appear and disappear in the weave's stripes, amusing
himself further on the long ride south with the funny thought, not so amusing come to think of it, that for boys his age, Emmett Till's age, colored boys
growing up in Northern cities, teenagers in the mid-1950s, boys taught in
school they owned no origins other than the dark skin covering them at
birth, no roots older than slave plantations, boys orphaned from their history by ignorance and shame, for them, us, the American South served as
a surrogate Africa. Our ancestral home. Our heart of darkness. South the
birthplace of grandparents, elderly aunts and uncles, many parents of the
boys, too, so the boys just a generation or so removed from the old ways,
old country that most likely they had never visited, a land vaguely understood from family stories, magazine pictures, movies, legends, myths, negative news items in the Negro press deploring ignorance, backwardness,
and violence. A shameful American Negro South, not shameful Africa,

337

his ancient, original home. A South darkened by slavery's long shadow. Source of manners and customs, half-understood, half-remembered language, music. A South preying upon Africa, hiding and preserving Africa. Though the boys couldn't have articulated why, nor appreciated the fact if confronted by it, Africa reborn in their walking and talking, singing, dancing, superstitions, ways of worship, ways of telling time, swimming in time clocks can't reckon, styles indisputably West African, by way of the South, the Caribbean, styles boys express simply by imitating one another, styles not associated in city boy minds with any particular region on earth except the urban turf on which they were born and raised, boys keeping the secret, dark heart thumping in spite of themselves.

Like Africa, their south a distant, primitive region. Dangerous, mysterious. Stuck forever in some old-timey ghetto of the past. South with savage natives who were not the boys' color, tribes of pale faces who would as soon catch, cook, and eat you as welcome you home. Bloodthirsty inhabitants, enemies time out of mind. Do not trust them. Their funny way of talking. Ghost color. Ghost blue eyes. Black eyes with no pity. They mean you no good, boy. Never have. Never will. They will hurt you, kill you if you don't stay on guard against the evil hearts and minds of those different colored natives down south. A trip south meant penetrating hostile territory, risking heat, wild animals, noxious insects, shitting in nasty outhouses, wiping your ass with a Sears catalogue. Skinny, vicious farm dogs. Skinny farms and skinny redneck farmers. City flair and flash lost in dark miles, in dark nights of rural isolation. Territory it could cost a boy's life to enter, a forbidding land no matter how fondly parents, grandparents, tottering uncles and aunts remembered it in funny down home tales they told each other and their progeny, tales full of laughing, patting, hugging, dance steps, pantomime, *mmmmm-mmmmm-mmmmm*, recalling good food, clear air, sweet water, hunting, fishing, sermons, funerals, weddings, baptisms, moonshine. No matter all that once-upon-a-time good stuff, those smiles, struts, city boys like Marlow had heard other tales, too, and remained more suspicious, more than reluctant to take the plunge south.

Marlow had said, *No sir,* and *Thank you, sir, can't go this summer,* declining many summers his grandfather's invitation to accompany him south, dodging the trip south until his grandpa Harry, born and baptized Hannibal in 1878, in South Carolina, not long after slavery days, got too old to go and stopped asking, and they missed the opportunity of traveling together, hanging out together in the old man's home place, Promised Land. Grandpa deprived of a chance to celebrate with Promised Land his successful trek to the big city and show off his grandson, first northern-born male child of the extended clan. A trip Marlow bitterly regrets missing. Lost golden summer in Grandpa's South Carolina briar patch, Old Harry's birthplace, Marlow's transplanted heart of darkness. His Africa of bloody tooth and claw. Crazy, white-sheet-wearing motherfucking peckerwoods running around down there in the woods, waiting to cut off your balls, string you up. *Dixie, wish I was in Dixie.* No thanks, Grandpa. Missing him, that Hannibal who called himself *Harry* out of shyness or shame after he settled in the North. Missing him terribly on the droning bus. Too late. Sorry, Grandpa. Wish you were here.

Marlow thinks that if he ever gets to the U.S. Army's Disciplinary Training Center at Metato, near Pisa in Italy, he'll be visiting another site, like the South, outside time. During World War II the DTC a heart of darkness, a black hole. Colored soldiers 25 percent of the four thousand unlucky internees at the mercy of white officers who ran the godforsaken camp, by all reports, as if they were possessed by devils. The camp at Metato alien territory then and now. Uncountable miles away from the known, the everyday, the acceptable. An American prison on conquered Italian soil, ominous and unsafe as any teeming jungle of a mythical dark continent, as the South for northern colored boys like Emmett Till and Marlow. Inmates of the camp exposed to bitter cold, withering heat, never-ending labor, humiliation, beatings. Prisoners born again as slaves, guards as vicious slave drivers in the DTC time warp. But if the famous American poet imprisoned with Louis Till was correct, a different Africa also abounding in the Metato inferno. Luminous traces of dark speech, dark faces, dark music, dark looks, the dark generosity of kind acts, *actes gratuity*, only dark hands dared perform. Africa surviving but only if you paid attention, looked around yourself, inside yourself, and knew how to look. The poet's desk a gift from an African spirit disguised as a colored prisoner. A writing desk ingeniously fashioned from a packing crate, just appearing one morning, no warning in the poet's bare cell, a desk compliments of quiet Saunders whose gleaming bronze forehead belongs on a Benin mask.

Whereas the sight of a good nigger is cheering, the poet wrote, a captive poet who plays Mistah Kurtz in Marlow's fantasy of the camp, an endangered soul Marlow must rescue, bring back alive. The poet a witness for the defense, his *Pisan Cantos* telling truths at the court martial of Till and McMurray.

Ain committed no federal crime
Jes a slaight misdemeanor

If any single voice guarantees that a hangman's noose will settle around the neck of Louis Till, one voice in the welter of ghostly voices rising like dust from the transcript's yellow gray pages Marlow reads again and again—invisible dust cloying his hands, eyes, nostrils as he sifts through the file asking dust to do what dry dust cannot do, assume shape, substance, breathe and speak—it's the voice of Private James Thomas, Junior, that dooms Till. A fawning, howling, lying, sly voice driven by fear profound as the weight on Louis Till's tongue, the dead weight of Till's silence. An unbudgeable weight stealing the power of words Till might have summoned to save himself, free himself. If he could say the words. If they could silence the voice of Junior Thomas.

What would have happened to Louis Till if he denied James Thomas's story, challenged it when interviewed by CID agents. What if Till had accused his accuser, Thomas, in a sworn statement of his own, delivered by his lawyer to court-martial judges. What if earlier, during investigation of the sugar theft that became an investigation of rape and murder, Till had scared Junior Thomas, shut him up with an evil stare, or wasted Thomas in a dark alley in Naples the moment Till caught the glint, the hang dog Iago smirk of complicity and betrayal in the eyes of Junior

Thomas. The innocent, imploring look of determination and helplessness in the eyes of a man who's fallen hopelessly in love and understands he is not loved in return and that nothing the loved or unloved can do, good or evil to the other, will ever unknot unrequited love.

Monroe Thomas, who everybody calls Money, the man who's the son of Private James Thomas, Jr. (16098325, Company 177 of Port Battalion 379), picks up Marlow at the Holiday Inn in Greenville, South Carolina, and they drive to Promised Land school. Louis Till's buddy, Money's father, James, is called Junior, but not because he bore the Christian name of his father. Edgar Clyde Thomas the father's name, and his son, James, became Junior because everybody who grew up in Promised Land with Edgar (*Glide* for Clyde) Thomas, all the folks working in the cotton fields, attending Promised Land AME Zion, going to Promised Land school the little-bitty time school open back then, all the elder folks who remembered little *Glide* Thomas recognized that his son, the chubby-cheeked, eyes set wide apart, small-nosed, small-eyed, always grinning, you better not never believe a word coming out his little, big-lipped mouth, that dark brown-skinned shortish, bowlegged boy named James, the spitting image of his daddy, Glide, when Glide was a boy. Edgar Clyde Thomas's son James's got to be a Junior, running around here so lookalike you'd swear it was lil Glide Thomas all over again.

They say my daddy, Junior, a real heartbreaker, mischief maker in his day, Money Thomas tells Marlow. Just an old quiet dude in a rocking chair to me. Never heard him say nothing about no war. Never heard the man say much of anything, Mr. Marlow. Even before his bad heart and the second stroke put him down for good. Wasn't really that old a man, I guess. Beat-up-looking more than old, but once that last stroke put him down he stayed down in that rocking chair by the door, sitting outside by day, inside at night. Sleeping in that damned chair the day he passed. Some folks say they saw him rocking in that empty chair after he passed. Never heard no stories from him. Which, come to think of it, kinda unusual, you know, being as how my daddy had the reputation around here of a fast talker, big talker. I wasn't born when my daddy first gone off. Then like I told you he was sick by the time he come back to settle for good. Why the man be telling me his business, anyway. I wasn't nothing but a little squirty boy. Even if I'd been the kind of kid likes to sit still and listen to old folks talk. Which I wasn't. He came back from the war, then my daddy up and left again. In and mostly out for years, and once he came back to stay, it's too late. He old and sick. Mouth sewed shut for good.

You lucky though, Mr. Marlow, coming through here this weekend when everybody be out at the school reunion. Promised Land school one hundred twenty-five years old this year. Bet you find one or two the older folks at the birthday reunion who was raised up with my daddy and can tell you more than me about him.

When I asked the girl at the motel desk how to get to Promised Land, she told me she wasn't sure, almost like she didn't know there was a place called Promised Land.

If she a local, she know. And knows how to get there.

A white girl. Maybe that's why she wasn't sure.

They know how to get to Promised Land. All of 'em. Black gals and white gals nowadays. Ask her how to get to Sugars. *Shugs*. She tell you exactly and right away, if she want to tell you, sure nuff. Most all young folks, black and white, hang out at Shugs. Still got they white joints and they black joints, but nowdays they all got Shugs, too.

Sugar's in Promised Land.

Yes and no. Ain't no Promised Land no more. Not the way it once was. You got two, three short blocks of raggedy houses hardly nobody lives in now. Shugs out behind the end block. The schoolhouse sits a little ways off from there and that's it, all's left of Promised Land those couple three short blocks just cross the old L M & N railroad tracks and some little farms nobody works no more. So when you ask the whereabouts of Promised Land, some folks say it's gone. Not on the new state highway maps what they mean. Everybody lives here knows about Promised Land, remembers Promised Land, and could take you right there if they want to remember. Some might wish Promised Land long gone, but it ain't true. There's a

Promised Land sign up the road a piece from where you staying in Greenville. Right where 10 comes into Route 65. Take 10 to the right like we did
and twelve miles you there, Promised Land, but ain't no sign telling you
you there when you there. You might easy could miss it. Pass on by. Not
much to see. Ain't no mystery, neither. If you know how to look. Promised Land sitting where it always sat. And gonna keep sitting whether
they mark it on the state map or not. Check out what I'm saying with
the folks partying at the school. They know what I mean. They Promised
Land people and always will be. School a hundred-twenty-five years old
this very day. Course the white gal at the desk didn't know nothing about
that. Didn't tell you Promised Land folks celebrating the school's birthday today, did she. Well, guess what. She knows even if she don't know, if
she's born around here. They all know even if white folks be choosing not
to remember and choose not to come out to Promised Land less there's
something they want real bad and can't get it nowheres else. Know what I
mean, Mr. Marlow.

Land flat as an old peckerwood's ass. Money Thomas laughs. Out the
red Dodge Ram window a stretch of runty, new growth pines, straight,
stiff bristles of a skinhead's shaved hair starting to grow back. No underbrush to hide the geometrical precision of the rows. Low slung houses
with sheds, junkyard yards behind or beside them. Some houses starkly
isolated, others in small clusters, some hugging the road, some shying
miles away it seems from Route 10. Quick pass through a time tunnel museum of weathered, wooden cabins occupied or not, impossible
to discern, dry, gray, flyaway flimsy, collapsing into the niggardly soil.
Here and there a big, scrawny, crooked tree, dying on the same bare
patch of ground where it had sprouted. A flurry of brand-new two- and
three-story homes, different models, colors to choose from, low down
payment, convenient terms, generous amenities the signs promise, just
choose your model, buy now, settle down today in this newly minted
mini-sprawl of lookalikes that, from the angle of the Dodge Ram passing
by appears, Potemkin-like, to go on forever, an endless village hunkered
down, house after empty house, surrounded by identical neighbors. The

quickie development, the scattered single houses or groups of three or four, the slavery-days shacks don't relieve the monotonous landscape, just make it more melancholy.

Brutal too strong a word for the land, *sparse* suggests the pervading quality of something missing, but *sparse* doesn't indicate what's missing. Marlow searches for another word to describe sparseness freighted, troubled with intimations of the thing reduced to leave behind sparse remnants. *Gaunt* maybe. Maybe *cadaverous*. Closing his eyes, he sees hordes of men clearing a towering forest, gangs of women stooped by heavy sacks slung over their shoulders, lives fed to the land, buried by the land, unmourned lives that scar it indelibly. Like land struck by lightning or overgrazed, or plowed up and salted, or polluted by poisonous sprays, land damaged by ravagings no longer spoken about, no voices keeping alive the land's history, only the silence of scarcity and emptiness begging for regrowth, reseeding, retaliation, renegotiation, reparations, greening, for some further clean distancing and settling of accounts to separate it at last from the blight that usurped what the land once was, what it could have been or will become.

Was it Tom Wolfe who came up with *red elbows*, a phrase Marlow had read just yesterday, it seems, but probably decades ago. Wolfe thought he was coining a clever, more accurate epithet than *rednecks*. Wolfe bringing news his southern brethren free at last from the incriminating pink collar of field work, free to bake their elbows red in open windows of pickups tooling round the mall. Why didn't Wolfe's tongue-in-cheek offering catch on, Marlow wonders, gazing out the open window of Money's truck at a bare, warm elbow which sun would never turn red exactly. Was he certain the arm belonged to him. If the arm framed in the window changed color, what color would it turn.

Greenville to Promised Land a short hop, Money Thomas promised. Eleven thirty on the motel clock when they met in the lobby, and only six minutes later by his watch, but Marlow's drowsy, exhausted like they've driven hours or like he's been up chopping cotton since dawn. Daydreamy. Betwixt and between. Anywhere. Anytime. *The contemporary*

Tom Wolfe, he footnotes his conversation with himself, distinguishing live Tom *Wolfe* from dead Thomas *Wolfe*, from the English lady Woolf, from the *wolf* whistle allegedly authored by Emmett Till. All *wolfs* sounding alike though spelled differently, and he can't recollect the proper word for female wolf—*wolfess*—no, no, you know better, no such thing, *wolfess, poetess, negress, mulatress* are obsolete, bad taste, Marlow. *She-wolf* for a female, as in the construction *were-wolf.* Or perhaps *wolf* the most enlightened option—one word equaling male, female, every gender, creed, color of wolf. Democracy, Marlow. Everybody's neck red, elbows red. Everybody blushes blood red. Blood-red color under his colored eyelids when he squeezes them shut against the disk of bloody sun risen nearly to mid-day height at the tail end of a Deep South morning, and Marlow imagines Route 10 at night, no sun, no moon, no stars. In pitch-black darkness a black man his color is driving a black car. The man's alone, in a hurry. Tightly grips the steering wheel. No other traffic until suddenly a pair of headlights in the rear view mirror bearing down on him. Wolf eyes. Glowing bright and hungry in the dark night as pine-pitch torches, a cross burning.

Uh-huh. Sure I members old Junior Thomas. Why wouldn't I. Dirt the onliest thing members more bout the goings on round here than me—I member Junior's daddy, too, old Clyde Thomas. Me and Glide tight way back when. Uh-huh. And who you, mister. What you want wit dead Junior Thomas.

Excuse me for not introducing myself. My name's Marlow, Mr. Jones. Pleasure to meet you, sir. Guess I missed what Mr. Thomas was saying. With all the talk and music. Thought he said my name to you when he brought me over and said your name, Mr. Jones.

Heard what Money said. Wanted to hear you say your entitles your ownself. How do, Mister Marlow. And I ain't Mister nothing. One name all I needs. Jones. One name, Jones.

Makes perfect sense to me, Jones. I prefer one name myself: Marlow.

What you looking to hear about that boy Money's daddy. Tell you one thing sure, Money favors Junior some, but Junior a spittin' image when he was a boy of his daddy Glide when his daddy Glide and me was picks. You being from up north, maybe you don't know the word *picks*. Short for pickininnies.

I've read it comes from *pequenos*, a Portuguese word for "little ones." Child. A baby. What Europeans called colored children during slavery days.

Little niggers what it mean. Don't know nothing about no Portugeechee. Me and Glide little nigger kids playing in this here Promised Land briar patch. Picks cause thas all white folks figured we was good for, picking cotton. Little niggers and the white folks come by peeking at us every now and then to see if one us picks ripe to carry to market. Spying to see if we grown enough give them a good day in the cotton field. Putting us out to work what they called it. Hired out soon's we can drag them sacks up and down a row. Picks pecking round in white folks yards like chickens till the boss man think we large enough to pick cotton. Picks, Marlow. So course I knew all the other little niggers with me growing up inside them chicken wire fences. Them ole chicken-wire days. All us happy scratching around in the dirt, didn't know no better. Some the best days lots of niggers ever gon get. The good ole days like some folks say. Sure didn't get no better for me after I start to working. Me and Glide Thomas was picks together.

Then maybe you watched his son Junior growing up here. I'm in Promised Land to piece together a story, and Junior Thomas a big part of it. An ugly story that took place in Italy many years ago during World War II when James Thomas, Junior, was a soldier. I'm searching for anybody who can help me understand more about what happened over there, more than I've been able to learn from books and government records. Anything you're willing to tell me about Junior Thomas will help, I'm sure. Grateful to hear anything you have to say.

Ain't about to 'buse the dead. Dead got a way of sneaking back and thumping you upside your skull you talk bad 'bout 'em. 'Sides, too close to dead my ownself to talk bad 'bout folks I be meeting up wit real soon. But I got to say, Marlow, since you done asked, Mr. Junior Thomas— excuse me, brother Glide, but I got to tell the truth—Junior Thomas wasn't worth shit. Not worth shit, man or boy. And you know it's true, Glide. I wish it wasn't so, much as you wish it, Glide, but you know just as well as I do what I'm saying the god's truth. Trouble with Junior, you couldn't get truth out him if you tied him down and give that boy a truth enema. Squeeze him like you squeeze a lemon, squeeze like womens used to squeeze clothes in those washbasins with wringers. Squeeze him dry as a bone, you still ain't squeezing no truth out Junior Thomas. Truth not in him. Once you understand that fact then you could go head and deal with Junior. Likes you deals with peckerwoods or any other body. Trouble is some folks don't figure out what I'm telling you bout Junior till it's too late. Skinning Junior's ass won't do them no good then 'cause Junior's done already messed up they business with lies. Junior Thomas— bless his sorry soul, Glide, but I got to tell it like it is—Junior a born liar. Couldn't help lying to save his soul. Once a person get past Junior's lying habit, Junior ain't much worse than nobody else. Better than some. Like they say, Marlow. Either praise the dead or let them rest in peace.

Here come Money again. Bet he's coming for you not me. Half way surprised, all these people in here, he bring you over to me. He knows I ain't a man holds his tongue. Anybody in here knows Jones knows that fact. People tell you Jones do too much truth telling for his own good. But ain't no such a thing as too much truth, Marlow. Truth is truth and don't need to lay my hand on no stack of Bibles to tell it. What come out my mouth about Junior true and nothing but the truth. Maybe Money Thomas wants you to hear the worst about his daddy first. No hiding place from truth. Every Promised Land man or woman ever been around Junior Thomas know what I know. But not all them would tell it. And here come Junior's son gon take you away so you can hear a good word about his daddy form some these other folks. And some good things them other people be saying true, too. Maybe.

Money a nice fella. Kinda slow some people say. See, Marlow, how long he taking to get over here. Money all right by me. Hell, his daddy, Junior, all right by me, too. Everybody all right with me 'cause I ain't studying none them. My time close at hand. These folks can't do nothing for Jones but stick me in the cold ground when my time come. I ain't studying them. Money decent, folks say. Got a new wife, grown children by an old wife and a new boy just come by the new wife. Lives up the road over in Greenville. Money's whole family around here somewheres today. Tell the truth, Glide, I wouldn't know em to see 'em in this crowd of negroes. Every Promised Land body can get here is here at the school today. This school and dirt onliest things black in Promised Land older than me.

James Thomas, Jr., fidgets. Squirms itchy inside his suntans. Rather be outdoors naked in the broiling sun loading hot steel barrels on hot goddamn trucks. No air in the tiny room. What passes for air stinks of white boy hair oil, aftershave, shit they rub up under they armpits think they shit don't stink. This one with a quart of tonic slicking down the little bit of GI haircut top his head. Pimples on his neck all shaved red. Uniform fresh and pressed from Naples this morning shit brown already and wetbacked as mine. Thinking he's cool, smelling like some damned ho, thinking he got him some dumbass nigger, sweat this coon, scare his black ass, get him twisted up and squeezed out, nigger say any damn thing I want this nigger to say. Then we can lynch him and his black-assed buddies in peace. Yes, sir. No, sir. Yessiree. Whatever you say, boss. Yessuh. No, ma'am. No sir and yes sir this officer chump to death. Yes, sir. Happened in the morning like you say. Yes, sir, in the afternoon. Yes, sir, you got it right, sir. At night. Happened at night, just like you say. Yes. Dark when I saw them do it. Yes, sir, in the afternoon. Dark. Uh-huh, dark like you say. Dark morning, dark afternoon that night, sir. Dark as a white crow's wings at midnight, sir. Yes, sir. Just like you say. Black as snow. Dark as daylight.

Junior Thomas can't wait to tell Till about big mouth Hite. Stupid, scared rabbit Hite piss his pants a white boy look at him crosswise. Till would know how to handle Hite. Shut his fat mouth. Till don't need to say one word. Till just stare Hite down with them cold ass eyes. Hite forget all about being scared of some cracker officer. Can't wait to get out here and tell Till. Till know just what to do to shut Hite up.

Till's good black. Don't crack. Till won't admit nothing. Don't give a good goddamn about nothing these crackers say. Till ain't afraid. Till crazy. If Till with me in the room wit this white boy, I wouldn't say shit, neither, Junior Thomas tells himself. Till's fault, he tells himself, if I talk. Why ain't Till here. Why ain't Till standing right beside me saying nothing. No fear. No words. *Fuck you*, loud and clear. Somebody got to look out for Junior Thomas. And it ain't Hite. Ain't McMurray. Ain't Kitchen. Ain't Till. Ain't nobody in this stinky room looking to help Junior Thomas but Junior Thomas. This sour pussy nasty-smelling peckerwood CID behind the desk looking to hang him a nigger. Four niggers. A dozen. One as good as another. Hite, McMurray, Till, Kitchen, hang 'em all, all these pack-mule niggers, mop-and-bucket niggers, sweep-up niggers, jeep-driving shoeshine niggers, every last one swinging at the end of a rope. You, too, Thomas. You first, Thomas. Mize well talk while you still got a neck to talk with. You better tell us everything, Private Thomas, or you'll swing like the rest. Got you dead to rights, Private. Save yourself. Fat-mouth chickenshit Hite squealing like a stuck pig and we all fucked now. How Till gon shut Hite up. Till locked in a cell just like you. Till standing at attention in a room with a white boy behind a desk asking Till questions night and day. Till singing like a canary, Thomas. Lying on your ass to save his ass. Till ain't said shit. Know Till ain't said word the first, but Junior Thomas sees Till nod his big hard black head. *Uh-huh, Uh-huh, Uh-huh*. Till ain't said a word. Just nod his head when the CID say my name. Was it that goddamn Private Thomas did it. *Uh-huh, Uh-huh*, big head nodding. Yessir. He the one.

Four of us, Thomas says. Names names. Nods his head up and down like Till. Yes, sir, after each name, each serial number the CID agent reads. Wearing masks, carrying guns. Yes, sir. Niggers busted in, fucked those Italian women at the waterpoint. Yes, sir, they did, them other three niggers did just what you say they did and I didn't do nothing but watch. No, sir. Not me. I swear it was the others inside the shack done it and me standing at the door watching, lighting matches to check out what's what, who's in there, what's going down. Wasn't me inside but I could sorta see a little corner of it happening just like you say it did, yes sir, with my back against the door I pulled shut tight behind me. Lit matches, yes, sir. How many, sir. Maybe six matches, maybe more, sir, how many you say, sir. Matches so I could kinda see what's going on in the dark with my back to the door where the four of us come in at. Yessir, Till, McMurray, the British guy go inside but I didn't go no farther than the door. Four of us went through the door, sir, not three like them Italian peoples say. They wrong, sir. Four busted in not three. Them Italians inside the shack ain't seen me at the door I guess. 'Cause I stopped. The others run in when the door opened, went after the women in there, beat up the old man. But I stopped.

First Till sent McMurray and the English guy, Chappie we called him. No, sir. Never knew his name. He call everybody *Chappie*, so we call him *Chappie*. Yes, sir. Till said you two go creep around the back of the shack and listen make sure no men inside before we all bust in. McMurray come back said he heard what might be one man snoring, all the rest women's voices, couple, three women talking he said when him and the Englishman come back to where me and Till sitting on the stone wall where we all been sitting since dark, drinking vino, making a plan to hit the shack, cop more wine, cop pussy. Four of us on the wall again after McMurray come back with the English guy from sneaking up to the shack. McMurray said there's women in there, and Till said, c'mon then, said pussy, said raid. Louis Till don't talk much and so when he does say something you best listen. And do what he says do. Till's wild, crazy. And Till got a .45 automatic in his pocket. Took it from a white boy sailor he punched out that night. Snatched the sailor's .45 out his belt when the sailor reaching for it. Knocked him down, stomped him, dared him to get up. Till just might have killed him if I didn't pull Till off. Let him be, man,

I said. Nothing but trouble, I said to Till. Said c'mon, man, let's go up the hill to the Italian camp and cop some vino.

Anyway, Till says raid and it's four us, not three, creeping up on the shack. Then *Pow. Boom. Boom.* Guns, sirens, search lights bright as day. Forty millimeters, nineties. Boom. Pow-pow-pow-pow. Shack door pops open.

Goddamn late, goddamn sleepy, he thinks, close to damn morning before they bring the statement to sign. Two a.m. anyway, later most likely, Thomas guesses. CIDs took a long break for dinner around ten, eleven. His stomach empty too, real empty. Real dark outside, barely could see black bars on the cell's window, damn bars on that peephole little as it was. Black outside when they locked him back in his cell and went to eat, letting him know sure enough they was getting food. Late, dark, and they gone a good, long while and lots more questions soon's they come traipsing back to get him. No dinner, not a fucking coke, just more questions back and forth, them asking, him yessing and noing, yessir, nossir, him saying shit over and over or different shit, yes sir, no sir, none of it making no damn sense no more no way. The more he says, the more he can't remember from one story to the next what story he told before and the white boys pick, pick, picking at each story as if he knew, as if he cared. Like any bit of truth anywhere in any of it. Not his story no more, don't matter no more what the fuck he say or don't say. One lie same as the one before, and just as true and not true as what he says next, so what the fuck's the difference, they be asking the same question again and again like Till say nothing don't mean shit. Tell the same lie or a different lie next minute. They ain't listening. Fuck it. So it's very goddamn late when the final statement comes. He plays at reading typed words, one page and half another page, because the two CIDs say read. Then he signs both sheets because that's what they order Private Thomas to do.

Don't say shit. Just run your tired eyes slowly a minute over the two sheets they bring. Like you're reading, like you care. Look at the pages long enough to say *fuck you* couple times under your breath. Lucky it's only a few words, only a page and a half. Not ten million pages. Not like goddamned big mouth squealing Hite telling the whole world every motherfucking thing in his dumb rastas busybody head. It's just a few skimpy words squared up all neat on a page and a half.

Hey, Till. Don't roll your evil eyes at me, man. Bet you singing away in your cage, man. Fuck you, man. All you niggers singing. So fuck it. Fuck your eyes. I ain't the one started it. Hite started it.

Till's damn eyes don't roll. Huh-uh. Till stab you in your chest with those icy motherfuckers. Leave me be, Till. Paper I'm signing ain't shit, man, just a couple, three words, no harm. G'wan away, Till. Somebody got to look out for James Thomas, Jr. Yessir. Zackly, sir. You got it right, sir. What you say is surely what happened. I don't want to hang by the neck until I'm dead. Who do. Do you, Till. Goddamn that Hite.

Second statement no hassle. Three weeks, maybe a month or so after the first statement another starched shirt CID in charge and then another one who bops in a second at the end to sign on the line below the line Thomas signs. Thomas in and out quick, too. At attention in front of the CID sitting behind his desk. A fan moving the air so officer stink not the only thing to breathe. No talk, talk, talk, talky, talking. No questions this time poking him like needles. Minute all it take the CID to say, We cleaned up your first statement, Private. You left out a few things we put in. We took out a few things you never said. Understand, Thomas. Read it if you wish to read it, but I've just told you everything you need to know. Yessir. Thank you, sir. Good. You're doing yourself a favor, Private. Sooner we finish this business, better it will be for everybody. Herlihy, c'mon. Need your John Hancock. Right. Good. Dismissed.

You weren't there in the CID lieutenant's office, were you, Marlow. You're reporting your imagination as fact again, right. You're as unscrupulous as the army investigators, Marlow. Worse because you claim to know better. Do you really believe you're exempt from telling the truth, just because you believe your project is serious business. Isn't the United States Army's duty to win a war and keep peace after war a more creditable, less despicable excuse for bending facts, stretching truth than your self-interested desire to entertain Chip's fans.

Private James Thomas, Jr., sees Private Louis (NMI) Till only once after they meet at the court martial in Leghorn, Italy. The truck transporting Thomas and fifteen other released prisoners to rejoin their units is routed through the MTOUSA (rhymes with *Medusa*) Disciplinary Training Center at Metato in order to pick up three inmates who have served out terms there. Through a hole created where a loop of rope has come undone from one of the steel poles to which the truck's canvas top is lashed, a missed stitch stretched open for a merciful breath of air and probably also out of curiosity, too, since men sweating under the truck's canopy might wish to check out the camp where they've halted, the granddaddy prison, largest and meanest of an archipelago of camps, a facility where some of them may have been interned before and all the others certainly would have heard tales about, hellish acres of blowing sand and wind, broiling in the summer, bitter cold, wet and muddy winters, the DTC at Metato notorious because a bunch of colored GIs attempting to escape were machine-gunned by guards on duty in towers that jut up next to the gate and at each corner of the razor-wired perimeter fence, through that improvised hole Thomas sights a group of men mustered at the far end of the football-field long DTC yard, a punishment not a work detail since the men's hands empty and no tools stacked nearby, men disintegrating in a buckling haze of Mediterranean heat, dust, and glare. To Thomas, squinting through the hole, the scene is a movie projected on a washboard. The men over there colored men, he assumes, though swirling grit and great distance separates them from where he squats on a rail inside the truck, colored probably like all the men packed inside the truck with him, a colored detail over there he's absolutely sure when a colored guy double-times past to join the group across the yard. No mixed details in the DTC.

Thomas sucks air, drips sweat. The guys crowded beside him shove in slow motion, silently, insistently to squeeze closer to the privileged spot, the little riff of less stale air. For a minute his chance to look and breathe, breathe and look, but soon he'll have to shift, lose sight of the men whose black silhouettes in the heat of the yard shiver and crack.

Colored soldiers in rows face an officer who's white, Thomas knows because all colored officers white. This one's got his baton in one hand, glint of silver whistle in the other. Whistle shrieks. Rows of men drop to the ground as if an invisible sickle slashed their ranks. All the prisoners, maybe twenty-five, thirty, freeze in the push-up position, a posture, a drill, a punishment way too familiar to Thomas. They are waiting for the whistle's next blast to commence the cadence count every man in the detail must shout at the top of his lungs. Loud enough to satisfy the officer or the whistle will throw a toot-toot shrieking fit, the count go back to zero, the sentence of ten or thirty or fifty push-ups start all over again. Hup-one-two-*One*-hup-one-two-*Two*-hup . . . All the troops mowed down except one. One sticking up like a hair the blade of whistle missed. For three or four counts two black shapes stand fact to face, white officer, colored soldier above rows of prone bodies that dip and rise in unison. Two dark silhouettes, too far away, too much hazy shimmer and glare to pick out features, but Thomas has no doubt one is Louis Till. Thick body, big head Till, Till ignoring the count. Till upright like the officer. Meeting the officer's hate, matching it stare to stare. Hate that would kill if it could. Thomas hears it hiss, catch fire. Searing white heat of blowtorches. Hate alive a second, a lifetime in the thick air. However long it needs to bond two men until they die. Hate zapping back and forth three, maybe four beats while Till refuses to drop to the ground. Time enough for Thomas to think, *Gotta tell the fellas this shit. Till crazy, boy.* And Thomas wonders how long he'll need to finish being a soldier, finish his life, finish with Louis Till. Till, no doubt about it. Goddamn St. Louis Till on his feet, after all the other men down. Till eye to eye with the peckerwood officer, hate traded for hate an instant, an eternity before Till drops to his hands, arms extended under his chest, the push-up position held one beat, then two, his big head looking round side to side like what the fuck all this shit spozed to be, before he begins to pump up and down, up and fucking down. Hup-one-two-*Six*-Hup-one-two-*Seven*. Faster and faster, chasing shrieks of the officer's whistle chasing him.

My sweet grand baby boy the spittin' image of you, Money. You all maybe should call him Junior, maybe.

Junior. C'mon, Mama. Junior stone country. Seem like every little back boy a Bo or June. Anyway, Junior Daddy's name and what Daddy been to me.

You carry the Thomas name. Carry your daddy's blood, Mr. Monroe Thomas.

Don't make a hill of beans, Mama. I was half grown when Daddy came back. You know as well as I do he never did really come back. Kept on leaving us and by the last time he came back after prison and the rest, just an old, old man in a rocking chair. Good for a whole lot of nothing. Never been a daddy to me. Sorry, but that's how I feel.

Don't disrespect your father.

Sorry, but I'm telling it the way it is. Deserted us. Then come back all crippled up to sit in that old rocking chair and die. Huh-uh. Why should I give a son of mine his name. Daddy give me a name and that's all. Damn lot of good it did me.

Your name's a good name. A good family in Promised Land. Your daddy's daddy a fine man. Thomas name worth something. Good name ain't nothing to let go and forget.

Thomas okay with me, Mama. Nothing against the Thomas part. But Junior not even a real name. Junior just something on the end of a name to keep track of generations. I gave my son a real name, not a countrified nickname everybody calls him by and forgets his Christian name.

Edgar Clyde Thomas your boy's great granddaddy. Thomas a good name way before it was your daddy's name. Always been Thomases in Promised Land. Your daddy's daddy a fine man. Owned land till the peckerwoods stole it. A proud man everybody say. A deacon. One them build up Promised Land AME Zion board by board.

All that's well and good. You told me those stories, Mama, and I'm proud of my grandfather and his father. But what the hell happened to Daddy.

War stole his spirit. Then that jail time hurt him bad. Wasn't the same Junior come back here as the Junior left Promised Land.

Heard those stories, too. It's sad. A shame. War messes wit a man's mind. Look at my homeboys come back from 'Nam. Come home dope addicts. Crazy. And black men Daddy's age. They a mystery to me. Don't see how they did it. I mean black men in a Jim Crow army fighting for a Jim Crow country. What kinda damn sense that make. Don't know how they did it. But not all black men come back from the army and abandon they family. Not all my old buddies dope addicts. Don't all black men run away and do they dirt till ain't nothing worth nothing left of them and creep back home to die.

Listen to your mother, Money. I don't believe your daddy, God rest his soul, ever had a chance to grow up. Junior still a boy when he signed up for the army. Gone for years and still silly, bad little boy silly, when he got back. Acting like he didn't have a care in the world. But Junior not a bad man. In and out of jail don't mean a man's evil natured. Your father just never learned how to be a grown-up family man. War took his growing up time. Put some mean in him. War stole something from your daddy. Wore hisself out chasing it. Dead now and still ain't never caught it. Running wild all those years till he dropped down in that sorry rocker by the door.

Why'd you wait, Mama. Why didn't you go on with your life.

Where Ima go. What I got to go wit. What I got sides my children. *Wait* didn't have nothing to do with it. No. Huh-uh. Busy every day God send here. Working and taking care my babies can to caint. Ain't no wait in it. Wish I'd had time to wait. Time to sit back and pick my teeth. No waiting. Not hardly. Busy every day doing everything I knew how to do to keep us scraping by.

He should have been here scraping with you. Daddy wasn't always in jail. Boy or no boy. War or no war. Prison or no prison. His place here with you. Us. I can't forgive daddy for running away. Leaving you and his children to rot, to die, for all he knew or cared. I don't forgive James Thomas, Jr.

Not about forgiving. Look at you, Monroe. You done made something of yourself. New wife. Starting a second family. Your first children grown up nice and out on they own. You got two families and both doing well. Forgiving a thing of the past. Whole lot today to be grateful for. No need crying over what's over. The plan in God's hands. Nobody need to be forgiving God's plan. Or forgetting it's His plan. Nobody's hands clean. You and Madeline can call my sweet grand baby boy whatever name you-all want to call him by. An me, Ima call him what you-all say call him when I'm around you-all. But every time it be just him and me and I pick him up and hug him and sugar one his chubby cheeks, Ima call him June, li'l Junebug, cause I see you, Monroe, in them big, brown eyes. Say June every time. June cause he's a good sweet child, the very image of you, his daddy, my baby, Monroe, and your daddy and granddaddy, and all them perfect babies God bless poor colored women folk to love.

His last night in Greenville's Holiday Inn, Marlow asks himself, Why didn't I tell anyone here about my family roots in Promised Land. Didn't know you didn't tell until this very moment, Marlow. Cat got your tongue. Are you still scared of the South. Like you're still scared of the dark. Why not claim your family name that appears in the community's earliest records, years before Promised Land the town's name, years before someone had the idea of breaking up the Willis plantation into small parcels of land and giving away or selling them cheap to newly freed slaves to farm, years before the rumored promise of forty acres and a mule to every ex-slave family got sidetracked by the state of South Carolina into a money-making scam to profit local whites who once owned both the land and human beings who worked it.

As far back as 1867, documents attest a Robert bearing Marlow's family name had presented himself and registered his X at a polling place. This despite the fact that roads and voting sites patrolled by white vigilantes brandishing guns and threats of violence, threats backed up by long memories of white power, white people's absolute prerogative to brutally punish or kill people of color during slavery days. Slavery days nobody white was saying they felt sorry about nor uncoupled from their understanding of a future which would replicate precisely the old ways of reckoning who votes and who doesn't, who counts and doesn't count, who's on top and who's on the bottom, who owns things and who's a thing owned. A vision just the opposite of change in the status quo between so-called blacks and so-called whites, a vision embodied by armed, hooded men on horseback who vowed *Never. Not here, nigger.* Words haunting perilous back country trails his ancestor Robert trekked to cast his first ever vote. Marlow's people also among the first in line when a few scanty parcels of the Willis plantation's worst land doled out to former slaves, and some of his people among the very few who managed to hold on to their farms in spite of punishing taxation, debt, intimidation, and swindles organized to systematically restore the land and colored people who worked it to their former lords and masters. Why not introduce himself as a homeboy. Say my family's from here. My grandfather left Promised Land in 1898 and went up north. Say, I'm the prodigal son come back to listen, to tell you my story, to make new stories from your words and mine. Hey, cuz. Hi auntie and uncle and great-grandmama and great-great-granddaddy.

We's all kin, ain't we folks. Who knows what went on down here after dark in these woods. Mama's baby, daddy's maybe, names and blood ringing the changes generation after generation of marriages and couplings and whatnot. Some folks gone for good, some never left home, some half-white, some half-black, some come back home to stay. Nobody knows and who cares, so here I am, and you-all my people.

But during his time in South Carolina, Marlow didn't, couldn't say to anyone, I'm Promised Land people. Didn't say, You're my people. Couldn't claim kinship with others so drastically severed from him and him from them by time, place. By evil lies, and worse even than lies, the years of foolishly believing lies, treating lies as true. Lies that cursed, shamed, and diminished people. Is that why he made no claim to belong to Promised Land or it to him, except once, alone in the churchyard out behind Mount Zion AMEZ which his great-grandfather had pastored, driving to his church each Sunday in a horse-drawn buggy with his impeccably dressed wife in her Sunday bonnet next to him on the wooden seat, according to one of the stories his grandfather Harry had told Marlow about the family's roots in South Carolina. In that Mount Zion AMEZ churchyard several gravestones bore Marlow's family name, three in particular, side by side, sturdy, rough hewn, broad-shouldered stones belonging to his grandfather Hannibal, *aka* Harry's brothers—Jordan, Foster, Baker—among the scattered graves of their wives, uncles, aunts, sisters, in-laws, elders, neighbors, and whatnot, the people Marlow had never met and never would because once upon a time he was scared to come south with his grandpa and too late now, Harry's eldest sister's son, Littleman, the last known survivor of the clan his grandfather had left behind when he went north in 1898, buried now behind one little country church or another down here. Only to them, the ones in Mount Zion's hallowed ground, only to them he said, *Yes. I'm back. Here with you again.* And that's about everything the hurt let him say. Overwhelmed by their silent greeting. And his. How could any of that business be anybody's business but family business. Amen. See you all soon again.

GUN TALE

How many .45s manufactured for U.S. military during World War Two—Louis Till allegedly stole a .45 automatic from a sailor on the night of June 27 and used it to kill Anna Zanchi—J. W. Milam's service .45 killed Louis Till's son—live by the .45, you son dies by the .45—justice or coincidence or irony—maybe none of the above—Louis Till not necessarily the intruder who shot Zanchi—J. W. Milam an MP—did he serve in Italy—could Louis Till and Milam have crossed paths during the war—did Milam bust colored soldiers from Till's battalion—in Marlow's script / treatment / notes / documentary daydreamed for Chip, will the same .45 kill Anna Zanchi and Emmett Till—perhaps a narrative constructed from the point of view of a .45—its serial number as its name—weapon in Zanchi shooting identified as a .45 by shell casings, by holes in door, big hole in stomach of dead woman—a .45 never recovered by investigators—did the mysterious English guy eventually identified by CID agents as Private Frank Emmanuel, 903787, 6th Battalion, Gordon Highlanders, C Company, CMF, borrow the .45 from Till the night of June 27—was the .45 in the Canadian/Englishman's possession a month later when he was shot and killed by an Italian civilian at Maenza, near Terracina during a hold-up attempt—who was robbing whom—did J. W. Milam bring his army sidearm back to the states or buy a different .45 after he returned home—who sold Milam a .45 in Mississippi—a .45 Milam liked to show off to his sharecroppers, people say—the war souvenir he shoved into Emmett Till's ear to scare him, smashed across Till's skull when Emmett didn't seem scared enough, pulled the trigger and blew out the boy's brains when scaring wasn't good enough—was the AWOL English-sounding guy a gay guy bunking in a U.S. Army colored barracks with Till, McMurray, and Thomas—was Chappie fucking Junior Thomas on the sly—did Thomas with his lover the foreign soldier, hustle and rob gay sailors, is that how Zanchi weapon obtained—after the Mari barracks attack, did Chappie and Thomas, not Till and McMurray perpetrate the raid on the Zanchi shack—who shot the .45 through the closed door—Marlow's plot thickens—to what end—where is the story headed—what does Marlow wish it to say—prove.

LOVE TALE

On December 3, 1944, Mrs. Joyce MB of Bonfire Close, Chard, Somerset, England, married and in her ninth month of pregnancy, left her home to walk to a cinema. She was followed by Corporal Robert L. Pearson and Private Cubia Jones, both colored, of Company A, 1698th Engineer Combat Battalion, United States Army. The men, strangers to Mrs. MB, walked up behind her, grasped her wrists, and despite her protests that she was married and pregnant, dragged her into Bonfire orchard and raped her.

The next day in a lineup at the U.S. camp, Pearson and Jones were identified by Mrs. MB as her assailants and arrested. At trial Mrs. Joyce MB testified that she begged the soldiers repeatedly *Don't do it*, but the men ignored her pleas. Attempted to calm and console her by saying they loved her.

Corporal Pearson, twenty-one years old, and Private Jones, twenty-four, despite their claims of love, were both found guilty of rape and subsequently hanged at Shepton Mallet prison, March 17, 1945, part of a wave of executions—including the judicial asphyxiation of Privates Till and McMurray—that resulted from a directive issued by General Eisenhower, supreme commander of Allied forces in Europe and later president of the United States of America, ordering expedient resolution of all pending cases alleging capital crimes committed by U.S. service personnel against civilians.

TALL TALE

Private Louis Till, interned at MTOUSA Disciplinary Training Center, Metato, wondered what kind of motherfucker so bad they got to weld steel bars to his steel wire cage to keep him locked up. Old skinny white motherfucker army gon hang they say. Dried up like a rattlesnake skin. In a cage cause he badder than a nigger they say. Till thinks, *Huh-uh. No.* and rolls his eyes, sucks his teeth, hisses *shee-it* at nobody in particular, then nods, says *shee-it* again, this time under his breath and says, *No goddamn way.* These motherfuckers crazy round here.

MORALITY TALE

Thomas believed the worst over. Pissing blood, lips raw meat, eyes bruised shut, hurt spots deep inside ain't stopped aching since they trapped him, beat him, no place to run, busted him up good in that dark alley till they got tired of busting. Thought they meant to kill him, thought he heard them arguing, *yes . . . no . . . kill this stool pigeon motherfucker*, him laid out almost dead in the alley rolling round on wet stones, bloody, piss in his pants, halfway passed out, can't feel a thing, then everything pops wide awake, on fire, a kicked rib, hears the boot land, hears his own scream but the damned hurt jumps up some other damn place, he's bits and pieces, broken, tossed round the alley, too many pieces, too many hurts, new hurt got to stand in line, wait a turn to catch up and hurt, blood from his nose chokes him, chunk of tongue or tooth swimming round in his jaw, a good right hook never seen it coming catch him square in the chops, tore him up, too slow, not ducking, falling, knocked out, he's already down and out, fuck you, mister, curled up hiding, nowhere to run if he could run, on his knees, crawling, wet drawers drooping off his bare behind, where are the pieces, can't find shit in the dark, can't hurt no more, too hurt, kicked and punched, chin bumping stones, they jerk him up, slam him down, *nigger ain't worth killing, killing too good for this nigger*, the worst almost over then, nother hour, nother day, picks hisself up, forget the scattered pieces he can't find, hopes the MPs find them, shovel them in the goddamn MP jeep, cussing him like they gon beat him some more, splashing fire on him, a needle rammed halfway up his ass, save me, save me, Jesus, Lord help me, save me from these white devils, and then finally maybe the worst really over, over and done, hurt bad, real bad, but not dead, not his time, not dead that night. Wondering how the niggers knew, how they found him. Niggers talk, don't they. Jungle telegraph. Niggers know shit before the generals. Niggers don't know nothing. Niggers ain't supposed to know shit but they found his sorry ass, didn't they, in the club, in the street, who saw him, who told, who knew him from nobody, knew he's not just another nigger soldier out getting drunk, hunting pussy, niggers knew something, didn't they, cause they found him, stomped him, mouth full of blood and teeth and ripped up tongue, one leg he still can't walk straight, two fingers broke, one eye blind under a bandage, other eye everything he sees swimming in blood—and now this fucking sheet of paper on his bunk, in this different barracks only white officers spozed to know where they hided the busted-up stool pigeon nigger but somebody put a paper on the bed and drawed two stick men hanged on two stick poles and it ain't over. Till and McMurray hanged and dead but it ain't finished yet. Till don't say shit, just nod that big head on his thick black neck, *huh-uh, huh-uh*, shit ain't over yet.

Resist the temptation, Marlow. No just desserts passed out to players at the end of the play. Nobody believes in fairy tales anymore. Did any grown-up ever. What does anybody believe anymore. Resist. Don't chronicle the fall of Junior Thomas like it's good news. Don't warn us that a snitch's reward is every little dog in town will have a bite of his lying tongue, the snitch's balls cut off and stuffed in his fat mouth to chew on, choke on until merciful death rescues him. And even then maybe not over. Sins of snitches punish snitch's children. Forever. Like a lie once told always a lie and poisons forever the possibility of truth. Truth busted forever by just one fucking lie, the very first lie cracking the sheen of truth, the crack spreading, generating more cracks, truth will never be the same. Never be. Broken neck of Louis Till holds his slump-shouldered body that shudders, wobbles below the tilted head, Till's wobbling, dangling weight disturbs the perfect perfect cycling of the spheres, the universe off-center for eternity, though after a second or two the mechanism seems to right itself, the shudder, the wobble cease, the corpse stops swaying, dark pendulum at the end of the plumb line stock still. All's right with the world again. Or is it. Over. If we turn to the next page, turn the next card, will it be clean or is truth marked always ever after by the sign of *no, not*, the bloody sign of a man on whom the sun has set crookedly.

Resist, Marlow. You may be reading things ass backwards. Maybe a lie's first and truth a phony something made up after the lie, truth a fiction trying to cover up the lie, usurp the lie's authority. A lie the very first word uttered by the very first person. *No. Not.* Lying. Afraid. Denying the clarity they behold. The beam of light they ride. Open eyes shutter themselves. Say *no* to the light. The rest, all the words that follow—truth included—a thicket of lies. Lies, so light won't return. Terrorizing, freezing light. Light nightmare or sweet dream. Who can say. What does it matter as long as it never returns. You, Marlow. If you can't speak of the light, then any word, any tale's as good as another. Let poor James Thomas, Junior, rest in peace. Let him be a man not a meaning. Lessons a plenty every minute of every day of every person's life to instruct them what they should and shouldn't do next. It's never over until it's over. Resist, Marlow. Let us speak for ourselves, teach ourselves, fabricate our own lies. We're the ones who must eventually pay the dues. Your fiction of evil James Thomas, Junior on the cross or Saint Louis Till on the cross can't pay for us. Save us.

WITNESS: A LETTER FROM FRANCE

2015

My people are being killed. Dying in great numbers everywhere, dying and disappearing.

At some point today, if the sky clears or if it doesn't, I will take a good, long walk in the French countryside. "Good" meaning good. "Long" meaning an hour or more. I will try to walk away from the conversation that I am having with myself at this moment, while my people are dying and I am wondering who is in charge and why so few of us notice or acknowledge the willful destruction of colored lives that I witness daily, and why I have no words to convince others of the losses, the evil, my stupefaction as I watch wave after wave of death, or one single quiet fall after another that disappears people I call mine, my people, though I'm guilty of not loving them enough and thus complicit in the killing that I hope will recede from my mind as I walk later in the French countryside.

I will walk and walk and regard nature's ageless, expressionless face, nature not watching me or barking at or sniffing me, nature that fears nothing in me and wants nothing from me, but simply takes me in and buries me with an utter lack of recognition, so that I am relieved of myself, emptied and erased from the reflections that I cast on nature and nature doesn't cast back. In the French countryside this afternoon, I will try to imagine that the walk will never end, and that the self who sees the killing will slip away, and I will never again need to deal with this, the annihilation of people I would love more if I could, protect more if I could, talk with, sit with, hold hands with, dance with, if I could. But daydreams won't stop the killing—no matter how many denials, how much shock or outrage or pretended surprise at each new victim, no matter how many hours I walk. The remorseless attrition goes on.

It starts with single lives, and turns into many, many deaths, too many anonymous colored faces, faces with no words, words with no faces. I have no more information than anyone else, no clues to connect the dots, no dots except those I glean by imagining myself among the dead, not exactly myself but a disembodied witness, a victim who also survives, as if a person could be in two places at once.

It starts with intimations of a grand plan for the wholesale slaughter and elimination of people of color. Voices from a room too far away for me to distinguish individual words. I can make out only the rise and fall of urgent conversation, arguments, deliberations, plans for war. Not my plan, obviously, but a plan that encompasses me, my color, my anguish, the anger at myself at those times when it seems that I do nothing but stand by and watch—not only strangers dying in the news, but mother, father, siblings, nephews, nieces ground down, overwhelmed, overcome. People I believe I love. And then I see that my people don't count because they can be snatched away or neglected or abused or forgotten, with no reckoning, no fault assigned, as if they, he, she, we had never been anything other than empty faces, empty words, smoke and mirrors.

I see the men of my family. My father—all skin and bones, after a lifetime of jobs that consumed his body, embittered his mind—slides down a waterproof sheet on a hospital bed that has been elevated to keep him awake and responsive. My middle brother holds on to my elbow, shuffles his Parkinsonian shuffle down the hall of a nursing home's locked ward. Youngest brother, fresh from bending over for a rectal inspection, pauses at the guard's kiosk to sign into the visiting room, suddenly too old, too small in his orange jumpsuit beside his fellow inmates, most of them colored guys, on average thirty years his junior, who pad their bulky, shapeless coveralls with jailhouse muscle and arrogance, decorate them with stylish gang ticks. His son, shot dead in front of a pregnant girlfriend, their two-year-old in her arms. A nephew cursing his daughter on the street, where she trades pussy for crack; a cousin's kid selling drugs; another relative who returned from war an addict and now deals big time to support his family, his habit; one of his sons, in Cleveland, following in Daddy's footsteps—or is he dead or in the slam for murdering some other mother's son?

The facts of my life materialize, no mere headlines or essayistic musing on human nature or theories of culture, no talk-show interpretations or testimonials of incredulous bystanders, no recitations of the numbing statistics of other holocausts to diminish what is happening here, now. Simply pain, punishment, deeply rooted, echoing pain that incarcerates and kills. A plan operating patiently, like the microscopic wound in my mother's breast that grew large enough to swallow all of her. It chokes me, makes me short of breath.

If you let yourself listen, you can hear them running. Trains of endless cattle cars that run all night and in the daytime, too, though the noise we make to keep ourselves company during daylight hours drowns out, for the most part, the trains' sound. You can hear them best when you are exhausted. When you need to rest, to empty yourself of distractions and finally slide down naked into that vast tub of black oblivion, so much more of it than you. It waits quietly to dissolve your small portion into its measurelessness, until you are among the missing persons you do not miss when you sleep.

Trains packed with my doomed people, removing them as sleep removes me from myself, removes me from them. My people stuffed into nasty, wobbly stacks of chicken-wire crates, *clackety-clack, yakkedy-yak*, and some nights the sound keeps me awake before it puts me to sleep.

In Pittsburgh, Pennsylvania, when I was a boy lying awake at night, waiting for trains to pass on the tracks on a hillside just across from our colored street, Finance, trains close enough to rattle windowpanes in our raggedy little house, I'd hear China. Hear Cleveland. "China" and "Cleveland" meaning somewhere else, anywhere far away and different, where the next train might be headed. On my long-awaited first trip outside Pittsburgh, outside my state to another state, to Cleveland, Ohio, with the Shadyside Boys Club under-twelve basketball team, I wanted to kick the ass of the first boy I saw, because he was no different in his Cleveland backyard than the stupid Pittsburgh boys I'd been seeing my whole life.

Imagine yourself very hungry. Only one place in town open that serves food. Awful food. Eat it or starve. Eat it and starve. You arrive at the last restaurant in Cleveland and it's not there.

Kimberly Black sits beside her best friend, Sharice Swain, in the front seat of Sharice's car in Kimberly's driveway, in Cleveland. Kimberly slits Sharice's throat with a razor, then runs inside her house, emerges with her kids. Car starts up and strikes two of them. One kid dies.

LeBron James, famous hoopster, busts out of Cleveland. Celebrates his liberation like it's Christmas, like he was in jail those seven years on the Cleveland Cavaliers. Leave that boy alone, man. Who wouldn't do exactly what LeBron did, if he were in LeBron's big shoes? Ask yourself that question, sucker, and go on away from here. Always getting on LeBron's case. Shit, man. You couldn't shoot a basket to save your life, nigger.

In Cleveland, Ariel Castro kidnaps three women and locks them up in his house for ten years.

I'm not picking on Cleveland to make my case. Cleveland's the rule, not the exception. LeBron returned to Cleveland, didn't he? The case is far older than Cleveland. As old as America, as China, as classifying people by a color. As old as stealing people, buying and selling people. Older than a decision by NBA team owners that athletes should be treated like livestock, raised, bought and sold, distributed to markets.

No beginning or end to it. No case. Only this witness, these words attempting to unravel and stitch back together evidence that proves conspiracy, complicity, words to out the unfolding plan.

Where does the history of one particular group's need to dominate—to love, hate, consume—another group begin? You tell me, because I can't say exactly, except to say inside of myself, where I feel the evidence accumulate. The way time accumulates and swirls in Cleveland. Swirls inside and outside me. All time. No time. Lots and lots and lots of dots. Follow the dots and they will lead. Infinitely complex technologies at your fingertips. Banal as painting by numbers. Follow them and they lead to street maps, statistics, graphs, words, faces. Genocide of colored faces, of anonymous colored faces, with no words or one word: *colored*. Color meaning what? Genocide meaning what? *Genocide* a word coined not long after my birth, which will certainly outlive me.

Are certain people destined to be fat or rich? Are certain people destined to be colored and die soon? Why are some babies born with a silver spoon in their mouths, and some born to lick empty spoons? Some dumped in vats of sugary drink to drown? The dead can't say. Don't ask LeBron—he bounced.

Ask Amanda Berry, Gina DeJesus, Michelle Knight, the three "white" women held in bondage by Ariel Castro. Ask how three women could be abducted, raped, chained in an ordinary house on an ordinary Cleveland street for so long, surrounded by so many witnesses.

Photos of colored Kimberly Black began to appear in May 2012, along with headlines: "Woman in Chaotic Confrontation on Cleveland's East 125 Street Charged With Murder." "$1 Million Bond for Ohio Woman Charged in Odd Stabbing." "Fatally Stabbed Woman Runs Over Alleged Assailant's 2-Year-Old Daughter." If you search for her online, other Kimberly Blacks show up. Plain or provocative. Some shopping for dates, mates. Some distinguished, professional, stylish. Some lost, desperate. Lawyer Kimberly, Dr. Black, young Kimberlys, old Kimberlys, the same

Kimberly in multiple poses vying with other Kimberlys and with herself for attention, until what seems to be the original array returns, recycling the photo that caught my attention first time around. I keep it lit by touching the screen every so often while I attempt to sketch Kimberly Black's face into my notebook, my version of the mask she wears in the photo, my representation of what can't be seen behind the mask, my portrait of a young colored woman often under psychiatric observation, a woman who according to the records pleaded guilty to aggravated assault (2005), permitting drug abuse (2007).

I study the straight-on, eyes-front, look-at-the-camera-miss mug shot. No background, no depth. The subject's eyes do not stare blankly into the camera. They stop short. Eyes withheld at the very last instant before the lens blinks. Kimberly Black's gaze fixed on the abyss that stretches between herself and the camera, searching for signs of life—her own, anyone's—while her heavy flesh sinks into the camera's bottomless stare. Does she muse on the fact that the abyss, immense as it may appear, holds no room for her? She's gone. Dead and gone. Who cares. Not her, not nobody, no one in the whole wide world.

I study other colored faces. Colored face designated by a color "black" that none of them wears. Words kill faces. Faces kill words. Photos record carnage that no one sees. I try to convince myself that it's impossible to get rid of us, even if we are willing to go, even if some of us, to save our own skins, are willing to become accomplices to our own disappearance. I try to reason away the possibility of our extinction. Way too many of us, too deeply embedded, too many colors and languages, our roots too tangled with everyone else's—but I cannot step beyond the shadow, the weight, the number of crimes, victims, prisoners, witnesses bearing down.

All the words above to say what? To say whatever they say. To follow dots. To string yellow tape around a crime scene: three female friends of Kimberly Black descend upon her wooden frame house, on the 3000 block of Cleveland's East 125th Street, to rescue her from a seizure of depression, which they must believe to be an especially severe one, given their knowledge of Kimberly's long history of psychiatric problems. After two or three hours, they take a break from their stressful mission or perhaps attempt to attack their friend's unhappiness from a different direction or maybe they simply wish to spare Kimberly Black's four young kids an overdose of adult talk and tension and secondhand smoke. The women, with Kimberly in tow, leave the house and go sit and smoke dope in Sharice Swain's car, parked in Kimberly's driveway.

One press account of the crime says that two of the three friends go off to attend to unspecified business while Kimberly and Sharice, best buddies since childhood, who always address each other as Cuz, stay together in the front seat. A disagreement or worse ensues that results in Sharice's throat being slashed, either by a knife or a razor, the weapon either in Kimberly's pocket since the women entered the car or fetched from the house by Kimberly after an argument exploded. Subsequent to the slashing or stabbing or combination of both in the car, Kimberly returns to her house, strips naked, emerges onto the driveway carrying one of her kids and holding another's hand. The car with Sharice Swain slumped almost dead behind the steering wheel suddenly accelerates and strikes Black and the children, then careens across the street with enough force to collapse the porch roof of a neighboring house. Both kids are down, and Kimberly Black picks up the bloody one, who's silent, not moving, and flees, butt-naked, several blocks to where neighbors find her squatting on the ground in hysterics cradling her fatally injured two-year-old, Kymshia. An ambulance, then cops arrive. Take pictures, take names.

Four blocks away, at 12205 Imperial Avenue, in a neighborhood called Mount Pleasant, the home of Anthony Sowell had stood until the previous December, when city officials decided to demolish it, to expunge the communal memories of bad smells and the deaths of eleven colored women. Sowell, the Cleveland Strangler, had raped, murdered, and buried there. Not far away, another hovering cloud of god-awful stink emanating from a garage had led police to the beaten bodies of three more colored women. A few months later, Ariel Castro was found hanged in his cell in an Ohio prison.

Crime scene swirls. I cannot stop the dots. Can imagine no point of view from which to grasp the extent of the damage or assess the extent of responsibility. Many, many people who might have helped me measure the damage, the blows, the crushing losses inflicted have already been removed, passengers on trains I hear running at night, so loud some nights I think I might be a boy in the old house in Pittsburgh again, or tied to steel rails waiting for the locomotive's wheels to rush out of the darkness and free me.

A good friend I used to hoop with back in the day, my age, my color, except several shades darker, listened, nodded, and, when I finished, shrugged his broad shoulders, raised his big hands chest high, one on either side of his body, fingers spread wide apart to display pale, unsoiled palms. Maybe a gesture of surrender, maybe despair or defeat. Shit happens, he said. Not just to us, my man. Not just to our people. Shit just happens, man. Yes, I answered. Shit happens.

This fall I received an email: "In 1975 your brother Oliver held up my pizza shop in the Shadyside section of Pittsburgh one evening. I testified at trial where I met you briefly. I saw Oliver a couple of times after that. Once at the University of Pittsburgh gymnasium. This may seem strange but I have thought about Oliver many times over the years. There was something gentle in his eyes at times and I had hoped he would turn his life around. Is he doing alright. If you're still in touch with him please let him know that I forgave him a long time ago and I hope he is well. I live in the Pocono Mountains now after 18 years in New York City, 94th and Riverside. I'm 61 years old. I was 23 at the time of the robbery. It's funny how some things stay with you. Regards, Allen."

Many years before that email arrived, I received a letter from a woman who may have been a victim of the same crime, or perhaps witnessed a crime in the same Shadyside pizza joint on a different day, because once my brother decided to become a predator, no rhyme or reason motivated his stickups. He might have been as easily attracted as deterred by the fact that our family lived just down the block and around the corner from the strip of businesses containing the pizza shop he robbed. Worried or pleased that his face, mine, our brothers' faces were probably quite familiar to anyone who worked in or around the shop, since our faces were colored differently than the faces of most people frequenting Walnut Street's upscale stores. My middle brother was a danger to himself and others because he acted on impulse, with no fear of consequences, often doing with little or no premeditation whatever the fuck he felt he needed to do. Answering to no one but himself, a self created, inhabited from moment to moment by whim, anger, shame, deception, self-deception, resignation, illness, boredom, curiosity; a self he ran with the way you can find yourself running around with a crazy partner, who infatuates precisely because he or she is unpredictable, erratic, dangerous; a surrogate self who fronts for you and frees you from responsibility for yourself.

Same crime scene or not, two witnesses victimized by my brother's crimes, a woman and a man, have seen fit to contact me.

Dear Allen, the email you sent to the University has caught up with me. I don't recall meeting you, but the circumstances of that encounter are indelible. I appreciate your effort to reach out and communicate your memories and thoughts re ugly events that occurred so many years ago. In answer to your question about my brother, he is a victim of Parkinson's and has spent the last two years confined to a nursing home. Fortunately, as you guessed he might, he did manage to turn his life around before disease struck him down—attended college, married twice, fathered three kids that I know of, designed and administered an award-winning program in Boston for teens attempting to turn their lives around after juvenile incarceration. You say you forgive my brother—forgave him long ago. Thank you—I envy your generosity and wish that I could be as generous. Of course I wish

*you and yours continuing health and prosperity, but I don't forgive—can't
say precisely what or whom I don't forgive and your note is not a request for
forgiveness, so I'll just say that I'm much more confused than you are about
who should be forgiving whom for what.*

Should I write more? Tell Allen that I received from a woman a very
different sort of letter, one as unexpected, unsolicited as his. She, like you,
Allen, was present at the scene of a crime my brother committed. Oddly
enough, perhaps the same crime. Like you, she described my brother's
eyes, only she wrote to inform me that she still suffered nightmares in
which his green eyes stared at her, cold and merciless, as she remembered
them during the robbery a decade before. She did not forgive him and
clearly did not forgive me, either. In her view, the fact that I taught at a
university and wrote books increased my complicity, my share of guilt
and blame for the ordeal my brother forced her at gunpoint to endure.
She meant to punish me for the terrifying abyss she saw in my brother's eyes, eyes she was certain I had never truly seen because he was my
brother. Should I tell Allen that, in spite of all the venom and bitterness
directed at my brother and me by this witness, I preferred receiving her
message to receiving his?

Perhaps I should remind the e-mail's author that he and my brother
are almost exactly the same age. *What did you two think of each other
when my brown-skinned, green-eyed brother entered your pizza joint and
you both stared across the gap separating you, a vastness that guaranteed
that one of you was much, much more likely to have a decent job and suc-
ceed, the other much, much more likely to be poor, to die young. I don't
forgive that divide, those unforgiving depths into which my people are slipping, disappearing. If I can catch my brother in one of his good moments—
he sleepwalks the abyss almost constantly now, but his mind still generates
flashes of withering lucidity—should I ask him if he remembers you, Allen,
and what he thought of you? Should I ask if he forgives?*

*P.S.: You mentioned owning a pizza shop at twenty-three. How should I
deal with that fact? Ignore it? Treat it as incidental? What about the apartment on N.Y.C.'s Upper West Side, where you resided for eighteen years, or*

the home in the Poconos today? What about the feeling of belonging in those privileged places and the feeling that they belong to you and the feeling that multitudes of others have of not belonging anywhere, never belonging, just hanging on, hanging out, accepting what comes or snatching a fistful and running, hiding, a fistful of nothing, nowhere?

In the sleeplessness of nights like this I compose many letters and pretend to send them. Words I obsessively yet meticulously write in air, each draft melting, drifting as I drift, perhaps as my brother, my father drift into deeper levels of almost sleep. Words bending, stretching, disintegrating.

On a night like this, when the rattle of trains was too loud to ignore, my wife awakened herself with a volley of coughs. I asked if she was okay. Told her that she'd coughed several times as she slept, and that her snoring was louder than usual. My feisty French wife doesn't like to be reminded of her occasional noisy sleep, and quickly accused me of snoring ten times louder than her. An intensely private woman, she resents the fact marriage allows a spouse to spy on her sleep. Extremely smart, wood-nymph shy, a swimmer as strong as a mermaid, she steps out of the water and walks toward me on the beach at Toulindac, on the Gulf of Morbihan, in Brittany, wide shoulders, waist deeply cut, a dark hood of Medusa snakey curls frame her face and neck, drip on her breasts, a lapis-lazuli sheen colors her wet skin, her color now, if I could pick her out in the darkness, quietly gliding from our bed to go pee, her naked body illuminated an instant as the bedroom door cracks open. But not tonight, it's too late, black middle of the night and I can't see her, can't sleep, and I write sentence after sentence, invisible as she is with no light from a hallway window, no early-morning glow that she passes through going or coming, no glimpse, no sighting, she's true and not true, a rumor, a story, a painting of Venus atop an oyster shell risen from the sea. The lapis-lazuli glow of her skin not the color a dictionary would define but something else, a color more like sounds shimmering inside me, invisible yet substantial, weighty as those replies to a letter and an e-mail that I attempt to picture until the words dissolve entirely and I'm wide awake, alone in the dark, waiting, wishing for her please, please to return.

For reasons I'm unable to state, I believe I'll find stashed in an archive at Harvard University, where, unaccountably, my papers are ware-housed, the tickets, or rather invoices, that brought my colored family north from South Carolina, Virginia, Georgia, and later removed them on trains to wherever they are disappearing from now. There, along with my journals, diaries, handwritten drafts of unpublished novels, sparse correspondence, manuscripts of my earliest tries at story-writing, are the poems I scribbled before my first stories. Poems with exotic words like *lapis lazuli*, which I hoped would disguise my colored face. Words that I had never heard anyone say and whose meaning I barely under-stood. Words for things I'd never seen with my own eyes but believed, because poets I'd been taught to revere were witnesses. Great poets used the words and didn't I want to write like them, desire to be like them? Writers who could put any word in a poem because all words belonged to them. Hungry, envious, I tried out their words, as if by using them I could make them belong to me. As if by writing those words I could bury my face, bury my peoples' faces, the way the ancient Egyptians, wealthy ones, anyway, buried their beloved dead with scarabs made of lapis lazuli framed in silver, to protect them in the underworld.

No peace, no magic in words. She returns or not. Lost forever or not. Skin the color it is. The dead don't hear words. Remember nothing. Go nowhere. Words don't belong to me. I only borrow them, employ them in places like an archive. I do not own words in this underworld, where my people are being systematically destroyed. My words do not stop the killing. I am permitted to name people, places, things only because I become less wary, less dangerous when I believe that words belong to me. I need unsaid words, the words of witnesses who hear and see but do not speak. Words to confirm my guesses, intuitions, the intimations received of a plan that produces losses, atrocities beyond words, to cut down my people. Where are those words? Who owns them? What are the words for this? This writing, this silence, this waiting, this knowing and not knowing what's coming.

(A few names and details have been changed to protect individuals' identities.)

DOO-WOP

2025

Mitchell—please excuse my whiny response to your email in which you offer to help publicize my forthcoming book of essays—though today, June 27, 2025, is only my thirteenth day of being eighty-four-years old, I feel very eighty-four, and DOO-WOP, understand even less about what's coming next than I understand about what's been happening up to this very moment, all those words for so many, many years written, said, read to make sense of things imagined, lost now and forever, except the certainty I'm quite old, and except clearly it ain't over yet, cause DOO-WOP, old as I am, I hear the music, hear us (we called ourselves the *Commodores* long before some other brothers took the name and gone) four or five about fourteen-, fifteen-, sixteen-year-olds, I forget which, and the numbers not the point, point a singing group, maybe calling ourselves Commodores, back and forth with a couple other names we would have called ourselves, till one of us or all smiling, biting, tasting the sound, the ships and ocean crossings and slick outfits, slick hair traveling and seeing places, stuff none of us ever had, except the curve and weight of some bright smooth spiraling galaxy, clean and sharp as a tack we glimpse bending into notes just beyond our fingertips, beyond our tongues saying *Commodores* each in his own silent way till the vast wave of it not exactly said aloud by the group, but each in his own peculiar, secret way taken, engulfed anyway, members of the wannabe group we wanna be, the *COMMODORES* working our sorry and celestial shit to sweetly turn out songs like we've heard others of us sing, our music before it was theirs, and theirs before ours, DOO-WOP.

About time. The mystery of eighty-four years of time. Time that seems to tick on and on, seems to start up and seems definitively will stop—DOO-WOP—time here where I am when I listen or sing or think how I see, and how I don't, do or don't almost the same thing sometimes because time's not here—no more here than thousands, millions, billions of stars are here—though stars not here excite me as if they are here shimmering. DOO-WOP.

Dew Drop where my daddy Edgar hung out. Among others. Other joints. Other Edgars. Two of my names, middle and family, his: Edgar Wideman. And Lawson (from somewhere) in the middle of my father's name. Edgar Lawson Wideman. John, my first name, my mother's father's first name. Going by John, as I grew up, John when not Doot or Spank or get your behind over here, Boy. The Dew Drop Inn sits on the same corner it sat when I was named. Sits empty with its name painted on a raggedy sign you can still almost read over the door. Same DOO-WOP in the Dew Drop you can see (hear) in my daddy's footsteps passing through the Dew Drop's narrow door. Slip-sliding, slide, slipping in and out. Among others.

We do work in progress, Mitch. Progress in this best of all possible worlds. *Best* cause it ain't gon get no better, snickers one of the men hunched over drinks inside the Dew Drop, unshuttering himself, unsheltering himself an instant from the bar's permanent hunched-over darkness to crack up the shadow next to him, or could be him amening himself, *tell the truth,* black indistinguishable from black the Dew Drop preserves whether it's narrow door wide-open or windows appear suddenly in black walls where there are no windows to let in daylight.

Do you remember the first time someone asked you to write a story. Who. Where. Why. When.

I think it was a teacher in grade school told me to try. I must have tried if I was told to try. I was a good boy. And good in school, a good student if I knew anybody who counted was watching me, and I think I remember I liked, perhaps even loved my boney lady teacher in her thick glasses, the thick glasses, I loved, too, for some odd reason, and loved the scent of her if she leaned down close enough to me to see what I'd written in my workbook on my hard little desk chair with one fat, flat wooden arm so when the occasion to write arose, you could start there, add your scratches to all the other scratches, scars, gouges of names, my teacher hovering in a faint perfumey cloud is how I must have thought of it then, loving whatever it was she did to her clothes, her skin, but very fearful she might discover how pleased I was, only inches away, to smell her. Smell her smelling the story she'd assigned. First maybe I ever wrote.

I think she praised it. Said nice things that surprised me as they pleased me since her words had nothing to do with mine printed on a page of workbook. Said a very good start and very far to go and hard work will make it better. As if the words and sentences mine, when in fact, I think I had more or less copied words and sentences recalled from sports pages of the *Pittsburgh Press* I read some mornings if the paper happened to be around. Most likely my first story about a player hitting a homerun to win a game story, told in a voice as I remembered it from the newspaper. Especially that voice's big, impressive words I'd memorize along with those tried-and-true, familiar newspaper writer phrases that convince me and other readers that sportswriters are masters of sports they write about. Words and phrases I wanted to pretend I understood and used all the time, too. No big deal.

A very nice start, she said, but the rest I probably lost sniffing perfume, wondering, wishing I knew its name.

Not an allegory. I don't want the writing to become like Flannery O'Conner's when she tries too hard to be good and gets bad despite how good she often is talking about her South, her people and right and wrong and sorrow and evil meanness and ruthlessness and niggers and preachers and lost, unserved kids, souls, orphans, despite how she gets so much right, and if and when our turn, or another's turn there is an attempt to suggest to readers or perhaps even convince readers that a writer writes to make or thinks she or he can make everything in a story truthful and right as if it is that way out here now or should be or we wish it were or wish what we are writing will teach how to make it get better out here in the world, then I think maybe it's better to listen to that guy hangs in the Doo-Wop Dew Drop Inn, the guy drinking the bar's black shadow he sucks up and perfumes and deepens till he and it become the Dew Drop's indoor darkness all day and all night too—Doo-Wop, Doo-Wop, Doo-Wop—the best way, only everlasting way anybody ever gon git.

Nobody who tells us what to write makes us write it. Nor has anyone ever even come close to casting that evil spell. Not while we are here in time as we surely always are and have been and won't be. Nobody's time a noose around nobody's neck, around nobody's world, around nobody's song. Take your time. Swinging in the breeze. The dark. Sing. Sing. Sing. Doo-wop—do-do . . .

ABOUT THE AUTHOR

John Edgar Wideman's books include, among others, *Look for Me and I'll Be Gone*, *You Made Me Love You*, *American Histories*, *Writing to Save a Life*, *Brothers and Keepers*, *Philadelphia Fire*, *Fatheralong*, *Hoop Roots*, and *Sent for You Yesterday*. He won the PEN/Faulkner Award twice and has twice been a finalist for the National Book Critics Circle Award and National Book Award. He is a MacArthur Fellow and a recipient of the Lannan Literary Award for Lifetime Achievement, and the PEN/Malamud Award for Excellence in the Short Story. He divides his time between New York and France.